MW01016552

Racism
and
Anti-Racism
in Canada

Edited by
David Este
Liza Lorenzetti
Christa Sato

Fernwood Publishing
Halifax & Winnipeg

Editing: Fazeela Jiwa
Text design: Brenda Conroy
Cover image: Sarah Epp
Cover design: Jesse Warkentin
Printed and bound in Canada

Published by Fernwood Publishing
32 Oceanvista Lane, Black Point, Nova Scotia, B0J 1B0
and 748 Broadway Avenue, Winnipeg, Manitoba, R3G 0X3
www.fernwoodpublishing.ca

Fernwood Publishing Company Limited gratefully acknowledges the financial support of the Government of Canada, the Manitoba Department of Culture, Heritage and Tourism under the Manitoba Publishers Marketing Assistance Program and the Province of Manitoba, through the Book Publishing Tax Credit, for our publishing program. We are pleased to work in partnership with the Province of Nova Scotia to develop and promote our creative industries for the benefit of all Nova Scotians. We acknowledge the support of the Canada Council for the Arts, which last year invested $153 million to bring the arts to Canadians throughout the country.

Library and Archives Canada Cataloguing in Publication

Racism and anti-racism in Canada / edited by David Este, Liza Lorenzetti, and Christa Sato.

Includes bibliographical references and index.
ISBN 978-1-55266-888-7 (softcover)

1. Racism—Canada. 2. Canada—Race relations. I. Este, David, 1953-, editor II. Lorenzetti, Liza, editor III. Sato, Christa, editor

FC104.R33 2018   305.80971   C2017-907905-0

MIX
Paper from
responsible sources
FSC
www.fsc.org   FSC® C013916

CONTENTS

ACKNOWLEDGEMENTS

The seeds of this book began to develop after I was approached by Wayne Antony, who one day walked into my office at the University of Calgary in the Faculty of Social Work and candidly stated that he would like me to consider doing an edited volume on racism in Canada. By January 2016, after a series of additional chats with Wayne, I decided to move forward. This was a great opportunity for me as the potential book would be my first as lead editor. At the time, I was supervising two graduate students — Liza Lorenzetti, who was completing doctoral studies in the Faculty of Social Work at the University of Calgary and is currently an assistant professor in the same faculty, and Christa Sato, who was in the MSW program with the Faculty of Social Work at the University of Calgary.

Throughout my career, I have attempted to find or create opportunities for graduate students. Given that Christa, Liza and I share similar interests in academic and social work practice, I invited both of them to work with me as co-editors. I appreciated their willingness to embark with me on this odyssey that has tested us individually and collectively. This book would have never materialized without their insights, contributions and patience with me as I learned the role of being the lead editor.

Special thanks to the contributing authors, who remained committed to the initiative despite the fact that we missed some critical timelines. Your patience is greatly appreciated. We strongly contend that, with your respective chapters, you have enriched the discourse of racism and anti-racism in Canada.

We would like to acknowledge the final chapter, "Racialized and Indigenous Youth: A Call for Change," which contains the experiences and perceptions of the five youth from diverse backgrounds and different regions of Canada. You responded to our request and we are extremely proud that you are our colleagues.

We would be remiss if we did not acknowledge the support provided by our families, friends and colleagues. It is impossible to list the myriad ways that these individuals sustained us while we worked on this project. Our gracious thanks to all of you.

A special thanks to the Fernwood staff who developed the promotional materials for our book — Bev, Nancy and Curran — and Jesse Warkentin, who designed the cover for the book. We would also like to acknowledge Fazeela Jiwa and Deb Mathers for their invaluable copy edits on the manuscript. Finally, we would like to express our sincere thanks and gratitude to Wayne Antony, who walked this journey with us. Your various contributions to the book are greatly appreciated. However, what sustained us was your extreme patience as we worked on this volume.

ABOUT THE AUTHORS

Glenda Tibe Bonifacio is a professor in Women and Gender Studies at the University of Lethbridge. She is the author of *Pinay on the Prairies: Filipino Women and Transnational Identities* (2013). Her research interests centre on gender, migration and globalization, and she is currently a research affiliate of the Prentice Institute of Global Population and Economy.

Emma Maryam Bronson is a seventeen-year-old, mixed-race, Brown female living in Montréal. Her mother is a White Anglophone and her father is Mauritian. She has studied music her whole life, plays four instruments and sings. She hopes to one day make music the biggest use of her time. She studied theatre for five years and dance for four years. Political activism came into her life at an early age, as her whole family is very engaged. It is one of her strongest interests, but she has many more to discover.

Bryan (last name not provided) was born in Montréal, Québec, and is an anti-racist and trans activist.

Clark Carreon-Alarcon was born in Montréal, Québec. From a young age, he has been exposed to community work (activism and such) by his parents, who were some of the forerunners in a Filipino activist group called Kabataang Montréal (KM), an organization that demanded equal rights for Filipinos and minorities and vocalized the struggles of the working class during the early 2000s. Being a part of that, Clark encountered many truths about the world (racism, sexism, corrupt politics, etc.) in his head before he even experienced any hardships. As such, he is very aware of how the system and people work. Clark is currently attending Vanier College in hopes of becoming an architect.

Wendy Chan is a professor in the Department of Sociology and Anthropology at Simon Fraser University. Her research interests are in the areas of racism and immigration enforcement; the criminalization of poverty; racialization and the criminal justice system; race, crime and mental health; violence against women; and gender issues in the legal system. She has published five books, including *Racialization, Crime and Criminal Justice in Canada* (2014).

David Este is a professor in the Faculty of Social Work at the University of Calgary. The majority of his research is focused on different aspects of the immigrant and refugee experience in Canada. David is co-author of *Race and Well Being* (2010).

Ilyan Ferrer is an assistant professor in the Faculty of Social Work at the University of Calgary. His research focuses on aging, im/migration and caring labour of racialized communities in Canada; qualitative and oral history methodologies; and anti-oppressive social work theory and practice.

Grace-Edward Galabuzi is an associate professor in the Department of Politics and Public Administration at Ryerson University. He is also a research associate at the Centre for Social Justice in Toronto. Grace-Edward's research interests include globalization from below — local community responses to global economic restructuring in the Global North and South, the racialization of the Canadian labour market, and social exclusion and the social economic status of racialized groups in Canada.

Sharon Goulet is Red River Métis and a member of the Métis Nation of Alberta. Sharon has lived in Calgary for thirty years and has worked at the City of Calgary for the past twenty-four years in a variety of positions that support and advocate social change for Indigenous people living in Calgary. Presently, Sharon is a Social Planner with Family and Community Support Services, and her work involves social planning, community development, research and advocacy on issues that concern the Indigenous urban community.

André Jacob est un professeur associé à l'École de travail social de Université du Québec à Montréal et ex-coordonnateur de l'Observatoire international sur le racisme et les discriminations. Sa contribution à la lutte contre le racisme et les discriminations est reconnues: – Prix « Droits et libertés ». Commission des droits de la personne du Québec (1991); et – Prix d'excellence en matières de relations interethniques (Heritage Canada) (1992).

André Jacob is an associate professor at the School of Social Work at l'Université du Québec à Montréal and the past coordinator of the International Observatory on Racism and Discrimination. His contributions in the struggle against racism and discrimation are recognized by the Rights and Liberties Award presented by the Québec Human Rights Commission (1991) and the Award of Excellence on Inter-Cultural Relations presented by Heritage Canada (1992).

Carl E. James is a professor and teaches in the Faculty of Education and the Graduate Programs in Sociology and Social Work, York University, Toronto. He is the Jean Augustine Chair in Education, Community and Diaspora; his research interest includes moving beyond essentialist representations and recognizing how accessible and equitable opportunities in education and employment for racialized youth account for their circumstances and achievements. Carl is the author of several books, including *The Equity Myth: Racialization and Indigeneity at Canadian Universities* (2017).

Aviaq Johnston is an Inuit author from Igloolik, Nunavut. Her debut novel is *Those Who Run in the Sky* (2017). In 2014, Aviaq won first place in the Aboriginal Arts and Stories competition for her short story "Tarnikuluk," which also earned her a Governor General's History Award. Aviaq is a graduate of the post-secondary program for Inuit students, Nunavut Sivuniksavut, and briefly studied English at the University of Ottawa. She is currently studying Social Service Work at Canadore College.

Nazilla Khanlou is the Women's Health Research Chair in Mental Health in the Faculty of Health at York University and an associate professor in its School of Nursing. Her overall program of research is situated in the interdisciplinary field of community-based mental health promotion in general and more specifically mental health promotion among youth and women in multicultural and immigrant-receiving settings. Her most recent book is *Women's Mental Health: Resistance and Resilience in Community and Society* (2015).

Edward Ou Jin Lee is an assistant professor at the School of Social Work at the Université de Montréal. Ed's interests include critical and anti-oppressive social work, critical and participatory research methodologies, social policy advocacy and community organizing, with a focus on queer and trans people of colour and migrants.

Liza Lorenzetti is an assistant professor in the Faculty of Social Work at the University of Calgary, on Blackfoot and Treaty 7 Territory. Her interest in social change is grounded by almost thirty years of practice and activism on interconnected social issues such as gender-based violence prevention, poverty elimination, peace-building and anti-racism.

Hieu Van Ngo is an associate professor in the Faculty of Social Work at the University of Calgary. Through his involvement with the Coalition for Equal Access to Education, he has worked with community members to advocate for access of immigrant and racialized children and youth to quality education and opportunities for equitable civic engagement.

Mahdi Qasqas is a psychologist at Qasqas & Associates (Q&A) and a PhD candidate in the Faculty of Social Work at University of Calgary. His research focuses on commitment, motivation and satisfaction among volunteer leaders of non-profit Islamic organizations. He has over seventeen years and fifteen thousand hours of community development and leadership experience and regularly provides consultation, training and motivational speeches to a range of diverse organizations.

Christa Sato completed her MSW (thesis route) in the Faculty of Social Work at the University of Calgary. She has worked on several projects focused on immigration, diversity and social justice.

Luz Vasquez is the research coordinator of the Office of Women's Health Chair in Mental Health at York University. Her PhD is from the Department of Sociology at York University. She possesses extensive research experience in Mexico, Belize and Guatemala.

Brittany Walker is a seventeen-year-old Jamaican-Indian girl, born and raised in Calgary. For many years she has worked with Liza Lorenzetti and many organizations, striving to make her community a better place. Brittany is currently in her final weeks of high school and aspires to become a social worker to create the life for others that she never had.

1

THE COLOURBLIND SOCIETY

David Este, Christa Sato and Liza Lorenzetti

In the May 2015 issue of *Toronto Life*, Desmond Cole, a project coordinator for City Vote Ontario and a political commentator, wrote an article that destroyed the myth that Canada had reached the pinnacle of multicultural success — that is, a so-called "colourblind society." The title of Cole's piece, "The Skin I'm In: I've been interrogated by police more than 50 times — all because I'm black," says it all. While the article focuses on his experiences in Kingston and Toronto, Cole also discusses the collective experiences of African Canadians with the criminal justice system in Canada.

The core of Cole's article is twofold: the first is his exposé of *carding*. The African Canadian Legal Clinic (2017: 29) defines the practice of carding as, "police fill[ing] out Field Information Reports (contact cards) which include a subject's personal information (skin colour, height, weight, reason for stop, location of stop and associates) and input this information into a massive database." Commenting on this practice, Cole (2015: n.d.) remarks,

> the police have never provided any evidence to show how carding reduces or solves crime. They've also failed to justify carding's excessive focus on black men. The *Toronto Star* crunched the numbers and found that in 2013, 25 percent of people carded were black. At that time, I was 17 times more likely than a white person to be carded in Toronto's downtown core.

Despite the lack of evidence to support this widespread and highly discriminatory practice, Mark Saunders, who heads Toronto's police force remarked, "abolishing carding is not the way in which we are going to say, everything is going to get better" (Ross 2015). An open letter from the Edmonton Police Association in July 2017 defends what they term "street checks" and positions it as a strategy for crime prevention and public safety. The Association's acting vice-president and author of the letter goes on to state, "during my twenty years of service, I have never seen a police officer act in a racist manner" (Huculak n.d.: 1–2). The open letter was a response to a report obtained by CBC showing that, between 2012 and 2016, *racialized persons* who had committed no crime were disproportionately stopped, questioned and documented by the Edmonton Police; in 2016, Indigenous women were ten times more likely than White women to be subjected to "street checks" (Huncar 2017).

The second theme that prevails in Cole's article is the pervasive practice of *racial profiling* experienced by African Canadians. In 2003, the Ontario Human Rights Commission defined racial profiling as

> any action undertaken for reasons of safety, security or public protection that relies on stereotypes about race, colour, ethnicity, ancestry, religion, or place of origin rather than on reasonable suspicion, to single out an individual for greater scrutiny or different treatment. (ONHR 2003: 6)

Racial profiling is not only imposed by police services across Canada but is also practised by an array of societal institutions such as commercial centres and nightclubs. Discussing the consequences of racial profiling and the impact on him as an individual, Cole (2015: 2) shares,

> I've developed habits to check my own behaviour. I no longer walk through upscale clothing stores like Holt Renfrew or Harry Rosen, because I'm usually tailed by over-attentive employees ... I'm terrified of anyone with a badge and a gun, since they always seem excessively interested in who I am and what I am doing. My eyes follow every police car that passes me. It has become a matter of survival in a city where, despite all the talk of harmonious multi-culturalism, I continue to stand out.

Several scholars and organizations (Kelly 1998; Wortley and Tanner 2006; Henry and Tator 2010; Nova Scotia Human Rights Commission 2013; Meng, Giwa and Anucha 2015) have explored the varied manifestations of racial profiling. However, it should be noted that racial profiling is not limited to African Canadian males. In 2005, Shoppers Drug Mart was ordered to pay $8000 to Mary McCarthy, who resided in Fredericton, New Brunswick, as a result of profiling her in a downtown location. Ms. McCarthy was wrongly accused of being a shoplifter. The Ontario Human Rights Tribunal ruled that McCarthy was singled out by the Shoppers employee because she is Black (Harrop 2015).

An additional burden to racialized and Indigenous women, racism can act as a key barrier to accessing services, as well as legal and support systems (Smith 2004). In cases of domestic violence, for instance, women often feel "forced to make a choice between 'delivering their men' to be treated unfairly by the police, or learning to live with the abuse" (Smith 2004: 27). With disproportionate rates of incarceration and collective histories of abuse by governments, Indigenous and African Canadian communities have particularly good reasons to question the concept of "justice" within Canada's justice system (Alexander 2010; Government of Canada 2013).

The objectives of this chapter are to:

- set the context for this book;
- introduce key definitions and fundamental concepts;
- introduce the theoretical framework; and
- provide an overview of the book chapters.

Racism and Race-Related Concepts

The section above provides a glimpse of some of the complexities associated with understanding racism in Canada. It is necessary to provide an initial conceptual understanding of *racism* and race-related concepts that are used throughout this chapter and the rest of the book. It is also important to keep in mind that these definitions are not exhaustive and contributing authors may have different conceptualizations of the terms depending on the purpose and/or context in which they are used. Nevertheless, these key terms provide a foundational starting point to begin situating oneself within discourses of racism and *anti-racism*.

Racialized Persons or Groups

The Ontario Human Rights Commission (OHRC) provides general guide-lines on the most inclusive terminology to use when describing individuals or groups of individuals, while recognizing that people within these groups may contest or disagree with the terminology used to describe them. The Commission posits,

> When it is necessary to describe people collectively, the term "racialized person" or "racialized group" is preferred over "racial minority," "visible minority," "person of colour," or "non-White" as it expresses race as a social construct rather than as a description

based on perceived biological traits. Furthermore, these other terms treat "White" as the norm to which racialized persons are to be compared and have a tendency to group all racialized persons in one category, as if they are all the same. (OHRC n.d.: S2.1.1)

Building on the notion that race and racism are social constructs, Matthew Clair and Jeffrey Denis (2015: 857) maintain that, through the process of *racialization*, "perceived patterns of physical difference — such as skin color or eye shape — are used to differentiate groups of people, thereby constituting them as 'races'; racialization becomes racism when it involves the hierarchical and socially consequential valuation of racial groups."

What Is Racism?

In the scholarly literature on racism in Canada, several conceptualizations of racism exist. Augie Fleras and Jean Leonard Elliot (2007: 362) refer to racism as

a relatively complex and organized set of ideas and ideals (ideology) that assert or imply natural superiority of one group over another in terms of entitlements and privileges, together with power to put these beliefs into practice in a way that denies or excludes those who belong to a devalued category.

Carl James (2003: 136) provides some critical detail in his definition:

Racism is the unconditional acceptance of a negative social definition of a colonized or subordinate group typically identified by physical features (i.e., race–black, brown, yellow, red). These "racialized groups" are believed to lack certain abilities or characteristics, which in turn constructs them as culturally and biologically inferior.

It is well understood that race does not exist as a biological category among humans, since there is more genetic variation within *racial groups* than between them; however, race as a social construct "has tremendous significance in structuring social reality" (Clair and Denis 2015: 857). As such, racialization occurs as a process whereby racial meaning is constructed to create categories attributed to particular groups and is reinforced through social processes that result in system-wide racial inequalities (Clair and Denis 2015).

Table 1.1: Racism, Violence and Health Study: The Meaning of Racism by Participants

> From a study that explored how racism impacted individuals of African descent residing in Toronto, Calgary and Halifax, the following are examples of the meaning of racism:
>
> - Racism serves to diminish, demean, belittle, exclude, marginalize and dehumanize people of colour (Caribbean male, Toronto).
> - Racism is people suppressing other people and trying to be controlling and claiming superiority and thinking they are better based on the colour of their skin, their beliefs, how they look, how they talk (African female, Calgary).
> - Racism means using privilege and position to oppress the group and keep those groups down (Caribbean female, Halifax).

Source: James et al. 2010.

Types of Racism

According to Frances Henry and Carol Tator (2010), there are three main forms of racism: individual, systemic and cultural. As well, we discuss structural racism, colourblind racism and structural violence.

Individual and Everyday Racism

Henry and Tator (2010: 42) define *individual racism* as "the attitude, belief, or opinion that one's own racial group has superior values, customs, and norms and, conversely, that other racial groups possess inferior traits and attributes." They further note that racist attitudes may not be overtly expressed by an individual, but rather through practices of racial discrimination. For example, when getting on the train, an individual may purposely avoid sitting next to an elderly Punjabi male wearing a turban.

In a similar vein, *everyday racism* was a term coined by Philomena Essed (1991). The notion of everyday racism is an "integration of racism into everyday situations through practices that activate underlying power relations" (Essed 1991: 50). This type of racism

> involves the many and sometimes small ways in which racism is experienced by people of colour in their interactions with the dominant White group. It expresses itself in glances, gestures, forms of speech, and physical movements. Sometimes, it is not even consciously experienced by its perpetrators, but it is immediately and painfully felt by its victims. (Henry and Tator 2010: 44)

Everyday racism is ingrained in personal interactions and community and institutional practices; the psychological distress from daily experiences of racism can cause chronic adverse effects on one's mental and physical health (Essed 1991).

Institutional or Systemic Racism

Institutional racism refers to "the policies, practices and procedures of various institutions, which may directly or indirectly, consciously or unwittingly, promote, sustain, or entrench differential advantage or privilege for peoples of certain races" (Henry and Tator 2010: 44). Similarly, Kwame McKenzie (2017: 5) defines institutional racism as "an ecological form of discrimination … [that] refers to inequitable outcomes for different racialized groups." Hence, it is maintained that, despite the presence of institutional racism, organizations do not appear to have the ability to address this behaviour or may simply ignore the existence of this form of oppression. A consequence of not dealing with institutional racism is the maintenance of the status quo.

Henry and Tator (2010: 45) differentiate institutional racism from *systemic racism*, which refers more broadly "to the laws, rules, and norms woven into the social system that result in an unequal distribution of economic, political, and social resources and rewards among various racial groups." Simply put, systemic racism occurs when an institution or set of institutions working together creates or maintains racial inequity (Government of Ontario 2017).

Cultural or Ideological Racism

Cultural or *ideological racism* permeates societal values and is therefore challenging to isolate because it is embedded within the collective beliefs of the mainstream or hegemonic society (Henry and Tator 2010). An example of a type of cultural or ideological racism is Essed's (1991: 143) conceptualization of *gendered racism*, which "refers to the racial oppression of racial/ethnic minority women and men as structured by historically situated racist perceptions of gender roles and behaviour." Gendered racism is a social construct that perpetuates, for example, the myth that violence is a form of cultural practice within racialized communities and specific racialized ethnocultural groups. Accordingly, "cultural racism creates a 'we' and 'them' mentality in which one's own racial group is considered to be better than other groups" (Henry and Tator 2010: 45). These forms of racism are learned through a set of ethnocentric beliefs and values, which are typically maintained through the socialization of new generations who are taught these beliefs from an early age (Henry and Tator 2010).

Structural Racism
Sociologist Eduardo Bonilla-Silva (2015: 1360) provides a useful definition that captures the structural nature of racism:

> Racism is, above anything, about practices and behaviors that produce a *racial structure* — a network of social relations at social, political, economic, and ideological levels that shapes the life changes of the various races. This structure is responsible for the production and reproduction of systemic racial advantages for some (the dominant racial group) and disadvantages for others (the subordinate races). Thus, racism as a form of social organization places subjects in common social locations. As subjects face similar experiences, they develop a consciousness, a sense of "us" versus "them." (emphasis in the original)

Accordingly, *structural racism* is the sum total of institutional racism in the labour market, housing market, education system, criminal justice system and other institutional domains (Mensah and Williams 2017: 34). These forms of racial discrimination within multiple institutions and systems create a structure of racial inequality that advantages certain groups over others to create a social hierarchy.

Colourblind Racism
Bonilla-Silva (2015: 1364) has written extensively on the concept of *colourblind racism*, which refers to "the racial ideology based on the superficial extension of the principles of liberalism to racial matters that results in 'raceless' explanations for all sort of race-related affairs." Colourblind racism is a form of racism embedded within liberal discourses wherein White people refuse to acknowledge the existence of racial inequality by denying that racism exists and essentially use this discourse as a tool "to avoid the appearance of racism" (Bonilla-Silva 2002: 63). Bonilla-Silva (2002: 42) argues that colourblind racism emerged as the dominant ideology of the post-civil rights era, and is characterized by four major themes:

- the extension of the principles of liberalism to racial matters in an abstract manner;
- cultural rather than biological explanations of minorities' inferior standing and performance in labour and education markets;
- naturalization of racial phenomena such as residential and school segregation; and

- the claim that discrimination has all but disappeared.

Accordingly, these strategies or tools for navigating contemporary racial landscapes are effective for White people to justify "our current racial situation as they see no reason for any kind of intervention or even to ameliorate the extent of racial inequality" (Bonilla-Silva 2015: 1364). Consequently, such strategies make White people "look good" as they no longer sound "racist" (Bonilla-Silva 2015: 1364), and contemporary racial discourses reinforce the notion that Canadians live in a colourblind society.

Structural Violence
A discussion of racism in North America, and Canada in particular, cannot be understood without the examination of racism as *structural violence*. As noted by Liza Lorenzetti, Lana Wells, Carmen Logie, and Tonya Callaghan (2017: 175),

> Structural violence theory conceptualizes the multiple levels (micro to macro), types (direct, indirect) and actors (individual, institutional) involved in producing violence against marginalized and oppressed communities.

Structural violence is most blatant in the high rates of abuse perpetrated against Indigenous women interpersonally and systemically and the targeting of racialized communities — particularly Black and Indigenous men — by Canada's "justice" system. A strong critique of state-imposed structural violence exposes the duality of policy and legislation in providing protections for some groups (White, male, wealthy) and enhancing risks for targeted groups (racialized, Indigenous, economically marginalized) (Lorenzetti 2016).

Anti-Racism
Broadly, anti-racism is defined as the study of how the dynamics of social difference (race, class, gender, sexual orientation, physical ability, language, education and religion) are mediated in people's daily experience. Anti-racism, therefore, can be understood as "forms of thought and/or practice that seek to confront, eradicate and/or ameliorate racism" (Bonnett 2000: 4). More specifically, anti-racism is

> an action-oriented educational strategy for institutional, systemic change to address racism and the interlocking systems of social oppression ... Anti-racism explicitly names the issues of race and

social differences of power and equity rather than as matters of cultural and ethnic variety. (Dei 2000: 27)

It is imperative that individuals who are committed to anti-racism engage in a series of activities or events that are designed to increase their awareness of racism and to begin to actively address racist attitudes and behaviours.

Racism-Related Stress and the Impact of Racism

An African American psychologist, Shelly Harrell (2000), notes that an adequate understanding of the stress in the lives of racialized persons must take into account experiences that are related to unique person–environment transactions involving race. Simply put, Harrell contends that we have to look at racism as it is experienced by those who have been its target. She advanced a typology that discusses six types of racism-related stress (Harrell 2002):

- racism-related life events;
- vicarious racism;
- daily racism micro-stressors;
- chronic contextual stress;
- collective experiences of racism; and
- the transgenerational transmission of group trauma.

Racism-related life events are types of stressors that include "significant life experiences that are relatively time limited although they may lead to other events or have a lasting impact on individuals" (Harrell 2000: 45). Examples include being harassed by police, as described by Desmond Cole, or being discriminated against when accessing housing.

Harrell (2000: 45) asserts that "racism exerts its influence not only through direct personal experience, but also through observation and report." This type of race-related stress is known as *vicarious racism*. As a Black male residing in Canada, the first author of this book (David), watched how his peers were treated by White police officers, either through racial profiling or when in custody, which caused him to become fearful of police; he felt that he would be subjected to similar behaviours. Vicarious racism is exerted by and experienced through observation and media reports, which "can create anxiety, a heightened sense of danger, vulnerability, anger and sadness, among other emotional and psychological reactions" (Harrell 2000: 45).

Daily racism micro-stressors represent another dimension of race-related stress. These are also known as "interpersonal forms of discrimination." Being ignored while waiting in line or being followed while in public constitute forms of this type of stress (Harrell 2000). Important results of these types of experiences are the negative impacts on people of African descent, Indigenous Peoples and other racialized groups, such as being demoralized or feeling disrespected.

The fourth form of race-related stress is *chronic contextual*. Harrell (2000: 46) remarks, "this source of stress reflects the impact of social structure, political dynamics or social role demands and the larger environment within which one must adapt and cope." The ongoing racism and discrimination experienced by Indigenous Peoples in what is now known as Canada captures the essence of this type of race-related stress. Chronic contextual stress results from the process of colonization, which impacted Indigenous Peoples' access to education, housing, food security, employment and health care services. As well, Indigenous Peoples continue to be overrepresented in the child welfare and criminal justice systems (Allan and Smylie 2015).

Collective experiences represent another type of race-related stress discussed by Harrell. Examples of this include the stereotypical images of Muslims presented in the media, or poor economic conditions or wealth inequality associated with an individual's racial/ethnic or cultural group, such as with Indigenous Peoples or African Canadians.

Finally, Harrell contends that *transgenerational transmission of group trauma* constitutes a strong type of race-related stress. Simply put, this type of racism-related stress takes into consideration the history of a racial/ethnic group and their relationship with the dominant group, which in the Canadian context are White people. For example, the systematic colonization of Indigenous Peoples in Canada and the traumatic impact of residential schools, which attempted to separate individuals from their families and strip them of their cultures, have had long-lasting negative consequences felt across generations. The finding from Canada's Truth and Reconciliation Commission underscored the causal relationship between the *Indian residential schools* (IRS) system and widespread *intergenerational trauma* among Indigenous communities (TRC 2015). This ongoing colonial project persists in present-day relationships between Indigenous Peoples and Canadian settlers (Lawrence and Dua 2005).

Racism leaves deep emotional, psychological and physical scars (Carillo and Tello 2008; James et al. 2010). A recent Canadian study confirms this disturbing reality. Interviews with nine hundred people in three major cities

(Calgary, Halifax, Toronto) found that, for over 70 percent of respondents, racism impacts or somewhat impacts their daily lives (James et al. 2010).

Cole highlights this point, recalling an incident when his family was stopped by a White police officer after his cousins threw a tissue from the family car. The officer informed Cole and the rest of the family that they would need to watch their behaviour, as any future infraction could result in being stopped and interrogated by the police at will. Cole (2015: 1) vividly remembered the impact of this incident on his family:

> We drove off, overcome with silence until my father finally exploded. "You realize everyone in this car is black, right?" he thundered at Sana. "Yes, Uncle" Sana whispered; his head down and shoulders slumped. That afternoon, my imposing father and cocky cousin had trembled in fear over a discarded Kleenex.

The experiences described by Cole may resonate with many African Canadians who have been confronted by similar incidents and even with those African Canadians who have been fortunate not to encounter this kind of racist behaviour. Navigating one's daily experiences through ongoing exposure to racialization carries heavy consequences and collective trauma. The media coverage of the deaths of several Black men in Canada and the United States during 2016 and the collective fear that they provoked are clear examples of the vicarious racism that has impacted both African American and African Canadian communities. Most disturbing is that the majority of those deaths resulted from police aggression, leading many to comment that the relationship between historical oppression and current articulations of state violence are still intact (see, for instance, Alexander 2010).

For Cole, the practices of carding and racial profiling are just two indicators of the systematic bias in Canada's justice system in relation to Black men and other racialized groups. Racialized groups are also highly over-represented in the prison system: between 2009 and 2013,

> fifteen percent of Black male inmates were assigned to maximum security compared to 10 percent overall. And racial bias is not limited to African Canadians. Today at least 25 percent of inmates in federal prisons are of indigenous descent and the proportion is much higher for incarcerated females and inmates in provincial jails. (Cole 2015: 4)

Systems, and in particular the criminal justice system, may be seen as repressive and untrustworthy in the eyes of racialized persons in Canada and the US (Kasturiangan, Krishnan and Riger 2004; Jolly and Reeves 2005; Guruge, Khanlou and Gastaldo 2010). Accentuating this point, a 2013 Government of Canada report confirms this stance: over the previous ten years, Canada's racialized incarcerated population increased by 75 percent. The incarceration of Indigenous people increased by over 46 percent, while the incarceration of Caucasian inmates decreased by 3 percent over this time period (Government of Canada 2013). Canadian and American experiences draw a number of parallels in that "the primary targets of [the penal system's] control can be defined largely by race" (Alexander 2010: 10–11).

It is important to stress that the criminal justice system is just one of many systems in Canadian society where racism exists. It is widely acknowledged by many scholars that, within these systems, institutionalized racism prevails (Henry and Tator 2010; James et al. 2010). This type of racism, or structural violence, contributed to the formation of Toronto's Black Lives Matter.

Black Lives Matter

After the shooting death of Michael Brown in Ferguson, Missouri, the emergence of the Toronto chapter of *Black Lives Matter* (BLM) underscored years of ongoing frustration by the city's Black community, particularly its relationship with the Toronto Police Services. In Toronto, the killings of Jermaine Carby in 2014 and Andrew Loku in 2015 provided more evidence of police brutality against African Canadian men. Just as important was the shattering of the image and myth that Black men and women are not targeted by Canadian police personnel.

Rodney Diverlus, a community organizer in Toronto who helped found BLM Toronto maintains there is no way for Black Canadians to be treated fairly if they do not talk about race:

> Americans talk about their history at least more than [Canadians] do ... we also had slavery in Canada, that we also had segregation of every form in Canada. What we do as Canadians is we say, "we are not the Americans." (Clarke 2015)

The presence of BLM in Toronto, not surprisingly, has garnered criticism from certain media outlets. Writing in the *Toronto Sun* in August 2016, Joe Warmington remarks, "Black Lives Matter protesters in Toronto don't abide by the rules, and since there are never any ramifications nor repercussions, why should anybody else?" He comments further:

BLM can set up a permanent protest centre in front of Toronto Police headquarters and nothing happens except they get a meeting with the chief. Pull an aggressive stunt to get the attention of the mayor outside his office and they are rewarded with a chance to sit down with him. (Warmington 2016: 1)

Such commentary is not unique, and the vilification of both BLM and its stance on human rights is commonplace in both media and mainstream White social circles. One has to question deeply, why is membership or alliance to BLM viewed as a threat to mainstream society? Black lives should matter, after all. However, the BLM movement centralizes all the ways that Black lives are in fact dehumanized in Canadian society, leading BLM to be interpreted as a threat to the status quo. The vitriol against BLM provides ample evidence that such critics continue to see the world through the prism of privileged White society that cannot comprehend the experiences that racialized Canadians encounter on a daily basis.

Those individuals who maintain that "all lives matter" clearly do not understand the historical and contemporary forms of anti-Black racism. In particular, as Cole noted, young Black men are extremely vulnerable to what Maynard (2017) described as *Policing Black Lives*. In a report released by the United Nations Human Rights Council (UNHRC) in fall 2017, entitled "Report of the Working Group of Experts on People of African Descent," the following commentary on its mission to Canada was put forth:

> The Working Group is concerned about excessive use of force and killings by police, especially in response to cases involving vulnerable people of African descent who are mentally ill or otherwise in crisis. Several Black Canadians have reportedly been killed by the police since 2010, including Andrew Loku, Jermaine Carby, Alex Wettlaufer, Kwasi Skene-Peters, Jean-Pierre Bony, Ian Pryce, Frank Antony Berry, Michael Eligon, Eric Osawe, Reyard Jardine-Douglas and Junior Alexander Mason. (UNHRC 2017: 8)

The Working Group recommends the Government of Canada ensures that "a psychiatrist or psychologist accompany police officers when responding to mental health calls" (UNHRC 2017: 18). As noted by Cole, Maynard and the UNHRC report, despite the "all lives matter" criticisms directed against BLM, both historically and in contemporary society Black Canadians have been and continue to be systematically and unfairly victimized as a direct consequence of state violence, often paying with their lives. This is the rationale for the emergence of the Black Lives Matter movement.

David Este, one of the authors of this chapter and editors of this book, is a third-generation African Canadian male. He has witnessed racism in all sectors of Canadian society as well as being a recipient of racist behaviours. As well, he possesses a strong fear of being stopped by White police officers while driving. He recalls being stopped by the police at least five times in various cities across Canada. While living in Montréal, he stepped out of his apartment while he was taking clothes to the drycleaners. He was seen by a passing police car, which stopped, turned around and approached him. The two police officers informed him that they stopped him because there had been a number of robberies in the neighbourhood and he "looked suspicious." The primary reason they let him go was the fact that, at the time, he was attending McGill University and he showed them his student identification card.

The killings of Alton Sirling in Baton Rouge, Louisiana, and Philando Castile in St. Paul, Minnesota, during the summer of 2016 by White police officers severely impacted Black males in North America and their families emotionally and psychologically. According to Harrell (2000), such actions induce vicarious forms of stress for African American and African Canadian men, who strongly fear that they may be the next victims of this form of police brutality. To understand Cole's perspective and the emergence of BLM as a means of confronting systemic violence against Black people and communities in Canada, one must understand the complex historical and current-day experiences of anti-Black racism.

Anti-Black Racism

Anti-Black racism (ABR) is, quite simply, racism that is directed against Black people (Kumsa et al. 2014). In his report on racism in Ontario, Stephen Lewis (1992: 2) elaborated on the conceptualization of ABR:

> First, what we are dealing with, at root, and fundamentally, is anti-Black racism. While it is obviously true that every visible minority community experiences the indignities and wounds of systematic discrimination throughout Southern Ontario, it is the Black community which is the focus. It is Blacks who are being shot, it is Black youth that is unemployed in excessive numbers, it is Black students who are being inappropriately streamed in school, it is Black kids who are disproportionately dropping-out, it is housing

communities with large concentrations of Black residents where the sense of vulnerability and disadvantage is most acute, it is Black employees, professional and non-professional, on whom the doors of upward equity slam shut.

Akua Benjamin (2003: 60) goes further:

> The concept of anti-Black racism emerged as an analytic weapon in the struggles against racism in policing by the Black community. This concept became a lightning rod that gave specific focus to the issues of police violence, harassment and shootings impacting the Black community in Toronto.

She goes on to stress that ABR essentially describes the practices and procedures of dominant and hegemonic structures and systems of power over Blacks.

Anthony Morgan (2015), an African Canadian lawyer, wrote in the *Toronto Star* about ABR:

> Being Black in Canada can sometimes be suffocating. This feeling does not only come from being subject to anti-black racism in multiple domains of social, economic, cultural and civic life in Canada. It is overwhelmingly the result of carrying the exhausting burden of having to convince others of the truth of your lived experience.

Two publications by the African Canadian Legal Clinic (ACLC) provided detailed descriptions depicting how ABR manifests in Canadian society (Smith and Lawson 2002; ACLC 2012). In both documents, the authors contend that this type of racism exists in the Canadian immigration, legal, education, child welfare and health care systems. A second important contribution of these publications is their detailed analysis of anti-Black racism from a historical perspective.

A recent report on hate crimes illustrates the basis of racism in Canada. In 2013, the police reported 1167 criminal incidents that were motivated by hate. Of these hate crimes, over half (51 percent) were motivated by hatred of a race or ethnic group, while another 28 percent were motivated by hatred of religion. Hatred toward an individual's sexual orientation constituted 16 percent of the reported hate crimes. Among hate crimes related to race, Black populations were the most frequently targeted (22 percent), while for religion-oriented hate crimes, 16 percent were directed at Jewish communities (Allen 2015). These statistics represent disturbing trends related to hate crimes in the nation. Another community against which hate crimes are on the rise is Canada's Muslim community. Recently, a vicious attack on innocent Muslims attending a prayer service at a local mosque in Québec further shattered the myth of Canada's successful multicultural dream, particularly as it pertains to religious interculturalism. The death of six Canadian Muslims and the shock and self-questioning that would follow did not deter ongoing intolerance toward Muslims, which has included numerous misguided protests outside mosques across Canada (Nasser and McLaughlin 2017).

Multiculturalism in Canada

In 1971, Prime Minister Pierre Trudeau introduced *multiculturalism* as a major Canadian policy. The underlying rationale for the policy stressed that Canada would respect the different forms of diversity that existed in Canada, such as the array of racial, ethnic, linguistic and religious communities. As time has progressed, multiculturalism has become a key identifier of Canadian society. In defining the concept, Sarah Song (2017: 1) remarks that multiculturalism is a body of thought in political philosophy, about "how to understand and respond to the challenges associated with cultural and religious diversity."

However, multiculturalism as practised in Canada has been criticized by academics, writers and journalists. Jeffrey Reitz and his colleagues (2009) state that multiculturalism is not meeting a core goal of ensuring that all Canadians possess equal opportunities to participate and be successful in Canadian society. Writers such as Neil Bissoondath (1994) and Richard Gwyn (1995) stress that multiculturalism leads to the formation of ghettos and promotes difference between ethnic groups instead of creating a common Canadian identity.

A Time for Reconciliation and Social Justice

Canada recently emerged from a six-year truth-telling process that centred the critical re-telling of Canada's colonial history, particularly the extensive and multigenerational violence perpetrated on Indigenous Peoples from the IRS system. Over six thousand testimonies were heard, leading to a final report with ninety-four Calls to Action for durable changes to systems and structures (education, justice, health, social services, etc.) across various levels of government and within settler communities (TRC 2015):

The Commission's focus on truth determination was intended to lay the foundation for the important question of reconciliation ... Getting to the truth was hard, but getting to reconciliation will be harder. It requires that the paternalistic and racist foundations of the residential school system be rejected as the basis for an ongoing relationship. Reconciliation requires that a new vision, based on a commitment to mutual respect, be developed ... Reconciliation is not an Aboriginal problem; it is a Canadian one. Virtually all aspects of Canadian society may need to be reconsidered. (TRC 2015: vi)

The work to establish meaningful routes to *reconciliation* and an anti-racist Canada is deeper than mere words, platitudes and false promises, which have characterized Canadian society. *The Canadian Reconciliation Landscape,* a study conducted in 2016 to assess the views of Indigenous and non-Indigenous peoples on reconciliation, provides key insights into our national climate (Reconciliation Canada 2017). Drawing responses from a representative sample of non-Indigenous Canadians (n=1,529) and Indigenous Peoples (n=521), findings from the report indicate that the majority of respondents agree that there is a need for reconciliation; Indigenous respondents, however, more frequently answered that there is a "great need." Further, while a majority of Indigenous and non-Indigenous respondents agreed that they would be willing to take a minimum of one action to promote reconciliation, only 22 percent of those who were non-Indigenous responded positively to the question of whether they would be "willing to re-examine your perceptions and attitudes and make a personal commitment to reconciliation" (Reconciliation Canada 2017: 5).

Broad engagement of Canadians in the work of reconciliation is an outstanding item on our national agenda. Justin Trudeau's belated apology to the Inuit, Innu and NunatuKavut residential school survivors of Newfoundland and Labrador in 2017 underscored this message. Having been shut out of the original governmental apology of 2008, survivors fought tirelessly for more than ten years to have Trudeau stand before them at Happy Valley-Goose Bay in Labrador. Tellingly, during his statement of apology, he twice emphasized that *all Canadians,* in addition to their government, were responsible for both the apology and the work of forging a new relationship with Indigenous Peoples. Trudeau's emphatic statement was reminiscent of the words of Justice Murray Sinclair, chair of the TRC, who reminded Canadians of all generations that we "must be clear, loud and united in expressing [our] heartfelt belief that reconciliation must happen in order for it to be effective" (*CBC Radio* 2015).

As various levels of government and other institutions table their action plans or responses to specific Calls to Action, it remains to be seen how the needed groundwork for authentic reconciliation and significant and durable changes in our collective colonial mindset will emerge. With more than ninety First Nations living in communities without access to assured clean drinking water (Council of Canadians n.d.), it seems that guaranteeing even the most basic human rights are still out of reach. Clean water and sanitation — what the United Nations Department of Economic and Social Affairs (UNDESA 2014: para 1) determined on July 28, 2010, as "essential to the realisation of all human rights" — is still not a reality for Indigenous communities in Canada.

What's in This Book?

What would Canada look like without racism? What are the steps to create an anti-racist society? Multiculturalism in Canada is regarded as a key feature of national identity, which is reflected in an increasingly diverse ethnocultural mosaic. Despite the changing demographic profile, racialized Canadians are systematically excluded politically, economically and socially from full participation in society through personal and structural forms of racism and discrimination.

Creating a society without racism is a complex task, which involves accounting for historical injustices, colonization, present-day ramifications of a society built on inequity, and the courage and optimism to articulate pathways forward. What is the roadmap to arrive at an authentically inclusive Canadian identity? Who needs to be involved? In this book, we invite and implore each of us to be architects in developing a just society built on values of equity and inclusion.

The primary purpose of this book is to provide a critical examination of how racism permeates Canadian society; how racism interacts with different types of oppression; and finally, how individuals, families and communities are impacted by these forms of domination. Although from diverse backgrounds, the contributors to this book are strong anti-racist scholars and advocates who are committed to the struggle against racism and colonization. Hence, each of the contributing authors presents anti-racism strategies that are designed to deal with the racism that prevails and is manifested in Canada. As activists, we truly believe in the words penned by Julian Bond, former American politician and chairperson of the National Association for the Advancement of Colored People, close to five decades ago. In his book, *A Time to Speak, A Time to Act,* Bond (1972: 8) argues that "without committed and sustained action designed to deal with the oppression, the scourge of racism will continue to negatively impact the recipients of the behaviour and attitudes."

It is important for us to share with you who we are. Susan Tilley (2016: 13–14), in talking about doing social research, stressed the importance of "tak[ing] into account the ways in which ... social locations and identities intersect and influence the design and focus of ... research." Her message also applies to us as a team of editors. The decisions we made about the subject matter of each chapter and who we invited to contribute chapters is a representation of our values, especially as they relate to social justice. We are not neutral in the social issues examined in this book. We hope that this book will not only provide new insights about how racism and other forms of oppressive behaviours impact an array of Canadians but will also serve to catalyze a lifelong commitment to creating a just society through resisting racism.

Who Are We?

These profiles are about who we are as individuals and as a team. The ongoing need to address oppressions such as racism and discrimination was indeed one of the major driving forces that brought the three of us together for this project. Our deep passion for social justice also served as a strong motivator, as we believe that all Canadians bear the responsibility of tackling issues of injustice.

David Este

I am a third generation African (Black) Canadian. My grandparents migrated to Canada between 1912 and 1928. They left their homes in Antigua and Barbados, settling in Montréal. My great uncle, Reverend Doctor Charles Este, played a key role in the development of Montréal's Black community for over forty years; he served as the minister of the oldest Black congregation in Montréal, Union United Church. In discussions with him, I learned about the history of the Black community in Montréal. In conversations with my grandparents, as well as several great uncles and aunts, I cultivated a strong interest in the history of people of African descent from a global perspective.

From 1967 to 1970, I lived in Dartmouth, Nova Scotia, as my dad, who was in the Canadian military, was stationed in Halifax. The time I spent living in this part of Canada proved to be quite insightful and started me on the journey to become "a Black nationalist." I recall two events that facilitated my awareness as a Black person living in White-dominated society. I attended Dartmouth Senior High (DHS) in the late 1960s. This was the largest high school in that city. I was aware of the longstanding presence of African Nova Scotians in the Halifax–Dartmouth region. However, out of a student population of fifteen hundred, there were only four Black students. I clearly remember asking myself and my parents, why were there so few Black students? The second question I posed was related: where are the Black teachers? The entire teaching staff was White. I also observed the absence, in both grade ten and eleven history classes, of content dealing with the people of African descent. The emphasis in these courses was on European and mainstream Canadian history.

The second event took place in 1968. During that year, a number of Black Panthers from the United States spent time in Halifax to understand the plight of African Nova Scotians and work with community activists such as Rocky Jones. I have read the book entitled *Burnley "Rocky" Jones: An Autobiography* (2016), where Jones provides considerable detail about this time period (Walker and Jones 2016). I attended a debate at DHS between two Black Panthers and two teachers who taught social studies. I walked away quite impressed and extremely happy to see and hear the two brothers educate the two teachers about the experiences of people of African descent in North America as well as directly confront their assumptions about African Nova Scotian students.

When I attended McGill and Carleton Universities for undergraduate studies, my areas of study were African and African American history. I completed a master of history degree under the supervision of Jim Walker at the University of Waterloo, who was a very good friend of Rocky Jones and who co-wrote his autobiography. At the time, Jim Walker was one of a handful of historians who specialized in "Black History." I became quite immersed in both African Canadian and African American history. Having this background helps me understand the issues/challenges that face these two broad communities today.

From 1980 to 1982, I attended the University of Toronto, where I completed my MSW degree. At this stage of my life, I became more aware of the daily struggles that confronted people of African descent residing in Canada's largest city — racial profiling, the killing of Black men by White police officers, and an education system that streamed considerable numbers of Black male students into the trades (propelled by the belief that they did not possess the knowledge and abilities required to be successful in the academic domain). Some of the places I enjoyed spending time were the Black barbershops on Bathurst Street. These were spaces that enabled me to take the pulse of Toronto's Black community and gain an understanding of major political developments in the Caribbean. I also recall spending hours at the Third World Bookstore owned by Leonard and Gwen Johnstone. They had a great collection of books focused on a wide range of topics on the African diaspora. However, just as important were the discussions we had on the injustices experienced by people of African descent throughout the world.

In 1992, I joined Calgary's Faculty of Social Work and, during the past twenty-five years, the majority of my research has focused on the experiences of immigrants and refugees in Canada along with the health and well-being of people of African descent. In reflecting on my work as a social work professor, there are a couple of events/contributions I would like to share. In 2003–09, I had the opportunity to work on a research study known as the "Racism, Violence, and Health Study." This project, conducted in Halifax, Toronto and Calgary, focused on how racism impacted African Canadian men, their families and communities in the three cities mentioned. An important aspect of the study was focused on understanding how racism impacted the various participants' health.

It was led by a team of African Canadian scholars who are also friends: Wanda Thomas Bernard with the School of Social Work at Dalhousie University, Akua Benjamin with the School of Social Work at Ryerson University and Carl James with the Faculty of Education at York University. One of the major insights I gleaned from this experience was that, although we were working with African Canadians in three cities, as researchers we were also exploring our experiences as people of African descent and professors in predominantly White spaces, such as the universities where we worked. Second, the study was well received and the community forums were well attended; 900 participants completed the survey while another 120 participated in in-depth interviews.

The history of Canadian social welfare essentially mirrored the dominance of mainstream Canadian history. During the past fifteen years, working with colleagues such as Dr. Bernard, we have been able to document the contributions of African Canadians to the history of social welfare and social work in Canada as well as contemporary practice with people of African descent. For me, this work is very important; one of the driving forces that prompted my decision to pursue social work as a profession was indeed to work with African Canadian communities.

I am currently involved in a research project with a community organization in Edmonton, Alberta, called the Shiloh Centre for Multicultural Roots. The primary purpose of this study is to research and document the stories of the first and subsequent generations of African Americans who migrated to Alberta primarily during 1909 to 1920s. Known as Black Pioneers, these early settlers and their descendants have received scant attention by Canadian scholars.

Christa Sato

Being asked to co-edit a book addressing issues related to race and racism is both an honour and a privilege. As a second-generation, racialized female of Japanese and Filipino ancestry, I have experienced the deleterious impacts of racism at an individual, family, community and societal level. While some racist behaviours may be dismissed by members of the dominant society, they undoubtedly have left a lasting scar that, in many ways, profoundly dehumanized the essence of who I am. I hope writing about who am I will motivate you to understand that, while racism is indeed structural and systemic, it is first and foremost experienced at a personal level.

My father and mother were immigrants who came from Japan and the Philippines, respectively. My father immigrated as an eight-year-old boy with his family and my mother arrived during the 1970s, sponsored by her aunt and trained as a skilled midwife. My parents met in Alberta, got married and had me and my four brothers. While both of them had high aspirations for their five children, as immigrants they inevitably encountered a plethora of barriers that hindered their ability to successfully settle and integrate into Canadian society. My parents struggled to provide us with basic necessities but always ensured our needs were met. For this, I am forever indebted to my parents for the tremendous sacrifices they made and the hardships they endured to ensure that my future was secure. Whether I was aware of it or not, witnessing the injustices experienced by my parents and so many other racialized Canadians in similar situations, I was drawn to the profession of social work and determined to effect change.

Furthermore, at a personal level I encountered a different set of challenges as a Canadian-born, bicultural daughter of two immigrant parents and can certainly relate to experiences of exclusion based on my ethnicity. One of the most salient forms of racism I encounter on a regular basis is being asked, "where are you from?" When I say Calgary, I can almost always expect the follow up question, "but where are you really from?" This is not an isolated incident of racism; I am constantly asked these questions. While it may seem like an innocent question of curiosity about cultural background, it implies that, as a racialized person, I do not fit conceptualizations of what it means to truly be "Canadian."

Growing up, I struggled to feel any sense of belonging. Although I could identify with aspects of my mother's Filipino culture, my father's Japanese culture and the Canadian culture into which I was born, I never truly felt a strong sense of belonging to any of these cultural communities. None of these ethnocultural communities truly accepted me as an "insider." Multiple and sometimes competing factors related to my social identity all contributed to feeling a need to prove my worth in each of these communities while simultaneously feeling hopeless. The core of who I am — born in Canada to two immigrant parents from different cultures, and female — undoubtedly presented challenges in coming to terms with my own ethnic identity. I learned that, no matter how much I tried to belong to any of these communities, I would always carry the burden of not being "good enough."

During my childhood and especially during adolescence, I constantly felt competing pressures to meet the cultural and familial expectations of my parents and wanting to fit in with the Canadian mainstream. This was compounded by the fact that, among the children in our family, I was the only daughter and there were differential gender expectations placed on me in comparison to my four brothers. Often times, I felt that I could never measure up to these expectations and, consequently, felt I had either disappointed my parents or did not truly fit in with my Canadian peers. This resulted in feeling depressed, as well as lacking self-esteem and confidence.

After a long and arduous journey of discovering myself, I have now come to a place where I can feel pride in who I am as a second-generation, racialized female. Attending university and studying social work enabled me to contextualize my own experiences and situate them within broader issues related to structural and systemic discrimination.

I completed a master of social work degree and specialized in international and community development at the University of Calgary. My practice as a social worker, particularly in community-based research with immigrant, refugee and racialized populations, has been informed by my own experiences of injustice. I believe obtaining education has afforded me a position of privilege that enables me to advocate with, for and on behalf of other marginalized groups. This has indeed been reflected in my practicum and research experiences, which have been directly related to practice with diverse ethnocultural populations.

My first immersion into professional social work was my BSW placement with Child and Family Services. There, I worked with an assessor who investigated allegations of child abuse in an area heavily populated by immigrant and refugee families. This experience provided me with the opportunity to have a glimpse of the everyday challenges, struggles and realities experienced by individuals and families who encounter the child welfare system. It taught me the value of direct frontline practice but also challenged me to critically question the relationship of these inherent challenges experienced at the personal level as symptomatic of broader societal issues. This compelled me to pursue my second placement in the area of community development.

My senior BSW practicum was as a community social worker with the City of Calgary. This placement had a strong focus on community development and social justice. I spent considerable time engaging and mobilizing neighbourhood residents in collective actions that responded to systemic underlying issues and effected sustainable change. I worked in an ethnically diverse neighbourhood in northeast Calgary, comprised mostly of new Canadians.

Finally, during my MSW practicum with Citizenship and Immigration Canada, I was involved with the Local Immigration Partnerships. These community-based partnerships engage a broad range of local stakeholders to improve accessibility and coordination of services that facilitate immigrant settlement and integration, leading to economic, social, cultural, and civic inclusion of newcomers.

In addition, during the past five years, I have been working as a research assistant at the Faculty of Social Work at the University of Calgary, under the mentorship of David Este. I was introduced to research as a form of social work practice during the summer of my third year as an undergrad and fell in love with it. My professional experience as a research assistant and project coordinator has enabled me to build strong relationships with diverse individuals from agencies serving immigrant and ethnocultural populations.

I was also involved in a national research project funded by the Movember Foundation, entitled "Strength in Unity," which was conducted in Calgary, Vancouver and Toronto. Strength in Unity was a community-based research study that attempted to reduce the stigma of mental illness among boys and men in Asian communities. This was done by educating participants about stigma and training them to become Community Mental

Health Ambassadors within their communities. It supported them in working to effect change for themselves, their families, their communities and the broader Canadian society.

My MSW thesis research explored the question, *what are the processes that enabled second-generation young Filipino males living in Calgary to complete university?* I engaged in the research process with the intention that the knowledge gained will contribute to the social inclusion of young, second-generation Filipino males, their families and their communities.

This reflexive process of writing about who I am has been transformative in realizing how far I have come in terms of my personal and professional journey. As I write this, I feel a renewed sense of agency and hope that addressing race-related issues in Canada can be achieved through socially just and equitable means. While oftentimes I have felt that I am tackling these issues alone, I am deeply humbled to be collaborating with such brilliant and passionate colleagues, who have made significant and meaningful contributions in addressing issues of racism across Canada. Having a chance to amplify the voices of those who have experienced racial discrimination and allies who believe in a more socially just and equitable society is a beginning that I believe can have a profound and rippling effect.

Liza Lorenzetti
I was born in Montréal, Kanien'kehá:ka (Mohawk) land and have been living in Calgary for many years, on the traditional land of the Blackfoot and Treaty 7 people. Many of my family arrived in Canada over the period of what is known as three historical waves of Italian migration to Québec and Canada. There was no "point system" for European migrants at the time; otherwise our family would not have been admitted. Largely from rural backgrounds, with limited education, and fleeing both poverty and, intermittently, war, our migration stories — like many — were propelled by the search for a "better life for the next generations." Hard work, simplicity and a strong intercultural support network would result in my parents being the first college-educated members of our lineage. As teachers, they would afford the privilege of "moving up" into the working-class neighbourhood where I was born.

I grew up in an intergenerational household (on an intergenerational street!), where collective well-being far outweighed the rights of any individual. In fact, when studying the concepts of "the nuclear family" and "adolescent individuation" in my psychology classes at McGill some years later, those of us from collective cultures would marvel that these foreign ideologies were taught to us as *normal and necessary* aspects of modern socialization. In earlier years, I was often confused when attempting to navigate the social cues of the dominant culture, despite my White privilege. With age and further confidence, I later reframed this phenomenon as the cult of individualism that drove the dominant White society of which I was a part.

Non-dominant language and cultural practices were a common reality for many of Montréal's ethnic groups, which attempted to find a place for themselves between the power struggles of English and French settler communities. A plethora of family and social responsibilities (many of these underscored by gendered roles) led me to seek relationships with people from similar collectivist frameworks.

The socioeconomic challenges experienced by Italian and other southern-European immigrant communities did not prevent our imposition of ethnocentrism, Eurocentrism and the perpetuation of racism. Unencumbered by the accents of our first-generation relatives and resourced by White privilege, strong networks and Canadian education, second- and third-generation Italian Canadians could see an end to our intergenerational acculturation process and find acceptance in dominant society.

My father was intolerant of racism or other forms of discrimination in our home and community. He often conflicted with other Whites in his workplace, as he would not be a silent witness to any form of dehumanization. As an educator specialized in working with children with diverse abilities, he taught us respect and humility through his actions. From his teachings, I grew to understand that I had a responsibility to speak and act against injustice. As with my father, this commitment would at times lead to workplace bullying within a social services field that values conformity and, for myself, the loss of employment on more than one occasion.

I began my anti-racist, feminist journey from these early teachings, which, over time, grew to a conscious understanding of intersectionality and a commitment to anti-oppression. Joining the anti-apartheid movement in Calgary at nineteen, I soon discovered that Canada's reserve system was a model for South Africa's racist segregation policies. I became involved in local and global anti-racism movements, making the connections between imperialism at home and abroad. I also began to work with women and girls impacted by gender-based violence, which became a lifetime commitment both personally and professionally. I am still waiting for one day without violence against women and girls.

After completing high school in Calgary, I returned to Montréal to study social work and joined with many students who supported the Kanien'kehá:ka (Mohawk) resistance in 1990. Military intervention and racist vitriol against Indigenous Peoples drew me to further uncover aspects of Canadian history that had been hidden or mythologized by our education system and my White privilege.

As a university student in Montréal with an emerging consciousness, I realized that racism permeated our corridors of "higher learning." A few of us among the social work study body formed a committee in the Faculty of Social Work at McGill University to address what we called "internal and external racism." Many students were too afraid to participate. We also worked with students outside our faculty to host what we hoped would become an annual inter-university conference on racism. Students from Montréal's main English and French universities attended, as well as a number of community members. The significant turnout and presentations by racialized students served to reinforce my dedication to anti-racism work.

My volunteer commitments with refugee communities in Montréal also taught me about Canada's neocolonial politics related to war, poverty, forced migration and ongoing oppression. Meeting refugee claimants who were locked away in hidden Canadian "detention centres" was a shocking and necessary part of my learning/unlearning. I became committed to working in solidarity with immigrants and refugees and have since participated in actions against deportation and for globalized rights.

Moving back to Calgary to care for a family member, I continued to pursue social justice through groups such as the Committee Against Racism, the Committee for Anti-Racism Education, Calgary Committee for Peace and Anti-Racism; I also did solidarity work with organizations such as the Ethno-Cultural Council of Calgary, the Calgary Centre for Culture, Equity and Diversity and Migrante Alberta. As a community organizer at the City of Calgary, I helped to initiate projects such as Rap for a Reason and Breaking Down Racism — Youth Unity Jam. A very important and recent formative experience in my ongoing learning journey was being witness to the truth-telling hearings hosted by the Truth and Reconciliation Commission of Canada in Calgary and Edmonton; anti-colonizing work has greatly influenced my praxis and evolving efforts to be a trusted social justice ally.

Somewhere in my journey, I discovered for myself that, to change structural relations of oppression, I needed to work to address my own privilege and internalized dominance. Working "internally and externally" isn't just about communities and institutions — it involves the hard truths of addressing the root causes of oppression and the underserved benefits of historical domination. Further, it is not enough to eradicate racism alone; all forms of *power-over relationships* dehumanize us all. For those with privilege, it means starting with ourselves, then working to dismantle the very systems that we, over history, have striven to create and maintain. It means overcoming denial, excuses, guilt, immobilization, false generosity (Freire 1970) and the very real choice to walk away and ignore the injustice done to "Others" who we think are not "Us." I believe that critical self-reflection, authentic relationships, deconstructing and exposing dominance, and enduring solidarity are some ingredients required for the groundwork to achieve lasting structural changes.

Theoretical Framework: Intersectionality

The theoretical framework that underpins this book is *intersectionality*. Intersectionality is a term first coined by Kimberlé Crenshaw (1989), who called into question the feminist and racial discrimination discourses at the time that insisted that the demands and needs of Black women were filtered through a single categorical analysis. Such single-axis analysis denies the multi-dimensionality of experiences and serves as a mechanism to further marginalize those who experience intersecting oppressions — for example, an African Canadian female who is living with a disability or a Muslim male who is gay.

Intersectionality is a complex and multi-layered phenomenon based on socially constructed realities of oppression and domination that influence and reshape each oppressive social location as it connects with another (Crenshaw 1989; Weldon 2006). *Oppression* and *domination* are fuelled by a systematic undermining and dehumanizing of individuals and groups that are targeted as inferior by those with power. Key aspects of this phenomenon are the exclusion from resources and participation in the dominant group based on one's social location (Dominelli 2002; Kivel 2011) and the creation of "oppressive relations [that] divide people into dominant and subordinate groups along social divisions" (Ngo 2008: para 5). These divisions are what create and perpetuate oppressed identities and social locations.

The concept of intersectionality is contested and continues to be regarded as controversial. While it has gained increased popularity, there is ambiguity around intersectionality. Kathy Davis (2008: 68), a sociologist from Europe, notes that "'intersectionality' refers to the interaction between gender, race, and other categories of difference in the lives, social practices, institutional arrangements, and cultural ideologies and the outcomes of these interactions in terms of power." Olena Hankivsky and Renée Cormier (2011: 217) contend that intersectionality involves "taking into account that social identities such as race, class, gender, ability, geography, and age interact to form unique meanings and complex experiences within and between groups in society." As noted by these authors, intersectionality stresses that identity markers do not exist independently of each other.

Intersectionality is a useful and essential term in understanding the ways in which race, class, gender and other characteristics interact to create power differentials between groups and marginalize certain individuals through complex relationships that shape contemporary power relations (Crenshaw 1989, 1991; Davis 2008; Hankivsky and Cormier 2011; Mattsson 2013). According to Seyla Benhabib (1999), these various forms of oppression will always potentially be incomplete as there will be new grounds upon which groups will feel discriminated against and new rights and claims from which they will feel excluded. This is also affirmed by Bonilla-Silva (2015: 1360), who speaks specifically to the socially constructed categories of race, arguing that "racism produced (and continues to produce) 'races' out of peoples who were not so before." Therefore, while social identities such as race, class and gender may be categorical ways of defining groups, the constructed meanings attributed to these categorizations are fluid and changing as well as contextual.

The contributors weave the concept of intersectionality throughout their work, paying particular attention to the key principles of intersectionality.

Intersectionality recognizes that, while race may be a pervasive factor that

Figure 1.1: Principles of Intersectionality

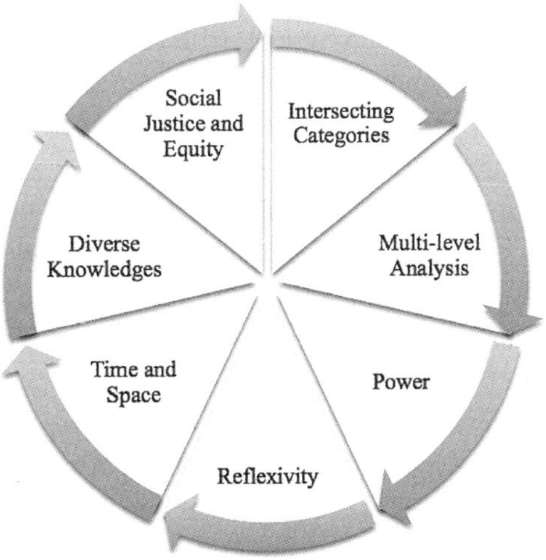

Source: Olena Hankivsky 2014.

impacts one's experience with oppression, other social identities simultaneously play a role in determining one's position in the social hierarchy both individually and collectively. For example, in Canada, racialized women may experience both racism and sexism as a result of their identities. As well, if these women are working in jobs that do not pay well, it is highly likely that from a class perspective, they are at the lower end of the socioeconomic ladder.

As depicted in figure 1.1, there are a series of principles that serve as the foundation of intersectionality. The notion of intersecting categories stresses that human lives cannot be reduced to a single category of experience. For example, David is not only an African Canadian male, but he is also a professor, a colleague, a son, a brother and a social worker. Intersectionality is concerned with understanding the interaction between and across various levels of society. We need to be aware of how global and national institutions influence each other and similar entities at the provincial level. In Canada, we need to understand the relationship between the three levels of government — federal, provincial and municipal. The policies and actions of these players impact various communities as well as individual Canadian citizens. Proponents of intersectionality contend that *power* is a critical construct and maintain that power is relational. It is manifested at a basic level in relationships between individuals. Of particular importance are the notions that expressions of power include power *over* people and power *with* individuals, which implies people are working together for the common good.

Intersectionality stresses the diversity of the types of knowledge that exists. In particular, it values hearing and including the perspectives and voices of people who are typically marginalized, such as Indigenous Peoples and racialized immigrants. Hankivsky (2014) maintains that intersectionality stresses the importance of time and space. This principle contends that how we as individuals experience and understand time and space is dependent on when and where we live and interact (Hulko 2009). The concept of *reflexivity* is also identified by scholars like Hankivsky as a key dimension of intersectionality. Reflexivity compels us to be introspective in relation to the power we possess as individuals and in the relationships we have with other individuals. As well, reflexivity also examines how power is manifested at the societal level.

While the focus of this book is racism in Canada, we are aware that race is not the categorical, singular issue upon which discrimination is based. Rather, in using an intersectional approach, we take into account other forms of oppression that intersect with racism.

Chapter Summaries

As previously mentioned, the primary purpose of this book is to provide a critical examination of how racism permeates Canadian society, how racism interacts with different forms of oppression and how individuals, families and communities are impacted by these forms of domination. It is important to stress that racism affects all Canadians (Mensah and Williams 2017). Each of the following chapters presents a series of action steps to address the interlocking nature of racism and other forms of oppression, such as sexism, Islamophobia and discrimination against LGBTQI communities. All of the contributors clearly recognize that sustained action is required to deal with the oppressive behaviours that are daily occurrences in Canadian society.

Chapter 1: The Colourblind Society
In this opening chapter, Este, Sato and Lorenzetti explore how Canada is perceived as a colourblind society despite the fact that racism has become a permanent feature of it. They draw on both historical and contemporary examples to illustrate the pervasiveness of this form of oppressive behaviour. The authors also engage in discussion focused on concepts that are critical to understanding the various chapters contained in the book. The authors conclude with an examination of the concept of intersectionality, which is the guiding framework used by the contributing authors.

Chapter 2: White Privilege: Racism, Anti-Racism
and Changing Oppressive Social Structures
In their chapter, Liza Lorenzetti and André Jacob focus on understanding and confronting White privilege by analyzing Canadian nation building from a critical and historical lens that interrogates European colonization and identifies key intersectional underpinnings that create our current context of structural oppression. Multi-levelled analysis and actions (personal to systemic) are proposed, which are grounded in personal accountabilities and the practice of trustworthiness to open the possibility for equity and lasting change.

Chapter 3: From Racism to Reconciliation:
Indigenous Peoples and Canada
Sharon Goulet's chapter will help learners understand the history of Canada as colonized land from an Indigenous lens that is critical to reconciliation efforts. Learners will also understand the connections between the historic treatment of Indigenous Peoples and the recurrent social conditions today.

Finally, Goulet asks readers to understand how the Truth and Reconciliation Commission's Calls to Action might be actioned in everyday life and social work practice.

Chapter 4: "Us and Them": Immigration and Barriers to a Diverse Canadian Identity

Glenda Bonifacio's chapter examines the connections between racism and contemporary immigration policies and the creation of a working under-class of temporary foreign workers and racialized immigrants. While racism and discrimination remain embedded in institutions and social practices, a cogent understanding of intersectionality and interconnectedness of nations, communities and peoples enables steps toward building a better place for all.

Chapter 5: The Colour of Poverty: Racialization and Inequality in Canada

In his chapter, Grace-Edward Galabuzi explores the racialization of poverty in Canada's urban centres. Drawing on a wealth of statistical evidence, he contends that the complex experience of racialized poverty disproportion-ately impacts racialized and immigrant populations concentrated in the country's major cities. He strongly asserts that, as a consequence, these groups are relegated to low-income neighbourhoods.

Chapter 6: Racism, Masculinity and Belonging: The Gendered Lives of Racialized Youth

Carl James examines the ways in which racism and "hegemonic masculinity" operate in the lives of racialized youth. He aims to understand how racial-ized youth have differentially experienced and responded to (or navigated and negotiated) their racialization and other inequitable mechanisms they encounter in their everyday lives.

Chapter 7: Racism in Canadian Education

Hieu Van Ngo's chapter examines Canadian schools as sites of complex intergroup relations that involve intricate interplay of personal attitudes, interpersonal interactions and institutionalized structures, policies and practices. In the context of power differentials, these relations have resulted in the marginalization of ethnoracial minority learners. Informed by the anti-racist education framework, it examines the experience of ethnoracial minority learners in Canadian schools, school responses to the changing student population and the impact of racism on ethnoracial minority learners and Canadian society. It further offers strategies to address educational inequities and to promote educational success for all learners.

Chapter 8: Sexual and Gender Diversity: Resituating within the Frame of Anti-Racism and Anti-Colonialism

The primary purpose of Ed Lee's chapter is to resituate the ways in which sexual and gender diversity contribute to an anti-racist and anti-colonial politics. As well as grounding its claims within reflexive and multidimensional ways of knowing, this chapter seeks to reframe how sexual and gender diversity is engaged on multiple registers: identities, theories and politics. This chapter highlights the ways in which queer and trans people of colour survive, thrive and resist multiple oppressions. Finally, key principles and action steps are suggested that centre queer and trans people of colour and affirm multiple identities within an anti-racist and anti-colonial politics.

Chapter 9: Dismantling Racism in the Canadian Criminal Justice System

Wendy Chan's chapter examines the relationship between race and crime in Canada, particularly the impact of this relationship on people of colour. Ideologies of race are deeply embedded in the Canadian criminal justice system, shaping criminal justice outcomes that reinforce racial inequality in Canada.

Chapter 10: Social Determinants of Newcomer Immigrant and Refugee Youth's Mental Health in Canada

Nazilla Khanlou and Luz Vasquez use the frameworks of social determinants of health and intersectionality to explore newcomer youth's experiences with racism. A major theme these authors stress is that prejudice, racism and discrimination can negatively affect youth's process of settlement and integration as well as their feelings of belonging to Canadian society. They maintain that immigrant youth may experience racism at the personal or institutional/systemic levels. The conclude their chapter by sharing a series of actions designed to address the discrimination faced by immigrant youth.

Chapter 11: Combatting Racism through the Intersectional Life Course: The Filipino Community in Canada

Based on his scholarly and community work with Filipino elders, Ilyan Ferrer's chapter explores how racism is directed against older racialized adults and immigrants in Canada. Guided by the life course perspective, he explores how older racialized adults experience social exclusion throughout their lives and across different generations. Ferrer also discusses a series of actions designed to acknowledge how this community is rendered invisible, as well as how to ensure that the voices of older racialized adults are heard and respected.

Chapter 12: Radical Resilience: Islamophobia and the New Canadian Muslim Reality

Mahdi Qasqas's chapter explores Islamophobia as a major form of racism directed against Muslims in Canada, particularly during the past two decades. In his work, he provides readers with a demographic profile of the Muslim population, both globally and in Canada. Qasqas then defines Islamophobia. The heart of the chapter is his examination of key issues confronting the Muslim community, such as crime, negative attitudes, stereotypical images and the increasing scrutiny that members of this community face on a daily basis.

Chapter 13: From Multiculturalism to Critical Multiculturalism

In this chapter, Christa Sato and Dave Este discuss the evolution of Canada's multicultural policy and how multicultural discourse is constructed and situated within the country. The authors critique traditional conceptualizations of multiculturalism and put forth the case for an alternative — critical multiculturalism. The chapter concludes with a series of strategies designed for the adoption of critical multiculturalism as a pathway to address issues of racism in Canada.

Chapter 14: Racialized and Indigenous Youth: A Call for Change

In the concluding chapter, the voices and experiences of racialized and Indigenous youth from different regions in Canada are presented. Aviaq Johnston, Brittany Walker, Bryan (last name not provided), Clark Carreon-Alarcon and Emma Maryam Bronson responded to the following question posed by the editors: What does a racialized Canada look like from the standpoints of our next generations, and how does this impact their hopes, aspirations and everyday lives?

References

ACLC (African Canadian Legal Clinic). 2017. "Making Real Change Happen for African Canadians. Toronto, ON: ACLC.

____. 2012. "Errors and Omissions: Anti-Black Racism in Canada. A Report on the Canadian Government's Compliance with the International Convention on the Elimination of All Forms of Racial Discrimination." Toronto, ON: ACLC. <tbinternet.ohchr.org/Treaties/CERD/Shared%20Documents/CAN/

INT_CERD_NGO_CAN_80_8297_E.pdf>.

Alexander, Michelle. 2010. *The New Jim Crow: Mass Incarceration in the Age of Colorblindness*. New York: New York Press.

Allan, Billie, and Janet Smylie. 2015. "First People, Second Class Treatment: The Role of Racism in the Health and Well Being for Indigenous Peoples in Canada." Toronto, ON: Wellsley Institute.

Allen, Mary. 2015. *Police-Reported Hate Crime in Canada, 2013*. Juristat. Ottawa, ON: Canadian Centre for Justice Statistics.

Benhabib, Seyla. 1999. "The Liberal Imagination and the Four Dogmas of Multiculturalism." *Yale Journal of Criticism*, 12, 2.

Benjamin, Akua. 2003. "The Black/Jamaican Criminal: The Making of Ideology." Unpublished doctoral dissertation, University of Toronto, Toronto, ON.

Bissoondath, Neil. 1994. *Selling Illusions: The Cult of Multiculturalism in Canada*. Toronto, ON: Penguin.

Bond, Julian. 1972. *A Time to Speak, A Time to Act*. New York: Simon and Schuster.

Bonilla-Silva, Eduardo. 2015. "The Structure of Racism in Color-Blind, 'Post-Racial' America." *American Behavioral Scientist,* 59, 11.

___. 2002. "The Linguistics of Color Blind Racism: How to Talk Nasty about Blacks without Sounding 'Racist.'" *Critical Sociology,* 28, 1–2.

Bonnett, Alastair. 2000. *Anti-Racism (Key Ideas)*. London, UK: Routledge.

Carillo, Ricardo, and Jerry Tello. 2008. *Family Violence and Men of Color: Healing the Wounded Spirit*, second edition. New York: Springer Publishing Company.

CBC Radio. 2015. "Reconciliation Is Not an Aboriginal Problem, It Is a Canadian Problem. It Involves All of Us." *As It Happens*, June 2. <cbc.ca/radio/asithappens/as-it-happens-tuesday-edition-1.3096950/reconciliation-is-not-an-aboriginal-problem-it-is-a-canadian-problem-it-involves-all-of-us-1.3097253>.

Clair, Matthew, and Jeffrey Denis. 2015. "Sociology of Racism." *International Encyclopedia of the Social and Behavioral Sciences,* second edition, 19.

Clarke, Kinsey. 2015. "Here's What Black Lives Matter Looks Like in Canada." *National Public Radio (NPR): Code Switch: Race and Identity Remixed*. August 7. <npr.org/sections/codeswitch/2015/08/07/427729459/heres-what-black-lives-matter-looks-like-in-canada>.

Cole, Desmond. 2015. "The Skin I'm In: I've Been Interrogated by the Police More Than 50 Times — All Because I'm Black." *Toronto Life*. Toronto, ON.

Council of Canadians. n.d. "Safe Water for First Nations: Troubled Waters in First Nations Communities." <canadians.org/fn-water>.

Crenshaw, Kimberlé. 1991. "Mapping the Margins: Intersectionality, Identity Politics and Violence against Women of Colour." *Stanford Law Review,* 43, 6.

___. 1989. "Demarginalizing Intersections of Race and Sex: A Black Feminist Critique of Anti-Discrimination Doctrine, Feminist Theory and Anti-Racist Politics." *Chicago Legal Forum,* 140.

Davis, Kathy. 2008. "Intersectionality as Buzzword: A Sociology of Science Perspective on What Makes a Feminist Theory Successful." *Feminist Theory,* 9, 1.

Dei, George J. Sefa. 2000. "Towards an Anti-Racism Discursive Framework." In George J. Sefa Dei and Alstair Calliste (eds.), *Power, Knowledge and Anti-Racism Education*. Halifax, NS: Fernwood Publishing.

Dominelli, Lena. 2002. *Anti-Oppressive Social Work Theory and Practice*. New York: Palgrave Macmillan.

Essed, Philomena. 1991. *Understanding Everyday Racism: An Intediscipliary Study*.

Newbury Park, CA: Sage Publications.

Fleras, Augie, and Jean Leonard Elliot. 2007. *Unequal Relations: An Introduction to Race, Ethnic, and Aboriginal Dynamics in Canada.* Toronto, ON: Pearson.

Freire, Paulo. 1970. *Pedagogy of the Oppressed.* New York: Continuum.

Government of Canada. 2013. "The Changing Face of Canada's Prisons: Correctional Investigator Reports on Ethno-Cultural Diversity in Corrections." <oci-bec.gc.ca/cnt/comm/press/press20131126-eng.aspx>.

Government of Ontario. 2017. "A Better Way Forward: Ontario's 3 Year Anti-Racism Strategic Plan." Toronto, ON: Anti-Racism Directorate.

Guruge, Sepali, Nazilla Khanlou and Denise Gastaldo. 2010. "Intimate Male Partner Violence in the Migration Process: Intersections of Gender, Race and Class." *Journal of Advanced Nursing,* 66, 1.

Gwyn, Richard. 1995. *Nationalism Without Walls: The Unbearable Lightness of Being Canadian.* Toronto, ON: McClelland and Stuart.

Hankivsky, Olena. 2014. "Intersectionality 101." Vancouver, BC: The Institute for Intersectionality Research and Policy, Simon Fraser University.

Hankivsky, Olena, and Renée Cormier. 2011. "Intersectionality and Public Policy: Some Lessons from Existing Models." *Political Research Quarterly,* 64, 1.

Harrell, Shelly P. 2000. "A Multidimensional Conceptualization of Racism-Related Stress: Implications for the Well-Being of People of Colour." *American Journal of Orthopsychiatry,* 20, 11.

Harrop, Catherine. 2015. "Fredericton Woman Wins Racial Profiling Case, Shoppers Drug Mart Must Pay $8K Human Rights Tribunal of Ontario Rules Employee Targeted Fredericton Woman Because She Was Black." *CBC News,* October 8. <cbc.ca/news/canada/new-brunswick/mary-mccarthy-shoppers-drug-mart-decision-1.3262361>.

Henry, Frances, and Carol Tator. 2010. *The Colour of Democracy: Racism in Canadian Society,* fourth edition. Toronto, ON: Nelson Education.

Huculak, Cory (Seargeant). n.d. "An Open Letter to the Citizens of Edmonton from the Edmonton Police Association: 'Carding' and Street Check Reports." Edmonton, AB: Edmonton Police Association. <s3.documentcloud.org/documents/3884939/EPA-Open-Letter-on-Carding.pdf>.

Hulko, Wendy. 2009. "The Time and Context-Contingent Nature of Intersectionality and Interlocking Oppressions. *Affilia,* 24, 11.

Huncar, Andrea. 2017. "Indigenous Women Nearly 10 Times More Likely to Be Street Checked by Edmonton Police, New Data Shows." *CBC News,* June 27. <cbc.ca/news/canada/edmonton/street-checks-edmonton-police-aboriginal-black-carding-1.4178843>.

James, Carl E. 2003. Seeing Ourselves: Exploring Race, Ethnicity and Culture. Third Edition. Toronto, ON: Thompson Educational Publishing, Inc.

James, Carl, David Este, Wanda Thomas Bernard, Akua Benjamin, Bethan Lloyd and Tana Turner. 2010. *Race and Well-Being: The Lives, Hopes and Action of African Canadians.* Halifax, NS: Fernwood Publishing.

Jolly, Susie, and Hazel Reeves. 2005. "Gender and Migration: Overview Report." Institute of Development Studies. <bridge.ids.ac.uk/sites/bridge.ids.ac.uk/files/reports/CEP-Mig-OR.pdf>.

Kasturirangan, Aarati, Sandhya Krishnan and Stephanie Riger. 2004. "The Impact of Culture and Minority Status on Women's Experience of Domestic Violence." *Trauma, Violence, and Abuse,* 5, 4.

Kelly, Jennifer. 1998. *Under the Gaze: Learning to Be Black in White Society.* Halifax, NS: Fernwood Publishing.

Kivel, Paul. 2011. *Uprooting Racism: How White People Can Work for Racial Justice.* Gabriela Island, BC: New Society Publishers.

Kumsa, Martha Kuwee, Magnus Mfoafo-M'Carthy, Funke Oba, and Sadia Gaasim. 2014. "The Contours of Anti-Black Racism: Engaging Anti-Oppression from Embodied Spaces." *Journal of Critical Anti-Oppressive Social Inquiry,* 1, 1.

Lawrence, Bonita, and Enakshi Dua. 2005. "Decolonizing Antiracism." *Social Justice,* 32, 4.

Lewis, Stephen. 1992. *Report of the Advisor on Race Relations to the Premier of Ontario, Bob Rae.* Toronto, ON: Government of Ontario.

Lorenzetti, Liza. 2016. "Engaging Men in Domestic Violence Prevention: Building A Collective-Cultures Approach." Unpublished doctoral dissertation, University of Calgary, Calgary.

Lorenzetti, Liza, Lana Wells, Carmen Logie and Tonya Callaghan. 2017. "Understanding and Preventing Domestic Violence in the Lives of Gender and Sexually Diverse Persons." *Canadian Journal of Human Sexuality,* 26, 3.

Mattsson, Tina. 2013. "Intersectionality as a Useful Tool: Anti-Oppressive Social Work and Critical Reflection." *Affilia,* 29, 1.

Maynard, Robyn. 2017. *Policing Black Lives: State Violence in Canada from Slavery to the Present.* Black Point, NS and Winnipeg, MB: Fernwood Publishing.

McKenzie, Kwame. 2017. "Rethinking the Definition of Institutional Racism." Toronto, ON: Wellesley Institute.

Meng, Yunlian, Sulaimon Giwa and Uzo Anucha. 2015. "Is There Racial Discrimination in Police Stop–and–Searches of Black Youth? A Toronto Case Study." *Canadian Journal of Family and Youth,* 7, 1.

Mensah, Joseph, and Christopher J. Williams. 2017. *Boomerang Ethics: How Racism Affects Us All.* Black Point, NS: Fernwood Publishing.

Morgan, Anthony. 2015. "The Suffocating Experience of Being Black in Canada." *Toronto Star,* July 31. <thestar.com/opinion/commentary/2015/07/31/the-suffocating-experience-of-being-black-in-canada.html>.

Nasser, Shanifa, and Amara McLaughlin. 2017. "Protesters Outside Masjid Toronto Call for Ban on Islam as Muslims Pray Inside." cbc *News,* February 17. <cbc.ca/news/canada/toronto/anti-muslim-protest-masjid-toronto-1.3988906>.

Ngo, Hieu Van. 2008. "A Critical Examination of Acculturation Theories." *Critical Social Work,* 9, 1.

Nova Scotia Human Rights Commission. 2013. *Working Together to Serve All Nova Scotians: A Report on Consumer Racial Profiling in Nova Scotia.* Halifax, NS: Nova Scotia Human Rights Commission.

ohrc (Ontario Human Rights Commission). n.d. "Part 1 – Setting the Context: Understanding Race, Racism, and Racial Discrimination." Policy and Guidelines on Racism and Raical Discrimination. <ohrc.on.ca/en/policy-and-guidelines-racism-and-racial-discrimination/part-1-%E2%80%93-setting-context-understanding-race-racism-and-racial-discrimination>.

___. 2003. *Paying the Price: The Human Cost of Racial Profiling.* Toronto, ON: Inquiry Report. <ohrc.on.ca/sites/default/files/attachments/Paying_the_price%3A_The_human_cost_of_racial_profiling.pdf>.

Reconciliation Canada. 2017. "The Canadian Reconciliation Landscape: Current Perspectives of Indigenous Peoples and Non-Indigenous

Canadians." <reconciliationcanada.ca/staging/wp-content/uploads/2017/05/NationalNarrativeReport-ReconciliationCanada-ReleasedMay2017_2.pdf>.

Reitz, Jeffrey, Rupa Banergee, Mai Phan and Jordan Thompson. 2009. "Race, Religion and the Social Integration of New Immigrant Minorities in Canada." *International Migration Review*, 43, 4.

Ross, Selena. 2015. "New Toronto Police Chief Saunders Turns Down Calls to End Carding." *Globe and Mail*, April 29. <theglobeandmail.com/news/toronto/new-toronto-police-chief-refuses-to-abolish-controversial-carding-process/article24168683/>.

Smith, Ekuwa. 2004. *Nowhere to Turn? Responding to Partner Violence Against Immigrant and Visible Minority Women*. Ottawa, ON: Canadian Council on Social Development.

Smith, Charles, and Erica Lawson. 2002. *Anti-Black Racism in Canada. A Report on the Canadian Government's Compliance with the International Convention on the Elimination of all Forms of Racial Discrimination*. Toronto, ON: African Canadian Legal Clinic.

Song, Sarah. 2017. "Multiculturalism." *The Stanford Encyclopedia of Philosophy* (Spring, 2017 Edition), Edward N. Zalta (ed.). <plato.stanford.edu/archives/spr2017/entries/multiculturalism>.

Tilley, Susan. 2016. *Doing Respectful Research: Power, Privilege and Passion*. Winnipeg, MB and Black Point, NS: Fernwood Publishing.

TRC (Truth and Reconciliation Commission of Canada). 2015. "Truth and Reconciliation Commission of Canada. Calls to Action." <trc.ca/websites/trcinstitution/File/2015/Findings/Calls_to_Action_English2.pdf>.

UNDESA (United Nations Department of Economic and Social Affairs). 2014. "The Human Right to Water and Sanitation." International Decade for Action "Water for Life" 2005–2015. <un.org/waterforlifedecade/human_right_to_water.shtml>.

UNHRC (United Nations Human Rights Council). 2017. "Report on the Working Group of Experts on People of African Descent to Canada, 16 August, 2017." <refworld.org/docid/59c3a5ff4.html>.

Walker, James St. G, and Burnley "Rocky" Jones. 2016. *Burnley "Rocky" Jones Revolutionary: An Autobiography by Burnley "Rocky" Jones*. Winnipeg, MB and Black Point, NS: Fernwood Publishing.

Warmington, Joe. 2016. "Black Lives Matter — Toronto Apparently Answer to Nobody." *Toronto Sun*. <torontosun.com/2016/08/15/black-lives-matter-toronto-apparently-answer-to-nobody>.

Weldon, S. Laurel. 2006. "Women's Movements, Identity Politics and Policy Impact: A Study of Politics on Violence Against Women in 50 United States." *Political Research Quarterly*, 59, 1.

Wortley, Scot, and Julian Tanner. 2006. "Immigration, Social Disadvantage and Urban Gangs: Results of a Toronto Area Study." *Canadian Journal of Urban Research*, 15, 2.

2

WHITE PRIVILEGE

Racism, Anti-Racism and Changing Oppressive Social Structures

Liza Lorenzetti and André Jacob

> If you are neutral in situations of injustice, you have chosen the side of the oppressor. If an elephant has its foot on the tail of a mouse and you say that you are neutral, the mouse will not appreciate your neutrality. (Bishop Desmond Mpilo Tutu, cited in McAfee Brown 1984: 19)

Western societies appear to be in the throes of a re-entrenchment of the colonial status quo, characterized by intentionally visible acts of *racist oppression*. Frequently the topic of mainstream and social media, this attempt to "roll back time," reverse any steps toward meaningful change and reaffirm White (and male) socioeconomic political privilege has equally catalyzed a collective response of demoralization, outrage and resistance. Concepts such as "Whitelash" (Van Jones 2016), or "White Rage" (Anderson 2016), have been used to explain this phenomenon, although the more silent and enduring (systemic) realities of racism are more revealing than individual acts.

Donald Trump's inauguration south of the Canadian border by more than sixty-three million voters, (the majority of whom were Whites) in 2016 was eclipsed only by his relentless use of government mechanisms and loopholes to isolate, ridicule and vilify an increasingly long list of people, communities and nations (including Muslims/people from predominantly Muslim nations, Indigenous and racialized peoples, women, the economically exploited, migrants and their children, LGBTQI and people with disabilities).[1] In response to this electoral win, the Ku Klux Klan held a victory parade in North Carolina to declare to the world that *White power* was back (as though it ever went away).

Similarly, in European nations, political candidates forwarding exclusionary or hate-promoting platforms are increasingly prevalent, with many eager supporters; an example is the election of several neo-Nazi candidates in Austria and the ensuing racist scandal.[2] These ongoing affronts in other Western states catalyzed a sense of national smugness among many White people in Canada. With our goverment and other Western nations proclaiming the Canadian multicultural project a success, and media coverage of families braving the trek across freezing border crossings to "escape" to Canada from our repressive southern neighbour, maybe Canada was not so bad after all.

However, these disturbing distractions from ongoing *structural oppression* and historical inequity in our own country were brief, and the daily injustices faced by racialized and Indigenous Peoples have not magically shifted. In fact, when six people were killed and nineteen others injured on the evening of January 29, 2017, while attending prayers at the Centre Culturel Islamique de Québec (Islamic Cultural Centre), Canada's self-imagination as the diversity-accepting nation to the North (of the US) was shattered. That innocent Muslim Canadians could be murdered while exercising their human right to practise their faith was a shock to many Canadians, as it demonstrated the depth to which oppression was firmly intact. It is important to underscore that a White male committed this hate-motivated act. While the prime minister labelled this massacre a "terrorist attack on Muslims" (Dougherty 2017), the assailant was later charged with murder and attempted murder — not terrorism.

This unfolding of current events nationally and globally occurs in a context where socioeconomic inequality is deepening; Indigenous land, water and resource rights are still largely ignored; and the killing and harassment of Black men is an expected item in the news. This is Canada.

To begin envisioning our collective living here as a healthy coexistence, broad, significant and enduring power shifts are required in social, economic, political and community life; "all aspects of Canadian society may need to be reconsidered" (TRC 2015: vi). This chapter centres on our shared commitments, as White anti-racists, to necessary reflexive and anti-oppressive actions toward a re-envisioned Canada — one without racism and one that must also include social, economic and environmental justice. This commitment is a necessary starting point, not solely because oppression is dehumanizing and unsustainable but because *we all live here.* Our continued coexistence on this land is dependent upon our dedication to significant structural changes that create the social conditions where peace, reconciliation and ecological justice become possible and attainable.

The objectives of this chapter are to:

- understand White privilege and practising trustworthiness;
- critically analyze nation building and current social structures that perpetuate race-based inequities and structural oppression in Canada; and
- deepen the commitment of White anti-racists toward confronting White privilege and the inequity of socioeconomic political relations and structures to open the possibility for equity, harmony and lasting change.

Racism as Structural Oppression

Racism is structural or systemic oppression, rooted in racialization and White privilege. *Race* is socially constructed and interlinked with other forms of power (Carrillo and Tello 2008), such as class, gender or sexuality. *Racialization* refers to the process by which superficial traits like skin colour become a platform for social arrangements, including a hierarchy that is reflected in socioeconomic and political arenas (Li 2008). Racism functions at multiple levels of social interaction (Mullaly 2010), creating "a system of social structures that produces and reproduces cumulative, durable" (Hinson, Healey and Weisenberg 2011: 4) forms of inequality. Agnes Calliste and George J. Sefa Dei (2000: 37) argue, "institutional or systemic racism occurs when established policies and practices of particular organizations reflect and produce differential treatment towards and outcomes for various groups" favouring the dominant White population (Li 2008), which are deeply embedded and often self-sustaining. Examples of this inequality can be seen in the presence (and expectations) of White Canadians in powerful roles in most organizations and institutions across the country, including the majority of our political leadership in all levels of government, our CEOs and business leaders, and our most wealthy 1 percent (*Canadian Business* 2017).

With impacts (including and) far beyond individual behaviours, racism as a form of *structural injustice* is supported by ideological representations or stereotypes (reinforced by mainstream media's positive representations of Whites compared to often negative depictions of racialized and Indigenous people and communities) and collective practices and political organizations (such as Canada's ongoing status as a member state of the British Commonwealth and legal relationship with the British monarchy). A historical and intersectional analysis of racism (Crenshaw

1989; Hankivsky and Cormier 2011) demonstrates that *White privilege* interacts with other forms of oppression (ethnicity, class, gender and sexual identities, nationality, language, abilities and religion) to create a status-quo system that continues to divide people according to superficial traits, with undue benefits and disadvantages according to this arbitrary system of classification.

Currently, our *neocolonial* era — marked by increasing global capitalism, transnational corporatism and an elevated inequality of wealth — has accelerated racist policies and practices. Étienne Balibar (1988: 27) referred to this era as one of neoracism, "*une nouvelle articulation de pratiques, de représentations, de doctrines et de mouvements politiques axés sur la catégorie de l'immigration*" (a new articulation of practices, imagery (representations), doctrine and political movements that are fixed on immigration).

Neoracism is structural and exemplified in the continued pursuit of racist policies and (inter)national transactions that ensure the socioeconomic dominance of Europeans and White North American settler elites (the famous "1 percent," or top income earners, are primarily White and male). This collective ideology, which can also be seen as an aspect of *White culture*, includes intensified opposition to racialized migrants (while at the same time exploiting their labour); this was underscored by the response to the plight of millions of Syrians escaping oppression and war or the anti-Mexican rhetoric in the US that focused on border controls and undocumented workers while negating the labour contributions of Mexican-Americans as well as their economic and health-care disadvantages (Zong and Batalova 2016). The neoracist agenda centres on the exaggeration of "cultural differences," (between racialized migrants and Whites) as irreconcilable and antagonistic (Ferréol and Jucquois 2003).

Speaking from the Position of Anti-Racism and Solidarity

We write from the perspective of *White anti-racists*. It is our view that *anti-racism* includes "forms of thought and/or practice that seek to confront, eradicate ... racism" (Bonnett 2000: 4) and White privilege (in tandem) through intersectional and multi-dimensional ways (micro/mezzo/macro), places (family/community/institutions/structures) and functions (individual/systems) where racism is (re)produced and maintained. White anti-racists commit to the *ongoing internal work* to "recognize the unearned privilege ... receive[d] from society's patterns of injustice and take responsibility for changing these patterns" (Bishop 2015: 3), while understanding the tensions, limitations and contradictions inherent to the discourse of White privilege constructed through the lens of White experiences (Carr and Lund 2008; Frankenberg 1993; Kivel 2011).

Our starting points are a practice of trust-building, including the acknowledgement that anti-racist does not mean "I'm not racist." In our view, the process of becoming trustworthy to those who are targeted by systemic injustice involves not replicating, denying or supporting oppression but actively working to eradicate it. We agree with Brazilian educator and activist Paulo Freire (1970) who viewed solidarity, in its most authentic form, as an act of love. *Trustworthiness*, an essential step toward anti-racist solidarity, means acknowledging that our current oppressive social structures call for our collective liberation (Freire 1970; Lenoir and Ornelas Lizardi 2007). While the benefits and "spoils" of power are highly coveted, as demonstrated by Peggy McIntosh's (1988) early work "Unpacking the Invisible Knapsack of White Privilege," they are inherently damaging and unhealthy, and they conflict with a greater human aspiration for a peaceful global community. As White anti-racist allies, we must learn to commit (as an ongoing practice) to interrogating, critiquing and refuting the rewards and benefits of oppression. Building on *intersectionality*, Sarita Srivastava (2005) emphasizes a critical need for those working toward solidarity to examine their commitment to anti-racist action (see Davis 1981; hooks 1981, 1994). It is through engagement in liberatory actions to dismantle oppressive social structures that humanizing alternatives become possible in a world increasingly dominated by a small group of wealthy, powerful people controlling structures and media which, in turn, forge public opinion in their favour.

Becoming Trustworthy

How we write "is a reflection of our own interpretations based on cultural, social, gender, class, and personal politics" (Creswell 2007: 179). However, a narrative from a privileged position is often accompanied by invisibility, which is easily portrayed as objective truth. The writing of Western history is a key example, as the accepted stories that are told and retold over generations paint a positive and redeeming image of those who maintained power, regardless of the brutality or coercion used to achieve their goals. Taking ownership of what is being shared and clarifying intentions in visible and accountable ways enhances trustworthiness. This practice helps prevent the implicit adoption of dominant theories of knowledge (Carter and Little 2007). The ongoing process for becoming — or better yet being regarded as — an anti-racist ally includes an inward-looking process of visibly claiming our positionality and opening this process to both critique and reassessment. We share our experiences below to illustrate this practice.

André: History Talks

On the road of my life, I have learned by studying as well as having some never-to-be-forgotten experiences. I grew up in rural Québec. My mother, a teacher in an elementary school, subscribed to several magazines related to global realities pertaining to Latin America and Africa. In that sense, my parents shared a desire to show to their twelve children the wide and interesting world that existed outside our rural area. Still today, I remember reading about different countries; as a teenager, I was dreaming of discovering the world. At eleven, I was accepted in a boarding school in Trois-Rivières because there was no secondary school in my village; my first discovery was to learn to cope with differences. As a kid from a rural area, living at a school where the majority of children were from rich or middle-class urban families was a tough experience. They made me feel different because my *patois* was quite specific, and my clothes were not as up-to-date as theirs. Many other kids in the same situation were not able to deal with the bullying, social differentiation and stigma. I learned that I had to be resilient and not give up. My parents were pragmatic and supported my personal challenge to succeed in my studies. On many occasions, the fact I spoke French made me feel like a stranger or lower-ranking citizen in my own country.

After high school, I moved to the University of Ottawa to obtain an undergraduate diploma in philosophy. Right after my studies, I went to Chile as a volunteer in a humanitarian non-governmental organization (NGO). I lived there for one year. Learning Spanish and getting involved in a *poblacion* (poor area) helped me to become part of another community. When I returned home to pursue a degree in social work, it was the end of the sixties and seventies era of civil and human rights in North America. In Québec in particular, October 1970 was when Pierre Elliott Trudeau sent the army to Québec, and this was supposedly justified because a small group called Front de Libération du Québec (FLQ) kidnapped a minister and UK commercial delegate (viewed as symbols of the colonialist British power). Canadian military forces occupied Montréal and Québec City and about five hundred union leaders and other activists were put in jail. What a nightmare! It was humiliating to be scrutinized by soldiers in our own country.

Years later, I also had the chance to work and live abroad in many different countries — France, Spain, Tunisia, Mali, Chile, El Salvador, Argentina, Nicaragua, Mexico, Costa Rica and Honduras. Through my experiences, I developed a clear understanding of what it means to be part of a minority. My life-long involvement in the struggle against racism and discrimination took place through the years living inside and outside Canada and forged the basis of my commitment.

Liza: From Action to Greater Awareness
I was born in Montréal, traditional Six Nations territory, Kanien'kehá:ka (Mohawk) land, and now live in Calgary, traditional Blackfoot Nation and Treaty 7 Territory. My family of origin is rooted in our her/history as Italian immigrants — the importance of the family and community collective ties me to other Southern and Eastern cultural ways of being. I speak my heritage language and three others. My partner Arya is from Iran and we have two daughters, Parisa and Brittany.

I navigate my various gendered and cisgendered social roles from my evolving understanding of anti-racist and intersectional feminism (Crenshaw 1989; hooks 1994; Calliste and Sefa Dei 2000). My Canadian/ Québec-born, English/French speaking, White and elite-educated status permits me to perpetuate racism, heterosexism and the imposition of dominance and privilege without structural accountability. This reality creates an unhealthy and imbalanced society.

When I was nineteen, guided by the influence of anti-racist mentors, I joined the anti-apartheid movement against South Africa's racist regime. I then "discovered" that Canada's reserve system was an inspiration for South Africa's racist segregationist policies. Understanding the connections between colonization at home and abroad, I became involved in local and global anti-racism work.

While completing my undergraduate degree in social work, I joined students and other activists who were in solidarity with the resistance of the Kanien'kehá:ka (Mohawk) people in what was erroneously labelled "The Oka Crisis" in 1990[3] (Warrior Publications 2014). This action was not a "crisis" for Indigenous people. It was a crisis for settler communities and the White Canadian system, which had long relied on oppressive policies and tactics to thwart Indigenous Peoples and their rights. Military intervention by the Canadian government and the Sûreté du Québec (Québec police) against Indigenous Peoples became unforgettable lessons in Canadian history that sharply refuted the colonial myths of my childhood (for instance, the romanticized view of the hardworking "settler" versus the reality of

land theft and displacement of the original inhabitants). Critical relearn-
ing of history compelled me to reconstruct my image of Canada, which
is incomplete. Ours is a country that renowned educator Dr. Leroy Little
Bear (2015), during the inaugural Redx Talks, labelled a "Pretend Nation"
that has not yet contended with and accounted for its past and present.[4]

Accounting for White Privilege

Public and critical debate is needed to further expose and refute the credibility of "*Whiteness*," a key category of ongoing sociopolitical and economic
dominance. Whiteness is a hierarchical, socially constructed, unstable
and contradictory concept (DiAngelo 2011) related to power. Whiteness
itself is not dominance; however, it exists only in reference to its privilege
over other social constructs (e.g., racialization). The social construction
of Whiteness has rendered it conveniently invisible (Frankenberg 1993)
to those who benefit from a myriad of undue privileges linked to cultural,
social, economic and political domination. It masquerades itself as "normal"
(Lorde 1984) or mainstream and brings with it the imagined personification
of "Canadian values." Moreover, White privilege is upheld by the "binary
of normal/deviant" (Hill Collins 2005) and essentialist, unchanging stereotypes through which racism in general is justified. As noted by Richard
Dyer (2005: 10), "as long as White people are not racially seen and named,
they/we function as the human norm."

It is rare for those with power to expose or highlight the nature and
benefits of undue privilege. In fact, Whiteness is a matter of power, domination and socioeconomic and political interests. For centuries, White
male Europeans have primarily controlled Canada's institutions; these
institutions reflect the values and aspirations of those they are meant to
serve. It is no surprise, then, that even among White anti-racists, examining
Whiteness has been largely ignored in favour of anti-racist theorizing and
"*allyship*"; the latter concept has been critiqued as being both self-serving
and reinforcing of existing power relationships (Indigenous Action Media
2016). Some important works on Whiteness include Ruth Frankenberg
(1993), Paula Rothenberg (2005) and, specific to Canada, an anthology
by Paul Carr and Darren Lund (2008). These texts shine a needed lens on
Whiteness, centralizing the often invisible source from which racism has
been conceived and maintained.

While the concepts of "White guilt" (Tatum 1994) and "White resistance" (Goodman 2011) have provided frames through which to examine
Whiteness, Robin DiAngelo (2011) moves the conversation further by

naming the fear and intolerance of dissent that underpins and maintains Whiteness/White privilege as socioeconomic and political hegemony. She forwards the concept of "*White fragility*," wherein "even a minimum amount of racial stress becomes intolerable, triggering a range of defensive moves" (Di Angelo 2011: 52). Anger and guilt, for example, are common defences linked to White fragility, which are ultimately aimed at reconfirming the status quo, silencing critique and even justifying or extracting sympathy for beneficiaries of oppression (e.g., "I wasn't born when this happened, so why should I be blamed?"). White fragility is exemplified when people with power decry that their individual freedoms are curtailed by so-called *political correctness* or when they are confronted for racist (as well as sexist, homo/bi/transphobic) propagations. As Toni Morrison (cited in Dreifus 1994: n.p.) rightfully asserts, the "political correctness debate is really about the power to be able to define. The definers want the power to name. And the defined are now taking that power away from them." Srivastava (2005: 29) explores the depth of this resistance to name and account for White privilege, noting the multiple strategies used to "block, diffuse and distract" accountability.

Teresa Guess (2006: 651) further interrogates Whiteness as a social construction, underscoring the "dynamics of racism by intent, a type of racism that is founded upon custom and tradition." Speaking to the strength of custom and tradition, the status and position of governor general (the representative of the British monarchy) as an enduring feature of our Canadian political structure is an example of a White colonial tradition that still has not been repealed. This points to the importance of history in the purposeful construction and creation of systemic inequities that favour Euro-American interests. As Guess (2006: 650) notes, to understand racism is to contend with the concept and culture of "whiteness as a social norm." Interrogating the fictional yet dominant concept of Whiteness in Canada requires a critical retelling of history intended to deconstruct the current image of nation and nation building.

Building a National Identity: Multiculturalism or Historical Domination?

There are several approaches and standpoints to an honest understanding of the concept of "nation" as it relates to Canada (that do not fit with the typical Confederation story). These include (Statistics Canada 2013):

- the "establishment" of a Canadian nation from the perspective of European conquest and slavery;
- the struggles of Indigenous Peoples (First Nations, Metis, Inuit) to resist cultural genocide (TRC 2015) imposed by the Europeans/settler governments and to gain land and Treaty Rights and full recognition as pre/existing Nations within and beyond current boundaries of the federation;
- the recognition of Québec as a nation within Canada with meaningful markers of statehood; and
- the establishment and contributions of multi-generational, non-Anglo/Franco citizens and new generations to Canada's evolving national identity/ies, where one in five Canadians is born outside of the country.

As noted by Ernest Renan, *"la nation est l'âme, le principe spirituel de l'État"* ("A nation is a soul, a spiritual principle," cited in Tardivel 2016: 55). This highlights both the imagery and at times romanticized invocations of nationhood. Canada is imagined and considered a progressive and hospitable country on the international stage and by the typical Canadian historical account of its formation. Yet, oppression and marginality are perpetuated through longstanding historical inequities and the targeting of specific individuals and groups, which continue to shape our current sociopolitical climate and policy frameworks (Jiwani 2006; Fong 2010; ACLC 2012).

Colonization of First Peoples

Canadian history cannot be uncoupled from European colonization, legislated slavery (Trudel 2004; Cooper 2006) and centuries of racist and discriminatory policies (Bannerji 2000; Wallis and Kwok 2008) based on greed and the consolidation of power into the proverbial colonial coffers. Canada's Truth and Reconciliation Commission (TRC 2015: 15) summarizes:

> The spread of European-based empires was set in motion in the fifteenth century when the voyages of maritime explorers revealed potential sources of new wealth to the monarchs of Europe ... it also unleashed an unceasing wave of immigration, trade, conquest and colonization. It marked the beginning of a European-dominated global economy.

For over five hundred years, the British Empire, its descendants and, to a certain extent, those of other (primarily northwestern) European heritage gained increasing political, economic, sociopolitical and cultural domination on land that is now known as Canada through policies and practices that attempted to eradicate existing Nations and ways of life. The elimination of Indigenous governing structures and rights, disregard for treaties, the spread of European diseases and numerous other strategies were implicitly and explicitly intent on creating a national climate where Indigenous Peoples "cease[d] to exist as distinct legal, social, cultural, religious, and racial entities in Canada" (TRC 2015: 1). Aggressive *assimilation* (Ajzenstat 2006; Legacy of Hope Foundation 2013; TRC 2015) was a core plan of action, marked by more than a century of Indian Residential Schools (IRS). Over 150,000 Indigenous children attended Canada's IRS. Those as young as four years of age were interned in these schools, primarily through coercion, legislation and enforcement. In the words of Duncan Campbell Scott, Deputy Minister of Indian Affairs in Canada in 1920, the IRS would "get rid of the Indian problem. Our objective is to continue until there is not a single Indian in Canada that has not been absorbed into the body politic and there is no Indian question and no Indian Department" (cited by the TRC 2015).

The IRS system perpetuated *cultural genocide* through countless forms of physical, sexual, psychological and spiritual violence and repression, resulting in multiple levels of intergenerational trauma (Bopp, Bopp and Lane 2003; TRC 2015). A climate of *structural violence* (formed by policies and social norms that attempt/ed to dehumanize and eradicate Indigenous Peoples) was imposed, marked by cultural denigration, social exclusion, creation of apartheid-like reserves (Castellano, Archibald and DeGagné 2008), overt political and legislative control and, particularly but not exclusively, punishment against children in IRS (TRC 2015). The Canadian government implemented and maintained the IRS system, often contracting Christian churches (Catholic, Anglican, Presbyterian, United) and charitable organizations as key partners (TRC 2015). Slavery, a brutal foundation of colonial nation building, targeted African and Indigenous men, women and children and consolidated wealth and power in European — White — hands.

Slavery and Oppression as Canadian Practices

Slavery was practised in Canada for over two hundred years. Yet, this part of Canadian history remains largely unrecognized as systematized and legislated violence committed upon thousands of Africans, African descendants and Indigenous Peoples (Hill 1993, 2007; Cooper 2006;

Whitfield 2016). Slavery was legally recognized in Canada up to 1834 and practised in what is now known as Ontario (Lower Canada), Québec (New France), Nova Scotia, New Brunswick and Prince Edward Island (Winks 1997; Trudel 2004). While many Canadians may prefer to read the stories of the Underground Railroad, which brought enslaved people to freedom in Canada, some historians underscore that their arrival in Canada did not necessary result in emancipation (Whitfield 2016). In fact, numbers of those fleeing from the United States "found themselves ether re-enslaved or living a discounted version of freedom" (ACLC 2012: 4).

There are important links between these historical atrocities committed against Black people in Canada and today's climate of *anti-Black racism* (Hill 2007). Canada's history includes several little-known, anti-Black stories. Until 1955, there were exclusionary anti-Black immigration policies. A campaign by the African-Canadian National Unity Association, led by Hugh Burnett and supported by the Jewish Labour Committee, confronted racial segregation in Dresden, Ontario in 1951; this part of Canadian history is unknown to many Canadians (Waters 2013). Further, the story of Viola Desmond (Reynolds 2016), who confronted segregation in a movie theatre in New Glasgow, Nova Scotia, in 1946 and was assaulted and charged, has only recently been recognized as Canadian history, most notably symbolized by Desmond's image appearing on a ten-dollar bill in 2018. The eradication of Africville in Nova Scotia (Hill 2007; Nelson 2008), a vibrant African Canadian neighbourhood demolished in the 1960s, its people displaced as an act of systemic, institutional racism, is another of many important historical facts that warrant a place in our history books and archives (Africville Museum 2012). Today, anti-Black racism endures through socioeconomic marginalization (poverty — see chapter 5 in this book) and judicial and police repression of African Canadians (Cooper 2006; James 2012; Maynard 2017). These persistent forms of oppression not only perpetuate intergenerational harm but also rob Canadian society of the talents within our communities and the richness of our diversity. As noted by Lawrence Hill (1993: 19–20),

> Canada's refusal to accept its racist past and simultaneous failure to recognize the historical contributions of people of African descent is partly responsible for the perpetuation of contemporary anti-Black racism. Specifically, denying Canada's history of slavery, segregation and racial oppression means that the modern day socio-economic circumstances of Canada's Afro-descendant

population cannot be placed in their proper historical context; at the same time, neglecting the numerous contributions of members of the African Canadian community leads to the portrayal of this community as "good-for-nothing."

Hill's assertion is well-articulated in a large-scale study of Canada's Black community (James et al. 2010), which pointed to the ongoing barriers created by anti-Black racism to the health and well-being of Canadians. Gathering responses from more than nine hundred people, a substantial number stated that their colour of skin significantly (43 percent) or somewhat (28 percent) impacted their everyday lives. Negative health outcomes are also related to anti-Black racism, including stress levels, physical and mental un-health, and a decreased sense of positivity. The damaging effects of racism on people's daily lives extends to quality of schooling, ability to obtain employment and advancements consistent with experience and education, access to quality housing and negative involvement with the police and judicial system (James et al. 2010).

Yet, there remains a deafening silence in the place of what should be societal, governmental and state-wide accountabilities. Instead, Black, Indigenous and other marginalized communities are often blamed or vilified, attested to by the treatment of *Black Lives Matter*[5] and, earlier, the *Idle No More* movement.[6] For example, a reactionary "*All* lives matter" counter-campaign was amplified across North America as a response to efforts by Black leaders to bring attention to the numerous inequities faced by Black communities on a daily basis). In Candian anti-racist circles, this response was often described not only as a dismissal of racism and erasure of the lived experiences of Black North Americans, but an attempt to reaffirm White privilege through silencing and manipulation. Prior to this, the targeting of Idle No More by corporate media can be viewed in a similar light. In Calgary, for example, the *Calgary Sun*, seemingly intent on denouncing the efforts of Indigenous people to gather through this movement, was eventually greeted by an Idle No More rally in 2013 (*Huffington Post* 2013). The focus of the demonstration was to underscore racist and anti-Indigenous reporting practices. As a participant at this rally, co-author Liza Lorenzetti was not surprised when the *Sun* later used their influence and access to readership to deny the racist lens that they employed in their columns and polls. The right to discussion and debate was again used by White people to avoid positionality and claim neutrality when dealing with issues of racism.

Racialized communities in Canada have all been subjected to historical and systemic aggressions by European settler groups. Well-noted examples, often omitted from our history lessons, include the systemic oppression of Chinese Canadians through the Chinese head tax of 1855 and *Chinese Immigration Act* of 1923 (Chan 2016), now known as the *Chinese Exclusion Act*, and the forcible internment of 22,000 Canadians of Japanese origin during the Second World War (Robinson 2017). A cogent reminder of our history of deeply rooted anti-Semitism is the murder of Jewish refugees who escaped Europe aboard the St. Louis. After being denied sanctuary by a number of countries, including Canada, the ship of over nine hundred people was forced to return to Europe, resulting in the death of 254 people, who were killed in concentration camps. Anti-Semitism is still practised, with Jewish Canadians accounting for 16 percent of victims of reported hate crimes in 2013 (Allen 2015). Racism and religious intolerance was further buoyed by the former conservative federal government's *Zero Tolerance for Barbaric Cultural Practices Act* and proposed tip line (Government of Canada 2015; Maloney 2015), unmistakably targeting Muslim and other non-Christian faith groups. Further, in 2017, efforts by one member of parliament to introduce a motion to denounce Islamophobia led to a national and often vitriolic debate on the issue, and Motion 103 was eventually passed by a large majority. The MP in question also received death threats after bringing this issue to the fore.

These brief examples describe the relationship between White privilege, systemic racism and violence — the historical framework that continues to maintain structural relationships of privilege/marginalization in Canada. Canada is much more than folkloric representations. Its development as a nation is underpinned by exploitation of immigrant and racialized workers and forcible removal of Indigenous Peoples from their lands through multiple unethical policies and practices. Instead, Canadian history as it is taught is made up of Mounties, peacekeepers, democracy, multiculturalism and so on — the actions of White people building a great nation.

Two Nations, One Country — A Myth?
The relationship between European settlers and the history of political conquest between colonial nations are important factors that sustain White privilege and domination in Canada today. Canadian history was profoundly altered after the victory of the British over France in the colony in 1760. In the Treaty of Paris of 1763, coming after the end of the Seven Years War, France gave up its colonized territories in mainland North America to Britain.

So began a long path to becoming "one" nation. Anglophones and Francophones have typically been defined as the "founding nations" of Canada. Both are considered equal according to the Canadian Constitution (from which Québec was excluded in 1982). In reality, the founding nations story is a myth. First of all, throughout Canadian history, Francophones have been excluded, discriminated against, ignored or suppressed by British conquerors. There is a deep gap between these two populations and many contradictions remain unresolved. More importantly, the founding nations idea attempts to erase the existence of multiple Indigenous Nations who were living on the land (that later became Canada) prior to and during European settlement, as well as the genocide perpetrated against them.

From the time of British conquest in 1760, Canada has never gained the political, linguistic, social and cultural allegiance of the majority of Francophones; the conquest was just the debut of an ongoing struggle for linguistic, social, cultural and political survival (Bouthillier and Meynaud 1972) The history of Québec in Canada contains numerous acts of resistance to British conquest, such as the 1837 Patriotes Rebellion. Since Canada's confederation, political and juridical struggles continue within Québec for national sovereignty (which have always been defeated by large campaigns waged by Québec's economic elites).

Among various measures of exclusion and discrimination against Francophones was the Durham Report, a British political reaction to uprisings in Québec between 1837 and 1839. After defeating French Canadians, the British government used that political policy to gain total control over the people. Lord Durham's conclusion was that, "in Lower Canada, with its francophone majority population ... the problems [are] racially rather than politically based." He found "'two nations warring in the bosom of a single state" (Durham Report, cited in the *Canadian Encyclopedia* n.d.: para 6). A description of Lord Durham notes:

> He was a cultural chauvinist and recommended assimilating the French Canadians — whom he called a people with no literature and no history ... through a legislative union of Canada, in which an English-speaking majority would, in his view, dominate. Thus the French Canadians could not pursue ethnic aims, and the largely Anglophone merchants could pursue a strong St. Lawrence economy to ensure future prosperity.

John Conway (2004: 17) illustrates the national and cultural differences between these two European settler groups:

> A large part of the problem is that English Canada and Quebec premise their actions on two different versions of the same history. [For instance], English Canada celebrates Confederation in 1867 as the birth of a nation. Quebec views it as the imposition of a two-layered constitutional stranglehold on national aspirations. English Canada sees the hanging of Louis Riel as unfortunate, an event best forgotten, and ambivalently contemplates making Riel a hero ... And so it goes, each solitude with its own version of the same history, even up to the present.

Conway's quote captures the essence of what is at times referred to as "English and French Canada" and the historical power relations and current tensions that frame Canadian nation building.

The dynamics between these two first ethnocultural settler groups and their colonial history continues to characterize Canada's sociopolitical environment. It also illuminates certain distinctions between Anglo and Franco colonialist claims and broader relationships with Indigenous Peoples, as well as with settler groups that are deemed by these colonial powers to have lesser claims on Indigenous lands. For example, Chinese, Greek, Italian and Sikh communities do not claim official language status in Canada. However, Southern European migrant groups and those that initially experienced discrimination by the first settler groups, the British in particular, adopted many cultural norms and habits of the prevailing colonialists. Benefiting from White privilege (which, over time, they were permitted to claim) and free from formerly unacceptable accents and cultural practices of their first-generation parents/grandparents, non-dominant European settlers would gain the benefits of European dominance in Canada (Guglielmo and Salerno 2003). While experiencing various discriminatory policies over time based on their ethnic heritage, European settlers who were not part of the English or French groups were active participants and beneficiaries of colonization and systemic racism. The "Othering" of racialized and Indigenous peoples (what Henry and Tator 2010 termed *cultural racism*) was a practice that reaffirms Whiteness among these communities and within the first-settler groups that continue to lay claims to land and resources within their appropriated jurisdictions.

Today's Multicultural Canada

The *Multiculturalism Act* of 1988 was considered in its time to be a basic national principle that put into policy the vision that individuals and groups could live according to their beliefs and traditions. However, the concept of a multicultural Canada continues to be controversial (Bissoondath 2002; Momin 2004) in its negation of history and the suppression of Indigenous Nations and racialized communities. Discussions on race in Canada have been subsumed under "the discourse of Canada's cultural mosaic and liberal multicultural discourse" (Berry 2011: 23). Further, the concept of a multicultural Canada downplays the fluidity, contextuality and evolution of culture (which includes multiple aspects of identity such as gender, sexual identity and class). The underpinnings of *multiculturalism* perpetuate the idea that culture is essential and unchanging, a stereotype that imprisons so-called "minority groups" based on cultural differentiation (McLaren 1994); in vogue for an extended period of time, the terms "minority" or "visible minority" lack clarity and create confusion without addressing racism or enforced minoritization. Racialization has increasingly become a relevant and commonly used concept, as it focuses attention more clearly on racism as a widespread and systemic practice.

Whiteness and, relatedly, the enforced minoritization of targeted groups creates a separation of cultures and privileges Euro-Canadian (particularly first-settler groups) norms and arbitrary standards (called Canadian/Québec values). Further, the perception (reinforced through experience) of an imagined mainstream promotes "cultural tourism" (Nylund 2006). This is exemplified primarily among English-speaking Whites who omit or disavow the presence of their own "culture," negate their migration history and express an exaggerated interest in mythologized and caricaturized cultures of racialized people (Kivel 2011). This reinforces one-on-one relations of marginality/dominance, which further entrenches the significance of binary cultural attributes where White culture is invisible/everyone else's culture is stereotyped and unchanging. As a result, multiculturalism fortifies the "hegemony of Whiteness" (Nylund 2006: 29). Hidden by the pervasive dynamics of multiculturalism is the right of all members to actively and equitably participate in social, political, economic and cultural aspects of Canadian society. Multiculturalism has not created equality; its myth perpetuates dominance by White settler communities (for more detailed analysis of multiculturalism, see chapter 13).

Based on the above description, the culture and race of "Others" is the topic of mainstream/dominant essentialist conclusions, while White cultural and racial identities are simply used and imposed as permanent, normalized and invisible traits — for example, a White person can claim to be an average Canadian or true Québecer while people from other groups are often questioned about where they are *really* from. In many aspects, culture is often used synonymously with race. Such an attitude can lead to global stereotypes, and it negates the complexity of multiple cultures and identities; ethnicity, faith, age and gender and sexual diversity influence the ways that we experience culture. It is our perspective that culture is not a vague abstraction that exists in itself. Rather, it is an outcome of socialization (which primarily teaches conformity), normative ideology (dominant ideas about life) and the social and economic system in which we live. What human beings think (ethics, beliefs, ideology and traditions) is often a direct result of conditioning by dominant social and economic forces that define the scope of social interactions, use of language and so on.

To overcome racial discrimination and exclusion may appear to be a Sisyphean task — rolling the stone forever uphill. An emphasis on individual attitudes and behaviours will not address the systemic nature of racism and can only have a limited effect. Even more troubling, Canada's current social context has become increasingly characterized by White people's obsession for "security," which is a code word for racism. On one hand, the image of the "feared other" (El Matrah 2018: n.p.) is reinforced by multiple strategies, including corporate media and our education system; simultaneously at play is the myth of "respected minorities," which reinforces difference. Both strategies collude to keep categories of citizens in their roles and statuses of inequality. Continuous manifestations of dominance by those defined as majority (for example, emphasizing White culture as authentically Canadian) maximize these differences, reinforcing "oppressive relations [that] divide people into dominant and subordinate groups along social divisions" (Ngo 2008: para 5) and exclude certain groups from social and economic resources and participation (Dominelli 2002; Kivel 2011).

This system of minority/majority differentiation gives rise to structured isolations that can appear to function almost seamlessly. The stability of the oppressive system fosters collective denial of the oppression committed on the part of the dominant group (Freire 1970). The socioeconomic relations within this system are punctuated by various forms of tokenism, such as minimal representation of Indigenous or racialized people on boards or committees or hiring into low-paying or menial jobs to claim organizational diversity; this is then claimed as evidence of equality and redistribution. Therefore, conceptualizing racism as a series of "individual acts" upholds oppressive systems and rewards those with privilege for individual acts toward those who are oppressed without actually challenging the status quo. It is a fundamental aspect of what Freire (1970) refers to as *"false generosity."* False generosity is particularly dangerous because it entrenches the notion that individual kindness or "generosity" (on the side of the oppressor) and individual worth (on the side of the oppressed) is the way to balance out injustice.

The sustained power gap between oppressor/oppressed may appear so entrenched that a desire for change may be superseded by a conviction that inequities are both inevitable and unmovable. However, history has shown (such as the case of the Dresden, Ontario, movement and the current work of the TRC, discussed in this chapter) the power and effectiveness of conviction, collective anti-racist and anti-colonial organizing to shift and abolish racist policies and practices over time. Assessing the effectiveness of current institutional mechanisms is important to illuminate the functions and failures of our current system.

A Canadian Way of Addressing Racism and Discrimination? Government and Its Institutions

> There must exist a paradigm, a practical model for social change that includes an understanding of ways to transform consciousness that are linked to efforts to transform structures. (hooks 1994: 184)

On December 21, 1965, the General Assembly of the United Nations ratified the *International Convention on the Elimination of All Forms of Racial Discrimination.* The Convention was a response to the Second World War, the horror of the Nazi-led Holocaust, and the political and migratory movements that had changed the demographic picture of the globe (for instance, Indian migration to England in the 1950s and 60s). In particular, the 1960s was an era of anti-colonial struggle in Canada and the United States that nourished the forces of liberation and anti-racist movements, women's rights and other anti-oppression organizing. In that context, the Convention proclaimed a role for nation-states in the struggle against racial discrimination. Article 2, for instance, obliges parties to "undertake to pursue by all appropriate means and without delay a policy of eliminating racial discrimination in all its forms" (United Nations 1969: article 2).

Canada's response to this international Convention was the *Canadian*

Bill of Rights in 1960 as well as the *Canadian Charter of Rights and Freedoms* in 1982, which, in article 15, affirms,

> Every individual is equal before and under the law and has the right to the equal protection and equal benefit of the law without discrimination and, in particular, without discrimination based on race, national or ethnic origin, colour, religion, sex, age or mental or physical disability.

After many years of political advocacy and social movement organizing, the *Canadian Human Rights Act* was amended in 1996 to include sexual orientation as a prohibited ground for discrimination, and gender identity and gender expression were added in 2017.

The Charter, in conformity with the United Nations Convention, introduced the concept of "race" but added "visible minorities," a quintessential notion of multiculturalism also used in the United Kingdom and other countries of the British Commonwealth (now refered to as the Commonwealth of Nations). The federal government was required to make certain decisions to actualize and implement the Charter's fundamental position in Canadian law so that it could not be superseded by any government of the time; However, section 33 of the Charter allows Parliament or provincial governments to override certain aspects of the Charter (commonly known as the "notwithstanding clause" or "veto power"); this problematic and contradictory clause has yet to yet to be addressed or repealed by a governing party (Department of Justice 2018).

The Canadian Race Relations Foundation

Following upon the Canadian Charter, the Canadian government created the Canadian Race Relations Foundation (CRRF) in 1997. Its specific vision is to be a "leading voice and agent of change in the advance towards the elimination of racism and all forms of racial discrimination, and the promotion of Canadian identity, belonging and the mutuality of citizenship rights and responsibilities for a more harmonious Canada" (CRRF 2015: para 2). The Foundation received a comprehensive mandate in terms of research, public education, annual awards and the advising of public institutions, which is currently active. Political leadership at all levels of government is needed in tandem with the current mandate of CRRF.

Provincial and Territorial Charters

Over time, provinces and territories developed their own charters and implementation mechanisms. This included the inception of human rights commissions with mandates to engage in research, education, inquiries, legal actions and public statements to compel governments, NGOs and private institutions to fulfill and enhance anti-discrimination mandates. Despite this, Canada's human rights record has been the subject of international critique by Amnesty International (2016) and the United Nations Human Rights Commission (Lum 2015) for the ongoing oppression of Indigenous and Black communities.

Municipalities

Another more recent governmental approach to addressing racism is the Canadian Coalition for Municipalities against Racism and Discrimination (CMARD). Canada joined as a member of the International Coalition in 2005, under the coordination of United Nations Educational, Scientific and Cultural Organization (UNESCO), which was launched internationally in 2004 as a follow-up to the World Conference against Racism, Racial Discrimination, Xenophobia and Related Intolerance. To date, more than sixty-nine Canadian municipalities representing larger and smaller cities have signed on to this convention, as well as a number of unions and other organizations, such as the National Association of Friendship Centres (Canadian Commission for UNESCO n.d.). Signatories to this convention are assigned ten core commitments, such as monitoring racism and supporting measures to promote equality in areas like housing and the labour force. However, the question of CMARD's ability to move its commitments toward tangible goals and structural change remains unanswered.

Municipalities are positioned to play an important role in eradicating racism and discrimination. In principle, according to the Federation of Canadian Municipalities, all municipalities could promote affirmative action programs to adopt concrete changes within municipal systems. Currently, this is not the case because anti-discriminatory measures are not mandated; rather, they depend on the elected councillors' good will. While cities are on the frontline of resettlement initiatives for new Canadians, municipalities are often involved in many strategies without addressing key resettlement barriers related to racism and discrimination. Various programs of action against racism could be expected from the Federation of Canadian Municipalities, but there are few proposed (see, for instance, FCM 2011).

Effectiveness of Current Structures and Policies

The ongoing system of White privilege confirms the ineffectiveness of government to address, let alone eradicate, structural racism. It was over fifty years ago that Canada signed the *International Convention on the Elimination of All Forms of Racial Discrimination*. Since then, provinces and territories have implemented charters and developed human rights commissions. More than twenty years ago, the Canadian Race Relations Foundation was formed. Even with these measures, approximately seventy cities across the country joining CMARD and the equity work of numerous civil society and labour organizations, racism is still a pervasive institutional problem in Canada.

Although charters and conventions open pathways to implement durable solutions to ongoing structural oppression, implementation bodies need the capacity to translate legislation into action. For instance, provincial human rights commissions and judicial bodies such as the Supreme Court need to be maintained at arm's length from political tides and, specifically, elected officials who use their roles to further entrench divisiveness or inaction as responses to structural racism. These mechanisms, if truly serving their functions, could challenge White dominance and other forms institutional discrimination. This is currently not the case, which, reminiscent of Audre Lorde's poignant assertion, "the master's tools will never dismantle the master's house" (1984: 110). Until now, very few implementation mechanisms have achieved a coherent and continuous program of action in the most important sectors of the society, such as the education and health care systems, public services, police, municipalities, corporations and unions, among others. The state has the responsibility and institutional mechanisms to require the implementation of specific internal policies inside institutions and corporations; it's not enough to say that human rights charters exist and should be the unique reference for remedial actions. Fundamentally, anti-racism in its current conceptualization requires the eradication of White privilege from within the very structures that have been created, which are largely overseen by Whites — hence the tensions and contradictions within this formula. While racism and discrimination remain the subjects of these various approaches, White dominance remains invisible, and the eradication of White privilege is not a stated objective of policies that contend with racism in Canada.

Envisioning the potential of Canada without racism means that intersecting and multi-layered forms of injustice are confronted through durable and mandatory implementation measures, developed by people who experience these injustices and underscored by legislation with visible consequences for inaction. Such a paradigm must be a universal principle and an inspiration to foster structural changes that are concrete and lasting, allowing people to live according rights and freedoms with collective responsibilities and accountabilities. Currently, the notions of rights, freedom and equality — the seemingly universal consensus portrayed in most charters — appear to be a matter of convenience, as they remain in the hands of those with dominance, lacking mechanisms to assure implementation and disregarded in favour of political gain or electoral popularity.

A less evident flaw is the enshrinement of individual rights within our charters, which ignore collective equity and social responsibility. For example, the individual "right" to amass extreme wealth while others suffer from extreme poverty is the imposition of colonial, liberal, capitalist economic principles that use the rhetoric of individual freedoms. Neoliberalism and capitalism, White enterprises, are predicated on economic inequality and exploitation to facilitate profit-making and have maintained the economic interests and dominance of White people (overwhelmingly, White men). Thus, anti-racism is limited within the confines of neoliberal capitalism, as Colleen Lundy (2011: 4) notes:

> Transnational organizations now determine the social, economic, and political policies of countries. The result is a profound increase in the polarization of wealth and disparity within and among countries as growing numbers of people within global village lack the basic needs for survival, while a small number of others accumulate the riches of the world.

With increasing economic disparity and inequity, anti-racism strategies must include the institutionalization of anti-poverty policies and address the rising income gap.

Personal Accountability as a Foundation for Structural Change

With inherent flaws in current anti-racist institutions, the institutionalization of social change is necessary to address the systemic and structural nature of racism and oppression. Yet, this approach can depersonalize individual and social accountabilities, shifting the responsibility to an invisible system or out-of-touch government, hence permitting those with undue privilege to remain passive and disengaged (e.g., "it's the government's problem"). For this reason, we propose key principles or learning companions to be contemplated by those seeking to be recognized as anti-racist allies. We use the word "recognized" intentionally, because one can claim to be an ally while still perpetuating/and benefiting from oppression. Working toward trustworthiness and dedication to anti-racist and anti-oppressive actions are critical steps to taking personal responsibility for individual acts of repression and collusion in the marginalization of "Others" through structural inequalities.

Effective structural change is grounded in *personal accountability* and connecting the systemic/public with the personal/community. To address undeserved privilege is not only a matter of self-consciousness. Changes in individual attitudes and behaviours are made possible by becoming more informed, more educated (or re-educated) and, in many cases, as a result of social pressures set up by movements, community organizations, political leadership, policies and so on. There is a need to integrate personal, collective/community and institutional accountabilities into a structural anti-racism. We therefore propose five key principles, with ideas for personal accountability and collective work, as learning companions and building blocks for White anti-racists working toward personal and collective responsibility and, ultimately, social change.

Understand that racism and colonization
in Canada is our collective story.

Personal accountability: Nation building in Canada was founded on numerous forms of explicit and implicit discrimination, including judicial and legislative marginalization, dehumanization and various forms of violence. These were/are meant to favour the interests of those with White settler identities. An understanding of racism in Canada requires an intersectional analysis of White privilege that includes class, gender, sexuality and other forms of dominance.

Collective work: It is not enough to focus on our own anti-racist consciousness. Working with other White people who are at various points in their own understanding of White privilege and racism is an integral aspect of White anti-racism work. It is unacceptable to keep the burden on Indigenous and racialized peoples to teach White people about White privilege and, at the same time, deal with its daily impacts. While acknowledging that our own learning journey is incomplete, White anti-racists who are engaged in our own self-work can be important resources in catalyzing critical thinking among others — always keeping in mind that this does not refute our complicity or involvement in structural oppression.

Open ourselves to critical self-examination
through the retelling of history.

Personal accountability: Many of us grew up with a faulty account of Canadian history, which included omissions and structural deception (including lies about particular nations or groups of people) and the reframing of conquest as heroism. A retelling/relearning of Canadian history is required, one that includes critical, diversely centred and previously marginalized perspectives that interrupt and mediate the concept of nation and nations, past, present and future.

Collective work: There is an increasing call for school-age history books, which are key to socializing a hegemonic Canadian identity, to be rewritten (this is already underway in certain jurisdictions). A collective will is needed to ensure that critical and multiple accounts of the Canadian nation building story are included, in all contexts and versions of "official" history (within our education system, government websites, official papers and documents). Included within these accounts should be the stories of resistance, strength, cultural knowledge, science, contributions and heroes that have been obfuscated by a racist colonial national agenda. Moreover, this retelling should not be attached solely to "special days" or specific commemorations. These changes to what should become our common stories should be accompanied by broad-reaching, anti-colonial training for the many generations that were indoctrinated into historical untruths that promote a false belief in White cultural superiority.

Refute inevitability; the concept of Canada and Canadian
society is socially constructed and based on dominance and conquest, so
it can be re-envisioned, reconstructed and revitalized.

Personal accountability: By understanding our collective history, we can challenge the belief that social relations (and racism and inequity in particular) are static and cannot be changed. Restoring our faith in our own potential for *social transformation* (Freire referred to this as "*refuting inevitability*") opens new inroads to needed structural changes, such as anti-racist policies at all levels. Refuting inevitability also compels us to take action and, for those with White privilege, to refuse the oppressive options of complacency, immobilization or ignorance.

Collective Work: We need to reconceptualize "nation" as "nations." The concept of nationhood is not static. The colonial redrawing and carving up of pre-existing land/people/relationships as a process of nation-claiming (based on conquest) is fairly recent in our long history; these lines, claimed to be borders, should not be *pris pour acquis*. Anti-colonialism and anti-racism require that settler communities, particularly White colonial settlers, unhinge themselves from the mythologized Canada to reconsider what it means to live the principle of reconciliation. There are several approaches to this, including efforts of Indigenous governments to reinstitute their own legal frameworks; a good example is the Akwesasne Justice System that the Mohawk Council instituted in 2016, which legislates all activities in their territory. We believe that contesting the concept of a Canadian nation with two founding settler groups is an intrinsic aspect of structural anti-racism.

Communicate authentically and accountably.

Personal accountability: *Personal transformation* is required, and difficult, for those in positions of dominance, as the benefits and invisibility of our status are barriers to an authentic understanding of our complicity. Therefore, communication within anti-racist work/movements must be interrelational and accountable (Gilbert and Sliep 2009) to be a catalyst for personal and social transformation. White fragility, as described by DiAngelo, can act as a destructive and silencing barrier to communication and personal accountability. *Authentic communication* exposes tensions and hidden truths within anti-racist organizing and establishing a foundation for the relationships of trust needed for this work. Accountable communication must be accompanied by social justice actions.

Collective work: From authentic communication, the possibility of (re)forming and implementing anti-racist, anti-oppressive governance and legislation (including our charters) can emerge with clear and timely accountability markers (including consequences for inaction). Structural change should be tied into legislation and policies that are infused into both public and private institutions. To ensure institutional accountability, mechanisms should be established so that civil society is intricately involved in assessing progress; they must become people's organizations that are empowered with the rights and roles to evaluate institutions and governments on their promises and strategies instead of just being "consulted" or "providing feedback."

Have the courage to act. Willingness to change in thoughts, words and actions to re-envision both ourselves and our relationship with Whiteness is foundational to re-envisioning Canadian national identity/ies without racism and other forms of oppression.

Personal accountability: Working for a healthier and more equity-based society requires the courage to denounce and work against a personal desire to hold onto power over others and continue to accrue the unfair benefits of Whiteness. At a systemic level, we envision this as the collective will of those with undue power to work together (and under the guidance of those who have experienced oppression) to transform policies into implemented practices with legislative and social accountability indicators.

Collective work: John Samuel (2002: 10) defines *systems advocacy* work as a "people-centred approach … to bridge the gap between micro-level activism and macro-level policy change." People-centred advocacy central-izes the concepts of rights, legitimacy, participation and communication and refutes the notion of "speaking for Others." Based on this approach, "advocacy is about mobilising the politics of the people to ensure that the politics of the state is accountable, transparent, ethical, and democratic. It is a mode of social and political action" (Samuel 2002: 9). Systems advocacy can be taken up in families, communities, business and particularly within our three levels of government (municipal, provincial/territorial, federal). Systems advocacy uplifts the roles and rights of each person to access those with power, particularly elected officials, to demand that significant changes be made that will target and eventually eradicate inequity. This includes a call for the dismantling and rebuilding of what is a blatantly racist and colonialist policing/judicial system in Canada. Undeniably, without changes to this system there will be no foundation of trust from which to build inclusive and protective norms and structures that promote equity and fair-ness. For White people, undue privilege can mask the realities of structural disadvantage. That is why we should follow and support the analysis and action agendas laid out by those with lived experiences of racial oppression. The ninety-four Calls to Action from Canada's Truth and Reconciliation Commission are key examples of this.

Working for Social Change

We cannot create a climate for social and structural change by simply look-ing at where we are today. As racism cannot be eliminated without being critical of the system of White privilege, so it is that poverty cannot be addressed without attention to wealth, women's inequality without men's privilege, and oppression of non-binary gender expression without problematizing cisnormativity and heterosexual privilege (for more information on cisnormativity, see Schilt and Westbrook 2009; Logie, James, Tharao and Loutfy 2012). The overriding message is the need to refocus from the "problems" of inequity to the *sources* of inequity.

Further, as systemic oppression is multi-layered and multi-levelled so must be a social justice response. For example, efforts to eradicate racism without attention to the racial and gendered nature of poverty, underemployment — and the White and masculine nature of wealth — will not be fruitful. In this vein, White privilege and racism cannot be uncoupled from the lack of national affordable daycare, and the imposition of White hegemonic masculinity (Lorenzetti 2016); it also cannot be removed from the regressive/aggressive immigration policies wilfully intended to enhance free movement of White people (and small handfuls of wealthy elites) across the globe and restrict those who are racialized and those who are labelled "poor." Racism and White privilege in Canada cannot be authentically addressed without limiting racist, patriarchal capitalism, which has now resulted in the supremacy of White-run corporations over nation-states.

While it can appear to be an overwhelming task to conceptualize, let alone address, these parallel areas of social injustice, it is our view, based on our experiences of social justice activism, that making the connections about how power is misused and marginality reproduced will strengthen the work for social change. As demonstrated in this chapter, our social locations and identities are reflected in structural relations of power/privilege and oppression/marginalization. The spaces we occupy and the influences we have intersect with both our conscious understanding of social change and the work needed to achieve it. The narratives shared in this chapter, and strategies for change we proposed, centre our positionality and the focus of this chapter: Whiteness.

Who's in Power?

The stronghold of White elites, specifically men, has not been significantly altered in Canadian society, although certain inroads and examples can be found. It is not acceptable that White people continue to occupy the majority of powerful positions and posts, while at the same time claiming Canada to be a society of diversity and opportunity. Structural racism cannot be addressed in a substantial way if this imbalance is not addressed. Most problematically, power, money, Whiteness and patriarchy are inextricably linked, meaning that shifting and diversifying power imbalances within Canadian society is complex and encounters multiple forms of resistance.

As discussed in this chapter, there are many ways that White people can move away from "passive positioning" (colluding with the racist system), which is often characterized by selective ignorance, denying or minimizing the depth to which racism is a structural problem in Canada, justifying a resistance to take action because there is a perceived economic cost, or defending the idea that other people or organizations will address these injustices. Personal accountability is a key starting point; however, a number of institutions and civil society structures should play important roles toward this end. Mandatory legislative accountabilities, evaluation measures and a focus on shifting the social and cultural acceptability of racism/White privilege through education for this generation and the next are paramount. All fields of action should bustle about in finding measures to prevent and end racism and, with it, all forms of discrimination.

We are all responsible for creating a common place where people will live with a sense of belonging and experience the conditions that foster equitable participation in all spheres of society including social, economic, cultural and political fields. That is what we call a dynamic and permanent dialogue for full and equitable civic participation.

DISCUSSION QUESTIONS

1. What did you learn about non-European cultures and Nations in Canadian history and nation building?
2. How does the concept of White privilege help you understand the dynamics of racism in Canada? How do other forms of oppression, like heterosexism, sexism, ableism and religious hegemony, contribute to a racist nation and maintain barriers for racialized and Indigenous people in Canada?
3. What roles should White people take in addressing racism and White privilege?

ACTION STEPS

1. Read, discuss and engage in learning opportunities that dispel historical myths regarding White privilege and Canadian nation building.
2. Participate in Indigenous or decolonizing activities, training and knowledge-sharing opportunities offered by First Nations, Métis or

Inuit Elders, cultural teachers or organizations.
3. Engage in work within communities, groups and organizations toward the development of policies and practices that dismantle White privilege and promote racial equity in areas such as hiring practices, leadership opportunities, equal pay for equal work, etc.

Supplemental Readings

English
Lund, Darren E., and Paul R Carr. 2015. *Revisiting the Great White North? Reframing Whiteness, Privilege, and Identity in Education,* second edition. Rotterdam, NE: Sense.
Siemerling, Winfried. 2015. *Black Atlantic Reconsidered: Black Canadian Writing, Cultural History, and the Presence of the Past.* Montreal, QC: McGill-Queens University Press.
The Truth and Reconciliation Commission of Canada. 2015. "TRC Final Report." <trc.ca/websites/trcinstitution/index.php?p=890>.

Français
Garner, Steve. 2007. "Le Paradigme de la Whiteness et les Identités Blanches dans l'Angleterre Contemporaine." In Michel Prum (dir.), *La Fabrique de la Race. Regard sur l'Ethnicité dans l'Aire Anglophone.* Paris: L'Harmattan.
Jacob, André. 2010. "La Diversité Ethnoculturelle: Entre la Peur et la Fascination." Texte d'une Conférence au Colloque "Psychologie et Diversité" organisé par l'Association des Professeurs(es) de Psychologie du Réseau Collégial du Québec (APPRCQ), Sainte-Adèle. June 8. <criec.uqam.ca/upload/files/Jacob_Div_ethno_juin10.pdf>.
Labelle, Micheline. 2006. "Un Lexique du Racisme. Étude sur les Définitions Opérationnelles Relatives au Racisme et aux Phénomènes Connexes." Report presented to UNESCO, « Montréal, Université du Québec à Montréal (UQAM), Centre de recherche sur l'immigration, l'ethnicité et la citoyenneté.» <criec.uqam. ca/upload/files/cahier/029.pdf>.

Additional Resources
Black Lives Matter Toronto
Kanehsatake: 270 Years of Resitance <archive.org/details/kanehsatake>
Redx Talks <vimeo.com/172822409>

Notes

Liza Lorenzetti would like to recognize Lemlem Haile for her guidance on this chapter.
1. For more information, see MSNBC: <msnbc.com/hardball/watch/the-389-people-places-and-things-trump-has-insulted-on-twitter-1103243331881>.
2. See, for example, Reuters: <reuters.com/article/us-austria-politics-nazi-scandal/austrian-freedom-party-politician-resigns-over-neo-nazi-scandal-idUSKBN1FL5GB>.

3. See also "Kanehsatake: 270 Years of Resitance" <archive.org/details/kanehsatake>.
4. Dr. Little Bear made this comment during an inaugural Redx Talks presentation in Calgary Alberta, December 2015. His statement is added here with his permission. To view Dr. Little Bear's presentation, go to <vimeo.com/172822409>.
5. See Black Lives Matter — Toronto <blacklivesmatter.ca/>.
6. See Idle No More <idlenomore.ca/>.

References

ACLC (African Canadian Legal Clinic). 2012. *Errors and Omissions: Anti-Black Racism and Canada: Report of ACLC to CERD.* <aclc.net/wp-content/uploads/CERD-Report-FINAL.pdf>.

Africville Museum. 2012. "The Community of Africville." <africvillemuseum.org/the-community-of-africville/>.

Ajzenstat, Janet. 2006. "Introduction." In Gerald M. Craig, *Lord Durham's Report.* McGill-Queen's University Press.

Allen, Mary. 2015. "Police-Reported Hate Crime in Canada, 2013." *Juristat*. Ottawa, ON: Canadian Centre for Justice Statistics.

Amnesty International. 2016. "No More Stolen Sisters." <amnesty.ca/our-work/campaigns/no-more-stolen-sisters>.

Anderson, Carol. 2016. *The Unspoken Truth of Our Racial Divide: White Rage.* New York: Bloomsbury.

Balibar, Étienne. 1988. "Y a-t-il un Néo-Racisme?" In Etienne Balibar and Immanuel Wallerstein (eds.), *Race, Nation, Classe. Les Identités Ambiguës. Paris, La Découverte.* ("Is There a Neo-Racism?" in *Race, Nation, Class. Ambiguous Identities.*)

Bannerji, Himani. 2000. *Dark Side of the Nation: Essays on Multiculturalism, Nationalism and Racism.* Toronto, ON: Canadian Scholars' Press.

Berry, John W. 2011. "Integration and Multiculturalism: Ways towards Social Solidarity." *Papers on Social Representations,* 20.

Bishop, Anne. 2015. *Becoming an Ally: Breaking the Cycle of Oppression in People,* third edition. Black Point, NS and Winnipeg, MB: Fernwood Publishing.

Bissoondath, Neil. 2002. *Selling Illusions: The Cult of Multiculturalism in Canada* (revised and updated version). Toronto, ON: Penguin.

Bonnett, Alastair. 2000. *Anti-Racism (Key Ideas).* London, UK: Routledge.

Bopp, Michael, Judie Bopp and Phil Lane. 2003. *Aboriginal Domestic Violence in Canada.* Ottawa, ON: Aboriginal Healing Foundation.

Bouthillier, Guy, et Jean Meynaud. 1972. *Le choc des language au Québec, 1960–1970.* Montréal, PQ: Les Presses de l'Université du Québec.

Calliste, Agnes, and George J. Sefa Dei. 2000. *Anti-Racist Feminism: Critical Race and Gender Studies.* Halifax, NS: Fernwood Publishing.

Canadian Business. 2017. "Canada's Richest People 2018: The Top 25 Richest Canadians." November 9. <canadianbusiness.com/lists-and-rankings/richest-people/top-25-richest-canadians-2018/image/26/>.

Canadian Commission for UNESCO. n.d. "Coalition for Municipalities Against Racism." <unesco.ca/home-accueil/ccmard-ccmcrd%20new/partners%20and%20resources>.

Canadian Encyclopedia. n.d. "Durham Report." *The Canadian Encyclopedia.* <thecanadianencyclopedia.ca/en/article/durham-report/>.

Carrillo, Ricardo, and Jerry Tello (eds.). 2008. *Family Violence and Men of Color: Healing the Wounded Spirit*, second edition. New York: Springer Publishing.

Carr, Paul R., and Darren Lund. 2008. "Antiracist Education." In F.E. Provenzo (ed.), *Encyclopedia of the Social and Cultural Foundations of Education*. Thousand Oaks, CA: Sage Publications.

Carter, Stacy M., and Miles Little. 2007. "Justifying Knowledge, Justifying Method, Taking Action: Epistemologies, Methodologies, and Methods in Qualitative Research." *Qualitative Health Research*, 17, 10.

Castellano, Marlene Brant, Linda Archibald and Mike DeGagné. 2008. "From Truth to Reconciliation, Transforming the Legacy of Residential Schools." *Aboriginal Healing Foundation*. <ahf.ca/downloads/from-truth-to-reconciliation-transforming-the-legacy-of-residential-schools.pdf>.

Chan, Arlene. 2016. "The Chinese Head Tax. The Canadian Encyclopedia." <thecanadianencyclopedia.ca/en/article/chinese-head-tax-in-canada/>.

Conway, John F. 2004. *Debts to Pay: English Canada and Quebec from the Conquest to the Referendum*. Toronto, ON: Lorimer.

Cooper, Afua. 2006. *The Hanging of Angelique: The Untold Story of Canadian Slavery and the Burning of Old Montreal*. Toronto, ON: HarperCollins Publishers.

Crenshaw, Kimberle. 1989. "Demarginalizing Intersections of Race and Sex: A Black Feminist Critique of Anti-Discrimination Doctrine, Feminist Theory and Anti-Racist Politics." *Chicago Legal Forum*, 140.

Creswell, John W. 2007. *Qualitative Inquiry and Research Design: Choosing Among Five Approaches*, second edition. Thousand Oaks, CA: Sage.

CRRF (Canadian Race Relations Foundation). 2015. "Our Values." <crrf-fcrr.ca/en/about/about-the-crrf-5>.

Davis, Angela Y. 1981. *Women, Race and Class*. New York: Random House.

Department of Justice. 2018. *Section 33 – Notwithstanding Clause*. Ottawa, ON: Government of Canada. <justice.gc.ca/eng/csj-sjc/charter-charte/check/art33.html>.

DiAngelo, Robin. 2011. "White Fragility." *International Journal of Critical Pedagogy*, 3, 3.

Dominelli, Lena. 2002. *Anti-Oppressive Social Work Theory and Practice*. New York: Palgrave Macmillan.

Dougherty, Kevin. 2017. "Canadian PM Says Mosque Shooting a 'Terrorist Attack on Muslims.'" *Reuters*, January 29. <uk.reuters.com/article/uk-canada-mosque-shooting/canadian-pm-says-mosque-shooting-a-terrorist-attack-on-muslims-idUKKBN15E04T>.

Dreifus, Claudia. 1994. "Chloe Wofford Talks About Toni Morrison." *New York Times Magazine*, September 11. <nytimes.com/1994/09/11/magazine/chloe-wofford-talks-about-toni-morrison.html>.

Dyer, Richard. 2005. "The Matter of Whiteness." In Paula S. Rothenberg, *White Privilege: Essential Readings on the Other Side of Racism*. New York, NY: Worth Publishers.

El Matrah, Joumanah. 2018. "The Feared Other: Peter Dutton's and Australia's Pathology around Race." *The Guardian*, January 7. <theguardian.com/commentisfree/2018/jan/07/the-feared-other-peter-duttons-and-australias-pathology-around-race>.

FCM (Federation of Canadian Municipalities). 2011. *Starting on Solid Ground: The Municipal Role in Immigrant Settlement*. <fcm.ca/Documents/backgrounders/Starting_on_solid_ground_the_municipal_role_in_immigrant_settlement_

Report_Overview_EN.pdf>.
Ferréol, Gilles, et Guy Jucquois (eds.). 2003. *Dictionnaire de l'Altérité et des Relations Interculturelles.* Paris, FR: Éditions Armand Colin.
Fong, Josephine. 2010. *Out of the Shadows: Woman Abuse in Ethnic, Aboriginal, and Refugee Communities.* Toronto, ON: Women's Press.
Frankenberg, Ruth. 1993. *The Social Construction of Whiteness: White Women, Race Matters.* Minneapolis, MN: Univeristy of Minnesota Press.
Freire, Paulo. 1970. *Pedagogy of the Oppressed.* New York: Continuum.
Gilbert, Andrew, and Yvonne Sliep. 2009. "Reflexivity in the Practice of Social Action: From Self-to Inter-Relational Reflexivity." *South African Journal of Psychology,* 39, 4.
Goodman, Diane J. 2011. *Promoting Diversity and Social Justice: Educating People from Privileged Groups,* second edition. New York, NY: Routledge.
Government of Canada. 2015. "Zero Tolerance for Barbaric Cultural Practices Receives Royal Assent." <canada.ca/en/news/archive/2015/06/zero-tolerance-barbaric-cultural-practices-act-receives-royal-assent.html?=undefined&wbdisable=true>.
Guess, Teresa J. 2006. "The Social Construction of Whiteness: Racism by Intent, Racism by Consequence." *Critical Sociology,* 32, 4.
Guglielmo Jennifer, and Salvatore Salerno. 2003. *Are Italians White? How Race Is Made in America.*New York: Routledge.
Hankivsky, Olena, and Renée Cormier. 2011. "Intersectionality and Public Policy: Some Lessons from Existing Models." *Political Research Quarterly,* 64, 1.
Henry, Frances, and Carol Tator. 2010. *The Colour of Democracy: Racism in Canadian Society,* fourth edition. Toronto, ON: Nelson Education.
Hill, Lawrence. 2007. *The Book of Negros.* Toronto, ON: HaperCollins.
___. 1993. *Trials and Triumphs: The Story of African Canadians.* Toronto, ON: Umbrella Press.
Hill Collins, Patricia. 2005. *Black Sexual Politics: African Americans, Gender and the New Racism.* New York: Routledge.
Hinson, Sandra, Richard Healy and Nathaniel Weisenberg. 2011. "Race, Power and Policy: Dismantling Structural Racism." *The Grassroots Policy Project.* <racialequitytools.org/resourcefiles/race_power_policy_workbook.pdf>.
hooks, bell. 1994. *Teaching to Transgress: Education as the Practice of Freedom.* New York: Routledge.
___. 1981. *Ain't I a Woman? Black Women and Feminism.* New York: Routledge.
Huffington Post. 2013. "Idle No More Protesters Accuse Calgary Sun Newspaper of Racism. January 14. <huffingtonpost.ca/2013/01/14/idle-no-more-calgary-sun-newspaper-racist_n_2473135.html>.
Indigenous Action Media. 2016. "Accomplices Not Allies: Abolishing the Ally Industrial Complex. An Indigenous Perspective." <indigenousaction.org/wp-content/uploads/Accomplices-Not-Allies-print.pdf>.
James, Carl E. 2012. "Students at Risk: Stereotyping and the Schooling of Black Boys." *Urban Education,* 47, 2.
James, Carl, David Este, Wanda Thomas Bernard, Akua Benjamin, Bethan Lloyd and Tana Turner. 2010. *Race and Well-Being: The Lives, Hopes and Action of African Canadians.* Halifax, NS: Fernwood Publishing.
Jiwani, Yasmin. 2006. *Discourses of Denial: Mediations of Race, Gender, and Violence.* Vancouver, BC: UBC Press.

Kivel, Paul. 2011. *Uprooting Racism: How White People Can Work for Racial Justice.* Gabriela Island, BC: New Society Publishers.

Legacy of Hope Foundation. 2013. "Canada Considers 'Aggressive Assimilation.'" November 28. <wherearethechildren.ca/watc_blackboard/canada-considers-aggressive-assimilation/>.

Lenoir, Yves, and Arturo Ornelas Lizardi. 2007. "Le Concept de Situation Existentielle Chez Paulo Freire: Au Cœur d'Une Pédagogie Critique et Émancipatoire." (Freire's Concept of the Existential Situation: The Heart of a Critical and Emancipatory Pedagogy.) *Centre de Research sur l'Intervention Éducative (CRIE) and Chaire de Researche du Canada sur l'Intervention Éducative (CRCIE).* <usherbrooke.ca/crcie/fileadmin/sites/crcie/documents/3-Freire_Lenoir_Ornelas.pdf>.

Li, Peter. 2008. "The Market Value and Social Value of Race." In Maria A. Wallis and Siu-ming Kwok (eds.), *Daily Struggles: The Deepening Racialization and Feminization of Poverty.* Toronto, ON: Canadian Scholars' Press.

Logie, Carmen, Llana James, Wangari Tharao and Mona R. Loutfy. 2012. "'We Don't Exist': A Qualitative Study of Marginalization Experienced by HIV-Positive Lesbian, Bisexual, Queer and Transgender Women in Toronto, Canada." *Journal of the International AIDS Society,* 15, 17392.

Lorde, Audre. 1984. *Sister Outsider: Essays and Speeches.* Berkeley, CA: Crossing Press.

Lorenzetti, Liza. 2016. "Engaging Men in Domestic Violence Prevention: Building a Collective-Cultures Approach." Unpublished doctoral dissertation, University of Calgary.

Lum, Zi-Anne. 2015. "Canada's Human Rights Record Under Review for the First Time." *Huffington Post,* July 6. <huffingtonpost.ca/2015/07/06/canada-un-human-rights_n_7737376.html>.

Lundy, Colleen. 2011. *Social Work, Social Justice and Human Rights: A Structural Approach to Practice,* second edition. Toronto University Press.

Maloney, Ryan. 2015. "Tories Pledge Tip Line to Combat 'Barbaric Cultural Practices.'" *Huffington Post,* October 2. <huffingtonpost.ca/2015/10/02/tip-line-barbaric-cultural-practices-tories_n_8234610.html>.

Maynard, Robyn. 2017. *Policing Black Lives: State Violence in Canada from Slavery to the Present.* Winnipeg, MB and Black Point, NS: Fernwood Publishing.

McAfee Brown, Robert. 1984. *Unexpected News: Reading the Bible with Third World Eyes.* Louisville, KT: Westminster John Knox Press.

McIntosh, Peggy. 1988. "White Privilege: Unpacking the Invisible Backpack." Wellesley College Center for Research on Women.

McLaren, Peter. 1994. "White Terror and Oppositional Agency: Towards a Critical Multiculturalism." In David T. Goldberg (ed.), *Multiculturalism: A Critical Reader.* Cambridge, UK: Blackwell.

Momin, A.R. 2004. "Multi-Communitarianism in a Fragmented World." *Asia Europe Journal,* 2, 3.

Nelson, Jennifer. 2008. *Razing Africville: A Geography of Racism.* Toronto, ON: University of Toronto Press.

Ngo, Hieu Van. 2008. "Cultural Competence: A Guide to Organizational Change." *Citizenship and Immigration Canada.* <albertahumanrights.ab.ca/Documents/CulturalCompetencyGuide.pdf>.

Nylund, David. 2006. "Critical Multiculturalism, Whiteness, and Social Work." *Journal of Progressive Human Services,* 17, 2.

Reynolds, Graham. 2016. *Viola Desmond's Canada: A History of Black and Racial*

Segregation in the Promise Land. Winnipeg, MB, and Black Point, NS: Fernwood Publishing.

Robinson, Greg. 2017. "Internment of Japanese Canadians." <thecanadianencyclopedia. ca/en/article/internment-of-japanese-canadians/>.

Rothenberg, Paula S. 2005. *White Privilege: Essential Readings on the Other Side of Racism.* New York: Worth Publishers.

Samuel, John. 2002. "What Is People-Centred Advocacy?" *PLA Notes,* 43. <pubs. iied.org/pdfs/G01974.pdf>.

Schilt, Kristen, and Laurel Westbrook. 2009. "Doing Gender, Doing Heteronormativity: 'Gender Normals,' Transgender People, and the Social Maintenance of Heterosexuality." *Gender and Society,* 23, 4.

Srivastava, Sarita. 2005. "'You're Calling Me a Racist?' The Moral and Emotional Regulation of Antiracism and Feminism." *Signs,* 31, 1.

Statistics Canada. 2013. *Immigration and Ethnocultural Diversity in Canada: National Household Survey 2011.* Ottawa, ON: Minister of Industry, Catalogue no. 99-010-X2011001.

Tardivel, Emilie. 2016. "Qu'est-ce qu'une Nation?" *Études: Revue de Culture Contemporaine,* 4231.

Tatum, Beverly Daniel. 1994. "Teaching White Students About Racism: The Search for White Allies and the Restoration of Hope." *Teachers College Record,* 95, 4.

TRC (Truth and Reconciliation Commission of Canada). 2015. "Truth and Reconciliation Commission of Canada. Calls to Action." <trc.ca/websites/ trcinstitution/File/2015/Findings/Calls_to_Action_English2.pdf>.

Trudel, Marcel. 2004. *Deux Siècles d'Esclavage au Québec.* Montréal, QC: Hurtubise.

United Nations. 1969. "International Convention on the Elimination of All Forms of Racial Discrimination." <ohchr.org/EN/ProfessionalInterest/Pages/CERD.aspx>.

Van Jones, Anthony Kapel. 2016. "Van Jones Tears Up on CNN: 'This Is a White Lash' and 'Nightmare.' *CNN Breaking News,* Nov 8. <youtube.com/ watch?v=QQly01LLe-I>.

Wallis, Maria A., and Siu-ming Kwok. 2008. "Daily Struggles: The Deepening Racialization and Feminization of Poverty in Canada." Toronto, ON: Canadian Scholar Press.

Warrior Publications. 2014. "Defending Territory: The Oka Crisis in Five Minutes." <warriorpublications.wordpress.com/2017/07/11/the-oka-crisis-in-5-minutes/>.

Waters, Rosanne. 2013. "African Canadian Anti-Discrimination Activism and the Transnational Civil Rights Movement, 1945–1965." *Journal of the Canadian Historical Association,* 24, 2.

Whitfield, Harvey Amani. 2016. *North to Bondage: Loyalist Slavery in the Maritimes.* Vancouver, BC: UBC Press.

Winks, Robin. 1997. *The Blacks In Canada: A History,* second edition. Montreal, QC, and Kingston, ON: McGill-Queen's University Press.

Zong Jie, and Jeanne Batalova. 2016. "Mexian Immigrants in the United Satates." *Migration Policy Institue, March 17.* <migrationpolicy.org/article/ mexican-immigrants-united-states>.

3

FROM RACISM
TO RECONCILIATION
Indigenous Peoples and Canada

Sharon Goulet

On January 22, 2015, Winnipeg received the notorious title of Canada's most racist city (MacDonald 2015). Just six months prior, Winnipeg mayoral candidate Robert-Falcon Ouellette began exposing the racism he encountered as an Indigenous man, describing the hateful emails he received during his campaign (*CBC News* 2014). Comments ranged from "you are lower-class," to angry obscenities about Indigenous and French people, to statements like,

> Go back to drinking. That's where Indians belong. You're that guy running for mayor. You're an Indian. I don't want to shake your hand. You Indians are the problem with the city. You're all lazy. You're drunks. The social problems we have in the city are all related to you. (MacDonald 2015)

Ouellette, program director for the Aboriginal Focus Programs at the University of Manitoba at the time, responded by talking publicly about the experience to expose "what's out there." Sadly, the experience of racism is not uncommon to Indigenous Canadians.

Racism can be described in many ways. Taiaiake Alfred (2009a: 50) defines racism as, "a construct that legitimate[s] white people's usurpation, and a feigned legitimacy [that] is constructed to normalize the structures ... built into notions of Indigenous peoples' land tenure and political rights." He goes on to associate the basic tenets of racism with the whole of colonization; specially, racism is and has been used to underpin the colonization experiences of Indigenous Peoples, as *colonialism* "consists of such things as resource exploitation of indigenous lands, residential school syndrome, racism, expropriation of lands, extinguishment of rights, wardship, and welfare dependency" (Alfred 2009a: 43).

Table 3.1: Racism and Racialization

Racism	The term racism first appeared in the English language in the 1930s. It can be traced to using the idea of race to justify that certain groups of people are alien and inferior (Darder and Torres 2004: 63).
Racialized	The term racialization extends the term racism to emphasize the social construction and place of racism in society, overall, for particular groups of people that have similar attributes (Darder and Torres 2004: 62).

For many Indigenous people, racism is a fact of life and a daily occurrence. The historically constructed premises upon which racism toward Indigenous people is built are still very much alive in mainstream Canada. Often termed "*micro-assaults*" (Sue and Constantine 2007), Indigenous people face a variety of judgements and biases every day about who they are — in arenas such as popular literature, media portrayals and the overall ideologies of many Canadians — which can do a great deal of damage to individuals, their families and communities. For example, Rosanna Deerchild, Indigenous writer and broadcaster, told *Maclean's Magazine* that, every few weeks, she is harassed for the simple fact that she is an Indigenous woman: "Someone honks at me, or yells out 'How much' from a car window, or calls me a stupid squaw, or tells me to go back to the rez. Every time, it still feels like getting punched in the face" (MacDonald 2015).

In many cases, for those who are victimized the self-fulfilling prophecies of "failure" further reinforce the "truths" of racism. While Ouellette was replying to racist comments, Jacinta Bear, who manages the North End Hockey Program in Winnipeg, was also struggling against racism in her daily life:

> Our team has heard it all, says Bear, whose husband, Dale, has coached the midget team for seven years. Even opposing coaches and refs call our kids "dirty little Indians." "Just keep smiling," she tells the kids. "Don't give them the reaction they're after. There's something not right in their lives and they're taking it out on you." (MacDonald 2015)

Bear, whose two sons both play for the local hockey team, the Knights, commented that, "although incidents like these are becoming less frequent, these are 'heartbreaking lessons' to teach eight-year-olds living in the city" (MacDonald 2015). Despite the belief that most Indigenous people live in rural areas, research (Goulet, Lorenzetti, Walsh, Wells and Claussen 2016: 16) has shown that Indigenous people continue to leave their reserves or home communities to live in the city and that they will likely face racism and discrimination (Muid 2006; Menzies 2009; Thurston, Soo and Turner 2013; Goulet et al. 2016). Daily occurrences of personal and systems-level racism impact people at a personal, family and community level, making things like finding a job or a home very difficult. In a report prepared for the City of Winnipeg (2012: 3) on the status of racism and discrimination in the city, the authors found that, "although racism and discrimination exist within a broad range of groups and communities in Winnipeg, literature on immigrants and Aboriginal people is the most dominant, suggesting that the problems are bigger within these communities."

As we are well into the twenty-first century, the question remains, how can we begin to move toward acts of reconciliation together?

The objectives of this chapter are to:

- understand basic concepts, from an Indigenous lens, that are important to the work of reconciliation;
- understand the connections between the history of colonization in Canada and the recurrent social conditions facing Indigenous and non-Indigenous Canadians; and
- demonstrate how the recommendations of the Truth and Reconciliation Commission (2015) and other social movements, such as the Missing and Murdered Women and Girls movement, can act as positive steps for all Canadians toward actionable social justice.

Stereotypes and Indigenous People

As an integral part of racism, many Indigenous people living in Canada suffer from inaccurate *stereotypes* or *myths*, which add to their daily burdens. Stereotypes are attitudes, assumptions and feelings that are ascribed to a group of people. Often, they are negative attitudes based in false information that has been socially created. One well-known example in the West is the image of the "Cowboy and Indian," a North American stereotype and common story arc in American Western films that portrayed a skewed image of many of the early interactions between Indigenous and non-Indigenous people. While this stereotype may be benign on the surface for some, Indigenous people have begun to fight back, insisting that they suffer as a community from these harmful, inaccurate and damaging historical images.

Another persistent and particularly damaging stereotype is seeing Indigenous people as childlike and requiring constant supervision, often as "wards of the state." This assumption not only degrades the autonomy of Indigenous Peoples as rights-bearing Canadians but has also damaged the self-concept of countless generations of Indigenous people who unfortunately internalize such demeaning stereotypes (Harding 2006: 223). Other common stereotypes are often seen in the media and include negative assumptions about the pervasiveness and causes of alcohol and drug addiction, unemployment and levels of violence (Backhouse 1999; de Leeuw, Kobayashi and Cameron 2011).

Historical Misconceptions

Myth: Indigenous Nations lost possession or gave up their land because they were inferior.

Reality: Indigenous Peoples died from colonizing practices, including but not limited to the introduction of diseases to which they had no immunity, by European colonizers (Rice and Snyder 2008: 55).

Physical Misconceptions

Myth: All Indigenous people do, or should, retain certain physical features. This practice is often seen in the film industry, where certain characteristics such as black hair, chiselled facial features and slim builds are cast as the "correct" way for Indigenous people to look.

Reality: Not only does this practice stereotype all Indigenous people regardless of their Nation, it produces a false reflection of the diversity between the over six hundred different Indigenous Nations in Canada alone, further damaging Indigenous identities and casting Indigenous people as museum caricatures (*Canadian Encyclopedia* n.d.).

Cultural Misconceptions

Myth: All Indigenous people still live in tipis or in other historical ways and are not suited for modern life.

Reality: Indigenous people have been portrayed over time as simplistic, one dimensional caricatures. Examples are fierce warriors, maidens and braves. These portrayals that lock people into romantic, historical stereotypes rather than modern contexts is not a fair or just reflection of skills and abilities (Rice and Snyder 2008: 54).

Myth: Indigenous people all have the same history, culture and speak the same language.

Reality: Section 35(2) of the Canadian Constitution defines the term "*Aboriginal*" as "Indian, Inuit and Métis peoples of Canada" and notes that they are rights-bearing peoples. Therefore, if you refer to someone as Aboriginal, this means, at a minimum, the person could be Métis, Inuit or First Nations (Indian) (Government of Canada 2017).

Each of the three groups has its own unique historical background, culture and political goals, and within each rights-bearing group — such as the many different First Nations — are many different communities with their own languages, cultures and histories. Canada has a variety of legal relationships with each of the three groups.

First Nation

First Nation replaced the generic and offensive term "Indian" except for in the Canadian Constitution, which still uses the term Indian. The term First Nation is generally used to identify specific groups of people whose relationship with Canada is grounded in the Treaties and/or the Indian Act (1876). There are 633 First Nations bands, representing fifty-two Nations or cultural groups and more than fifty languages (*Canadian Encyclopedia* n.d.).

Métis

The word *Métis* comes from the Latin "miscere," to mix, and was used originally to describe the children of First Nations women and European men from the time of first contact onward. The Métis represent a unique Nation in Canada with a history, culture and language distinct from their First Nations and European parentage (Logan 2008: 73).

Inuit

The *Inuit* are the original inhabitants of the Arctic, including Nunavut, the Northwest Territories, the coast of northern Labrador and northern Québec (Canada's First Peoples 2007).

Legal Misconceptions

Myth: All Indigenous people have treaties, with entitlements to free land, housing, education, health and social services.

Reality: This is untrue. *Treaties* are legal settlements arrived at through negotiation between two or more nation-states. A treaty is a binding contractual obligation, outlining the rights and responsibilities of the parties as they are agreed upon. Treaties were historically used by the European nations to recognize Indigenous Peoples' existing occupancy, ownership and governance of the countries they wanted to colonize (McKay 2008: 110).

Table 3.2: Legal Milestones

1763 – Royal Proclamation	The King of England declared that Indigenous people had ancestral rights and ownership of the land and resources of what would become Canada. This set the stage for treaties, in that no land could be ceded to private interests but only to the Crown. The Proclamation still stands in the Canadian Constitution (Rice and Snyder 2008: 50).
1876 – *Indian Act*	The first *Indian Act* legislated almost all aspects of a First Nations person's life, including their identity, where they could live, if they could travel, and whom they could marry without losing their status (Jacobs and Williams 2008: 122).
1982 – Canadian Constitution	Section 35 reaffirmed the ancestral rights of all Aboriginal (Indian, Métis and Inuit) people and that they are rights-bearing people (Government of Canada 2017).
1985 – Bill C-31	Bill C-31 amended the portion of the *Indian Act* that discriminated against First Nations women who married non-Indigenous and Métis men. Prior to the amendment, First Nations women with "status" (which defines them as Indigenous according to the federal government) who married a non-Indian man (whether non-Aboriginal or non-status) would lose her status. In contrast, non-Indigenous women could gain status by marrying a First Nations man with status. The same held for children of either union (Jacobs and Williams 2008: 124). Status or registered Indians are individually recognized by the federal government as being registered under the *Indian Act*.

It is important to note that, while many Nations did sign treaties, several Nations across Canada did not. For those Nations that did sign treaties, the quality and amount of rights afforded to members (education, housing) differs between each Nation. Further, Métis and non-Status Indians do not get free housing or post-secondary education. Métis people may obtain a Métis card, which allows access to minimal Métis services and proves their Métis background (Métis Nation n.d.).

There are many different legal agreements, political and social policies and government relationships that have been developed with Indigenous groups across Canada. For example, Métis people do not live on reserves and do not have signed treaties, but instead they have negotiated agreements with their respective provincial governments. Some First Nations and Inuit people have federal land and resource agreements, but these differ greatly by Nation.

Several major legal milestones demonstrate the complexities of treaties and other federal social policies, as noted in table 3.2. Legal activity is ongoing and many more important cases are before the courts on a continuing basis.

Intergenerational Trauma, Colonization and Indigenous Peoples: Understanding the Truth

There are many factors that have contributed to the current situation of Indigenous Peoples in Canada. Prior to European contact, Indigenous Peoples were thriving in their environments. Colonization brought with it poverty at all levels and a destruction of traditional medicines, governance and social structures. Indigenous Peoples were never conquered, but control of lands, languages, cultures and worldviews was taken away (Menzies 2009; Christensen 2011, 2012).

The many social problems seen in Indigenous communities are a direct result of colonial practices and systemic destruction of Indigenous families and communities. One notable example is the imposition of *residential schools*. Colonialism and the removal of Indigenous Peoples from the knowledge contained in their traditional territories, communities and families has had devastating and enduring psychological effects on survivors and their families. According to Alfred (n.d.: 8), colonialism can be defined as

> a theoretical framework for understanding the complexities of the relationship that evolved between Indigenous peoples and Europeans as they came into contact and later sustained those initial relationships in building a new reality for both peoples in North America. Specifically, colonialism is the development of institutions and policies by European imperial and Euro-American settler governments towards Indigenous peoples.

One of the many ways in which this was accomplished was through the residential schools system.

Residential schools within Canada operated for nearly 150 years, between the 1840s and into the 1990s. The last residential school operated by the Canadian government, Gordon's Indian Residential School in Saskatchewan, was closed in 1996. While residential schools taught some basic academic content, the purpose of these schools was to transform Aboriginal communities … for assimilation, segregation, and integration into mainstream Canadian society. Separation from their family for months, even years, at a time resulted in children losing their language, culture, and spiritual beliefs, as well as sense of belonging to a family or kinship network. (Menzies 2009: 2)

Even more devastating was the widespread sexual abuse that came to public awareness in the late 1980s. In "Disordered Dependencies: The Impact of Language Loss and Residential Schooling on Indigenous Peoples," Leona Makokis (2009: 10) describes her experience in residential school as akin to being kidnapped:

> Our schooling was made up of rote memory, spelling bees, and multiplication. The nuns taught. We listened. We remembered. This was very different from our parents and grandparents "Idsklnohamewasowlna" (learnings and teachings), which taught children by modeling, showing, experiencing, and interacting. Instead, we read "Dick and Jane" and learned about their dog, Spot. They lived in a white house with a picket fence, and they had an immaculately kept yard. They did not have a "mosom" or "kokom" (a grandfather or grandmother), they did not have a large extended family, what we read had no meaning to our own experiences and our own world. Our schooling was not connected to anything that we brought with us from our communities; our schooling totally disconnected us from our life force.

Living for years in such harsh conditions, many parts of the child were lost — most notably cultural morals and values as they relate to a way of life. Returning home, the children soon became parents, but they found they were missing many, if not all, important cultural teachings. Makokis describes her own experience: "we have been so separated from these teachings (that are defined in our language), we cannot transmit them to our children; therefore, they lack the guidance they need to help create a world in balance and health" (2009: 12). When they could, grandparents also tried to pass on some aspects of culture when children were home from residential schools, but this lacked consistency.

After the residential schools slowly began to close, Indigenous communities began to see the devastating effects of residential schools at a community level. As Elizabeth Fast and Delphine Collin-Vézina (2010: 131) describe, a whole generation of survivors were being created "given the lack of parental role modeling and widespread physical and sexual abuse while attending residential schools." Having no positive parental role models to draw from opened the door to what is termed the *Sixties Scoop*.

Many writers have captured the intent of the Sixties Scoop, which was a period in the 1960s after most of the schools were closed when thousands of First Nations, Métis and Inuit children were removed from their parents and placed in ("adopted out" to) non-Indigenous homes (Blackstock, Prakash, Loxley and Wien 2005). Kristine Morris (2007: 135) describes this time as "a phenomenon of huge numbers of Aboriginal children being apprehended from their families … which was all done in the name of the 'best interest of the child.'"

Believed to be a conservative figure, a total of 11,132 Status Indian children alone were adopted out largely to White, middle-class families between 1960 and 1990 (Gough, Trocmé, Brown, Knoke and Blackstock 2005). This number does not account for Métis or non-status children who suffered the same fate.

Social problems such as substance abuse, poverty, low educational attainment and homelessness have all been traced back through research to the long-term effects of colonialism, specifically the removal of Indigenous children from their homes and birth families and their placement in non-Indigenous homes (Baskin 2007; Peters 2012; Whitbeck, Crawford and Sittner Hartshorn 2012; Thurston, Soo and Turner 2013). Coined the *"child welfare impact,"* studies show an intergenerational connection between presenting factors such as growing up in poverty or child welfare involvement and current homelessness or child welfare involvement (Blackstock and Trocme 2005; Fast and Collin-Vézina 2010).

Finally, *poverty* is a prevailing, compounding factor that also amplifies most of the social conditions that Indigenous people face. For Indigenous Peoples, poverty is a direct result of colonization. As traditional economies were destroyed, they were replaced "with foreign systems such as education, justice, health and child protection [that] have left Aboriginal peoples in a 'cycle of economic dependency'" (Baskin 2007: 33). Although education rates are increasing, breaking out of poverty is, in large part, dependent on acquiring formal education and employment, which is a difficult task as decades of racism and stereotyping follow people through the school system and into their jobs.

Intergenerational or Historical Trauma

Most troubling is that, due to colonization, many Indigenous people have lost their connection to spirit. Through the oftentimes invisible transmission of trauma, many Indigenous people are passing on to their children self-defeating and negative behaviours and ideas about who they are and their place in Canada. In addition to this, many Indigenous Peoples have lost their connection to their own worldviews, languages and cultural practices outright, leaving a legacy of colonial myths and stereotypes in their place. These erroneous and negative impacts are not only transmitted to individuals, but also through the prevailing structures and beliefs that people operate within daily. As Catherine Kingfisher (2007: 95) states quite eloquently,

> On one side were those who felt that a focus on Aboriginality was the necessary response to an empirically verifiable deficiency among that population, indicating, thereby, that if any problems with homelessness were structural in nature, they had to do with the structure of an inherently dysfunctional Aboriginal culture that produced dysfunctional individuals. In contrast, and fewer in number, were those who felt that a focus on Aboriginality was the necessary response to an empirically verifiable racism seen to be rampant in Woodridge [a suburb of Logan City, Australia], indicating that problems with homelessness were both personal and private and public and structural, in specific reference to dominant white, as opposed to Native, culture and society.

Despite the nature of response to colonial myths, the historical and ongoing devastation caused by colonialism cannot be overestimated.

There is no shortage of research documenting the massive and negative impacts of *intergenerational trauma* on Indigenous people and communities (Brave Heart-Jordan 1995; Brave Heart 2003; Sotero 2006; Evans-Campbell 2008; Solanto 2008; Fast and Collin-Vezina 2010; Brave Heart, Chase, Elkins, and Altschul 2011; Gone 2013). The term "intergenerational trauma" is found in a great deal of the literature and used interchangeably with terms such as "*historical trauma*," "*transgenerational grief*," and "*historic grief*." A pioneer in uncovering the root cause of many of the social issues facing Indigenous communities, Maria Yellow Horse Brave Heart defines historical trauma as "cumulative emotional and psychological wounding across generations, including the lifespan, which emanates from massive group trauma" (Brave Heart et al. 2011: 282). According to Brave Heart et al. (2011: 283), "the historical trauma response (HTR) has been conceptualized as a constellation of features associated with a reaction to massive group trauma. Historical unresolved grief, a component of this response, is the profound unsettled bereavement resulting from cumulative devastating losses." Some common examples that have not been acknowledged as unresolved grief are high rates of suicide and cumulative poor health outcomes, such as stress and anxiety disorders, in many Indigenous communities.

In response to this work, researchers are now beginning to emphasize the importance of understanding the social, political and economic conditions faced by Indigenous people within the overall context of trauma and colonialism (Brave Heart 2003; Evans-Campbell 2008; Fast and Collin-Vezina 2010; Brave Heart et al. 2011; Gone 2013). Denis Bracken (2008: 21) calls these conditions the social "symptoms" of trauma, recognizing that "the context of those social characteristics are the result of colonialism and related policies of discrimination, attempts at forced assimilation and economic marginalization experienced by Aboriginal people."

In her work, Marlene Brant Castellano (2006–07: 5) highlights that therapists treating troubled Indigenous people quickly began to note similarities to post-traumatic stress disorder (PTSD) symptoms: "hyper arousal such as being excessively alert, anticipating the next traumatic event, and easily made anxious or angry; flashbacks to the original traumatic event set off by minor triggers; and blunted feelings, which make it difficult to maintain relationships."

Intergenerational trauma helps to articulate, in clinical terms, the well-known and lived experiences felt daily by survivors of residential schools and their offspring from one generation to the next. It can also open doors to policymakers and funders who can then provide the necessary resources to assist in healing from the effects of residential school exposure. Indigenous communities across Canada are at different places in terms of healing from residential school impacts and trauma. In their work on trauma and addictions, Don Coyhis and Richard Simonelli (2008: 1929) highlight the positive impact of programs like the Wellbriety Movement, which emphasizes "the need to go beyond sobriety to heal the deep wounds of intergenerational trauma carried by almost all Indian people."

Similarly, the Healing Forest Model has been noted as both an inspiration and a basis for community healing and change at a deeper level. Coyhis and Simonelli describe the deep work of the model:

Alcoholism and other addictions are symptoms. The many social issues associated with alcohol and substance misuse are also symptoms. It is important to address the underlying spiritual and cultural issues that give rise to the anger, guilt, shame, and fear that create unhealthy soil in the forest metaphor. These four poisons in the soil of the sick forest lead to the onset of addictive behaviours and are one cause of intergenerational trauma. For American Indians and Alaska Natives, the trauma of the historical period is continually passed down from generation to generation. It is not only a thing of the past. (Coyhis and Simonelli 2008: 1931)

Indigenous communities continue to lead and promote spiritual and cultural healing approaches rather than symptom-based interventions that reinforce colonial stereotypes.

Murdered and Missing Indigenous Women and Girls Movement and Reconciliation

Probably the most damaging "Canadian-made" stereotypes have been directed toward Indigenous women. Although the origin is unknown, the term "squaw" has been, until recently, used quite liberally to describe Indigenous women, despite being universally offensive. Tied to the negative connotations of the term squaw, Indigenous women are frequently sexually objectified. This has led to alarming rates of violence directed toward Indigenous women and girls, documented by the mounting evidence of the *Murdered and Missing Indigenous Women Movement* (Government of Canada 2014). According to a Native Women's Association of Canada report (2015), as of March 31, 2010, approximately 582 cases of missing and murdered Indigenous women and girls had been identified. Of these, 67 percent are murder cases (death as the result of homicide or negligence); 20 percent are cases of missing women or girls; 4 percent are cases of suspicious death — deaths regarded as natural or accidental by police but considered suspicious by family or community members; and 9 percent are cases where the nature of the case is unknown — it is unclear whether the woman was murdered, is missing or died in suspicious circumstances. The same report found that only 53 percent of murder cases involving Indigenous women and girls have led to charges of homicide, once again demonstrating the pervasive devaluing of Indigenous women in Canadian society.

By 2014, a second report commissioned by the RCMP identified that the number had doubled to "1,181 missing and murdered Indigenous women and girls" (Government of Canada 2014: 7). Specifically, the report states,

> In 1991, Aboriginal females accounted for 14% of all female victims, compared with 21% in 2014. The lowest proportion of Aboriginal female homicides was 8% in 1984, and the highest proportion was 23% which occurred in 2004 and 2007, as well as in 2012 and 2013.

This operational overview also found that, while homicide rates for non-Indigenous women in Canada are declining, the homicide rate for Indigenous women has remained unchanged.

On August 3, 2016, the Government of Canada launched an independent national inquiry into missing and murdered Indigenous women and girls. The *National Inquiry into Missing and Murdered Indigenous Women and Girls* is independent from the federal government and, with the help of an independent commission, is directed "to examine and report on the systemic causes behind the violence that Indigenous women and girls experience by looking for patterns and underlying factors that explain why higher levels of violence occur" (Government of Canada 2014: n.p.). While the inquiry will most certainly report on the causes behind such elevated levels of violence, Indigenous communities are uncertain if any substantive and systemic changes will result. If this is the case, solutions must also be sought by turning back to traditional forms of healing and understanding of the value of Indigenous women, which can most often be found in women's stories.

Bringing Back the Indigenous Woman Through Stories

Seneca scholar Mishuana Goeman (2008: 295) has written that "Stories are a narrative tool that must be a part of Native feminism." *Native feminism* centres on the power of Indigenous women in finding their own voices and telling their own stories. These same stories also have the potential to be used as the tools to rebuild cultural answers to contemporary problems. Reclaiming and understanding these stories is also critical as Indigenous communities grapple with the monumental task of how to rebuild and enhance their community health. Pre-contact stories can be used as tools to empower Indigenous women, men and children while at the same time elevating *Indigenous knowledge* as a pre-contact practice. According to several Indigenous academics, Elders and Knowledge Keepers, this type of knowledge is primarily about relationships (Bastien 2004; Little Bear 2009). According to Betty Bastien (2004: 77), "Knowledge, accordingly, is not something contained in a book, a CD or other memory mechanisms. Knowledge, from an Indigenous perspective, is the relationships one must attend to, 'all my relations.'"

In traditional communities, stories, ceremonies and spiritual teachings played a central role in defining and valuing the specific roles of women, men, children and *Elders* within families and Nations. Language, songs, stories and ceremonies are all important practices that worked in the past and can help with decolonization efforts. Sarah Deer (2015: 116) suggests that the best way for communities to respond to widespread community issues such as violence against women may be through "the reclaiming and understanding of [pre-contact] stories."

According to respected Elder Dr. Reg Crowshoe of the Piikani Nation, in the absence of Elders to assist in the many facets of change communities can also look to original stories to help guide us back to who we are as Indigenous Peoples (Personal communication, Crowshoe 2016). In thinking about the usefulness of pre-contact stories, Deer also describes how Indigenous women "traditionally passed on information concerning community perceptions and sanctions … through stories, ceremonies and songs" (Deer 2015: 119).

In the absence of an understanding of the value of Indigenous women, communities in trauma have no other option than to continue to rely on imposed patriarchal and colonial structures, which were not in practice prior to colonization, to deal with family and community issues. Victorian ideals of gender roles, parenting and child care roles — right up to male-dominated tribal leadership — are a few examples of how patriarchy continues to devalue Indigenous women. Consequently, incorrect or stereotyped information is created to define Indigenous women and their roles and value in post-colonial Indigenous communities. With no other information to counter these ideas, they become internalized and continually reproduced with no end in sight. Glen Coulthard (2014: 31) describes this process of "internalization of forms of racist recognition" by Indigenous people as one of the greatest tools of continued colonization. He also suggests that

> the subjective realm of colonization be the target of strategic transformation along with a return to pride and empowerment instead of programs and services that serve only to help people fit into colonial structures that continue to be a "bad fit." (45)

This process requires turning away from the colonial structures that have never served Indigenous women, families or communities. This is not so much an act of reconciliation; it is one of resurgence. *"Resurgence"* is as an ancestral movement that is re-emerging among some Indigenous thinkers and Indigenous and settler-ally activists in North America (Alfred 2009b). Alfred has publicly spoken against the term reconciliation — suggesting that reconciliation does nothing to realign the very power structures that keep Indigenous Peoples oppressed, letting the oppressors off "with a simple apology" (Alfred 2009a: 48). Resurgence, instead, demands fundamental shifts to foundational worldviews and a reframing of power structures and relationships by Indigenous Peoples for real change to occur.

Reconciliation: Moving Forward

> My people will sleep for one hundred years; when they awake, it will be the artists who give them their spirit back. (Louis Riel 1885)

In May 2015, the *Truth and Reconciliation Report* (TRC 2015), with a highlighted refocus on the United Nations Declaration on the Rights of Indigenous Peoples (UNDRIP), was released (United Nations 2008). The report prepared a comprehensive historical record on the policies and operations of Canada's residential schools, as well as smaller report with ninety-four Calls to Action for the Government of Canada and other levels of government and institutions that have a historic or present-day relationship with Indigenous communities. According to the Truth and Reconciliation Commission, *reconciliation* is defined as "an ongoing individual and collective process that will require participation from all those affected by the Indian Residential School (IRS) experience. This includes activities such as public education and engagement, commemoration and recommendations for action to the parties" (TRC 2015: 16).

On September 2007, the UNDRIP was adopted by the General Assembly by 144 states in favour and four votes against. While Canada initially voted against the UNDRIP, Canada eventually signed the declaration in 2010. While the document is not legally binding, it should be a guidepost that may be used to support positive change in Indigenous communities.

In 2016, the federal government commissioned Canadian lawyer Thomas Isaac[1] to produce a report entitled, *A Matter of National and Constitutional Import: Report of the Minister's Special Representative on Reconciliation with Métis: Section 35 Métis Rights and the Manitoba Métis Federation Decision* (Isaac 2016). This further clarified the rights of Métis citizens

— an ongoing issue that had yet to be resolved since the repatriation and inclusion of Métis citizens as Aboriginal people in the 1982 Canadian Constitution. He goes on to say, "reconciliation is more than just platitudes and recognition. Reconciliation flows from the constitutionally protected rights of Indigenous people enshrined by Section 35, is inextricably tied to the honour of the Crown, and must be grounded in practical actions" (Isaac 2016: 3).

Section 35 of the 1982 Canadian Constitution is binding, federal legislation that recognizes and affirms *Aboriginal Rights* and must be used hand in hand with both the TRC and UNDRIP to move forward reconciliation.

Table 3.3: Section 35 of the *Constitution Act, 1982*

(1) The existing aboriginal and treaty rights of the aboriginal peoples of Canada are hereby recognized and affirmed.
(2) In this Act, "aboriginal peoples of Canada" includes the Indian, Inuit and Métis peoples of Canada.
(3) For greater certainty, in subsection (1) "treaty rights" includes rights that now exist by way of land claims agreements or may be so acquired.
(4) Notwithstanding any other provision of this Act, the aboriginal and treaty rights referred to in subsection (1) are guaranteed equally to male and female persons.

Source: Government of Canada 2017.

It is important to understand that section 35 recognizes Aboriginal Rights but did not create them, as Aboriginal Rights existed before section 35.

While section 35 of the *Constitution Act* of 1982 recognizes and affirms existing Aboriginal rights, it does not define them (Government of Canada 2017). What Aboriginal Rights include has been the topic of much debate and discussion, being defined over time through Supreme Court cases. Recognition has been further defined for each group over time (as most recently for Métis in the 2016 *Daniels v. Canada* decision). Finally, section 35 falls outside of the *Charter of Rights and Freedoms*. This allows section 35 to be exempt from the "notwithstanding clause" that applies to the Charter (Hirschl 2004: 196). In other words, the federal government cannot override Aboriginal Rights. Section 35 is also underpinned by the concept known as the "*Honour of the Crown*," and "is an important cornerstone to the work of reconciliation" (Saul 2014: 36).

In his book, *The Comeback*, Canadian writer John Ralston Saul describes how the honour of the Crown — which broadly suggests that the Crown should act honorably in its dealings with Indigenous Peoples — should be

considered the central Canadian constitutional principle on which reconciliation should be built and is at the very heart of the relationship between
Canada and Indigenous Peoples. Law in this area has developed rapidly in
recent years and is still a work in process. The honour of the Crown applies
any time the government contemplates policy, legislation or action that
may have an impact on established or claimed Aboriginal Rights and Title,
including Treaty Rights. Three key obligations flowing from the honour of
the Crown (Dickson 2014: 1–2) are:

> (a) the duty to consult and, where indicated, accommodate appli-
> cable Aboriginal interests prior to acting in a manner adverse to
> those interests;
> (b) the duty to bring a demonstrably purposive and diligent
> approach to the fulfillment of constitutional obligations owed
> applicable Aboriginal peoples; and
> (c) the (residual and, as will be shown, fundamentally unre-
> solved) fiduciary duty to act with reference to the best interests of
> a First Nation, Inuit, or Métis community in circumstances where
> the Crown has assumed a sufficient measure of discretion over
> cognizable legal interests of that community.

Most recently, the honour of the Crown has been again established as valid
in the 2013 Supreme Court of Canada decision regarding the Manitoba
Métis Federation, which stated that "the unfinished business of reconciliation of the Métis people with Canadian sovereignty is a matter of national
and constitutional import" (Isaac 2016: 3).

With respect to understanding the relationship between reconciliation
and the honour of the Crown in Haida Nation (2004), the Supreme Court
judgement (*Haida Nation v. British Columbia* 2004) provides key insights.

This Supreme Court judgment established an important precedence
regarding the obligations of the Crown, the importance of the treaties and
their application, and the overall rights of Indigenous Peoples.

The Fight for Social Justice

Social justice is "the idea of creating a society or institution that is based
on the principles of equality and solidarity, that understands and values
human rights, and that recognizes the dignity of every human being" (Zajda,
Majhanovich and Rust 2007: 10). The Centre for Social Justice (n.d.) also
suggests that social justice for Indigenous Peoples is tied specifically to
addressing the many long-term experiences of oppression such as residential

Table 3.4: *Haida Nation v. British Columbia* (2004: 16–19 and 25)

16. The government's duty to consult with Aboriginal peoples and accommodate their interests is grounded in the honour of the Crown. The honour of the Crown is always at stake in its dealings with Aboriginal peoples … It is not a mere incantation, but rather a core precept that finds its application in concrete practices.
17. The historical roots of the principle of the honour of the Crown suggest that it must be understood generously to reflect the underlying realities from which it stems. In all its dealings with Aboriginal peoples, from the assertion of sovereignty to the resolution of claims and the implementation of treaties, the Crown must act honourably. Nothing less is required if we are to achieve the reconciliation of the pre-existence of Aboriginal societies with the sovereignty of the Crown.
18. The honour of the Crown gives rise to different duties in different circumstances. Where the Crown has assumed discretionary control over specific Aboriginal interests, the honour of the Crown gives rise to a fiduciary duty …
19. The honour of the Crown also infuses the processes of treaty making and treaty interpretation. In making and applying treaties, the Crown must act with honour and integrity, avoiding even the appearance of sharp dealing …
25. Put simply, Canada's Aboriginal peoples were here when Europeans came, and were never conquered. Many bands reconciled their claims with the sovereignty of the Crown through negotiated treaties … The honour of the Crown requires that these rights be determined, recognized and respected. This, in turn, requires the Crown, acting honourably, to participate in processes of negotiation. While this process continues, the honour of the Crown may require it to consult and, where indicated, accommodate Aboriginal interests (Supreme Court of Canada 2004).

Source: *Haida Nation v. British Columbia* 2004.

schools, the Sixties Scoop and other paternalistic experiences. Specifically,

> Aboriginal people have a long and proud history that includes rich cultural and spiritual traditions. Many of these traditions, however, were altered or even taken away upon the arrival of European settlers. The forced introduction of European culture and values to Aboriginal societies, the dispossession of Aboriginal lands, and the imposition of alien modes of governance began a cycle of social, physical and spiritual destruction. You can see the effects of this today. Some effects include poverty, poor health, and substance abuse. Underlying these problems is a loss of identity and a learned helplessness from having their values oppressed and their rights ignored. (Centre for Social Justice n.d.: para 1)

It is through rich and historical traditions, noted above, that social justice can also be a tool used by Indigenous Peoples to return to traditional ideas that help rebuild the natural laws that existed in Indigenous communities prior to colonization.

In response to the many oppressive forces that Indigenous Peoples have faced and continue to deal with, many have long expressed a frustration with "justice," preferring instead a return to self-governance, *healing and cultural practices* as a form of social justice. As one Elder said,

> I believe there is a warehouse, somewhere — with all of the reports that have been written about our people and our problems. The only thing is nothing is done with them but they all say the same thing. That we want our sovereignty, language, values and natural laws recognized as important tools to bring Indigenous people back to who we are. (Personal communications, Moore 2012)

Although this may be true, what has recently changed is the public's recognition of the "issues" as symptoms of something larger and a desire to be part of the healing as an ally. For example, many levels of government, universities and other large systems are actively co-creating Indigenous strategies and policies in reaction to the Truth and Reconciliation Commission's ninety-four Calls to Action with Indigenous Elders and communities. Through these dialogues, the public is better able to understand the real effects of colonial practices and, in turn, how much more necessary healing approaches are than ensuring the absence of disease. As Makokis (2009: 11) describes,

> Unlike the western or capitalist worldview, which encourages the exploitation of mother earth, the Indigenous worldview indicates that the health of our future generations is at stake. Our relationship with the universe is governed by reciprocity: you invite into your life, and the life of future generations, optimum health or illness, by the way you conduct yourself.

These concepts pre-date colonization and speak to the holistic health that existed in Indigenous communities.

In conjunction with healing work being undertaken by Indigenous communities is the role of the ally. An "*ally*" has been defined by many, but according to Anne Bishop (2002: 125), ally work requires "a structural and historical approach ... wherein people are seen as part of larger systems, shaped by [their] context. The assumption is that we can change our institutions and culture only through collective organization and action." There are many sources of literature defining the role of the ally in relation to Indigenous Peoples, marginalized groups and social justice. Overall, the key points are outlined in table 3.5.

Table 3.5: Key Points on the Role of an Ally

- Being an ally requires a critical lens where our "normal" practices and process are redefined and changed to suit the needs of the people being supported, but it is not an identity.
- Being an ally is an ongoing practice where the ally may experience many failures as they learn how to shift previous roles and power relationships.
- Ultimately, the process and answers come not from the mandate of the ally but that of the "Other."

This new form of integrity can only be created if both parties understand the concept of *"ethical space"* and how this space both challenges and scaffolds the elevation of community mandates as well as defines the places where allies can assist instead of lead. According to Willie Ermine,

> Ethical space is formed when two societies, with disparate worldviews, are poised to engage each other. This includes conversations that evolve opportunities to live, plan and manage ourselves, and our process from an Indigenous perspective and ultimately from the environment. (Ermine 2007: 193)

The work of the ally is neither easy, nor accepted in all realms of Indigenous decolonization work, as it will require a significant shift in power and resources from historically dominant systems to Indigenous communities:

> The enemy is not the white man in racial terms, it is a certain way of thinking with an imperialist's mind. The enemy of our struggle is the noxious mix of monotheistic religiosity, liberal political theory, neo-capitalist economics and their supportive theories of racial superiority, and the false assumption of Euro-American cultural superiority. (Alfred 2009b: 102)

Alfred, founding director of the Indigenous Governance Program at the University of Victoria, summed up this struggle to transition influence in an authentic way.

Reconciliation in Action: One Example

There are many ways to be involved in reconciliation work. It is critical however, that any social programs, policy development or systems change be co-created, implemented and evaluated with the unique needs and strengths of Indigenous Peoples at the forefront. One such avenue is through the lens of sports and culture.

As an example, before settlement on reserves, some Indigenous Peoples lived in small nomadic groups and subsisted from hunting and gathering activities. Active lifestyles, healthy foods, natural medicines and a balanced approach to life has changed dramatically for many Indigenous people over the past several decades due to the massive changes in lifestyles as a result of colonizing practices (Dawson, Karlis and Georgescu 1998). One way to combat lifestyle changes is through the reintegration of sports and traditional games into community life. Traditional games that rebuild traditional values and knowledge is an easy approach toward reconciliation that brings together young people, parents, Elders and traditional people to develop collectively.

According to Lynn Lavallee (2007: 3), Indigenous games not only nurtured the physical needs of individuals but also taught social and personal values, which were a "curriculum for a cultural way of life." Recreation and sports had a significant role in Indigenous communities before colonization. Activities such as lacrosse and certain dance styles that were meant as healing practices, as well as the values and beliefs that they taught, were lost due to historical trauma. One way to bring back these activities is through the active involvement of community. Indigenous community development advocates for local community to be the primary driver for the development and operation of programs. This is an important concept for reconciliation activities with partners that consider themselves allies. In the *Truth and Reconciliation Report* (TRC 2015: 10–11), the value of sports and reconciliation was identified in five Calls to Action.

In several cities across Canada, the process of reconciliation with Indigenous people through specialized Indigenous sports and recreation programs has already begun. A longstanding and prime example is the work of the City of Saskatoon's Community Development and Leisure Services, initiated in April 1999. InMotion is a partnership of Saskatoon Regional Health, the City of Saskatoon, the University of Saskatchewan and ParticipACTION to develop a healthy community and a healthy workplace, which involves developing and implementing a community-wide active living strategy (City of Saskatoon 2016). The goal of InMotion is to

Table 3.6: TRC Calls to Action Related to the Value of Sports

87. We call upon all levels of government, in collaboration with Aboriginal peoples, sports halls of fame, and other relevant organizations, to provide public education that tells the national story of Aboriginal athletes in history.

88. We call upon all levels of government to act to ensure long-term Aboriginal athlete development and growth, and continued support for the North American Indigenous Games, including funding to host the games and for provincial and territorial team preparation and travel.

89. We call upon the federal government to amend the *Physical Activity and Sport Act* to support reconciliation by ensuring that policies to promote physical activity as a fundamental element of health and well-being, reduce barriers to sports participation, increase the pursuit of excellence in sport, and build capacity in the Canadian sport system, are inclusive of Aboriginal peoples.

90. We call upon the federal government to ensure that national sports policies, programs, and initiatives are inclusive of Aboriginal peoples, including, but not limited to, establishing:

  i. In collaboration with provincial and territorial governments, stable funding for, and access to, community sports programs that reflect the diverse cultures and traditional sporting activities of Aboriginal peoples.

  ii. An elite athlete development program for Aboriginal athletes.

  iii. Programs for coaches, trainers, and sports officials that are culturally relevant for Aboriginal peoples.
  iv. Anti-racism awareness and training programs

91. We call upon the officials and host countries of international sporting events such as the Olympics, Pan Am, and Commonwealth games to ensure those Indigenous peoples' territorial protocols are respected, and local Indigenous communities are engaged in all aspects of planning and participating in such events.

Source: TRC 2015.

increase the level of participation in sport, culture and recreational activities among Aboriginal youth, adults and families who are not active on a regular basis. The Aboriginal Leadership Program is an umbrella for a variety of exciting experiences that teach Indigenous youth how to be a leader in Saskatoon, including the Aboriginal Lifeguard Program, Aboriginal Fitness Certification Program, Adult and Community Leadership Development, recruitment of Summer Program Staff, Atoske Skills and Employment Summer Training Camp, and yearly Youth Leadership Summits.

In addition, the Mē Ta Wē Tān Centres (Cree word for "Let's Play") offer Indigenous people of all ages to get active in sport, culture and recreation, such as annual pow wows and Indigenous summer camps.[2]

Finally, a cornerstone to Indigenous sport and recreation is the

Maskwachees Declaration (Indigenous Sport Council Alberta 2000), created in 2000 by an intergovernmental advisory committee on fitness and recreation in Hobbema, Alberta. This document lauds physical activity as a crucial way to "improve the health, wellness, cultural survival and quality of life of entire communities in their fight against intergenerational trauma and return to wellness through traditional practices" (Indigenous Sport Council Alberta 2000: n.p.). This can be done through several integrated partnership approaches, including community education, the development of traditional practices, changing social norms, leadership development, community development, role modelling, using team approaches, increased coaching, increased community pride, increased self-confidence, improved nutrition, improved identity and, finally, healing the effects of colonization and trauma.

Resurgence and Reconciliation

Human relationships are at the core of the work of reconciliation. Many wrongs have been committed against Indigenous Peoples across Canada and, sadly, they continue. Reconciliation will not happen from attending to a "shopping list" of activities that are checked off and then forgotten but, instead, will only be advanced through respectful and difficult conversations. Reconciliation will take time. In some cases, work will look more like resurgence or the use of oral tradition. It will look like the rebirth of traditional knowledge and understanding and the emergence of silenced worldviews.

Most importantly, reconciliation will come from the Elders — those people who still retain the language, practices and worldviews that many have forgotten. The sad reality is that our Elders are passing faster than change can occur, so we must not sit idly by.

DISCUSSION QUESTIONS
1. How will I act as an ally and supporter of reconciliation?
2. How will I support Indigenous Peoples to lead reconciliation efforts?
3. What can I do to challenge those systems and power structures that maintain colonialism?

ACTION STEPS

1. Western or mainstream people and systems must embrace true reconciliation, which includes examining and addressing power and privilege at all levels of society. This includes (but is not limited to) significant changes to our key institutions such as education, child welfare, judicial and health systems, respect for Treaty and land rights protections and the implementation of the United Nations Declaration on the Rights of Indigenous People (UNDRIP).
2. New systems, approaches and programs must be built from Indigenous DNA. Indigenous DNA includes original stories, ceremonies and understanding of Indigenous worldviews and cosmology prior to contract.

All my relations — Wahpi osaw pihesiw iskwew — Yellow Thunderbird Woman.

Supplemental Readings

Alfred, Taiaiake. 2009. *Wasáse: Indigenous Pathways of Action and Freedom.* Toronto: ON: University of Toronto Press.

Coulthard, Glen Sean. 2014. *Red Skin, White Masks: Rejecting the Colonial Politics of Recognition*. Winnipeg, MB: University of Minnesota Press.

Saul, John Ralston. 2014. *The Comeback*. Toronto, ON: Penguin Group Publishing.

Additional Resources

Additional readings on *intergenerational trauma* can be found through a series of reports from the Aboriginal Healing Foundation: <ahf.ca/publications/research-series>.

Additional reading on *Indigenous Women* and *the Murdered and Missing Women and Girls movement* can be found at: Canada: Stolen Sisters, A Human Rights Response to Discrimination and Violence against Indigenous Women in Canada, *Amnesty International October 2004* <amnesty.ca/sites/amnesty/files/amr200032004enstolensisters.pdf>.

Additional readings on the *Truth and Reconciliation Report (TRC)* can be found at: <trc.ca/websites/trcinstitution/index.php?p=890>.

Notes

1. Editor's note: Thomas Isaac is a nationally recognized expert in colonial–Indigenous relations.
2. More information on the program can be found at <saskatoon.ca/parks-recreation-attractions/recreational-facilities-sportsfields/youth-and-m%C4%93-ta-w%C4%93-t%C4%81n-centres>.

References

Alfred, Taiaiake. n.d. "Colonialism and State Dependency." Prepared for the National Aboriginal Health Organization Project Communities in Crisis. School of Indigenous Governance, University of Victoria.

___. 2009a. "Colonialism and State Dependency." *Journal de la Santé Autochthone*, 5, 2.

___. 2009b. *Wasáse: Indigenous Pathways of Action and Freedom*. Toronto, ON: University of Toronto Press.

Backhouse, Constance. 1999. *Color-Coded: A Legal History of Racism in Canada. 1900–1950*. Toronto, ON: Osgoode Society of Canadian Legal History.

Baskin, Cyndy. 2007. "Aboriginal Youth Talk About Structural Determinants as the Causes of Their Homelessness." *First People Child and Family Review*, 3, 3.

Bastien, Betty. 2004. *Blackfoot Ways of Knowing: The Worldview of the Siksikaitsitapi*. Calgary, AB: University of Calgary Press.

Bishop, Anne. 2002. *Becoming an Ally: Breaking the Cycle of Oppression in People*, second edition. Black Point, NS, and Winnipeg, MB: Fernwood Publishing.

Blackstock, Cindy, and Nico Trocme. 2005. "Community Based Welfare for Aboriginal Children: Supporting Resilience Through Structural Change." Centre of Excellence for Child Welfare University of Toronto: *First Nations Child and Family Caring Society*, 24.

Blackstock, Cindy, Tara Prakash, John Loxley and Fred Wien. 2005. "Wen:de: We Are Coming to the Light of Day." *First Nations Child and Family Caring Society of Canada*.

Bracken, Denis C. 2008. "Canada's Aboriginal People, Fetal Alcohol Syndrome and the Criminal Justice System." *British Journal of Community Justice*, 6, 3.

Brant Castellano, Marlene. 2006–07. "Healing Narratives: Recovery from Residential School Trauma." The Vanier Institute of the Family: *Transition*, Winter.

Brave Heart, Maria Yellow Horse. 2003. "The Historical Trauma Response Among Natives and Its Relationship with Substance Abuse: A Lakota Illustration." *Journal of Psychoactive Drugs*, 35, 1: Special Issue: Morning Star Rising: Healing in Native American Communities.

Brave Heart, Maria Yellow Horse, Josephine Chase, Jennifer Elkins, and Deborah B. Altschul. 2011. "Historical Trauma Among Indigenous Peoples of the Americas: Concepts, Research and Clinical Considerations." *Journal of Psychoactive Drugs*, 43, 4.

Brave Heart-Jordan, Maria Yellow Horse. 1995. "The Return to the Sacred Path: Healing from Historical Trauma and Historical Unresolved Grief among the Lakota." *Dissertation Abstracts International*, 56.

Canada's First Peoples. 2007. "The Inuit." <firstpeoplesofcanada.com/fp_groups/fp_inuit1.html#>.

Canadian Encyclopaedia. n.d. "Social Conditions of Indigenous People." <thecanadianencyclopedia.ca/en/article/native-people-social-conditions/>.

CBC News. 2014. "Robert-Falcon Ouellette Faces Racism During Mayoral Campaign: Aboriginal Winnipeg Mayoral Candidate Target of Online Abuse After Speaking French in Debate." June 25. <cbc.ca/news/canada/manitoba/robert-falcon-ouellette-faces-racism-during-mayoral-campaign-1.2686918>.

Centre for Social Justice. n.d. "Aboriginal Issues." <socialjustice.org/index.php?page=aboriginal-issues>.

Christensen, Julia. 2012. "They Want a Different Life: Rural Northern Settlement

Dynamics and Pathways to Homelessness in Yellowknife and Inuvik, Northwest Territories." *Canadian Geographer.* 56, 4.

___. 2011. "Homeless in a Homeland: Housing (In)security and Homelessness in Inuvik and Yellowknife, Northwest Territories, Canada." Doctoral thesis, McGill University, Montreal, QC.

City of Saskatoon. 2016. "Youth and MĒ TA WĒ TĀN Centres." <saskatoon.ca/parks-recreation-attractions/recreational-facilities-sportsfields/youth-and-m%C4%93-ta-w%C4%93-t%C4%81n-centres>.

City of Winnipeg. 2012. *The Status of Racism and Discrimination in Winnipeg.* Prepared in 2012 for Winnipeg CMARD. Citizen Equity Committee: CMARD – Coalition of Municipalities Against Racism and Discrimination. <winnipeg.ca/clerks/boards/citizenequity/pdfs/RacismDiscriminationStatus2012.pdf>.

Coulthard, Glen Sean. 2014. *Red Skin, White Masks: Rejecting the Colonial Politics of Recognition.* Minneapolis, MN: University of Minnesota Press.

Coyhis, Don, and Richard Simonelli. 2008. "The Native American Healing Experience." *Substance Use and Misuse,* 43, 12–13: Special Issue on Recovery.

Darder, Antonia, and Rodolfo Torres. 2004. *After Race: Racism After Multiculturalism.* New York: New York University Press.

Dawson, Don, George Karlis and Denisa Georgescu. 1998. "Contemporary Issues in Recreation and Leisure for Aboriginal People in Canada." *Journal of Leisurability,* 25, 1.

de Leeuw, Sarah, Audrey Kobayashi and Emilie Cameron. 2011. "Difference." In Vincent J. Del Casino Jr., Mary E. Thomas, Paul Cloke and Ruth Panelli (eds.), *A Companion to Social Geography.* Oxford, UK: Wiley-Blackwell.

Deer, Sarah. 2015. *The Beginning and End of Rape: Confronting Sexual Violence in Native America.* Minneapolis, MN: University of Minnesota Press.

Dickson, Jamie D. 2014. *The Honor of the Crown: Making Sense of Crown Liability Doctrine in Crown/Aboriginal Law in Canada.* Saskatoon, SK: University of Saskatchewan.

Ermine, Willie. 2007. "The Ethical Space of Engagement." *Indigenous Law Journal,* 6, 1.

Evans-Campbell, Teresa. 2008. "Historical Trauma in American Indian/Native Alaska Communities: A Multilevel Framework for Exploring Impacts on Individuals, Families, and Communities." *Journal of Interpersonal Violence,* 23, 3.

Fast, Elizabeth, and Delphine Collin-Vézina. 2010. "Historical Trauma, Race-Based Trauma, and Resilience of Indigenous Peoples: A Literature Review." *First Peoples Child and Family Review,* 5, 1.

Goeman, Mishuana. 2008. "(Re)Mapping Indigenous Presence on the Land in Native Women's Literature." *American Quarterly,* 60, 2.

Gone, Joseph P. 2013. "Redressing First Nations Historical Trauma: Theorizing Mechanisms for Indigenous Culture as Mental Health Treatment." *Transcultural Psychiatry,* 50, 5.

Gough, Pamela, Nico Trocmé, Ivan Brown, Della Knoke and Cindy Blackstock. 2005. "Pathways to Overrepresentation of Aboriginal Children in Care: CECW Information Sheet #23E." Toronto, ON: Centre of Excellence for Child Welfare.

Goulet, Sharon, Liza Lorenzetti, Christine A. Walsh, Lana Wells and Caroline Claussen. 2016. "Understanding the Environment: Domestic Violence and Prevention in Urban Aboriginal Communities." *The Frist Peoples Child and Family Review,* 11, 1.

Government of Canada. 2017. "Constitution Act, 1982: Canadian Charter of Rights and Freedoms." Justice Laws Website. <laws-lois.justice.gc.ca/eng/Const/page-15.html>.

___. 2014. *Missing and Murdered Aboriginal Women: A National Operational Preview.* Ottawa, ON: Her Majesty the Queen in Right of Canada as Represented by the Royal Canadian Mounted Police (RCMP). <rcmp-grc.gc.ca/wam/media/460/original/0cbd8968a049aa0b44d343e76b4a9478.pdf>.

Haida Nation v. British Columbia, 2004, SCC 73.

Harding, Robert. 2006. "Historical Representations of Aboriginal People in the Canadian News Media." *Discourse and Society,* 17, 2.

Hirschl, Ran. 2004. *Towards Juristocracy.* Cambridge, UK: Harvard University Press.

Indigenous Sport Council Alberta. 2000. "Maskwachees Declaration — What Has Changed in the Communities Since." <aboriginalsports.org/resources/articles/maskwachees-declaration.html>.

Isaac, Thomas. 2016. *A Matter of National and Constitutional Import: Report of the Minister's Special Representative on Reconciliation with Métis: Section 35 Métis Rights and the Manitoba Métis Federation Decision.* Ottawa, ON: Her Majesty the Queen in Right of Canada as Represented by the Minister of Indigenous and Northern Affairs.

Jacobs, Beverly, and Andrea Williams. 2008. "Legacy of Residential Schools: Missing and Murdered Aboriginal Women." In Marlene Brant, Linda Archibald, and Mike DeGagne (eds.), *From Truth to Reconciliation: Transforming the Legacy of Residential Schools.* Ottawa, ON: Aboriginal Healing Foundation.

Kingfisher, Catherine. 2007. "Discursive Constructions of Homelessness in a Small City in the Canadian Prairies: Notes on Restructuration, Individualization, and the Production of (Raced and Gendered) Unmarked Categories." *American Ethnologist,* 34, 1.

Lavallee, Lynn. 2007. *Assessing the Impact of Sport Using and Indigenous Research Framework.* Toronto, ON: SIRC.

Little Bear, Leroy. 2009. *Naturalizing Indigenous Knowledge: Synthesis Paper.* University of Saskatchewan, Aboriginal Education Research Centre, Saskatoon, SK, and First Nations and Adult Higher Education Consortium, Calgary, AB.

Logan, Tricia 2008. "A Métis Perspective on Truth and Reconciliation." In Marlene Brant, Linda Archibald, and Mike DeGagne (eds.), *From Truth to Reconciliation: Transforming the Legacy of Residential Schools.* Ottawa, ON: Aboriginal Healing Foundation.

MacDonald, Nancy. 2015. "Welcome to Winnipeg: Where Canada's Racism Problem Is at Its Worst." *MacLeans,* January 22. <macleans.ca/news/canada/welcome-to-winnipeg-where-canadas-racism-problem-is-at-its-worst/>/.

Makokis, Leona. 2009. "Disordered Dependencies: The Impact of Language Loss and Residential Schooling on Indigenous Peoples." *Rural Social Work and Community Practice,* 14, 2.

McKay, Susan. 2008. "Criminalization of Indigenous Human Rights and Environmental Activists." Panel Discussion to the Shock Doctrine: Indigenous Peoples' Experience in Canada: Symposium of Indigenous Human Rights and Environmental Activists. (Unpublished.)

Menzies, Peter. 2009. "Homeless Aboriginal Men: Effects of Intergenerational Trauma." In J. David Hulchanski, Philippa Campsie, Shirley B.Y. Chau, Stephen Hwang and Emily Paradis (eds.), *Finding Home: Policy Options for Addressing Homelessness in Canada* (e-book). Toronto, ON: Cities Centre, University of Toronto.

Métis Nation. n.d. "Métis Nation Citizenship." <metisnation.ca/index.php/who-are-the-metis/citizenship>.

Morris, Kristine. 2007. "(A Literature Review) Re-Examining Issues Behind the Loss of Family and Cultural and the Impact on Aboriginal Youth Suicide Rate." *First Peoples Child and Family Review*, 3, 1.

Muid, Onaje. 2006. *"...Then I Found My Spirit: The Meaning of the United Nations World Conference Against Racism and the Challenges of the Historical Trauma Movement with Research Considerations.* Edmonton, AB: The Residential School Experience: Syndrome or Historic Trauma. CASAC Healing Our Spirit Worldwide (HOSW) 5th Gathering.

Native Women's Association of Canada. 2015. "Fact Sheet: Missing and Murdered Aboriginal Women and Girls." <nwac.ca/wp-content/uploads/2015/05/Fact_Sheet_Missing_and_Murdered_Aboriginal_Women_and_Girls>.

Peters, Evelyn. 2012. "'I Like to Let Them Have Their Time.' Hidden Homeless First Nations People in the City and Their Management of Household Relationships." *Social and Cultural Geography*, 13, 4.

Rice, Brian, and Anna Snyder. 2008. "Reconciliation in the Context of Settler Society: Healing the Legacy of Colonialism in Canada." In Marlene Brant, Linda Archibald, and Mike DeGagne (eds.), *From Truth to Reconciliation: Transforming the Legacy of Residential Schools.* Ottawa, ON: Aboriginal Healing Foundation.

Saul, John Ralston. 2014. *The Comeback.* Toronto, ON: Penguin Random House Canada.

Solanto, Joe. 2008. "Intergenerational Trauma and Healing." Video recording from the 2008 Aboriginal Justice Forum. Heartspeak Productions. <heartspeakproductions.ca/intergenerational-trauma>.

Sotero, Michelle. 2006. "A Conceptual Model of Historic Trauma: Implications for Public Health Practice and Research." *Journal of Health Disparities Research and Practice*, 1, 1.

Sue, Derald Wing, and Madonna G. Constantine. 2007. "Racial Micro Aggressions as Instigators of Difficult Dialogues on Race: Implications for Student Affairs Educators and Students." *The College Student Affairs Journal*, 26, 2.

Thurston, Wilfreda E., Andrea Soo and David Turner. 2013. "Are There Differences Between the Aboriginal Homeless Population and the Non-Aboriginal Homeless Population in Calgary?" *Pimatisiwin: A Journal of Aboriginal and Indigenous Community Health*, 11, 2.

TRC (Truth and Reconciliation Commission of Canada). 2015. *Honouring the Truth, Reconciling for the Future: Summary of the Final Report of the Truth and Reconciliation Commission of Canada.* <nctr.ca/assets/reports/Final%20Reports/Executive_Summary_English_Web.pdf>.

United Nations. 2008. *United Nations Declaration on the Rights of Indigenous Peoples (UNDRIP).* <un.org/esa/socdev/unpfii/documents/DRIPS_en.pdf>.

Whitbeck, Les, Devan Crawford and Kelley Sittner Hartshorn. 2012. "Correlates of Homeless Episodes among Indigenous People. *American Journal of Community Psychology*, 49, 1–2.

Zajda, Joseph, Suzanne Majhanovich and Val Rust. 2007. "Introduction: Education and Social Justice." *Review of Education*, 52, 1.

4

"US AND THEM"
Immigration and Barriers to a Diverse Canadian Identity

Glenda Tibe Bonifacio

The intrinsic connection between racism and contemporary immigration policies and practices in Canada occurs as a systemic exercise of oppression directed at racialized immigrant populations in society. The ways in which they have been historically and currently affected by immigration policies demonstrate overt and subtle racism. This chapter presents the realities of immigrants as well as *temporary foreign workers* (TFWs) as shaped by immigration policies and practices; some examples of social exclusion as framed by the intersections of race, class and gender; and the effect of unequal relations between economically rich and poor countries.

Through colonization, which included social constructions of a hegemonic Canadian national identity, the White population (especially French and British) established rule over sovereign independent Indigenous communities to form the Dominion of Canada. While the continued racism in Canada is certainly experienced by First Nations, it differs considerably from the racism that immigrants experience. This chapter focuses on immigrants and TFWs. During the next three years, it is anticipated that Canada will admit over 900,000 permanent residents (Governent of Canada 2017a). As well, the TFW program will continue to be an integral component of the country's immigration policy.

This chapter is divided into four sections. The first section presents contemporary immigration policies and related practices of the federal ministry Immigration, Refugees and Citizenship Canada (IRCC), formerly Citizenship and Immigration Canada (CIC), that determine the eligibility of various classes of immigrants into the country. The second section discusses the creation of a working underclass under several temporary foreign worker schemes such as the Live-in Caregiver Program (LCP), Seasonal Agricultural Worker Program (SAWP) and the Provincial Nominee

Program (PNP). In all these contexts, an *"us" and "them" dichotomy* has been fostered. The third section explores the dynamics beyond the individual, particularly the relations between countries to explain and break down this dichotomy. In the fourth section, recommendations are offered to create inclusive social practices for immigrant communities, and a more equitable immigration process involving pre-migration and post-migration services. This bridges the gap between theory and practice to eradicate barriers to a diverse Canadian identity for today and tomorrow.

The objectives of this chapter are to:

- outline contemporary immigration programs directed toward permanent migration and their exclusionary practices;
- highlight the creation of a working underclass of temporary foreign workers; and
- offer recommendations for inclusive social practices and equitable immigration processes.

Contemporary Immigration Policies

Immigration means permanently or temporarily moving to another country, involving a favoured country of destination granting the immigrant a visa through a rigid, bureaucratic process of admission. This exercise presumably guarantees that those who enter the receiving country have passed certain eligibility requirements, broadly including scrutiny of their health status and obtaining security clearance from origin countries or places they have lived for certain periods of time (Rudolph 2006; International Business Publications 2014). By and large, voluntary immigration is a desire to enter a country subject to state policy that is in effect at the time of application. In other words, it is not easy to become an immigrant because of all the required documentation and fees.

In Canada, contemporary immigration is set out in the *Immigration and Refugee Protection Act* (IRPA) of 2002. The objectives of IRPA are set out in table 4.1. These objectives recognize the importance of immigration in the economic, social and cultural aspects of Canadian society. Immigration also addresses the greying population of Canada, where more people aged 65 years and older compared to those under 14 years old were recorded for the first time in its history in 2015 (Mehler Paperny 2015). The trend continued in 2016, as seniors outnumbered children (5.9 million and 5.8 million, respectively) and showed a radical growth of a 20 percent share

Table 4.1: 2002 *Immigration and Refugee Protection Act* Objectives

(a) To permit Canada to pursue the maximum social, cultural and economic benefits of immigration;
(b) to enrich and strengthen the social and cultural fabric of Canadian society, while respecting the federal, bilingual and multicultural character of Canada; (b.1) to support and assist the development of minority official languages communities in Canada;
(c) to support the development of a strong and prosperous Canadian economy, in which the benefits of immigration are shared across all regions of Canada;
(d) to see that families are reunited in Canada;
(e) to promote the successful integration of permanent residents into Canada, while recognizing that integration involves mutual obligations for new immigrants and Canadian society;
(f) to support, by means of consistent standards and prompt processing, the attainment of immigration goals established by the Government of Canada in consultation with the provinces;
(g) to facilitate the entry of visitors, students and temporary workers for purposes such as trade, commerce, tourism, international understanding and cultural, educational and scientific activities;
(h) to protect public health and safety and to maintain the security of Canadian society;
(i) to promote international justice and security by fostering respect for human rights and by denying access to Canadian territory to persons who are criminals or security risks; and
(j) to work in cooperation with the provinces to secure better recognition of the foreign credentials of permanent residents and their more rapid integration into society.

Source: Government of Canada 2015a; IRPA 2002.

of seniors since 2011 (Grenier 2017). This trend has social and economic implications, as slow population growth means, for instance, fewer people working to contribute to domestic production and taxation. Since the 1960s Canadian women have shown decreasing fertility rates and, after the 1990s, immigration became the "key driver of population growth" (Statistics Canada 2017). More than anything else, immigration is important to sustain Canada's growth and prosperity as set out in IRPA policy objectives and in practice (Verbeeten 2007; International Organization for Migration 2008; Bodvarsson and Van den Berg 2013).

IRCC is the federal ministry tasked with the authority to issue related policies and directives to meet the objectives set out in the IRPA of 2002. Immigration programs are thus subject to change at the discretion of the political party in power. For example, when the Conservative Party under Stephen Harper formed government in 2006, the historical preference for permanent labour migration was eclipsed by the rise of temporary labour migration schemes (Lenard and Straehle 2012). The number of TFWs increased dramatically, from 101,098 in 2002 to 338,221 in 2012 (Ball 2015). The number of TFWs grew by 70 percent from 2006 to 2010 compared to 12 percent for permanent residents or immigrants (Geddes 2012). However, restrictions were subsequently placed by the Conservative government after reported abuses of the program were exposed in the media (CBC News 2015). As a result, TFWs declined in number to 90,211 by 2015 (Curry 2016), a further decline from the total number of 94,109 TFWs as of December 31, 2014 (CIC 2014). In 2016, 78,535 individuals were admitted to the TFW program (Government of Canada 2017a).

Immigration to Canada directly with IRCC through its new electronic *Express Entry* system became effective in January 2015. There are now three major economic streams: *Canadian Experience Class* (CEC), *Federal Skilled Worker Program* (FSWP) and *Federal Skilled Trades Program* (FSTP) (Government of Canada 2015b). Two additional programs are in place for family sponsorship and immigrant investors; the former is the *Provincial Nominee Program* (PNP) and the latter, under the Immigrant Investor Venture Capital Pilot Program, was open for applications from May 25, 2015, to December 30, 2015 (Government of Canada 2015c). Each of these federal immigration programs has different eligibility requirements. Applicants under the CEC must demonstrate a minimum of one full year's work experience in Canada, in the last three years before an individual applies, with proper authorization while in the country as an international student or a foreign worker, and, depending on the occupation applied for, required language levels based on the National Occupation Classification (NOC) system (Government of Canada 2017b). For example, in this immigration category, jobs classified as NOC 0 (managerial) or NOC A (professional) must have at least the required Canadian Language Benchmark (CLB), or the scale of language proficiency in English as a second language, score of seven for English language or Niveau de compétence linguistique canadiens (NCLC) score of seven in French for listening, speaking, reading and writing. Jobs under NOC B (technical jobs and skilled trades) must have CLB 5 or NCLC 5 (Government of Canada 2015d). Attainment of the required level of language proficiency means getting the necessary points for immigration purposes; less than the required CLB means ineligibility to immigrate to Canada.

The FSWP has six selection criteria: language level at CLB 7 with a language test; education with Canadian equivalency as indicated in the Educational Credential Assessment (ECA) report; ten years of work experience in NOC O. A or B; age; valid job offer; and adaptability. The FSTP has its own eligibility requirements that include two years of full-time skilled work experience within five years prior to application; offer of employment for a year; qualified for the job based on NOC; and language level at CLB 5 for speaking and writing and CLB 4 for reading and writing, with a language test (Government of Canada 2015d).

To date, these immigration programs — except the family sponsorship — are, in effect, geared toward addressing the economic needs of Canada. This scenario is no different from the premise of immigration policies since Confederation in 1867 (Whitaker 1991; Kelley and Trebilcock 2010). Immigration is intrinsically tied to the economy as clearly stated in the objectives of IRPA.

While generally geared toward economic need, Canada's immigration policies and practices historically also had clear racial objectives. The *Immigration Act* of 1910 prohibited the admission of "any race deemed unsuited to the climate or requirements of Canada" (Knowles 1992: 80). Other measures were racially restrictive, such as the Chinese "head tax," which affixed an extra fee to every Chinese person entering Canada as a way to discourage their immigration, or the Japanese "gentlemen's agreement," during which the governments of Canada and Japan negotiated to voluntarily limit the number of Japanese immigrants arriving in Canada yearly (Historica Canada n.d.; Van Dyk 2016). These were both examples of how racism is institutionalized within systems and policies. While policies like these were openly racist, contemporary immigration policies project the illusion of openness and inclusion of diverse groups of people from different parts of the world. The introduction of the *points system* in 1967 reformed overtly racist immigration policies by assessing the admissibility of immigrants to Canada based on certain suitability criteria such as education, age, language and skills. Consequently, a large pool of immigrants coming to Canada shifted from primarily European source countries to emerging and developing economic countries, particularly Asia, which contributed to a changing and more ethnically diverse Canadian demographic (Chui, Tran and Maheux 2007). In 2016, those coming from the Philippines and India registered the top two highest number of permanent residents in Canada. Syrian refugees constituted the third largest group of new Canadians. The People's Republic of China was fourth (Government of Canada 2017).

However, critics argue that contemporary immigration programs resulting from the implementation of the points system employ practices that are inherently racist and exclusionary based on gender, class and ability. Rather than being overtly written in its policies, racism is hidden in the structure of how points are awarded, which still heavily favours immigrants from Western or European countries (e.g., the United States and United Kingdom). Also, since the needs of the economy is a prime concern, there is an implicit gender bias in favour of male immigrants in skilled and trades occupations. Males often become the principal applicants, and females are considered to be their dependents. For example, in 2016, male economic immigrants who were the principal applicants outnumbered females by 28,340 to 1,657 (Government of Canada 2017a). Further, gender impacts the job category of intended work of permanent residents, where males are found mostly in managerial, professional and skilled occupations compared to females, found mostly in the intermediate, elemental and labourer categories (table 4.2).

Table 4.2: Intended Work of Permanent Residents by Gender, 2014

Job Category	Male	Female
Managerial	2,230	715
Professional	9,014	6,791
Skilled and technical	3,790	2,071
Intermediate level	512	2,071
Elemental and labourers	7	410

Source: Government of Canada 2015e)

Class is a measure of status in a society. It is defined in various ways and means depending on its context. In the practice of seeking immigration to another country, class plays a role because only a select group with certain income levels has access to resources to be able to pursue an application for immigration. Immigration to Canada requires significant investment, including application fees and other costs. As of October 2015, application fees for permanent residents under the economic class are as follows, in Canadian dollars: principal applicant at $550, spouse of applicant or family member over twenty-two years old at $550, family member under twenty-two years old at $150 and a right of permanent residence fee at $490 each for the principal applicant and spouse (Government of Canada 2015f). Assuming a family of three, with a child under twenty-two years old, the total fee for immigration is $2,230. These costs, together with other travel expenses associated with immigration, illustrate the fiscal drain on immigrants and suggest that entry into Canada is highly selective of those who can afford it. Thus, contrary to popular belief, immigrants are generally not poverty-stricken in their home countries. Applying through the immigration stream necessitates capital and other resources in their home countries.

Passing a language test in English or French is another practice that seemingly favours applicants coming from traditionally English-speaking or French-speaking countries. The minimum level of language proficiency in reading, writing, listening and speaking appears high to those who study these languages on their own. The International English Language Testing System (IELTS) is often used as the gauge of English proficiency and is administered in cities around the world. For instance, in the Philippines IELTS is administered by the British Council and offers the language test three times a month in selected cities at a cost of 9,400 pesos (CAD 238) in 2015 (British Council 2015). Sometimes it takes more than one test to attain the desired level for immigration. As well, IELTS fees vary depending on test date, location and type of test.

Consistent with the needs of the economy, there is a presumption that able-bodied applicants make up the pool of likely immigrants (Messamore 2004; Ayukawa 2008). Healthy and able immigrants are considered productive contributors of the economy and in society. The rigid medical examination conducted only by Canadian government–approved doctors in countries of origin ensures that immigrants and their dependents do not burden the health care system in Canada. This implies that immigrants admitted at their prime years have the ability to use their skills for a longer period to help sustain the economy and not be incapacitated upon entry into the country.

The bureaucratic processes surrounding the entry of immigrants to Canada negate the huge investment by many to do so. Immigration is a lifelong commitment to belong and be accepted as an equal. However, acceptance in Canadian society is still predicated on the desirable "White race" and non-accented English. *Racialized Canadians* or *naturalized Canadians* — immigrants who acquire Canadian citizenship — face the "origin question" when they venture out in public spaces: "where do you come from?" The question is insulting and demeaning to Canadian-born descendants of immigrants whose families have lived in Canada since Confederation, like many South Asians, and implies that all non-White immigrants have recently arrived in Canada.

Immigrants experience an extensive assessment process in order to migrate to Canada. However, when they arrive in the country they face many challenges including *deskilling, underemployment* and lack of services for settlement and integration. Immigrants possess higher educational attainment than the native-born population but are found mostly in low-paying jobs (Galarneau and Morissette 2008). Immigrants, on average, possess master and doctoral degrees at twice the rate of the Canadian-born population (Curry 2017). The 2006 census noted first-generation immigrants earned 12.6 percent less than the average wage of individuals born in Canada. Ten years later, this gap climbed to 16 percent (Magesan 2017). However, non-recognition of foreign credentials and the practice of requiring Canadian experience prior to employment lead to deskilling and underemployment (Bonifacio 2013). The often-cited example of a foreign-trained doctor driving a taxi represents the challenges experienced by some newcomers in Canada (*Globe and Mail* 2017). In some of my personal encounters with underemployed, skilled immigrants, they depict the paradox of getting the best education in the world for immigration purposes but then being trapped in low-end jobs upon settlement in Canada due to the rigours of professional accreditation. While immigrants possess the requisite educational background and skills for admission into the country, labour market practices and professional regulations place significant constraints on their use. Those immigrants who are racialized face more challenges in being accepted by Canadian society. The impact of lacking services for settlement and integration is discussed in the next section.

Working Underclass

Canada has perpetuated a *working underclass* through racist and discriminatory immigration policies since the nineteenth century through the continued practice of creating a group of people who work at meagre wages with less protection of their rights or access to resources compared to the Canadian-born population (Ley and Smith 1997). For example, the Chinese, mainly men, had a long history of settlement and work on the Canadian Pacific Railway that forged nation building. However, they were subjected to harsh exclusions after its completion, particularly the payment of the head tax under the *Chinese Immigration Act* of 1885 (Goutor 2007; Chan 2014). In recent history, the racialization of domestic work and care work by Caribbean and Filipina women means they are under strict rules of entry and qualification to become permanent residents.

Arguably, the first source of dividing "us" from "them" in immigrant-receiving countries like Canada is *immigration policy*. Governments, through their legislated authority to define who enters the country's borders, shape the realities of people affected — the locals and the immigrants. Immigrants are lumped into categories based on the type of programs through which they are admitted into Canada, and this consequently creates in the national imaginary the idea that certain groups of people exist only as a particular type of worker and not as a full human being with rights and entitlements. The immigration policy through which particular groups of immigrants are admitted into Canada helps shape how these immigrants are perceived by the local residents. For example, live-in caregivers under the Live-in Caregiver Program must have a minimum requirement of grade twelve equivalency, yet most of those accepted into this stream hold university degrees from the Philippines. In general, immigrants tend to have higher qualifications than the Canadian-born population, but they are popularly constructed to have low education and receive fewer earnings (Bonifacio 2013; Morissette and Sultan 2013).

To cope with widespread racism, even to this day so-called "*ethnic spaces*" are formed. According to Kay Anderson (1994: 241), "Chinatown," for example, is a "social construct that belonged to Vancouver's 'White' European society ... according to an influential culture of race." The predominantly White community created a social divide based on perceived racial difference that permeated ethnic cultures and ways of living. Racialized immigrants then created safer havens of belonging, or what are known as "*ethnic enclaves*." Ethnic enclaves are responses to exclusionary practices in host societies where immigrants find modes of survival, community and belonging (Andersson and Hammarstedt 2012; Hassan 2014). Ethnic enterprises provide opportunities for employment and venues for networking, for example, for those unable to get jobs in mainstream labour market.

The race and culture of immigrants become markers of difference that separate them from the rest of the dominant White Canadian mainstream population. Their representation in the popular psyche of Canada did not occur overnight but through the systemic reproduction of being the "Other," or "not us." These systemic reproductions range from immigration policy that denotes that such groups of individuals deserve less than what the Canadian-born population deserves, to popular media that preys on immigrants' so-called essential characteristics of "Otherness" (Fleras 2011; Aldama 2013). Consequently, immigrant women from Muslim countries who continue to wear the hijab or niqab often face discrimination when they venture into public spaces. The intersections of race and culture, as well as gender, are factors to consider in the making of the working underclass in Canada.

In the twenty-first century, Canada maintains a working underclass through variants of its immigration policy surrounding temporary foreign workers (TFWs). The number of temporary residents in Canada exceeded that of permanent residents for the first time in 2008, with populations of 399,523 and 247,243 respectively (Pang 2013; Carman 2015). The numbers of TFWs have grown steadily since 2003, with an average growth rate of 15 percent until 2008 when Canada hit recession. Still, during the period from 2002 to 2014, the number of TFWs grew rapidly, from 76,787 to 177,704 (Dharssi 2016). TFWs who are allowed to enter Canada after an employer has received a positive Labour Market Impact Assessment (LMIA) are restricted in where they are entitled to work and the type of employment they are allowed to do (Lemieux and Nadeau 2015). The LMIA is essentially a test used by Employment and Social Development Canada to determine if there are available Canadians who could fill a job vacancy (Lemieux and Nadeau 2015: 4).

TFW programs include the *Seasonal Agricultural Worker Program* (SAWP), the *Live-in Caregiver Program* (LCP) and the *Provincial Nominee Program* (PNP). SAWP and LCP are federally administered programs. SAWP was initiated in 1966 to allow foreign workers from the Caribbean countries and, later, Mexico to work in the seasonal agricultural sectors in Ontario, British Columbia, Québec, New Brunswick and Prince Edward Island (Basok 2000; Todoroki, Vaccani and Noor 2009).

Table 4.3 Seasonal Agricultural Worker Program — SAWP

• The program is conducted based on bilateral agreements between Canada and sending countries.
• Foreign workers are subject to the control of employers and their own governments to return to Canada upon expiry of contracts.
• In 2013, 37,595 agricultural workers were issued work permits, the highest since 2004.

Source: Government of Canada 2014: n.p.

LCP was established in 1992 and developed from the previous Foreign Domestic Movement program of the 1980s (Arat-Koc 2002; Stasiulis and Bakan 2008). Live-in caregivers work with children, seniors and the physically incapacitated in their households. Filipina women account for more than 90 percent of LCP participants (Bonifacio 2013). In November 2014, the LCP became the Caregiver Program, which made the live-in requirement optional to foreign care workers but essentially removed the universal access to *permanent residency* after completion of the program (Black 2014). Caregivers are now subject to two categories — those caring for children and those caring for people with high medical needs (Black 2014). LCP was the only temporary program that guaranteed permanent residency, and removing this feature made it consistent with the rest. More importantly, the removal of the live-in requirement, which had previously made the program akin to modern-day slavery, was touted as a long-awaited overhaul (Levitz 2014).

Table 4.4: Live-in Caregiver Program — LCP

- Caregivers are required to work for a minimum of two years within a four-year period before they can apply for permanent residency.
- Caregivers are subject to the control of employers and cannot transfer to another employer without securing another work permit.
- In 2007, 29,571 live-in caregivers were issued work permits, the highest number between 2004 and 2013.

Source: Government of Canada 2014, n.p

The PNP is a shared framework agreement between the federal and provincial governments. Under it, the foreign worker applies to the province without going through the federal standard point system assessment for skilled workers (Gabriel and MacDonald 2011). Then the applicant uses the approved nominee status to apply for permanent residency. Since this program started in 1999 in Manitoba, New Brunswick and Newfoundland and Labrador, it has expanded to fill the labour shortages in almost all provinces (Government of Canada 2012; Satzewich 2015). The number of provincial nominee admissions in 2016 was 46,170 (20,486 principal applicants and 25,684 immediate family members) (Government of Canada 2017a).

Unlike the SAWP and the LCP prior to 2014, the provincial nominees have the freedom to live outside their workplace. TFWs under the PNP can bring their families with them, subject to certain regulations based on age, health and financial capacity. Despite the various ways that TFWs come to Canada, most of these individuals initially arrive alone and, if able, their families follow later. Those coming from the United States and other Western countries and those in highly skilled occupations take advantage of this privilege as compared to those arriving from developing countries in low-skilled jobs.

TFWs are mostly concentrated in low-skilled occupations and viewed as the "disposable workforce" with fewer rights and protections (Byl 2011).

Table 4.5: Provincial Nominee Program — PNP

• Only Québec does not participate in the Provincial Nominee Program (as of October 2017). • Over fifty Nominee Program streams are operating in eleven jurisdictions. • Males represented 65 percent of the PNP admissions, while females accounted for 35 percent.

Source: Government of Canada 2017a

In fast-food outlets, hotel chains, nursing homes and other low-end jobs, TFWs provide the backbone of the service industry to sustain the comfort of the middle-class lifestyle Canadians are accustomed to (Bonifacio 2013). Many TFWs endure the blatant disregard of their human rights. Mostly, this remains unreported due to fear of deportation and to comply with the employment contract and earn money, often sent to their families left behind. Securing another work permit while in Canada takes about three to six months, as potential employers must have a LMIA, at the cost of $1000 as of June 2014, issued by Employment and Social Development Canada (Government of Canada 2016). The LMIA ensures that no Canadian is available to fill the position, justifying the need to hire a foreign worker. While waiting for a new work permit in Canada, the TFW is in limbo with no proper documentation to seek an alternative job to survive. This situation possibly leads to working in the *"underground economy"* of spot cash payment with no labour rights at all; if caught, the worker is deported. The uncertainty of securing another work permit gives workers no recourse but to complete the employment contract under an abusive employer.

TFWs form the working underclass. They contribute to taxation and employment benefits but often do not have access to employment insurance if they need it. "Temporary" is a condition imposed by the immigration program, but many migrant workers view it as a transition to permanent residency status (Bonifacio 2013). Many of them labour under challenging conditions with the hope of becoming permanent residents and being reunited with their families in Canada in due time.

Immigration policies shape the particular experiences of immigrants and temporary foreign workers compared to the Canadian-born population, which produces and reproduces a bifurcated society of "us versus them." There is a need to not only explain this dynamic but to overcome it.

Beyond the Individual: Intersecting Realities

Immigration exemplifies the intersection of categories, practices and experiences; it is a form of institutional arrangement that categorizes those entering into Canada based on their economic identity as federal skilled worker, temporary foreign worker, family sponsored, etc. But in lived experience, immigrants arrive and experience Canada through several identities based on their race, gender, ability, etc. As noted earlier, the type of program that an immigrant enters under shapes life trajectories in ways quite different from the Canadian-born population who might have the same economic identity. The identity constructed by the immigration program usually affects how the Canadian-born perceive them in the community. The female Filipina foreign worker, for example, is popularly known as the caregiver or nanny because of the high numbers participating in the LCP from the Philippines.

In attempting to eradicate the "us" and "them" dichotomy, it is important to examine relations between and among nation-states that connect immigrant-sending countries with immigrant-receiving ones. Understanding how systems of relation between countries enables us to recognize how people become connected and how an "us versus them" can develop and persist.

Immigrant-receiving countries tend to be more developed than immigrant-sending countries; Canada and the Philippines are good examples. Particular histories and cultural ideologies operating between these two countries imply relations of control and hierarchy, not of equality. In terms of gendered cultural ideologies, women from the Philippines are constructed as family-oriented, respectful to authority and better suited to work in the domestic sphere, which helps to explain why Filipina women are sought after as caregivers in Canada (Bonifacio 2013). Filipino workers in general are considered by their Canadian employers as industrious and hardworking people who do not complain, with work ethics that are good for business. These cultural ideologies contribute to Philippines being one of the top source countries of immigrants and temporary foreign workers in Canada since the 1980s.

Nation-states are positioned differently; some countries are industrialized and prosperous but lack the population to sustain their growth, while many countries have a high population growth rate and are economically underdeveloped. The global standing of a country facilitates the ways in which its citizens are treated in the international arena, as indicated by the issuance of visas. Citizens from developing countries are generally subjected to stringent requirements to enter Western countries like Canada compared to those coming from developed countries; they are often perceived as economic migrants, while those coming from Western countries are considered tourists.

Canadians appreciate the contribution of immigrants as workers and citizens. Human connectedness is very much evident in the rationale for immigration; Canada *needs* immigration and immigrants are *part* of Canada. A holistic view of immigrants compels us to connect the ways in which mutual advantage takes place, not only for their labour but in enriching local communities and the country in general. Immigration allows us to see how sending nation-states lose their "best and brightest" to live and work in Canada, often in menial jobs that Canadians tend to reject because they do not provide a decent standard of living. As the backbone of the economy, immigrants comprise the working class that perhaps deflates labour wages and ensures the stability of domestic production (Carbaugh 2015; Fleras 2015).

Historically, European imperialist colonists entered Indigenous lands around the world in search of resources and to convert members of these communities to Christianity, which formed part of the so-called trilogy of "God, gold, and glory" (Nugent 1999: 25). At this time, colonists simply occupied lands with force and intimidation, and these occupied areas did not require any immigration control. Now, immigrants from formerly colonized territories seek entry to Canada with their skills and talents to find better opportunities.

Further, regardless of origin an immigrant envisions a good life achieved by hard work through the opportunities available for them. In practice, however, immigration is hyped in popular discourses and politics to set a narrow view of immigrants as, for example, welfare dependents or terrorists who do not have the same aspirations of a better life as everybody else.

Reshaping the Immigration Process

Canada is a destination country for immigrants and temporary foreign workers. The nation benefits immensely from their productivity, as most of them enter the country at their prime years. Since immigrants play a crucial role in fostering economic growth, it follows that immigration is a form of investment by receiving countries. Governments have established a bureaucratic mechanism to screen the best applicants for immigration, often with readily transferrable skills in the labour market, and arrange services for settlement and integration upon their arrival. This section offers suggestions to reshape the immigration process to be more inclusive to people of diverse backgrounds by looking at *pre-* and *post-migration services*.

Services, both pre-migration and post-migration, form an integral aspect of the settlement and integration of newcomers and immigrants in Canada. The provision of services to newcomers in Canada by governmental and non-governmental organizations is an essential aid that aims to fully enhance the capacities of immigrants to contribute to Canada. Yet, there are some significant deficiencies in service delivery (Richmond and Shields 2005) and the types of services available to immigrants. Since the 1970s, immigrant service organizations based in different communities across Canada have become designated frontline agencies to respond to the challenges of a diverse society (Bonifacio 2008).

According to Usha George, Eric Fong, Wei Da and Rega Chang (2004), the basic settlement needs of newcomers include a general orientation to Canadian life; establishing community connections; securing housing, employment and language training; and obtaining information on available services. Political and social participation in the new society becomes of increasing importance as immigrants further their integration into Canadian society (George 2002). Canadian laws like the *Multiculturalism Act*, however, recognize respect for the diverse cultures of immigrants and others. In Canadian practice, services provided to immigrants fall under *settlement and integration services*, which "encompass activities that are specifically designed to facilitate the early economic and social integration of newcomers to Canada" (CIC 2004). IRCC offers four main settlement programs, namely the Immigrant Settlement and Adaptation Program, Language Instruction for Newcomers to Canada, the Host Program, and the Resettlement Assistance Program for refugees. These generally comprise the major post-migration services in Canada and the major support from the government to landed immigrants, but these are not available to TFWs.

Offering pre-migration services, on the other hand, is a recent approach to serving the needs of potential immigrants. In February 2015, Migration Policy Institute Europe released a policy brief that looks at the advantages of pre-departure programs in relation to the labour market performance and other contributions of immigrants (Desiderio and Hooper 2015). It argues that cooperation between source and destination countries is important for the long-term successful integration of migrants. Victoria Esses, Meyer Burstein, Zenaida Ravanera, Stacey Hallman and Stelian Medianu (2013) noted the types of services that are considered helpful in Canada, particularly the assessment of foreign credentials prior to migration. They further argued that the type of immigration category under which an individual enters into Canada affects the type of services they need. For example, professional and skilled workers prefer establishing connections with professional regulatory associations, while refugees need support in language training and translation services. Pre-arrival services they consider useful include assessment of international education and experience, skills training, connections with employers and professional associations, language assessment, orientation to Canadian culture, assistance in developing a plan before and after arrival in Canada, and housing and translation services (Esses et al. 2013).

As a form of pre-arrival service, the *Canadian Immigrant Integration Program* (CIIP) was launched as a pilot program in 2007 and became a full program in 2010 (CIC 2013b). This voluntary program is administered by the College and Institutes Canada (CIC 2013a). CIIP has three components: a one-day workshop about the job market in Canada, personalized planning and online advice (assuming immigrants accessing this service have access to a computer and the internet) (ACCC 2008). It primarily provides assessments of foreign credentials and knowledge about the Canadian labour market. China, India and the Philippines were the three initial countries with a Foreign Credential Referral Office to prepare immigrants destined to Canada. The United Kingdom was added later.

In reshaping the immigration process in Canada, based on the current thrusts of post-migration services and the limited pre-migration CIIP, I suggest three areas to create more equitable and inclusive practice for immigrants, including TFWs who are currently excluded from accessing these services:

- an integrated system of settlement service delivery;
- open client access points; and
- intergovernmental and multi-sectoral coordination.

An *integrated system of settlement service delivery* refers to the continuity of pre-migration services and post-migration services. *Open client access points* would consist of making settlement services open to all immigrants, regardless of status and type of entry program. *Intergovernmental and multi-sectoral coordination* involves the various levels of government and the participation of private sectors in immigrants' welfare and inclusion in local communities. Arguably, the recognition of these areas provides optimal benefits for immigrants and their host society.

Immigrants, particularly principal applicants, are presumed to be "responsible" for their own decision to leave their countries of origin and for processing the necessary information to their advantage. Countries of origin like the Philippines offer a government-mandated, compulsory pre-departure orientation of TFWS, at a cost, to prepare them for life in the destination country. Those leaving the Philippines with permanent immigration statuses are not required to undertake this orientation. Receiving countries like Canada provide general information about services upon arrival, online and in print media. Immigrants are presumed to access these services on their own volition. An integrated system of settlement service delivery considers the needs of immigrants at various stages. Pre-migration services require information about living in Canada, in which area to reside, what to do upon arrival, etc. Post-migration arrival requires both information and support services to adjust and adapt well into the community. As it is now, these two stages of migration seem independent from each other.

Post-migration services in Canada have a limited scope. Landed immigrants with permanent status can access these services provided by accredited immigrant-serving agencies, but generally this is not available for TFWS. The most vulnerable immigrant population is "fairly" excluded, because the service mandate (for example, provision of language services, access to shelters and health care) does not include them. Open client access to settlement services allows for all residents in the area have the opportunity utilize them when needed. With the increase of TFWS, cities such as Calgary and Lethbridge have added this group of newcomers as target clientele for migration services. While employers provide on-the-job orientation, TFWS need access to community-based services for their general welfare. This group of newcomers contributes to the local economy through their labour and consumption and should have the same access to services as other immigrants.

Immigration is a federal jurisdiction in Canada, but immigrants live in towns, cities and provinces. While most provinces participate in the Nominee Program, IRCC remains the government authority to issue visas and establish settlement programs for immigrants, while the majority of services are provided by the provinces, primarily by immigrant-serving agencies. The provinces, on their own, provide support to newcomers through recognized organizations. Cities also include servicing newcomers through regular community programming. Small towns have fewer resources to provide this type of support. Intergovernmental coordination suggests that all levels of government — federal, provincial and municipal

— have vital roles in the successful integration of immigrants. Multisectoral coordination invites other stakeholders in the community, such as schools, businesses and other public interest groups, to actively engage with immigrants from diverse backgrounds in their own spaces and activities, demonstrating openness and inclusion.

After over a century of immigration programs, Canada is now a country with diverse cultures and is well positioned to examine the impact of its current pre-migration and post-migration services to immigrants. Integrating these services with wider participation of different levels of governance and other sectors will consequently promote a more inclusive approach that will benefit immigrants, TFWs and their families.

Immigration is an important avenue toward achieving economic development and stability in Canada. The variety of economically directed immigration programs, attracting immigrants from around the world, is indicative of the importance of immigration in promoting prosperity in the country. But the ways in which immigration programs and practices have worked since the nineteenth century have produced different realities for racialized immigrants. Constructing racial difference as the imaginary line between "us and them" still permeates the immigration process, through which racialized groups are reduced to working in certain occupations with fewer rights. Immigration continuously subscribes those participating in entry programs to differential treatment, especially the temporary work regimes that produce the working underclass.

The treatment of those coming from developing countries exposes the multiplicity of oppression ranging from the individual to nation-states. Nation-states are differentially positioned in relation to each other; the difference is particularly clear between developed countries and developing ones, who have less power to protect their citizens while they are in other countries. Immigrants from developing countries like the Philippines are subjected to more stringent requirements to prove their admissibility as temporary workers, such as language skills, education and work experience. However, understanding how immigrants and TFWs contribute to Canada and the challenges that shape their lives, as well as recognizing the relations between countries, may lead us to adopt more inclusive practices.

DISCUSSION QUESTIONS

1. In which ways do the needs of Canada's economy influence Canadian immigration policy?
2. What do immigrants contribute to Canadian society?

ACTION STEPS

1. Organize temporary foreign workers to push the federal government for more access to the pre- and post-migration services provided by immigrant serving agencies.
2. Advocate for the need for additional resources to deal with the issue of underemployment.
3. Meet with all levels of government to make the case for improved intergovernmental collaboration and coordination.

Supplemental Readings

Edmonston, Barry. 2016. "Canada's Immgiration Trends and Patterns." *Canadian Studies in Population,* 43, 1–2.
Salami, Bukola, Salima Meherali and Azeez Salami. 2015. "The Health of Temporary Foreign Workers in Canada: A Scoping Review." *Canadian Journal of Public Health,* 106, 8.
Tungohan, Ethel. 2017. "Temporary Foreign Workers in Canada: Reconstructing 'Belonging' and Remaking 'Citizenship.'" *Social and Legal Studies,* 27, 2.

Additional Resources

Anti-racism Toolkit Now Available for Municipalities, Union of Nova Scotia Municipalities. <unsm.ca/anti-racism-toolkit-now-available-for-municipalities.html>.
Ignite! An Anti-Racist Tool Kit. <antiracist-toolkit.users.ecobytes.net/>.
Stop Racism and Hate Collective, Canadian Anti-Racism Education and Research Society. <stopracism.ca/content/canadian-anti-racism-education-and-research-society-caers>.

References

ACCC (Association of Canadian Community Colleges). 2008. <collegesinstitutes.ca/wp-content/uploads/2014/05/annualreport2008-2009.pdf>.
Aldama, Frederick Luis. 2013. *Latinos and Narrative Media: Participation and Portrayal.* New York: Palgrave Macmillan.
Anderson, Kay. 1994. "The Idea of Chinatown: The Power of Place and Institutional Practice in the Making of a Racial Category." In Gerald Tulchinsky (ed.), *Immigration in Canada: Historical Perspectives.* Toronto, ON: Copp Clark Longman.
Andersson, Lina, and Mats Hammarstedt. 2012. "Ethnic Enclaves, Networks and Self-Employment among Middle Eastern Immigrants in Sweden." *International Migration,* 53, 6.
Arat-Koc, Sedef. 2002. "From 'Mothers of the Nation' to Migrant Workers: Immigration Policies and Domestic Workers in Canadian History." In Veronica Strong-Boag, Mona Gleason and Adele Perry (eds.), *Rethinking Canada: The Promise of Women's History.* New York: Oxford University Press.
Ayukawa, Michiko Midge. 2008. *Hiroshima Immigrants in Canada 1891–1941.* Vancouver, BC: UBC Press.

Ball, David. 2015. "Canada Does Not Know What 154,000 Foreign Workers Do." *The Tyee,* March 13. <thetyee.ca/News/2015/03/13/What-Foreign-Workers-Do/>.

Basok, Tanya. 2000. "Migration of Mexican Seasonal Farm Workers to Canada and Development: Obstacles to Productive Investment." *International Migration Review,* 34, 1 (Spring).

Black, Debra. 2014. "New Rules for Federal Live-In Caregivers Program." *The Star,* November 28. <thestar.com/news/canada/2014/11/28/new_rules_for_federal_livein_caregivers_program.html>.

Bodvarsson, Örn, and Hendrik Van den Berg. 2013. *The Economics of Immigration: Theory and Policy,* second edition. New York: Springer.

Bonifacio, Glenda. 2013. *Pinay on the Prairies: Filipino Women and Transnational Identities.* Vancouver, BC: UBC Press.

___. 2008. "I Care for You, Who Cares for Me? Transitional Services of Filipino Live-In Caregivers in Canada." *Asian Women: Gender Issues in International Migration,* 24, 1 (Spring).

British Council. 2015. "Test Dates, Fees and Locations." <britishcouncil.ph/exam/ielts/dates-fees-locations>.

Byl, Yessy. 2011. "Temporary Foreign Workers in Canada: Disposable Workforce?" *Canadian Issues* (Spring).

Carbaugh, Robert. 2015. *International Economics,* fifteenth edition. Boston, MA: Cengage Learning.

Carman, Tara. 2015. "Canada Favours Temporary Residents to Permanent: Report." *Vancouver Sun,* September 1. <vancouversun.com/Canada+favours+temporary+residents+permanent+report/11333380/story.html?__lsa=59b0-e20e>.

CBC News. 2015. "Stephen Harper Won't Allow 'Permanent Underclass' of Temporary Foreign Workers." May 8. <cbc.ca/news/politics/stephen-harper-won-t-allow-permanent-underclass-of-temporary-foreign-workers-1.3066236>.

Chan, Arlene. 2014. *The Chinese Head Tax and Anti-Chinese Immigration Policies in the Twentieth Century.* Toronto, ON: James Lorimer.

Chui, Tina, Kelly Tran and Hélène Maheux. 2007. *Immigration in Canada: A Portrait of the Foreign-Born Population, 2006 Census* (Catalogue no. 97-557-XIE). Ottawa, ON: Minister of Industry, Statistics Canada.

CIC (Citizenship and Immigration Canada). 2014. "Facts and Figures 2014: Immigration Overview-Temporary Residents." <open.canada.ca/data/en/dataset/052642bb-3fd9-4828-b608-c81dff7e539c?_ga=1.55618795.156575898.1473525794>.

___. 2013a. "Changes to Improve Immigration System Pass; Consultations Next Step." <cic.gc.ca/english/department/partner/bpss/ciip.asp>.

___. 2013b. "Canadian Immigrant Integration Program." <cic.gc.ca/english/department/partner/bpss/ciip.asp>.

___. 2004. "Agreement for Canada-British Columbia Cooperation on Immigration. Annex B: Responsibilities for Immigrant Settlement Services, 2004." <cic.gc.ca/english/department/laws-policy/agreements/bc/bc-2004-annex-b.asp>.

Curry, Bill. 2017. "Census 2016: Canadians Including Recent Immigrants Are Most Educated in the World." *Globe and Mail,* November 29. <theglobeandmail.com/news/national/census-2016-education-labour-employment-mobility/article37122392/>.

___. 2016. "Ottawa Poised to Ease Rules for Temporary Foreign Worker." *Globe and Mail,* August 10. <theglobeandmail.com/news/politics/ottawa-

expected-to-introduce-new-rules-for-temporary-foreign-worker-program/
article31365448/?page=all>.

Desiderio, Maria Vincenza, and Kate Hooper. 2015. "Improving Migrant's Labour
Market Integration in Europe from the Outset: A Cooperative Approach to
Pre-Departure Measures." *Migration Policy Institute Europe.* Policy Brief Series
Issue No. 6. <migrationpolicy.org/research/improving-migrants-labour-market-
integration-europe-outset-cooperative-approach>.

Dharssi, Alia. 2016. "Desperate Canadian Businesses Seek Changes to Temporary
Foreign Worker Program." *Calgary Herald*, September 18. <calgaryherald.com/
news/national/desperate-canadian-businesses-seek-changes-to-temporary-
foreign-worker-program>.

Esses, Victoria, Meyer Burstein, Zenaida Ravanera, Stacey Hallman and Stelian
Medianu. 2013. *Alberta Settlement Outcomes Survey.* Report prepared for Alberta
Human Services by the Pathways to Prosperity Partnership. <work.alberta.ca/
documents/alberta-outcomes-settlement-survey-results.pdf>.

Fleras, Augie. 2015. *Immigration Canada: Evolving Realities and Emerging Challenges
in a Postnational World.* Vancouver, BC: UBC Press.

___. 2011. *The Media Gaze: Representations of Diversities in Canada.* Vancouver,
BC: UBC Press.

Gabriel, Christina and Laura MacDonald. 2011. "Citizenship at the Margins: The
Canadian Seasonal Agricultural Worker Program and Civil Society Advocacy."
Politics and Policy, 39, 1.

Galarneau, Diane, and Rene Morissette. 2008. "Immigrants' Education and Required
Job Skills." *Perspectives*, December. Statistics Canada Catalogue No. 75-001-X.

Geddes, John. 2012. "Canada's Foreign Worker Boom." *Macleans,* February 21.
<macleans.ca/news/canada/a-disposable-workforce/>.

George, Usha. 2002. "A Needs-Based Model for Settlement Service for Newcomers
to Canada." *International Social Work,* 45, 4.

George, Usha, Eric Fong, Wei Da and Rega Chang. 2004. *Recommendations for
Delivery of ISAP Services to Mandarin Speaking Newcomers from Mainland
China: Final Report.* Toronto, ON: Joint Centre of Excellence for Research
on Immigration and Settlement. <atwork.settlement.org/downloads/atwork/
ISAP_Mandarin_Final_Report.pdf>.

Globe and Mail. 2017. "Overqualified Immigrants Are Really Driving Taxis
in Canada." March 26. <theglobeandmail.com/globe-debate/editorials/
overqualified-immigrants-really-are-driving-taxis-in-canada/article4106352/>.

Goutor, David. 2007. *Guarding the Gates: The Canadian Labour Movement and
Immigration, 1872–1934.* Vancouver, BC: UBC Press.

Government of Canada. 2017a. *2017 Annual Report to Parliament on Immigration.*
Ottawa, ON: Immigration, Refugees and Citizenship Canada.

___. 2017b. "Who Can Apply as a Skilled Immigrant (Express Entry)." <canada.ca/
en/immigration-refugees-citizenship/services/immigrate-canada/express-entry/
become-candidate/eligibility.html>.

___. 2016. "Hire a Temporary Foreign Worker in a High-Wage Position-Program
Requirements." <esdc.gc.ca/en/foreign_workers/hire/median_wage/high/
requirements.page>.

___. 2015a. "Justice Laws Website." <laws-lois.justice.gc.ca/eng/acts/i-2.5/page-1.
html#h-1>.

___. 2015b. "Immigrate as a Skilled Worker through Express Entry." <cic.gc.ca/

english/Immigrate/skilled/index.asp>.

___. 2015c. "Immigrant Investor Venture Capital Pilot Program." <http://www.cic. gc.ca/english/immigrate/business/iivc/index.asp>.

___. 2015d. "Determine Your Eligibility — Skilled Immigrants (Express Entry)." <cic. gc.ca/english/immigrate/skilled/apply-who-express.asp>.

___. 2015e. "Facts and Figures 2014 — Immigration Overview: Permanent Residents. <cic.gc.ca/english/resources/statistics/facts2014/permanent/10.asp>.

___. 2015f. "Fee List." <cic.gc.ca/english/information/fees/fees.asp#visas_permits>.

___. 2014. "Facts and Figures 2013 — Immigration Overview: Temporary Residents." <cic.gc.ca/english/resources/statistics/facts2013/temporary/3-1.asp>

___. 2012. "Evaluation of the Provincial Nominee Program." <cic.gc.ca/english/ resources/evaluation/pnp/section3.asp>.

Grenier, Eric. 2017. "Canadian Seniors Now Outnumber Children for 1st Time, 2016 Census Show." *CBC News*, May 3. <cbc.ca/news/ politics/2016-census-age-gender-1.4095360>.

Hassan, Hwiada AbuBaker. 2014. "Loyalty Shifts and Alliances Establishments: Ethnic Enclaves as a Pattern of Creating Ethnic Identity among Southern Sudanese Women in Vienna, Austria." *Ahfad Journal*, 31, 2.

Historica Canada. n.d. "Japanese Canadians." <thecanadianencyclopedia.ca/en/ article/japanese-canadians/>.

International Business Publications. 2014. *Canada Immigration Handbook Volume 1 — Strategic and Practice Information*. Washington, DC: International Business Publications.

International Organization for Migration. 2008. *World Migration 2008: Managing Labour Mobility in the Evolving Global Economy*. Geneva, Switzerland: International Organization for Migration.

Kelley, Ninette, and Michael J. Trebilcock. 2010. *The Making of the Mosaic: A History of Canadian Immigration Policy*, second edition. Toronto, ON: University of Toronto Press.

Knowles, Valerie. 1992. *Strangers at Our Gates: Canadian Immigration and Immigration Policy, 1540–1990*. Toronto and Oxford: Dundurn Press.

Lemieux, Tracy, and Jean-François Nadeau. 2015. *Temporary Foreign Workers in Canada: A Look at Regions and Occupational Skill*. Ottawa, ON: Office of the Parliamentary Budget Officer. <pbo-dpb.gc.ca/web/default/files/files/files/ TFW_EN.pdf>.

Lenard, Patti Tamara, and Christine Straehle (eds.). 2012. *Legislated Equality: Temporary Labour Migration in Canada*. Montreal, QC, and Kingston, ON: McGill-Queen's University Press.

Levitz, Stephanie. 2014. "Government Changes Live-In Caregiver Program." *Global News*, October 31. <globalnews.ca/news/1647685/government-c hanges-live-in-caregiver-program/>.

Ley, David, and Heather Smith. 1997. "Is There an Immigrant 'Underclass' in Canadian Cities?" Vancouver Centre of Excellence, Research on Immigration and Integration in the Metropolis. Working Paper Series #97–08.

Magesan, Arvind. 2017. "New Figures Show Just How Big Canada's Immigrant Wage Gap Is." *Macleans*, October 25. <macleans.ca/news/canada/ new-figures-show-just-how-big-canadas-immigrant-wage-gap-is/>.

Mehler Paperny, Anna. 2015. "Greying Nation: Canada Has More Seniors than Kids for the First Time Ever." *Global News*, September 29. <globalnews.ca/

news/2247372/greying-nation-what-the-latest-population-numbers-mean-for-canadas-workforce-health-care-and-the-budget/>.

Messamore, Barbara J. (ed.). 2004. *Canadian Migration Patterns from Britain and North America*. Ottawa, ON: University of Ottawa Press.

Morissette, René, and Rizwan Sultan. 2013. "Twenty Years in the Careers of Immigrant and Native-Born Workers." Statistics Canada: Minister of Industry. <statcan.gc.ca/pub/11-626-x/11-626-x2013032-eng.pdf>.

Nugent, Walter. 1999. *Into the West: The Story of Its People*. New York: Knopf.

Pang, Melissa. 2013. "Temporary Foreign Workers." Parliament of Canada, Library of Parliament Research Publications. <http://www.lop.parl.gc.ca/content/lop/ResearchPublications/2013-11-e.htm>.

Patychuk, Dianne. 2010. *Action for Reducing Health Inequalities, Strategies for Racialized Youth*. Prepared for Across Boundaries Ethnoracial Mental Health Centre.

Richmond, Ted, and John Shields. 2005. "NGO–Government Relations and Immigrant Services: Contradictions and Challenges." *Journal of International Migration and Integration*, 6, 3/4.

Rudolph, Christopher. 2006. *National Security and Immigration: Policy Development in the United States and Western Europe Since 1945*. Stanford, CA: Stanford University Press.

Satzewich, Vic. 2015. *Points of Entry: How Canada's Immigration Officers Decide Who Gets In*. Vancouver, BC: UBC Press.

Stasiulis, Daiva K., and Abigail B. Bakan. 2008. "Marginalized and Dissident Non-Citizens: Foreign Domestic Workers." In Barrington Walker (ed.), *The History of Immigration and Racism in Canada: Essential Readings*. Toronto, ON: Canadian Scholars' Press.

Statistics Canada. 2017. "Population Size and Growth in Canada: Key Results from the 2016 Census." *The Daily*, February 8. <statcan.gc.ca/daily-quotidien/170208/dq170208a-eng.htm>.

Todoroki, Emiko, Matteo Vaccani and Wameek Noor. 2009. "The Canada-Caribbean Remittance Corridor: Fostering Formal Remittance to Haiti and Jamaica Through Effective Regulation." The World Bank Working Paper No. 163. Washington, DC: The International Bank for Reconstruction and Development/The World Bank.

Van Dyk, Lyndsay. 2016. "Canadian Immigration Acts and Legislation." Canadian Museum of Integration at Pier 21. <pier21.ca/research/immigration-history/canadian-immigration-acts-and-legislation>.

Verbeeten, David. 2007. "The Past and Future of Immigration to Canada." *Journal of International Migration and Integration*, 8, 1.

Whitaker, Reginald. 1991. *Canadian Immigration Since Confederation*. Ottawa, ON: Canadian Historical Association.

5

THE COLOUR
OF POVERTY
Racialization and Inequality in Canada

Grace-Edward Galabuzi

This chapter addresses the process of the *racialization of poverty* in Canada's urban centres. The complex experience of poverty disproportionately impacts racialized and immigrant populations concentrated in Canada's urban centres and relegates racialized groups to low-income neighbourhoods. The key to understanding *poverty* in Canada in the twenty-first century is acknowledging that the experience of poverty is not generic but highly differentiated — by race, gender and class, among other bases of differentiation. It is subject to social hierarchies that determine its intensity, because race, gender, religion, Indigenous status, immigrant status and other bases for social distinction intersect with class to compound the experience of poverty. In periods when race or religion become more pronounced as bases of distinction, the burdens and disadvantages borne by these groups translate into intensified *social exclusion*; economic marginality accentuates the status of "Other." This is the story of racialized poverty in the Canadian context — it is a product of structural processes of economic restructuring and racialization that determine differential access to economic opportunity for groups on the basis of race, gender, Indigenous status, immigration status, etc. An intersectional approach to poverty allows us to better understand the dimensions of vulnerability to poverty, as well as the sources of disadvantage that racialized and Indigenous women in particular experience at the bottom of Canada's economic pyramid.

Poverty is a condition of material and social deprivation. It causes individuals, families and communities misery, pain and, ultimately, marginalization and social exclusion. Indicators of social exclusion and denied well-being — such as uneven access to employment associated with discrimination in employment and devaluation of skills and immigrant human capital, unequal access to housing, disproportionate contact with the criminal justice system and decline in community safety, among others, are accentuated by the experience of poverty. This ultimately matures into a denial of full citizenship and possible threats to social cohesion. Poverty is also a key *determinant of health* (Mikkonen and Raphael 2010) and intersects with processes of racialization and feminization to produce disparities in health and well-being. The overall picture of poverty in Canada receives greater social concern when identifiable groups such as Indigenous people, immigrants, women or racialized people are the disproportionate victims of poverty. In a liberal democratic society that promises equality for all and claims multiculturalism as a core value, this has far reaching implications for social cohesion.

Today, the data show that racialized group members are two to three times more likely to live in poverty than other Canadians (Block and Galabuzi 2011). It is an experience that is compounded by other historical disadvantages that often become the popular cultural explanations for racialized poverty. As a society, we attempt to explore the complexity of these processes of social exclusion, whose various dimensions manifest in the particular experience of poverty suffered by racialized groups and accentuate their vulnerability to marginalization, hopelessness, voicelessness and stigmatization. *Racialized poverty*, understood as persistent disproportionate exposure to low income as popularly measured by the *low income cut-off (LICO)* or low-income measure, adversely impacts racialized groups members and harms their dignity and citizenship.[1]

This chapter argues for a comprehensive, multi-sector response to racialized poverty with adequate policies and programs from the various levels of government. This response must recognize the complexity of the experience and focus on mitigating existing forms of poverty as experienced by racialized groups in Canada. In making that argument, the chapter seeks to open a conversation about the conventional insistence on generalized notions of poverty that tend to ignore the characteristics that mark those living in poverty and structure their experience. The "generic conception of the poor," as Joe Feagin (1975) puts it, is a misnomer and needs to be addressed to open space for understanding identity-based dimensions of poverty. It is also necessary to challenge the premise of the conventional *anti-poverty policies* informed by liberal, individualistic notions of generic poverty. Using comparative data on income attainment, exposure to low income and evidence of residential segregation, this chapter argues for an understanding of poverty in Canada from an intersectional standpoint as increasingly feminized and racialized. Intersectional analysis is an essential starting point for effective anti-poverty or poverty elimination strategies.

The objectives of this chapter are to:

- gain a greater understanding of the process of the racialization of poverty in Canada's urban centres;
- enhance readers' knowledge of the intersectional approach to poverty; and
- understand the actions/interventions required to deal with racialized poverty in Canada.

The Structural Dimensions of Poverty in Canada

In 1989, the federal Parliament of Canada pledged to end child poverty by the year 2000. Yet, over fifteen years after that deadline Canada continues to have one of the highest poverty rates among individuals and families in the industrialized world (UNICEF 2005).[2] An important part of the explanation for that sad reality is that, although the root causes of poverty in Canada are structural, they have not always been treated as such. Too often, the connection between what is happening in the economy and in society generally has not been sufficiently made to inform our understanding of poverty; it is preferred, instead, to see poverty as a problem for which individuals should take moral responsibility. While Canadian research is limited in this area, a US research shows that a majority of Americans espouse individualistic explanations of poverty (Brown 2013; Shelton and Greene 2012). The impact of this misdiagnosis on anti-poverty policy has undermined the efforts of various levels of government and communities to effectively deal with poverty. *Poverty stigma* distorts the policy landscape in real, substantive ways. Linda Reutter et al. (2009) have presented evidence of how poverty stigma is both a key element of social exclusion but also impacts policy considerations in terms of responses to poverty.

Another critical observation that policymakers and anti-poverty activists have routinely ignored is that poverty is not a generic experience. It arises out of and bears the marks of the various social distinctions that determine access to society's resources. To understand existing poverty, specific characteristics that mark the poor are important to note (Block and Galabuzi 2011). Different groups in society experience poverty differently, some more profoundly than others. For instance, Canada has high levels of child poverty and women living in poverty. Average poverty among seniors has declined, partly due to public policy interventions, though not for all seniors (Block and Galabuzi 2011). Canada has disproportionately more poverty among

Indigenous Peoples, women, racialized groups and persons with disability, to name but a few identifiable groups that experience poverty differently.

This is because poverty-generating structures and processes are key features of a *capitalist economy*. While these processes systematically create economic winners and losers, class differences are compounded by the racial and gendered experiences of inequality. As capitalist structures that generate inequality in society and create poverty in communities become more entrenched, poverty transforms into a source of deep marginalization and exclusion. It then becomes a real threat to social cohesion, provoking securitized responses that inevitably focus on the marginalized "Other" as a threat to society. We now know that poverty and social inequality breed alienation, marginalization and, ultimately, social strife, social instability, unrest and often violence. These manifestations of social exclusion represent a threat to the very social fabric of society (United Way 2007; Myles and Picot 2010).

Poverty is a multi-dimensional phenomenon, encompassing inability to satisfy basic needs; inadequate control over access to resources; lack of education and skills; lack of shelter; poor health; malnutrition; poor access to water and sanitation; vulnerability to shocks, violence and crime; and lack of political freedom and voice in society (Galabuzi 2006). To better understand poverty, we need to consider both quantitative and qualitative indicators. We need to look at a number of key *qualitative indicators* that show the constraints poor people face in access to opportunities, quality of life and dignity within the context of their own societies. Among these are experiences such as racialization, which act to structure access to society's resources, benefits and burdens (Taylor, James and Saul 2007). We also need to use some *quantitative social indicators* such as income security, use of housing, health status and infant mortality. While we are more familiar with the quantitative measures and routinely use the low income cut-off as a measure of poverty, we need to pay close attention to all the factors that contribute to the weak base of livelihood for poor people and their security-related concerns.

It is essential to understand the vulnerabilities the poor face, as manifested by the risks associated with their everyday life experiences and arising from the sociopolitical and cultural relationships they have in society. These relationships generate experiences of powerlessness, voicelessness and marginality and demonstrate the need for empowerment and social inclusion. It is also important for our understanding of poverty to be informed by how those living in poverty perceive their own lives, circumstances and challenges, as well as their own desires and priorities for addressing them.

An effective, comprehensive response to poverty requires us to diagnose the various drivers that provoke and reproduce the conditions under which existing poverty festers.

Poverty is a human rights issue that harms the dignity of the poor and may represent a violation of their Charter rights as an identifiable group (Shaw 2007). It denies too many Canadians their fundamental rights to adequate food, shelter and a decent quality of life — standards of life a wealthy nation can afford for all its citizens. More importantly, it denies Canadians the right to be treated with respect and dignity as human beings. In the context of other grounds of discrimination and other hierarchies of oppression, it is compounded by experiences of social exclusion that make its elimination more intractable and its violations of rights more profound.

Poverty is also an expensive social condition. A 2008 study by Metcalf Foundation and the Ontario Association of Food Banks (2008: 4), entitled *The Cost of Poverty: An Analysis of the Economic Cost of Poverty in Ontario*, documents that the federal and Ontario governments lose at least $10.4 to $13.1 billion a year due to poverty — on such things as health care costs, negative social impacts of poverty and transfers. This is a loss equal to between 10.8 to 16.6 percent of the provincial budget (4). In real terms, poverty costs every household in the province from $2,299 to $2,895 every year. In Ontario alone, Canada's largest province (and the province with the biggest population of racialized people), when both private and public (or social) costs are combined, the total cost of poverty is equal to 5.5 to 6.6 percent of the province's gross domestic product (GDP) (4).

The annual cost of child or *intergenerational poverty* is also very high. If *child poverty* were eliminated, the extra income tax revenues nationally would be between $3.1 and $3.8 billion (4). Opportunity costs or lost productivity due to poverty also represents a great economic cost. Federal and provincial governments across Canada lose between $8.6 and $13 billion in income tax revenue to poverty every year (4).

The Rhetoric of Poverty:
Racialized Discourse on Poverty and Stigmas

There is a disturbing silence when it comes to talking about the structural nature of poverty and its root cause. There is also a deep denial that the widening problem of poverty in Canada increasingly has a racialized and gendered character to it. We need a conversation on poverty that broaches the taboo subjects of race and class.

In Canadian society, there is a reality gap between the experiences of many groups and the dominant narratives about poverty from the media and our business and political leaders. It corresponds to the polarization in incomes and well-being in Canadian society, which has been shaped by the neoliberal restructuring of the economy. But aside from the public moments of such movements as Occupy, which have highlighted the issue of gross income disparity in North American societies — the "1 percent versus the 99 percent" — poverty is not well articulated in the mainstream media or in the political arena, to the detriment of policy choices that can realistically address income inequality and poverty. This is largely because the victims of economic polarization have not had their voices or their claims to the state heard due to the individualization perpetuated by neoliberal capitalism.

The gap between media representations of how people live and what the majority experience as daily struggles to maintain a quality life is widening by the day. The precariousness in employment and livelihood structured by the neoliberal economy is not the dominant narrative, however prevalent it is. Income inequality and polarization are masked by the illusion of a society of winners and losers. It is an illusion manufactured to shield the winners — those with power — from social accountability for the violence of poverty; it is used to blame the poor for their condition of indigence or the "Other" for snatching from those who are impoverished the opportunities they are rightly entitled to.

Using selective reporting on the performance of the stock market and narratives of Canada as a prosperous country because it is globally competitive, we are counselled to accept inaction on social problems by our governments and subject ourselves to the discipline of the market — meaning that we must live with job insecurity and lower wages through free trade regimes run by undemocratic and unaccountable corporations. We are told that the globalized race to the bottom for workers and communities is inevitable.

In Canadian society, inequality and poverty are structurally inevitable, but the environment is rarely discussed in its complexity or substantively. Action at many levels of government in Canada must conform to the ideas that poverty is a by-product of an infallible market and what can be done is limited by the reality of limited government. Occasionally, one may hear talk from the government of homelessness, concerns about child care or the need for more proliferation of food banks. However, given the illusion of a prosperous Canada, these are largely limited to society's musings about moral failure. People living in poverty are largely stereotyped based on urban legends about welfare recipients driving Cadillacs, teenage mothers with "illegitimate children," able-bodied men and women choosing to collect welfare and spend their days drinking and smoking instead of looking for work, immigrants cheating their way into Canada so they can collect welfare (McCormack 2007). According to Judith McCormack (2007), the reality is starkly different: only 3 percent of single parents on welfare are under twenty years old and nearly half of all single parents on welfare have only one child while 31 percent have two children (McCormack 2007). But these stereotypes persist and inform the public debate because they converge with racialized pathologies of the "Other" in Canadian society — Indigenous Peoples, Blacks, Arabs, South Asians, Latinos, Vietnamese, and immigrants in general.

The stigmatization of the poor is highly racialized and gendered. For instance, Allison Harell, Stuart Soroka and Kiera Ladner's (2014) analysis of Canadian election data shows that *racialization* is an important factor in public support for redistributive programs. Their study tests how portrayals of recipients as Indigenous negatively impacts support for cash benefits. They find that support for redistribution is lower when recipients are Indigenous rather than white. When Canadians are cued to think about recipients as Indigenous, this activates negative racial stereotypes that reflect larger discourses of race and poverty, with the effect being dramatically lower support for the program (Mirchandani and Chan 2008; Harell, Soroka and Ladner 2014). The point is that racial stereotypes stigmatize redistributive programs, leading to low public support, punitive and discriminatory delivery of programs, excessive regulation and burdensome surveillance of the beneficiaries.

The Racialization of Poverty

The racialization of poverty is a process by which poverty becomes disproportionately concentrated and reproduced among members of racialized groups, in some cases intergenerationally. The racialization of poverty emerges out of structural socioeconomic features that predetermine the disproportionate incidence of poverty among racialized groups. Some of the contributing factors to this trend include racialized Canadians experiencing higher levels of unemployment and earning less income than non-racialized Canadians. As well, scholars contend that racialized Canadians are over-represented in a range of traditionally low-paid business services such as call centres and janitorial services (Block and Galabuzi 2011: 3), the result of which is this disproportionate vulnerability to poverty among racialized communities. The emergence of precariousness as a major feature of Canadian labour markets is an important explanation for the racialization and *feminization of poverty*, some of the most significant developments arising out of precarious labour conditions.

Racialized groups are disproportionately immigrant communities (67 percent) and also suffer from the impact of immigration status. Current trends indicate that the economic inequality between highly racialized immigrant groups and those who are Canadian-born is becoming greater and more permanent (Picot and Hou 2003; Picot, Hou and Coulombe 2007). Increasingly, racialized people live on the margins of society, surrounded by others in similar circumstances, excluded from the job market and other "avenues of upward mobility" (Picot and Hou 2003; Picot, Hou and Coulombe 2007). Increasingly, they live in neighbourhoods of deep poverty with high unemployment, welfare dependency and high school dropout rates, conditions that reproduce poverty.

The racialization of poverty is also linked to the entrenchment of disproportionate privileged access to the economic resources of Canadian society by a small but powerful segment of the majority population. This also explains the polarizations in income and wealth in society. The concentration of economic, social and political power that has emerged as the market has become more prominent in social regulation in Canada, which explains the growing gap between rich and poor as well as the racialization of that gap (Dibbs and Leesti 1995; Yalnizyan 1998; Kunz, Milan and Schetagne 2000; Galabuzi 2001; Jackson 2001).

Growing Polarization in Income and Wealth in Canada

In 2007, Armine Yalnizyan and the Canadian Centre for Policy Alternatives published a report entitled *The Rich and The Rest of Us: The Changing Face of Canada's Growing Gap*. The report notes that Canada's economy has doubled in size since 1981 — it is now the ninth-richest nation in the world (Yalnizyan 2007). These observations preceded the financial crisis that led to the economic recession and the destruction of many livelihoods. But while the new century has largely been defined as one of prosperity for Canada, scratch the surface of Canada's stellar GDP and below it you will find a country faced with growing economic polarization. The report concluded that the income gap between rich and poor is at a thirty-year high, there is greater polarization as the rich are getting richer, the bottom half are shut out of economic gains, and people are working longer to maintain their earnings (Yalnizyan 2007: 3–4).

Yalnizyan's report suggests that the problem is not the creation of adequate levels of wealth by the Canadian economy; rather, the prosperity is not being equitably distributed. According to Statistics Canada (2006), between 1999 and 2005 the median net worth of families in the top fifth of the wealth distribution increased by 19 percent, while the net worth of their counterparts in the bottom fifth remained virtually unchanged. The share of total household wealth of the top 20 percent of Canadian families continued to grow to 75 percent in 2005, up from 73 percent in 1999 and 69 percent in 1984 (Morissette and Zhang 2006). According to the CCPA report,

> The poorest 10% of families earned less than $9,400. Five percent of families earned less than $1,050 in 2004. The poorest 10% of families raising children — more than 376,000 households in Canada — lived on less than $23,300, after taxes, in 2004. Half of these families lived on less than $17,500 a year. (Yalnizyan 2007: 7–8)

In addition to the income gap, studies show that most Canadian families are working longer in the paid labour force than families were in the late 1970s, but their incomes are lower today than they were a generation ago. As a result, today even having a job is not enough (Jackson 2005).

In a federal government report entitled *Towards a Poverty Reduction Strategy: A Background on Poverty in Canada,* it was stated that, in 2014,

> about 746,000 Canadians live in a household where the main income earner is considered "working poor." These individuals work similar hours to the average Canadian worker but earn less money and their hours are more likely to rise and fall unpredictably. This can make it hard to balance work and family responsibilities. (Government of Canada 2016: 10)

Incidentally, the data show a significant difference between before-tax earnings and after-tax incomes, which includes government income supports and income taxes, suggesting that the governments can have a positive impact on income distribution and can mitigate income disparities. But while Canada's system of taxes and transfers has helped families in the last ten years, the system of social supports has been weakened by cuts to taxes and cuts to social services, the former benefiting the wealthy and the latter disadvantaging all other citizens (Yalnizyan 2007: 26).

Wealth and power have become increasingly concentrated in the hands of a relatively small group of citizens (and noncitizen investors). Such rising concentration of wealth and power, coming as it does at the expense of so many, undermines a national vision of an equitable society in which all can aspire to full participation and full and equal citizenship. There is now little doubt that this choice of economic system produces more and more poverty and income insecurity for many, even as it produces more and more profits for the few through massive concentrations of wealth and power.

The dominance of *neoliberal* ideas — the call to get "government out of the way" and let markets run their course — has meant that Canadian workers have lost much of their power to bargain effectively as partners in production with corporations. The ensuing result has been more income and social inequality. This has led to the deterioration of wages, job security and conditions of work, which hase impacted the most vulnerable groups in society most adversely. A growing body of research now shows clearly that the increasing *precariousness* in the forms of work available for working-class people, immigrants, youth, women, Indigenous and racialized peoples has led to a consolidation of poverty among these populations in many urban centres (Kazemipur and Halli 2000; Picot and Hou 2003; Fleury 2007; Picot, Hou and Coulombe 2007; Block and Galabuzi 2011).

Research data show that the precariousness arising from economic restructuring is not equally shared. According to numerous reports, women, racialized peoples, Indigenous Peoples and disabled people bear a disproportionate brunt of it (Vosko 2005; PEPSO 2013). Likewise, they encounter disproportionate and persistent experiences of low income. Increasingly, these experiences are intergenerational and deeply entrenched because they influence other determinants of social mobility, such as educational attainment, access to more secure employment, access to neighbourhoods and housing, health status or contact with the criminal justice system, all of which have a compounding effect on opportunities and future prospects. Hence, I use the concept of the *racialization of poverty* to describe the phenomenon that is unfolding.

Poverty and Social Inequality
as a Structural Phenomenon

> Poverty has many faces. It is much more than low income. It also
> reflects poor health and education, deprivation in knowledge and
> communication, inability to exercise human and political rights
> and the absence of dignity, confidence and self-respect. (UNDP
> 1997: iii)

In a sense, while the current deepening polarization in income and wealth
can be traced to the economic restructuring of the last quarter century and
state deregulation, enabling the market to dictate how the economy should
be organized, the persistence of poverty has its roots in the structures and
hierarchies of class, race, gender and disability that determine who the
winners and losers are in Canadian society.

These trends are not just passing concerns. Rather, they are enduring
because the structures that create inequality are built into the very foundation of Canadian society and the Canadian economy. Canada was founded
as a settler capitalist colony that required the subordination of Indigenous
Peoples and their way of life and economy so that their resources could be
harnessed for the capitalist machine, first in Europe and then domestically.
From its early days, the Canadian state created institutions that operated in
a way that economically, socially and politically disadvantaged some people
along the lines of class, gender, race, ability, sexual difference and others.
These have subsequently determined opportunities, quality of education,
access to resources, dwelling, location and participation in society and its
various institutions.

These different forms of exclusion are hierarchical and often intersecting
in the way they determine the experience of individuals and communities
in Canada. The Canadian experience suggests that structural inequality
is a product of gender, race and colonial relations, with the compounded
experience leading to deep experiences of social exclusion for particular
subjects of these processes. That is why Indigenous and racialized women
are particularly vulnerable to poverty.

Poverty and Social Exclusion

Poverty is a key cause and product of processes of social, political and economic exclusion. Canada, like all modern capitalist societies, has a division
of functions and social differentiation within society. Such differentiation

has become the basis of social stratification and social inequality as it acts to determine access to society's economic, social, cultural and political resources. Elsewhere, I have used the concept of social exclusion to describe the nature of these processes on individuals, communities and societies (Galabuzi 2006). I have suggested that social exclusion describes structures and processes of inequality and unequal outcomes among groups in society. It is a form of alienation and denial of full citizenship experienced by particular groups of individuals and communities. In industrialized societies, a key determinant of social exclusion is uneven access to the processes of production, wealth creation and power. In a capitalist economy, access to the labour market is central to the process of exclusion (Galabuzi 2006).

Poverty, Race and Health

The effect of income inequality on health reflects a combination of negative exposures and lack of resources held by individuals, along with systematic underinvestment across a wide range of human, physical, health, and social infrastructure. (Lynch, Smith, Kaplan and House 2000: 1202)

Poverty has a direct influence on the risk factors or protective conditions that lead to poor or good health. National Population Health Survey data show that 73 percent of Canadians with the highest incomes reported their health as excellent, while only 47 percent of Canadians with the lowest incomes rated their health as good or very good. Canadians at the bottom of the economic ladder are more likely to die from cancer, heart disease, diabetes, respiratory disease and other ailments than those who are well off.

Moreover, poverty, racism and other forms of oppression undermine the health and well-being of Indigenous people, racialized group members, women, children and the poor. Health disparities related to racism compromise health status and lead to disproportionate exposure to such conditions as diabetes and hypertension (James et al. 2010).

It is now widely documented that social inequalities in the labour market, education, housing and health service utilization lead to negative health outcomes (Lewchuk, Clarke and de Wolff 2008; Scott-Marshall and Tompa 2011). But there are also sociopsychological impacts related to historical and enduring modes of oppression and marginalization (colonization, everyday forms of racism and sexism, displacement) that account for traumas, stresses and distresses, which also influence health outcomes. The psychological pressures of resisting racism daily, for example, add up to a complex set of factors that undermine the health status of racialized and immigrant group members (James et al. 2010).

The death rate from injury among Indigenous infants is four times the rate for Canada as a whole, and three times among teenagers. Indigenous people are twice as likely to report fair or poor health status than non-Indigenous people with the same income levels. According to Sara Gartner and Rosemary Thompson (2004), "Young Blacks are four times (10.1 per 100,000) as likely to be victims of gun-related homicides as other members of the population (2.4 per 100,000)" (cited in Galabuzi 2016: 406).

Economic Exclusion

Attachment to the labour market is central to full membership in any society and, in a capitalist liberal democratic society, it is the foundation of full citizenship. It represents a source of livelihood as well as a means of identity formation and provides a sense of belonging. Attachment to the labour market is particularly central to the successful redress of all forms of exclusion, whether that be reconciling marginalized groups to society or integrating immigrants into host societies — challenges that increasingly face Canadian society. Research on income disparities shows that uneven attachment to the labour market has adverse impacts on social well-being through health status, housing status, educational attainment, political participation, etc. (Galabuzi 2008).

A key aspect of *economic exclusion* is related to the rise of precarious employment, which disproportionately affects women, racialized groups, Indigenous populations and youth. It represents the shift from a norm of standard employment based on full-time, continuous work with good wages and benefits toward work with low wages, job insecurity and minimal control over labour conditions — work arrangements, schedules — with no benefits but high health risks (Fuller and Vosko 2008; Fuller 2011).

There is a need to challenge the normalization of the distinction between good and precarious jobs by demanding secure employment as a standard for our society. Public policy should bring relief for those who are working long hours but for much the same pay; those working multiple jobs because of low wages; those seeking to escape precarious conditions of work; those clamouring for recognition of their international qualifications or experience; and those whose labour continues to be devalued because of their gender, race, disability, sexual difference, immigrant status or neighbourhood of residence (Hou and Coulombe 2010).

Economic Exclusion and Poverty among Indigenous Populations
Indigenous people in Canada experience a significant and persistent income gap compared to the rest of the Canadian population. The income gap contributes to the disproportionate exposure to poverty among Indigenous people. As a group, they are at least three times as likely to be living in poverty, with sub groups such as rural Indigenous populations, women and children facing even higher rates of poverty (Galabuzi 2006). Much of this disadvantage relates to their differential access to the labour market and unequal income attainment. Table 5.1 shows the persistent income gap over four census periods.

Table 5.1: Median Employment Income for Indigenous and Non-Indigenous Populations

	1996	2001	2006	2010
Indigenous	12,003	18,306	18,962	20,060
Non-Indigenous	21,413	25,081	27,097	27,622
Income gap	44%	27%	30%	27%

Source: Statistics Canada (Census 1996, 2001, 2006); 2015

Economic Exclusion and Poverty among Racialized Groups
Two key processes underway in Canadian society have made poverty among racialized groups an increasing source of concern for public policy. One is the changing economy under the assault of neoliberal restructuring, which has imposed new vulnerabilities on working populations as precariousness has become more prevalent in the labour market (Stanford and Vosko 2004). The other is the numerical significance of racialized groups as the major sources of immigrants to Canada; it has shifted from Europe to mostly countries in the Global South. These events are proceeding within the context of historical processes of social stratification that make race and gender socially significant as bases for the distribution of opportunities in the labour market. The compound effect is that these processes of social stratification have intensified in the last few decades under the neoliberal regime. This is largely because neoliberal restructuring and demands for "flexibility" in the workforce have made precarious employment the fastest-growing form of work, creating a prevalence of irregular work arrangements, non-standard contracts, self-employment and temporary, part-time, piece work or shift work, coupled with job insecurity, poorer working conditions and loss of control over workplace decision making (Cranford and Vosko 2006).

While these new developments have placed all workers in a very vulnerable position, these vulnerabilities are unevenly distributed — women, persons with disabilities, Indigenous Peoples, racialized workers and new immigrants are the hardest hit (Zeytinoglu and Muteshi 2000; Vosko 2005). The impacts of flexible deployment of labour and the attendant insecurity have combined with historical processes of discrimination in employment to impose added vulnerability on racialized groups in the Canadian economy (Galabuzi 2004). As a consequence, racialized groups are exposed disproportionately to the adversities of precarious work. Research shows that this translates into disproportionate exposure to lower incomes and occupational status in comparison to other Canadians (Galabuzi 2006).

Immigration and the Changing Profile of the Racialized Population in Canada

In 2006, Canada was home to about five million racialized people, or 16.4 percent of the Canadian population. Their share of the population is projected to increase to 33 percent by the end of 2031 (Statistics Canada 2017). Much of that growth can be accounted for by immigration but also higher-than-average birth rates. Since 2012, Canada has admitted at least 257,887 immigrants every year, with 296,346 coming to the country in 2016 (Statistics Canada 2013, 2014, 2015, 2016, 2017). In 2017, it was projected that at least 300,000 new permanent residents would be admitted to Canada (Canadian Council for Refugees n.d). According to a study by Human Resources and Skills Development Canada, immigration was expected to account for virtually all of the net growth in the Canadian labour force by the end of 2017 (Fleury 2007). In the last fifteen years, over 75 percent of Canada's newcomers were members of racialized groups.

According to the 2006 census, immigrants made up 19.4 percent of Canada's population and this figure was projected to rise to 25 percent by the end of 2017. Of particular note is that, since the 1970s, increasing numbers of immigrants to Canada have come from Asia and the Middle East. Asian-born immigrants accounted for more than half (57 percent) of the immigrants who arrived since 1991 (Statistics Canada 1996, 2001, 2006).The percentage of racialized minorities in the Canadian population, which was under 4 percent in 1971, grew to 9.4 percent by 1991, hit double digits (11.2 percent) by 1996 and was projected to be 20 percent by the end of 2017. With Canada's continued reliance on immigration for population growth, and with globalization escalating, these trends are likely to continue.

Canada's racialized groups are mainly concentrated in urban centres, with Toronto, Vancouver and Montréal accounting for about 75 percent of the total racialized population (42, 18 and 13 percent, respectively). In 2001, racialized groups accounted for an increasing number of people in the major Canadian urban centres as well as the most populous provinces.

Overwhelmingly, the changes in immigration composition have been most felt by Canada's three biggest urban areas — Toronto, Vancouver, and Montréal. The cumulative increase in the number of racialized group members over the last forty years is most noticeable in the major urban areas, where, in the 1990s, more than 80 percent chose to settle. Immigrants have transformed these areas into diverse cultural centres, and their increased contributions to the life and economies of cities like Toronto have led many Torontonians to proclaim diversity as their city's strength.

Immigration and Racialized Poverty

The changing Canadian demographic profile has given the issue of the socioeconomic status of racialized groups new significance as a public policy issue. That racialized groups are impending majorities in a number of Canada's urban centres represents a concern, because their exposure to low income can mature into threats to social cohesion. Yet, increasingly, research shows that there are significant and enduring disproportionalities in the experience of poverty in Canada, particularly in the urban centres. National and census metropolitan area (CMA) data from the census now show that racialized people are two or three times more likely to be poor than other Canadians (Kazemipur and Halli 2000; Lee 2000; Ornstein 2000; Hou and Picot 2003; Picot and Hou 2003; Fleury 2007; Picot, Hou and Coulombe 2007). The rates are even higher among recent immigrants and some select groups such as youth, women and seniors of Arab, Latin American, Somali, Haitian, Iranian, Tamil, East Indian and Vietnamese origin. The levels of poverty are especially high among some racialized groups of women, youth and seniors.

In urban centres like Toronto, Vancouver, Montréal and Calgary, where racialized populations are statistically significant, the cumulative impact of racially segmented labour markets — accounting for the income and employment gap between these groups and Whites — is not just the racialization of poverty. It is combined with other social patterns, such as the sustained school dropout rates, the racialization of the penal system and the criminalization of racialized youth, and the racial segregation

Table 5.2: Low Income in Ontario by Age and Racialization

	Indigenous	Racialized	White/Other	Total
Under age 15	0.9%	11.7%	0.5%	23.1%
Age 15–24	0.5%	7.3%	8.9%	16.7%
Age 25–44	0.7%	12.9%	14.8%	28.4%
Age 45–64	0.5%	6.8%	13.9%	21.2%
Age 65+	0.1%	2.5%	7.9%	10.5%
Total	2.7%	41.3%	56.0%	100%

Source: Statistics Canada, 2006; Patychuk 2010.

of urban, low-income neighbourhoods. These conditions have created a deepening social marginalization such that, in a number of low-income neighbourhoods in Toronto where racialized group members are dispro-portionately tenants of poorly maintained public housing and substandard private housing, the process of immiseration, desperation, hopelessness and disempowerment has degenerated into a level of violence that has claimed many young lives and threatens to spiral out of control. These are all signs of what has been referred to as *deep poverty* (Ley and Smith 1997).

Patterns of high school dropout and low literacy rates in predominantly racialized, low-income communities in urban centres or on Indigenous reserves reinforce the deepening experience of poverty in communities. These processes, in turn, reinforce school non-achievement, alienation and even higher dropout rates. The implications of these indicators are that children growing up in poor families are more likely to repeat the cycle of poverty, making the experience of poverty intergenerational (Burnaby, James and Regier 2000).

Racialized poverty can be observed by looking at five key qualitative and quantitative indicators: differential rates of exposure to low income, unequal income attainment, differential access to the labour market, neighbourhood selection, urban residential segregation and contact with the criminal justice system.

Differential Exposure to Low Income

National and cma data show that racialized groups experience deepening levels of poverty (table 5.3). The most basic measure of low income exposure is the lico, generally used by Statistics Canada and most official sources.

According to that measure, the low-income rate for racialized populations is approximately three times that of the rest of the Canadian population.

Table 5.3: After-Tax Low Income by Select Racialized Group

	2005	2016
Arab	32.5	36.2
Black	24.0	23.9
Chinese	19.5	23.4
Filipino	8.2	7.4
Latin American	20.6	19.8
Japanese	9.4	12.9
Korean	38.2	32.6
South Asian	16.4	16.5
South East Asian	18.5	17.6
West Asian	32.4	34.7
Multiple Vis. Min.	14.3	16.7
Total Racialized	19.8	20.8
Total Non-Racialized	6.4	12.2

Source: Statistics Canada (2006, 2016)

The experience is generalized among racialized groups, although it is deeper for some than others. Except for a minority of groups — Japanese and, to some extent, Filipino communities — most racialized communities experience a negative gap in low-income exposure compared to the general Canadian levels. As indicated, gender differentials as well as youth, children, single parenthood and immigrant status tend to exacerbate the experience of poverty among racialized groups.

Unequal Income Attainment and Differential Access to Labour Market

Racialized workers, Indigenous people, women and new immigrants are disproportionately over-represented in precarious work. The result of these patterns of attachment to the labour market is a disproportionate exposure to low income and poverty. This is partly because of what has been going on in the economy in the last two decades. Neoliberal restructuring and demands for flexibility have made precarious employment the fastest-growing form of work for the vulnerable — meaning contract, temporary, part-time, piece-meal, self-employed or shift work with low pay, no job security, poor and often unsafe working conditions, intensive labour, excessive hours and low or no benefits (Galabuzi 2006). Deregulation and restructuring have combined with persistent experiences of racist discrimination in employment to make racialized groups the most vulnerable in the Canadian economy. Their participation in the labour market is also characterized by overrepresentation in the sectors of the economy that feature precarious employment — a form of labour market segmentation.

Racialized and Indigenous women are particularly vulnerable to these problems. They are segregated into low-paying sectors and occupations. Many take on more than one job to survive. As a result, many racialized women make up the growing population of working poor in Canada. The situation is increasingly similar for another, doubly vulnerable group — racialized youth. Data show that racialized youth are more likely to experience higher unemployment rates and have lower income levels than their counterparts, raising their exposure to poverty and its effects on opportunities later in life. This holds true even among youth who are Canadian-born (Block and Galabuzi 2011).

Neighbourhood Selection, Urban Residential Segregation and Criminalization

Racialized groups are also spatially concentrated in *racial enclaves* and a growing set of racially segregated, low-income neighbourhoods. Immigrants in Toronto, Vancouver and Montréal are more likely than non-immigrants to live in neighbourhoods with high rates of poverty. Canada's urban neighbourhoods have been impacted by the restructuring of the economy as well as immigration patterns over the last quarter century that have established racialized countries as the predominant sources for immigration. As the changing economy has generated a growing gap between rich and poor over the last twenty-five years, that polarization has been felt in the neighbourhoods.

The racialization of poverty has had a major impact on neighbourhood selection and access to adequate housing for new immigrants and racialized groups. In Canada's urban centres, the *spatial concentration of poverty* or *residential segregation* is intensifying along racial lines. Increasingly, they are concentrated in what have come to be called racialized enclaves — a growing set of racially segregated neighbourhoods. As urban housing markets become more segregated, racialized groups are relegated to substandard, marginal and often over-priced housing (Philp 2000; Myles and Picot 2010).

In 2006, the overall poverty rate in Canada was 11 percent (Government of Canada 2013). However, for racialized persons it was 22 percent compared to 9 percent for non-racialized persons (Government of Canada 2013). As urban centres with sizeable numbers of racialized persons living in poverty, Toronto was home to 41 percent of all racialized persons living in Canada, Vancouver with 18 percent and Montréal at 17 percent (Government of Canada 2013). So, Canada's urban areas have seen residential segregation intensifying along racial lines, creating segregated poor communities.

Among the three largest racialized groups in Toronto, Vancouver and Montréal from 1981 to 1996, the number of ethnic enclaves increased from six in 1981 to seventy in 1991 (Qadeer and Agrawal 2009). In Toronto, the percentage of Chinese population living in ethnic enclaves increased from 28 percent in 2001 to 48.2 percent (Qadeer and Agrawal 2009).[3] These racialized enclaves have above-average levels of unemployment, low income, single-parent households and school dropout rates — all characteristics of deep and enduring, intergenerational poverty (Clark 1989).

Studies by Abdolmohammad Kazemipur and Shiva S. Halli (2000), Eric Fong and Kumiko Shibuya (2000) and David Ley and Heather Smith (1997), among others, suggest that these areas show characteristics of "*ghettoization*" or spatial concentration of poverty: racial concentration in urban cores, high density, tight clustering and limited exposure to majority communities. Vancouver had more racialized enclaves than Montréal, most of which reflect the three largest racialized communities in Canada — Chinese, South Asian and Black. These neighbourhoods, segregated by poverty, race and immigration status, have become increasingly defined by the distresses that come with the lacking allocation of resources by the various levels of government.

Racialized spatial concentration of poverty means that racialized peoples live in neighbourhoods that are heavily concentrated and "hypersegregated" from the rest of society, often with disintegrating institutions and social deficits such as inadequate access to counselling, skills training, child care, recreation and health care services (Kazemipur and Halli 1997, 2000). They also intensify the social distance between racialized and non-racialized groups in Canadian society, thereby reproducing residential or neighbourhood segregation (Massey 1981; Driedger 1989). Young immigrants living in low-income areas often struggle with alienation from their parents and community of origin, as well as from the broader society. This has led to, among other things, an increase in various forms of violence, including the explosion of gun violence among youth in low-income neighbourhoods in Toronto.

One way to understand such violence is setting it in the context of high levels of alienation, marginalization, hopelessness and powerlessness in these neighbourhoods, as they have been subjected to social service deficits and denied key government interventions and resources, allowing for conditions under which generalized violence can thrive. The connection between the socioeconomic crisis and violence is well documented. Research on murder in Canada, from a historical perspective, has established that young victims and perpetuators of violent crime tend to be impacted by developmental and social ecological factors such as family breakdown, poor parenting, poverty, social alienation and violence in popular culture and the mainstream media (Boyd 1988, see also Fagin 1989).

Other research on community violence suggests that it is largely a function of social breakdown deeply connected to social inequality (Leonard, Rosario, Scott and Bressan 2005; Welsh and Farrington 2005). It represents a form of nihilism that arises out of the alienation, disconnection from society and its values, despair, powerlessness and hopelessness in many socially excluded environments. So, young people are more likely to be the victims of violence, especially lethal violence, than other members of society. This is particularly true of racialized youth living in low-income areas.

They are also more likely to be criminalized because of the targeted policing that goes on in these areas, subjecting many to racial profiling, over-policing and, therefore, higher levels of contact with the criminal justice system, as the data on arrests and incarceration shows. The prison population in major urban centres is disproportionately Indigenous and racialized (Galabuzi 2006). However, it is important to note that, while they have real and persistent challenges and weaknesses, these neighbourhoods also have a complex role as nurturing communities for their immigrant and racialized residents by providing a space in which a sense of belonging is created.

Homelessness is also said to be proliferating among racialized people because of the prevalence of poverty and housing crises in many urban areas (Lee 2000). Homelessness is an extreme form of social exclusion that suggests a complexity of causes and factors. Increasingly, recent immigrants and racialized people are more likely to be homeless in Canada's urban centres. It compounds other sources of stresses in their lives. Homelessness has been associated with health factors such as substance abuse, mental illness, infectious diseases, difficulty accessing health services and early mortality (City of Toronto 1999).

Policy Responses to Poverty

Poverty is not a generic phenomenon but one that is highly racialized and gendered. Colonization, racialization and patriarchy determine access to economic opportunities and resources in Canadian society. The twin processes of racialization and feminization of poverty help explain the persistence of poverty in the Canadian population. They should be a central consideration in both our understanding of poverty and in the design of policy responses to poverty. There has been a growing effort to address poverty at the provincial level, with Québec, Newfoundland, Prince Edward Island, Nova Scotia, Ontario, Alberta and British Columbia enacting policies for poverty reduction (Parliament of Canada 2010). A key focus of *poverty elimination strategies* should be the social characteristics of the people living in poverty and the extent to which their identity impacts their vulnerability to poverty. Such consideration will ensure that the design of reduction strategies targets the root causes of poverty.

The diminishing commitment by the state toward income redistribution, income supports, social services and adequate funding for health care and education are combined with racial inequality in access to employment income. Other important factors are the shift toward flexible labour deployment and precarious forms of work in the urban economies, as well as the marked increase in South–North immigration. Also, isolated and racially defined, low-income neighbourhoods are vulnerable to disintegrating social institutions and anti-social outcomes such as violence (Galabuzi 2009). These growing neighbourhood inequalities limit access to social services, increase contact with the criminal justice system, create exposure to violence and engender higher health risks (Galabuzi 2009).

In the midst of the socioeconomic crisis that has resulted from racialized poverty, the different levels of government have responded by disengaging and abandoning anti-racism programs and policies aimed at removing the barriers to economic equity. The resulting powerlessness, socioeconomic marginalization and loss of voice compounds the racialized peoples' inability to put social inequality and the racialization of poverty on the political agenda. They are unable to seek remedy effectively through political representation.

An *intersectional approach* to policymaking will ensure that poverty is not concentrated among the most vulnerable populations because of the historical disadvantages they face. This concept is often referred to as "*targeted universality*" — the idea that a program is aimed at addressing the totality of poverty in the population but targets the most vulnerable as the starting point to achieve the most effective outcomes. A focus on improved access to unionization for workers in highly precarious sectors of the economy so as to institutionally address the power imbalance in the labour market between workers and employers, government interventions such as a national child care system, provincial minimum wages to align with living-wage levels, employment equity laws to address racial and gender discrimination in employment, job creation in low-income neighbourhoods by leveraging government procurement for community benefit, and a basic guaranteed income could go a long way to address the inequalities and associated racialized poverty discussed in this chapter.

Conclusion

Poverty in Canada is caused by structural processes and ideological forces that are responsible for concentrating wealth in the hands of fewer and fewer people. It is a part of a larger crisis of wealth and income distribution, as well as the distribution of power in labour markets, that makes workers increasingly vulnerable to deteriorating conditions of work and income. But the story of poverty is complicated by the fact that it is not a generic experience. Women experience poverty at significantly higher levels than men, even those in married family arrangements. Using the most basic measure of low-income exposure — the LICO, generally used by Statistics Canada and most official sources — we find that racialized and Indigenous populations are three times as likely as other Canadians to experience poverty. This is consistent with their unequal participation in the Canadian labour market. The disparity in exposure to poverty can also be documented by neighbourhood. The neighbourhood has an impact on the health outcomes of the groups that are particularly vulnerable to poverty. These populations carry the disproportionate burden of both the experience of poverty and its stigmas.

Poverty is feminized and racialized, as the data increasingly show. An effective poverty elimination approach must consider these dimensions and address them with strategies focused on race, class and gender. Along with addressing the key problems relating to the neoliberal economy — structural forces that are generating economic and income inequality and poverty in Canada — it is essential to understand the other underlying causes of vulnerability to poverty among particular populations in Canada. Targeted universality is an effective way to undertake this strategic approach to eliminating poverty.

DISCUSSION QUESTIONS

1. What are the major factors that contribute to the racialization of poverty?
2. What are some strategies that can deal with the plight of the working poor in Canada?
3. What specific polices should the federal government implement to help immigrants avoid being relegated to living in low-income neighbourhoods?

ACTION STEPS

1. Advocate to all levels of government (municipal, provincial, federal) for the implementation of poverty reduction policies and strategies.
2. Organize racialized Canadians who are underemployed and document the impact of this status on these individuals and their families. Prepare a policy brief and send it to your local councillor, member of legislative assembly (MLA) and/or member of parliament (MP).

Supplemental Readings

Bernhardt, Nicole. 2015. "Racialized Precarious Employment and the Inadequacies of the Canadian Welfare State." *Journal of Workplace Rights*, 5, 2.
Block, Sheila, and Grace-Edward Galabuzi. 2011. *Canada's Colour-Coded Labour Market: The Gap for Racialized Workers*. Canadian Centre for Policy Alternatives and the Wellesley Institute.
Galabuzi, Grace-Edward. 2006. *Canada's Economic Apartheid: The Social Exclusion of Racialized Groups in the New Century*. Toronto, ON: Canadian Scholars' Press.
Sethi, Bharati, and Alison Williams. 2015. "Employment Experiences of Visible Minority Immigrant Women: A Literature Review." *International Journal of Humanities and Social Science Research*, 1.

Additional Resources

Government of Canada. 2016. "Towards A Poverty Reduction Strategy." Discussion Paper. Ottawa, ON: Her Majesty the Queen in Right of Canada. <canada.ca/en/employment-social-development/programs/poverty-reduction/discussion-paper.html>.
The Canadian Observatory on Homelessness/Homeless Hub <homelesshub.ca/resource/poverty-profile-snapshot-racialized-poverty-canada>.

Notes

1. Racialized group members are persons, other than Indigenous Peoples, who are non-Caucasian in race or non-white in colour as defined by the federal *Employment Equity Act* of 1995; a fuller definition of racialized poverty is provided elsewhere in this chapter and in other work by the author.
2. Low income is used here as a quantifiable measure of poverty based on the Statistics

Canada "low income cut-off." This measure varies from region to region because it is relational, taking into account the varied cost of living. But in this chapter, it is complemented by qualitative measures of deprivation.

3. These enclaves represent census track areas with at least 30 percent of the population belonging to the designated group. In 2001, each census track included about five thousand people.

References

Block, Sheila, and Grace-Edward Galabuzi. 2011. *Canada's Colour-Coded Labour Market: The Gap for Racialized Workers.* Canadian Centre for Policy Alternatives and the Wellesley Institute.

Boyd, Neil. 1988. *The Last Dance: Murder in Canada.* Scarborough, ON: Prentice-Hall Canada.

Brown, Hana. 2013. "The New Racial Politics of Welfare: Ethno-Racial Diversity, Immigration and Welfare Discourse Variation." *Social Service Review,* 87, 3.

Burnaby, Barbara, Carl James and Sheri Regier. 2000. "The Role of Education in Integrating Diversity in the Greater Toronto Area." Toronto, ON: CERIS Working Paper 11.

Canadian Council for Refugees. n.d. "2017 Immigration Levels – Comments." Montréal, QC. <ccrweb.ca/en/2017-immigration-levels-comments>.

City of Toronto. 1999. *Taking Responsibility for Homelessness: An Action Plan for Toronto.* Toronto, ON: Toronto Mayor's Homelessness Action Task Force Report.

Clark, W.A.V. 1989. "Residential Segregation in American Cities: Common Ground and Differences in Interpretation." *Population Research and Policy Review,* 8, 2.

Cranford, Cynthia J., and Leah F. Vosko. 2006. "Conceptualizing Precarious Employment: Mapping Wage Work Across Social Location and Occupational Context." In Leah F. Vosko (ed.), *Precarious Employment: Understanding Labour Market Insecurity in Canada.* Montreal, QC., and Kingston, ON: McGill-Queen's University Press.

Dibbs, Ruth, and Tracey Leesti. 1995. *Survey of Labour and Income Dynamics: Visible Minorities and Aboriginal Peoples.* Ottawa, ON: Statistics Canada.

Driedger, Leo. 1989. *The Ethnic Factor: Identity in Diversity.* Toronto, ON: McGraw-Hill Ryerson.

Fagin, Jeffrey. 1989. "The Social Organization of Drug Use and Drug Dealing among Urban Gangs." *Criminology,* 27, 4.

Feagin, Joe R. 1975. *Subordinating the Poor.* Englewood Cliffs, NJ: Prentice Hall.

Fleury, Dominique. 2007. *A Study of Poverty and Working Poverty among Recent Immigrants to Canada.* Ottawa, ON: Statistics Canada, Human Resources and Social Development Canada.

Fong, Eric, and Kumiko Shibuya. 2000. "The Spatial Separation of the Poor in Canadian Cities." *Demography,* 37, 4.

Fuller, Sylvia. 2011. "Up and On or Down and Out? Gender, Immigration and the Consequences of Temporary Employment in Canada." *Research in Social Stratification and Mobility,* 29, 2.

Fuller, Sylvia, and Leah F. Vosko. 2008. "Temporary Employment and Social Inequality in Canada: Exploring Intersections of Gender, Race, and Migration." *Social Indicators Research,* 88, 1.

Galabuzi, Grace-Edward. 2016. "Social Exclusion." In Dennis Raphael (ed.), *Social*

Determinants of Health: Canadian Perspectives, third edition. Toronto, ON: Canadian Scholars' Press.

___. 2009. "Social Exclusion." In Dennis Raphael (ed.), *Social Determinants of Health: Canadian Perspectives,* second edition. Toronto, ON: Canadian Scholars' Press.

___. 2008. "In the News: To End Poverty, We Need Equity in Employment." Regional Diversity Roundtable. <regionaldiversityroundtable.org/?q=node/49>.

___. 2006. *Canada's Economic Apartheid: The Social Exclusion of Racialized Groups in the New Century.* Toronto, ON: Canadian Scholars' Press.

___. 2004. "Racializing the Division of Labour: Neoliberal Restructuring and the Economic Segregation of Canada's Racialized Groups." In Jim Stanford and Leah F. Vosko (eds.), *Challenging the Market: The Struggle to Regulate Work and Income.* Montreal, QC, and Kingston, ON: McGill-Queens University Press.

___. 2001. *Canada's Creeping Economic Apartheid: The Economic Segregation and Social Marginalisation of Racialised Groups.* Toronto, ON: Centre for Social Justice Foundation for Research and Education.

Government of Canada. 2016. *Towards a Poverty Reduction Strategy.* Discussion Paper. Ottawa, ON: Her Majesty the Queen in Right of Canada. <canada.ca/en/employment-social-development/programs/poverty-reduction/discussion-paper.html>.

___. 2013. "National Council of Welfare Reports: Povery Profile: Special Edition." <canada.ca/content/dam/esdc-edsc/migration/documents/eng/communities/reports/poverty_profile/snapshot.pdf>.

Harell, Allison, Stuart Soroka and Kiera Ladner. 2014. "Public Opinion, Prejudice and the Racialization of Welfare in Canada." *Ethnic and Racial Studies,* 37, 14.

Hou, Feng, and Simon Coulombe. 2010. "Earnings Gaps for Canadian Born Visible Minorities in the Public and Private Sectors." *Canadian Public Policy/Analyse De Politiques,* 36, 1.

Hou, Feng, and Garnett Picot. 2003. *Visible Minority Neighbourhood Enclaves and Labour Market Outcomes of Immigrants.* Research Paper Series. Ottawa, ON: Statistics Canada, Business and Labour Market Analysis Division.

___. 2004. "Visible Minority Neighbourhoods in Toronto, Montreal and Vancouver." *Canadian Social Trends.* Statistics Canada. Catalogue no. 11-008. <statcan.gc.ca/pub/11-008-x/2003004/article/6803-eng.pdf>.

Jackson, Andrew. 2005. *Work and Labour in Canada: Critical Issues.* Toronto, ON: Canadian Scholars' Press.

___. 2001. "Poverty and Racism." *Perception* (Canadian Council on Social Development), 24, 4.

James, Carl, David Este, Wanda Thomas Bernard, Akua Benjamin, Bethan Lloyd and Tana Turner. 2010. *Race and Well-Being: The Lives, Hopes and Action of African Canadians.* Halifax, NS: Fernwood Publishing.

Kazemipur, Abdolmohammad, and Shiva S. Halli. 2000. *The New Poverty in Canada: Ethnic Groups and Ghetto Neighbourhoods.* Toronto, ON: Thompson Educational Publishing.

___. 1997. "The Invisible Barrier: Neighbourhood Poverty and Integration of Immigrants in Canada." *Journal of International Migration and Integration,* 1, 1.

Kunz, Jean Lock, Anne Milan and Sylvain Schetagne. 2000. "Unequal Access: A Canadian Profile of Racial Differences in Education, Employment and Income." Report prepared for Canadian Race Relations Foundation by the Canadian Council on Social Development. <atwork.settlement.org/downloads/

Unequal_Access.pdf>.

Lee, Kevin Kaalip. 2000. *Urban Poverty in Canada: A Statistical Profile*. Ottawa: Canadian Council on Social Development.

Leonard, Lucie, Giselle Rosario, Carolyn Scott and Jessica Bressan. 2005. "Building Safer Communities: Lessons Learned from Canada's National Strategy." *Canadian Journal of Criminology and Criminal Justice*, 47, 2.

Lewchuk, Wayne, Marlea Clarke and Alice de Wolff. 2008. "Working Without Commitments: Precarious Employment and Health." *Work, Employment and Society*, 22, 3.

Ley, David, and Heather Smith. 1997. "Is There an Immigrant 'Underclass' in Canadian Cities?" Vancouver Centre of Excellence. Research on Immigration and Integration in the Metropolis. Working Paper Series #97–08.

Lynch, John W., George Davey Smith, George A. Kaplan and James S. House. 2000. "Income Inequality and Mortality: Importance to Health of Individual Income, Psychosocial Environment, or Material Conditions." *British Medical Journal*, 320, 7243.

Massey, Douglas S. 1981. "Social Class and Ethnic Segregation: A Reconsideration of Methods and Conclusions." *American Sociological Review*, 46, 5.

McCormack, Judith. 2007. "Why Myths About Poor Endure." *Toronto Star*, March 2. <thestar.com/opinion/2007/03/02/why_myths_about_poor_endure.html>.

Mikkonen, Juha, and Dennis Raphael. 2010. *Social Determinants of Health: The Canadian Facts*. Toronto, ON: York University School of Health Policy and Management.

Mirchandani, Kiran, and Wendy Chan. 2008. *Criminalizing Race, Criminalizing Poverty: Welfare Fraud Enforcement in Canada*. Black Point, NS: Fernwood Publishing.

Morissette, René, and Xuelin Zhang. 2006. "Revisiting Wealth Inequality." *Perspectives on Labour and Income*, 7, 12.

Myles, John, and Garnett Picot. 2010. Neighbourhood Inequality in Canadian Cities. *Horizon*, 5, 1.

Ontario Association of Food Banks. 2008. *The Cost of Poverty: An Analysis of the Economic Cost of Poverty in Ontario*. Toronto, ON: Metcalf Foundation.

Ornstein, Michael. 2000. "Ethno-Racial Inequality in the City of Toronto: An Analysis of the 1996 Census." Access and Equity Unit, Strategic and Corporate Policy Division Chief Administrator's Office. <www1.toronto.ca/static_files/equity_diversity_and_human_rights_office/pdf/ornstein_fullreport.pdf>.

Parliament of Canada. 2010. *Federal Poverty Reduction Plan: Working in Partnership Towards Reducing Poverty in Canada*. Ottawa, ON: Report of the Standing Committee on Human Resources, Skills and Social Development and the Status of Persons with Disabilities. <parl.gc.ca/content/hoc/Committee/403/HUMA/Reports/RP4770921/humarp07/humarp07-e.pdf>.

pepso (Poverty and Employment Precarity in Southern Ontario). 2013. *It's More than Poverty: Employment Precarity and Household Wellbeing*. <pepsouwt.files.wordpress.com/2013/02/its-more-than-poverty-feb-2013.pdf>.

Philp, Margaret. 2000. "Poor? Coloured? Then It's No Vacancy." *Globe and Mail*, July 18. <theglobeandmail.com/news/national/poor-coloured-then-its-no-vacancy/article4166031/?page=all>.

Picot, Garnett, and Feng Hou. 2003. *The Rise in Low Income Rates Among Immigrants in Canada*. Ottawa, ON: Statistics Canada, Analytical Studies Branch Research

Paper Series.

Picot, Garnett, Feng Hou and Simon Coulombe. 2007. *Chronic Low Income and Low Income Dynamics Among Recent Immigrants*. Ottawa, ON: Statistics Canada, Business and Labour Market Analysis, Analytical Studies Branch Research Paper Series.

Qadeer, Mohammad and Sandeep Agrawal. 2009. "Ethnic Enclaves in the Toronto Area and Social Integration: The City as Common Ground. Toronto, ON. <metropolis.net/pdfs/Evolution%20of%20Ethnic%20Enclaves-Oct27.pdf>.

Reutter, Linda, Miriam J. Stewart, Gerry Veenstra, Rhonda Love, Dennis Raphael and Edward Makwarimba. 2009. "'Who Do They Think We Are, Anyway?': Perceptions of and Responses to Poverty Stigma." *Qualitative Health Research*, 19, 3.

Scott-Marshall, Heather, and Emile Tompa. 2011. "The Health Consequences of Precarious Employment Experiences." *Work: Journal of Prevention, Assessment and Rehabilitation*, 38, 4.

Shaw, Mary. 2007. "The Politics of Poverty: Why the Charter Does Not Protect Welfare Rights." *Appeal*, 12, 1.

Shelton, Jason E., and Anthony D. Greene. 2012. "Get Up, Get Out, and Git Sumthin': How Race and Class Influence African Americans' Attitudes about Inequality." *American Behavioral Scientist*, 56, 11.

Stanford, Jim, and Leah F. Vosko. 2004. *Challenging the Market: The Struggle to Regulate Work and Income*. Montreal, QC, and Kingston, ON: McGill-Queens University Press.

Statistics Canada. 2017. "Annual Report to Parliament on Immigration." Ottawa, ON: Government of Canada.

___. 2016. "Annual Report to Parliament on Immigration." Ottawa, ON: Government of Canada.

___. 2016. "Data Tables, 2016 Census; Visible Minority, Low-Income Status." <www12.statcan.gc.ca/census-recensement/2016/dp-pd/dt-td/Rp-eng.cfm?APATH=3&DETAIL=0&DIM=0&FL=A&FREE=0&GC=0&GID=0&GK=0&GRP=1&LANG=E&PID=110563&PRID=10&PTYPE=109445&S=0&SHOWALL=0&SUB=0&THEME=120&Temporal=2016&VID=0&VNAMEE=&VNAMEF=>.

___. 2015. "Aboriginal Statistics at a Glance, 2nd Edition." Catalogue 89-645-X. <statcan.gc.ca/pub/89-645-x/2015001/income-revenu-eng.htm>.

___. 2014. "Annual Report to Parliament on Immigration." Ottawa, ON: Government of Canada.

___. 2013. "Annual Report to Parliament on Immigration." Ottawa, ON: Government of Canada.

___. 2006. Census data.

___. 2001. Census data.

___. 1996. Census data.

Taylor, Leanne, Carl E. James and Roger Saul. 2007. "Who Belongs? Exploring Race and Racialization in Canada." In Genevieve Fuji Johnson and Randy Enomoto (eds.), *Race, Racialization and Anti-Racism in Canada and Beyond*. Toronto, ON: University of Toronto Press.

UNDP (United Nations Development Program). 1997. *Human Development Report, 1997*. New York: Oxford University Press. <hdr.undp.org/sites/default/files/reports/258/hdr_1997_en_complete_nostats.pdf>.

UNICEF. 2005. *Report Card No.6. Child Poverty in Rich Countries 2005: The Proportion of Children Living in Poverty Has Risen in a Majority of the World's Developed*

Economies. United Nations International Children's Emergency Fund (UNICEF) Innocenti Research Centre. <unicef-irc.org/publications/pdf/repcard6e.pdf>.

United Way of Greater Toronto. 2007. *Losing Ground: The Persistent Growth of Family Poverty in Canada's Largest City.* Toronto, ON: United Way of Greater Toronto. <urbancentre.utoronto.ca/pdfs/gtuo/UWGT-LosingGround-2007.pdf>.

Vosko, Leah F. 2005. "Precarious Employment: Towards an Improved Understanding of Labour Market Insecurity." In Leah H. Vosko (ed.), *Precarious Employment: Understanding Labour Market Insecurity in Canada.* Montreal, QC, and Kingston, ON: McGill-Queen's University Press.

Welsh, Brandon C., and David P. Farrington. 2005. "Evidence-Based Crime Prevention: Conclusions and Directions for a Safer Society." *Canadian Journal of Criminology and Criminal Justice,* 47, 2.

Yalnizyan, Armine. 2007. *The Rich and the Rest of Us: The Changing Face of Canada's Growing Gap.* Toronto, ON: Canadian Centre for Policy Alternatives. <policyalternatives.ca/sites/default/files/uploads/publications/National_Office_Pubs/2007/The_Rich_and_the_Rest_of_Us.pdf>.

___. 1998. "The Growing Gap: A Report on the Growing Income Inequality Between the Rich and Poor in Canada." Toronto, ON: Centre for Social Justice. <policyalternatives.ca/sites/default/files/uploads/publications/reports/docs/The%20Growing%20Gap%20-%20A%20report%20on%20growing%20inequality%20between%20rich%20and%20poor.pdf>.

Zeytinoglu, Isik Urla, and Jacinta Khasiala Muteshi. 2000. "Gender, Race and Class Dimensions of Nonstandard Work." *Industrial Relations,* 55, 1.

6

RACISM, MASCULINITY AND BELONGING
The Gendered Lives of Racialized Youth

Carl E. James

Recently (May 2016), I attended the seventh annual *Stand Up* conference for male students[1] in grades 7 and 8 at George Brown College in downtown Toronto. The conference slogan was "Redefining the colour of success" and that year's theme was "The power of believing in yourself" with the catch phrase, "Why not me!" Attending were about two hundred mostly racialized (about 80 percent) students from schools in the downtown, low-income areas of the Toronto District School Board. My letter of invitation to the conference was signed by vice-principal, Ainsworth Morgan (a friend and colleague), who conceived of the program with principal Gary Crossdale as they were both working in different schools in the downtown area. The letter reads,

> We believe that every young person deserves and has the ability to be successful. We know from data that young men of Colour are at risk in terms of meeting the Ontario standard at grades 7 and 8. Only 40% of students born in the English-speaking Caribbean and 45% of students born in East Africa achieve or exceed the provincial standard in all four subjects in grades 7 and 8. These young men represent one of the largest groups of students at risk of failing the grade 10 literacy test and graduating from high school. They can sometimes feel powerless to navigate the barriers to their success.
>
> As a response to the high number of young men of Colour underachieving in schools, The Toronto District School Board launched the inaugural Young Men Conference in May of 2010. The conference was a tremendous success!
>
> For students, the conference provided a very special opportunity to synthesize their learning and to meet successful men of Colour and hear directly from them about the challenges ahead and how

through hard work and education they can achieve their dreams … Students left the day expressing optimism and hope for their futures and were able to visualize a path to success as outlined by the men at the conference.

Through the nearly thirty Black male conference speakers and facilitators — most of them dressed in suits (mainly dark colours) and ties (a few in bowties)[2] — who work in careers such as teaching, banking, law, politics, policing, broadcasting, media, sports and social services, it was hoped that the students would be able to visualize the types of careers to which they might aspire or in which they might work.

The idea behind the conference is that, like us (Black male conference speakers and facilitators), these male youth would come to imagine that "success" is possible if they "believe in themselves." To drive home this point, the master of ceremonies talked to the students about having grown up in a marginalized community with a single mother but stressed that this did not prevent him from attaining the broadcasting career in which he now works. He attested to the importance of reading and how education can be a source of empowerment, and he encouraged them to "think big and not let anything stand in your way." He continued on to say, "You have the ability to attain your aspirations" and while "there's going to be bumps in the road — don't ever give up." From the keynote speaker, a former football player and manager, the youth heard how he too grew up in "the projects" in the United States with a single mother who "believed in him" and "stressed education." Calling two youth to come on the stage with him, he demonstrated that individuals start at different points when working toward the same goal. The two youth were told to run and get the twenty-dollar bill he held. One youth was asked to come forward about one to two feet, while the other — who had said he could run faster — was asked to stay back. Needless to say, when prompted, the youth who was closer to the finish line easily retrieved the money. The moral of the exercise was that they must pay attention to the differences, "have a focus" and take advantage of the opportunities available to them.

I reference this occasion with marginalized youth to demonstrate the efforts of educators and community members to change the narrative and imagery of Blacks — and Black men in particular — with the hope that these 13- and 14-year-old, marginalized and racialized Toronto youth would aspire to, and come to imagine themselves, achieving professional careers. While I have reservations about liberal-framed "role model" programs (see

James 2012a), I happily participate in this annual *Stand Up* conference (the last one was my fifth time). I see it as an opportunity to introduce young people to adult males who have managed to seize opportunities and attain careers in a variety of fields. The message I hope that the youth take from the event is not that one can simply go from a marginalized community with single mothers and/or absent or uninvolved fathers to the careers represented by the suited men at the conference. I hope that they learn — as I tried to communicate to the boys in two sessions I facilitated — that it does not only take high aspirations, hard work and passion for education to attain those careers; structures — as represented in policies, programs and opportunities — must also be in place to enable them to attain their aspirations. I see the conference as a scaffolding mechanism for the youth — that is, it helps nurture their optimism and hope so that they might hold on to a belief that, despite what they see around them, there are still possibilities for them to make it in this society. The *Stand Up* conference, then, can be seen as an opportunity structure in which "successful" men are not merely props or "evidence" but individuals whose stories tell of possibilities — about the social capital or assets that marginalized and racialized people possess that can be deployed in ways that will enable them to attain their occupational goals and effectively participate in society.

The objectives of this chapter are to:

- explore the ways in which racism and "hegemonic masculinity" (Connell and Messerschmidt 2005) operate to limit the opportunities of racialized youth;
- understand the differentiated experiences of racialized youth within the context of inequitable social and economic systems; and
- appreciate that the disadvantages experienced by racialized youth might be addressed through programs that inspire young people's optimism, hope and efforts.

In addition to these objectives, the chapter concludes by submitting that the situation and experiences of racialized youth can be enhanced by their critical knowledge of and attention to the structural factors that enable or limit their participation and attainment in society. As such, they need to engage in activities and programs that build on and inspire their youthful effort, energy, optimism, hope and entitlement in the face of the structural factors that conspire to limit them.

Critical Consideration of Multiculturalism, Masculinities and Race Theories

In Canada, the 1971 Multicultural Policy, which became the *Multiculturalism Act* in 1988, claims that Canadians of any cultural group are free to maintain and practise "their culture" — negating the dynamism, variability and changing nature of culture. And as a number of scholars have argued, Canadian *multiculturalism* promotes a discourse of difference ascribed to individuals considered foreign (Sensoy et al. 2010; James 2012a; Kaur 2014). It is a difference that is tolerated, for it is, as Loveleen Kaur (2014: 72) writes, "something one would prefer did not exist and requires a constant managing of the presence of this undesirable thing ... [and] an unspoken understanding that the 'Other' will not interfere with the functioning of the status quo." Further, Canadian multiculturalism takes diversity to be what Ozlem Sensoy and colleagues (2010: 2) describe as "a superficial, additive study of culture and culturally rooted differences and inequities." It focuses on *celebration,* which, as Sarita Srivastava describes, takes the form of a "3–D approach" — "dance, dress, and dining," and in so doing "fails to take into account the multiple dimensions of racial and social inequality" (cited in Sensoy et al. 2010: 1). This state-sponsored additive approach to recognizing and preserving the "multicultural heritage" of Canadians, in practice, serves to maintain the myth of two founding nations and adds, rather than integrates, the contributions of other ethnoracial groups "to the 'main story'" (Sensoy et al. 2010: 4).

Premised on ethnic culture — where ethnicity is conflated with race and foreignness — Canadian multiculturalism fosters a perception of culture as a set of ideas, values, morals and behaviours that individuals inherit from their affinity groups and maintain over the years — even though their group might have resided in Canada for generations. The claim is that these groups have been able — as the *Multiculturalism Act* asserts — "to keep their culture" (James 2010). And their differences — cuisine, dress, language, accent, recreational preferences and religious practices — are attributed to the culture that their ancestors bring to Canada. Interestingly, English and French Canadians are not similarly assigned cultural attributes from away. They tend to be considered "Canadians" with Canadian cultures and accents that are accepted as the norm. It is against these accepted norms that "Others" are judged as different — people with "other" cultures and accents. And since "visibility" or "observable" behaviours and practices (pertaining to such things as language, accent and religion) enable easy identification of those with culture, race has become a principal signifier of those with culture — the "Others." Whiteness, therefore, remains the norm against which "Others" are measured. This process is also a form of racialization — a term that is discussed later.

This racial discourse has to do with the supremacy of *Whiteness*, which is less about "White people" representing "a socially constructed identity, usually based on skin color" (Leonardo 2009: 278), and more about how Whiteness operates as an invisible marker "asserting its normalcy, its transparency, in contrast with the marking of others on which its transparency depends" (Frankenberg 1997: 6). Scholars such as Robin DiAngelo (2011) and Ruth Frankenberg (1997) proffer that Whiteness seeks to disavow its particular social, historical and political structures while simultaneously bolstering its "taken-for-granted" constructions as universal (see also Wadham 2004).

It is within this sociopolitical and cultural context that patriarchy as an ideology operates to structure masculinity and the gender norms, values and mores of society into which men (and women) are socialized and by which they are expected to live. *Masculinity* transmits, as Mike Leach (1994: 36) writes, "a set of cultural ideals that define appropriate roles, values and expectations for and of men" that, over time, become part of their cultural practices and behaviours. Indeed, as Leach contends, masculinity "is the cultural interpretation of maleness, learnt through participation in society and its institutions." Hence, as residents of the society and participants in its institutions, minoritized and racialized males (and females) cannot escape the hegemony or power of masculinity — particularly as it is informed by Whiteness — that serves to legitimize the structures of social inequity and sustain the oppressive relationship between men and women, as well as White men and racialized men.

Scholars refer to this male ethos and its practices as "*hegemonic masculinity*," a social category in which "the dominance of white heterosexual masculinity is maintained and reproduced" (Leach 1994: 36). Most boys and men seek to perform hegemonic masculinity — specifically, the repudiation of things seen as feminine, while they strive to be daring, fearless, aggressive, successful and powerful (Kimmel 2008: 45–46) — but few are ever successful at doing so. Carolyn Jackson and Steven Dempster (2009: 342) proffer that hegemonic masculinity is an

> idealised form of masculinity which very few boys or men can ever attain ... Nevertheless, it is a standard against which boys and men

measure their manliness, and it influences their understandings of how they need to act in order to be "acceptably" male. Masculinity is a relational construct — which only exists in a contrasting relationship to femininity — being "unacceptable" or "insufficiently" masculine is equated with being "too feminine." So hegemonic masculinity is constructed in *opposition* to femininity, and also to other "subordinate" forms of masculinity. (emphasis in the original)

Accompanying this masculine–feminine binary — with its sets of behaviours, traits and social roles — is the cultural pressure "on males to be masculine in traits and heterosexual in orientation or else be viewed as feminine and socially unacceptable" (Theodore and Basow 2000: 31; see also McCready 2010). Boys and men — notably those who are racialized, immigrant and non–gender conforming — who fail to meet expectations or are unable to mask their inability to perform hegemonic masculinity, are thought to practise a form of *subordinate masculinity*. The fact is, there is a hierarchy to masculinities; nevertheless, masculinities are not fixed entities and they have not maintained a particular or consistent body of personality traits over time. Albeit, Ken Dolan-Del Vecchio (1998: 164) asserts that "oppressions experienced by men of colour create different dilemmas centered around masculinity for [their] group."

An incriminating consequence of the binary structured by masculinity, and the tendency to see it as a fixed entity, means that boys and men — particularly those seen as performing subordinate masculinity — will adopt survival behaviours to ensure their well-being and resist the alienation and violence inherent in hegemonic masculinity. Indeed, scholars submit that there is a link between boys' and men's violent behaviours (especially toward girls and women) and their social marginalization and historical suppression (Messerschmidt 2000; Groes-Green 2009). According to James Messerschmidt (2000), in addition to competitive individualism and aggressiveness, men generally perceive violence as an appropriate reference for constructing their masculinity that allows them to mediate their relationships with other people. To them, violence — which, over time, becomes normalized — is thought of as a "masculine resource" that serves in their affirmation and shields their vulnerabilities. In some cases, and in some contexts, men's orientation to aggression and violence as a form of their masculinity is connected to their responsibility to provide for (i.e., being the "breadwinner") and "protect" their families (see Groes-Green 2009; Hope 2010).

R.W. Connell and James Messerschmidt (2005: 847–48) also write of *"protest masculinity"* which they define as

> a pattern of masculinity constructed in local working-class settings, sometimes among ethnically marginalized men, which embodies the claim to power typical of regional [or area-specific] hegemonic masculinities in Western countries, but which lacks the economic resources and institutional authority that underpins the regional and global patterns.

With reference to Connell's discussion of protest masculinity, Heather Frost writes that, for some men, it is

> a means for confronting and challenging their powerlessness and exclusion using their limited resources, resorting to excessively macho behaviors and hypermasculine practices including violence, criminal activity and drug and/or alcohol abuse. In this way, protest masculinity amounts to a "frenzied and showy" performance ultimately resembling "a cul-de-sac" leading nowhere. (cited in Frost 2010: 221)

Whether racialized individuals' or groups' responses to their racialization and related marginalization or stigmatization are able to effectively counter the hegemony of Western White masculinity is not clear. Nevertheless, as Connell and Messerschmidt (2005: 848) also mention, because of the hegemony of dominant White masculinity, its ethos and practices are likely to be incorporated into "functioning" gender practices by minoritized and/or racialized males, or people generally, rather than being discredited by them.

Relatedly, in a society where race matters, experiences with masculinities and the ways in which they are understood and performed by racialized boys and men are informed by the prevailing meaning and significance ascribed to particular physical characteristics or differences. In other words, *racialization* — "the process of categorization through which social relations between people [are] structured by the signification of human biological characteristics in such a way as to define and construct differentiated social collectivities" (Miles 1989: 75) — plays a critical role in mediating the lives of racialized men and boys. And racialization is inherent in the cultural ideology that is produced and reproduced through institutional policies and practices that support particular constructions of "difference" (James

2010), including that which is particular to maleness and masculinity (such as Black males commonly being constructed as athletes). But compliance with, or conformity to, the prevailing notions of masculinity by racialized people — for example, Black, Asian, South Asian and Filipino — is not assured; individuals do exercise agency in varying ways and in relation to the context and issues they might encounter or with which they are expected to live. But in exercising their agency, individuals might adapt accordingly, critically engage or resist the norms to which they are subjected.

Central to my discussion of racialization is the role of racial inequity, which is sustained by racism in today's sociocultural context where claims of democracy, meritocracy and multiculturalism (premised on colourblindness) mask racial inequity's impact on the lives of racialized people. Critical race theorists such as David Gillborn (2015: 278) assert that "the majority of racism remains hidden beneath a veneer of normality and it is only the more crude and obvious forms of racism that are seen as problematic by most people." Therefore, if we are to effectively address the attendant concerns, issues and problems faced by racialized men and boys, doing so from the perspective of *critical race theory* (CRT) allows analyses in which race — recognized as a social construct — is "the point of departure for critique, not the end of it" (Leonardo 2005: xi). CRT gives attention to *intersectionality*,

> a concept that enables us to recognize the fact that perceived group membership can make people vulnerable to various forms of bias, yet because we are simultaneously members of many groups, our complex identities can shape the specific way we each experience that bias. (Gillborn 2015: 278)

Therefore, while CRT recognizes the intersectional relationship of various identity markers (e.g., gender, race, ethnicity, language or sexuality), and how together they might interact to produce oppression, it nevertheless insists on privileging race, and by extension "the primacy of racism," as a starting point for examination, since the apparatus of White supremacy has historically operated "to create and maintain the subordination of racialized people" (Gillborn 2015: 284) and resist the tendency to obviate the legitimacy of race as a major or central factor in individuals' oppression.[3] For this reason, unlike anti-oppression theory, which seeks to address the issues and concerns of all "oppressed" groups, CRT promotes examination that identifies the specific ways racial group members are oppressed. Predicated on this paradigm, *anti-Black racism* (ABR), for instance, "promotes examination of the specificity of Black people's experiences with racism — cognizant of the contextual realities of race as it intersects with gender, class, sexuality, citizenship and other identity markers" (James 2018).

Theorists of anti-colonialism, anti-racism, CRT and feminism serve as key references for ABR, which centres the lived experiences of Black individuals and their relationship to Whiteness. ABR explores the agency Black people exercise in fostering and maintaining optimism and hope in the face of doubts about their Canadianness — a notion that is sustained by the prevailing multicultural discourse (James 2018). ABR gives attention to the ways in which Black people negotiate the structural barriers and hurdles of inequity and racism (including stereotypes) through commitment to hard work, proving that they are law-abiding citizens, having culturally diverse friendships, demonstrating that they are friendly (for example, smiling a lot), becoming politically involved (even participating in student government) and being "better than" their White peers. Writers refer to the extra work or responsibilities that Black individuals take on to do these things as the "*Black tax*" (Ulysse 2015/17) or "*race tax*" (Rockquemore and Laszloffy 2008). Notwithstanding the particular experiences of Blacks, other racialized groups are similarly burdened with the "race tax" with the consequence that, if they engage in resistive actions and insist on their rights and entitlement like all other citizens, chances are they will be perceived as aggressive, divisive, anti-social and oppositional — the very stereotypes that they seek to eschew, especially as males.

Masculinity, Racialization and the Experiences of Racialized Young Men

Let us return to the boys who attended the *Stand Up* conference. I conducted two sessions with about eight youth in each. After I introduced myself — telling them of my background (including that I was born in the Caribbean) and that I teach teachers at a university — I asked them to tell me about themselves and how they felt about attending an exclusively male conference. Of the sixteen youth only two were first-generation (born elsewhere) Canadians and the others were second- and third-generation Canadians — altogether, they were of South Asian, Caribbean, Middle Eastern and Eastern European descent. The youth felt that being able to converse with adult males and their peers provided them the opportunity to "hear things that you understand," "hear from different boys" and "feel important." What these grades 7 and 8 students had to say about schooling and education was consistent with the message they had earlier received from the speakers at the opening session; they went on to reference similar encouragement they received from their "strict" (for some of them) parents, such as "concentrate on education," "[education] is best for me," "behave and get good grades," and "you must study, study, study." They seemed to get the message from their parents that "to get things [i.e., succeed], you have to maintain good grades," and, as one youth explained, "my parents want me to be happy [in] what I want to do." But despite the message about education and grades, there was also a critical insight offered by one boy: "Grades do not define you."

There was also mention of the social and cultural contexts in which these youth were growing up. From their observation of the practices among youth in the society generally (i.e., White youth), these boys claimed that "kids today are spoilt"; they "are drifting, [and they] need focus"; and they reasoned that some of this has to do with the fact that "Now, parents allow things to go too easy." They went on to say that youth "need" parental support as they try "to find the right path" in life.

Generally, the youth conceded that gender played a role in their experiences, as well as their parents' and teachers' responses to and expectations of them. Few believed that "guys have it easier" than girls, whom they believed "mature faster than boys." But most of them felt that boys had "more responsibility" than girls. The evidence for one boy was that "my parents expect more from me than my sister." Also supporting their reading of the differences between boys and girls were teachers' behaviours toward the girls. They reported that teachers were "more lenient with the girls," gave girls "more one-on-one time" and judged boys "more harshly than girls." The boys reasoned that the attention and leniency the girls received at school, and their tendency to be "less engaged in physical activities," made it possible for girls to "do better than boys. It is not that boys aren't as smart, it's just that they need more" from their teachers. Additionally, they talked about the effects of race on their schooling life. According to one boy, "Being the only racialized person in your class affects you."

These boys understood gender and race as influencing expectations of them and the treatment they received from their parents, teachers and members of the society generally. They were clear that racism and prejudice based on gender had significant effects on their social and educational circumstances. For this reason, they seemed to think that racialized youth, especially young men like them, do not have the luxury of being spoilt or drifting, or of having parents who go easy on them. This thinking seems to be related to how they internalized the messages they received from their parents: that they must behave well, concentrate on their education and maintain a commitment to their parents and community. For example, one student indicated that he wants "to become a police officer [because] I want to help my community." So, despite mentioning how "strict" their parents were (indeed, it might have been a complaint), these youth ostensibly understood that the strictness of their parents was in their interest and a product of their cultural backgrounds.

It is not surprising that the young students, in the one-hour discussions I facilitated, would come to construct their masculinity in relation to girls in that, as boys, they perceived themselves as having more responsibility, being judged more harshly and being more physical. They seemed to understand their parents' and the conference presenters' claims about the promise and potential of education. Education, then, was packaged to them as the means by which they would succeed in Canadian society, resist or contest racism and obtain respect for their "difference."

Did they accept these claims? Were these mentorship occasions merely to train them or reinforce the belief that having the "right" attitude, deportment/demeanour and aspirations (as modelled by suit-and-tie-wearing Black men) would work for them? Frankly, I am not sure what the youth made of these occasions; we did not have time to discuss this. But it is fair to suggest that, whatever the limitations, these occasions offer rare opportunities for young people, with the guidance and support of adults, to critically reflect on their situation and hopefully develop tools with which they might challenge the prevailing constructs of masculinity and become assured in their differences. It is possible that, in encouraging young people to become educated, the conference organizers, participating men (the "role models") and parents are cultivating the development of a masculinity in which education could be used to resist racialization, as a means of exercising agency or a form of protest masculinity. In other words, in the absence of other effective means of counteracting their racialization and marginalization, which in some cases serve as sources of motivation, racialized people use education as a requirement toward attaining respectable careers, satisfactory employment and creditable social standing in society (as evidenced by the professional Black men). They hold onto these notions even as they acknowledge the existence of inequities, racism and discrimination, which call into question claims of merit.

In the case of Black youth, numerous scholars have written of how schooling has failed to provide them the education needed for their effective participation and success in society (James 2009, 2012b; Dei and Kempf

2013; Tecle and James 2014). As I have written elsewhere, Black male students tend to be constructed or stereotyped as "immigrants, fatherless, athletes, troublemakers and underachievers," and as such are considered to be "at risk" — a label that contributes "to their racialization and marginalization that in turn structure their learning processes, social opportunities, life chances, and educational outcomes" (James 2012a: 465). Essentially,

> the cultural context of schooling, with its Eurocentric curriculum, homogeneity in its approach to the teaching/learning process, and reliance on culturally inappropriate assessments, functions as an incubator of the stereotyping that takes place. So the idea that schools operate on principles of cultural freedom (or multiculturalism), democracy, merit, racial neutrality (or colour blindness) and equality of opportunity is not borne out in the experiences of Black male students whose experiences in schools are affected by constructions of Black masculinities that are linked to fatherlessness, hopelessness, deviance, low expectations, and poor academic performance. (James 2012a: 484–85)

The web of stereotypes, which operates to disadvantage Black youth in schools, social services and society generally, is sustained by the discourses of hegemonic masculinity and neoliberal multiculturalism that mask the ways in which racism and racialization function to structure their lives and limit their social, educational, economic and political opportunities, possibilities and trajectories.

For Asian and South Asian young men, the "*model minority*" construct or stereotype is a trope that affects their education and their social and cultural lives. The problematic "model minority" concept is differentially used to position Asians and South Asians as exemplars. They are constructed as models for other racialized or minoritized group members to aspire to "be like," particularly in terms of "fitting into" society by adopting its prevailing norms, values and behaviours (see Pon 2000; Cui and Kelly 2012; Mahalingam 2012; Johal 2014). From their study of Chinese Canadian male and female youth in Edmonton, Alberta, Dan Cui and Jennifer Kelly (2012: 86) observe that, within their culturally heterogeneous group of respondents, who did not share the same "academic aspirations, or resources to facilitate their academic success," Chinese Canadian students were usually "stereotyped as model minorities and rendered invisible in identity debates. Their struggle with stereotypical representations in the media, or their daily lives in school and family, are typically ignored or overshadowed by an emphasis on academic achievements" while in fact, as the authors reveal, their Chinese Canadian research participants did not lack interest in social activities and sports.

Similarly, in arguing about the limits to the "model minority" stereotype, Gordon Pon (2000: 223) contends that, "at first glance this stereotype does not seem all that bad. Indeed, it even seems positive compared to the prevalent stereotypes of Blacks and Natives ... However, it is often quite harmful." He goes on to relate occasions in which teachers expected him and other Chinese students to be "smart," get good grades in math and be compliant students. And in his case, teachers did not believe that his English essays were written by him. Stereotyping, Pon (2000: 244) surmises, "places limits on what is expected of [Chinese people] and inhibits an understanding of the complex differences among the members of that group." Understandably, Pon shows that male high school peers did unwittingly or deliberately engage in activities that resisted or challenged the "model minority" trope. For instance, Pon recalls that one of his peers in junior high school took it to be a joke that teachers would think that they were "superior" at math when they knew they were not. One student probably, as Pon (2000: 232) writes, being "tired" of the teacher's essentialization of them, or "maybe just sick of math, became a chronic skipper of the class."

Similarly, in her study of Punjabi young men living in Surrey, British Columbia, Frost (2010: 206) observed that, while education was generally valued within the community, and

> its young people are encouraged to do well in high school and go on to receive post-secondary credentials, for certain young men who are unable or unmotivated to attend college or university, the gang or criminal lifestyle is appealing in that it represents an alternative mobility strategy and a means for earning the community's respect. (see also Sumartojo 2012)

Frost (2010: 221) highlights that the Punjabi teenage boys' conceptions of masculinity was constructed and contextualized within three competing versions of masculinity: "their father's first generation Punjabi version; the White variety of their peers; and the Surrey Jack, a form of protest masculinity constructed by other Punjabi young men." While rejecting, or distancing themselves from what they perceived to be their parents' version of masculinity (by doing things like drinking alcohol), participants (especially the males) commonly used the term "Brown" to refer to themselves, as opposed to other ethnocultural categorizations such as Canadian,

Indo-Canadian, Punjabi or South Asian. For them, the self-referential term "Brown" apparently served as a "middle ground" between their fathers' version of masculinity and that of their White peers. Frost's respondents also thought of "themselves as 'slackers,' who don't try very hard in school but are more 'manly' and popular with [White] girls" (223), as well as, in the words of one respondent, "more athletic [and] confident" (226). And in distancing themselves from the media portrayal of the Surrey Jack as "gang" members, they claimed that those other "Brown guys" were mainly groups of friends who do and "say stupid things" (222).

What might be gleaned from these "getting-by" high school students is a way of being male and performing maleness that seeks to challenge White male supremacy and normative masculinity. Nevertheless, the hegemony of masculinity as framed by Whiteness remains. For while these Brown young men might claim White masculinity to be subordinate to Brown masculinity, their ideas and behaviours re-inscribe White ideals, as well as traditional and universal constructs of masculinity, such as the female–male binary, physical and sexual prowess and White women's attraction to them. It is difficult to conclude the extent to which the actions or responses of these youth can be considered a form of protest masculinity but, as Frost notes, the racialized masculinities of South Asian youth in Surrey were in reaction to readings of their raced bodies in and relation to that of their White peers.

In "Asian and White Boys' Competing Discourses about Masculinity," Athena Wang (2000) established that, in addition to gender, culture and race played a significant role in how boys negotiated hegemonic masculinities. From her interviews with Asian and White male students at two high schools in British Columbia, she found that the boys simultaneously conformed to and resisted hegemonic masculinity. For instance, when asked to describe "What image comes to your mind when you hear the word 'masculine' or 'masculinity?'" both the Asian and White male students referenced the physical build and strength of men. For instance, one respondent said, "big beefy guy ... who has a lot of self-respect, is fairly big in size ... and also a lot of what society thinks ... all the girls like him. He's big. He has muscles. He's athletic." Another stated, "Some big-ass guy, just harsh-ribbed, like huge biceps, 6 pack [with very well-defined abdominal muscles] ... that's masculinity" (Wang 2000: 116). However, the responses began to diverge noting the differences between Asian and White male students. One Asian student indicated that in Asian cultures masculinity is also defined and measured by familial responsibility, noting that the personality of a Chinese guy is to basically keep face, I think. I've heard [it] lots of times. Like if the Chinese man was like to lose his business, he loses face basically ... he loses his status in society. (Wang 2000: 116–17)

Wang (2000: 117) explains that, within Asian cultures, face-saving "is central to Asian cultures and not only achieved by a man's social status but also expressed in his quiet demeanour." So, the popular Western notion of men being physical and aggressive, which the youth articulated as masculine, is contrary to Asian men's quiet, nurturing, face-saving demeanour, which, according to Wang (2000: 117), results in a racialized masculinity that is perceived as "effeminate and passive, and thus unmanly."

Recall Michael Kimmel's (2008) assertion that masculinity is structured on the rejection of feminine qualities and being strong, aggressive and fearless (see also Jackson and Dempster 2009). But for many racialized young and adult men, these "masculine" characteristics have become things that are used to racially profile them, and as a consequence they are placed under surveillance of police, customs officers and other correction agents. In the case of Sikh males, Kaur (2014: 69) writes that, following 9/11, there have been recurring Canadian images of Sikh men as "extremists, militants and terrorists" — people who "carry a sword" and "dress like warriors" (Kaur 2014: 74). In contrast with the "model minority" construct discussed above, Sikh males do not enjoy the same privileges with their religious symbols as do Christians. As Kaur (2014: 77) suggests, Sikhs in Canada

> are regularly lauded as a "model minority" and are regularly courted during election season. It is then not surprising that members of the Sikh community expressed great disbelief when the media, government officials and the general public were so quick to place a negative marker on them.

Indeed, as Máirtín Mac an Ghaill and Chris Haywood (2014) point out in their study of British South Asian males, the legacy of *Orientalism* — the tendency to essentialize and hold inferior Asian cultures — equally impacts upon how Sikh bodies are read and constructed.

That South Asians and all other racialized bodies (except those of Indigenous Peoples) are read as foreign means that the "aggressive practices" of racialized males will get attributed to their foreign origin — even though they are second- or third-generation Canadadian-born. Similar to Sikhs, and particularly significant, is the racial profiling of Arabs and Muslims since 9/11 and the heightened racialization of minority religious groups since then. In fact, Reem Bahdi (2016: 1) states that "social science literature and reports by community organizations conclusively demonstrate that Arabs and Muslims face stereotyping and discrimination post-9/11, despite Canada's commitment to equality." Noting that they are stereotyped as "violent bombers and terrorists," Bahdi (2016: 6) continues to point out how Arabs and Muslims are imaged as "dangerous precisely because they cannot be predicted, trusted or civilized." In reflecting on the effects of racial profiling on her sons, one Pakistani mother in Vancouver stated that the fact that her Canadian-born-and-raised sons "had Muslims names and they 'looked Muslim and/or Pakistani' took precedence over their rights as citizens ... She believed that citizenship was not protective enough for them as Muslims in the face of government scrutiny and profiling" (Jamil 2016: 2). Black men are also racially profiled. We have already cited that Black young men are profiled as troublemakers, among other characteristics. The *Toronto Star* reporter Jim Rankin (2010) has shown that, based on street checks, Black males aged 15–24 were stopped and documented two and a half times more often than White males of the same age (cited in Tardiel 2016). Such profiling and surveillance affects the social, psychological and educational well-being of these youth, including their sense of belonging as Canadians; hence, it will be incorporated into their construction of masculinity and how they perform that masculinity.

Beyond Multiculturalism

In a society where race matters, racialized people will share many similar experiences and conditions, particularly with regard to their respective ethnic backgrounds and related histories — including their group migration to and settlement in Canada. As such, racialized men and boys must navigate and negotiate the economic, social, political and cultural structures that have significant psychological effects on their relations to the state, their family members and other socializing agents. Critical theorists maintain that understanding the experiences, positional status and social situation of racialized men and boys necessarily requires attention to how, historically and contemporarily, inequity, colonialism and racism — and the by-products of hegemonic masculinity — have operated in these males' racialization processes to affect their lives. This understanding of their racialization has helped to drive attempts by parents, community leaders, educators and social service workers to obviate and/or interrupt its impact.

But to what extent can mentorship efforts, confidence in the promise of education, strategies of resistance and political mobilizing actions help? Whatever we do to address the situation of racialized men and youth must include examining and eradicating the forces that keep the structures of racism and racialization in place. This means providing education and other supportive programs that focus on the structures of inequity, colonialism, racism, patriarchy and hegemonic masculinity.

Mentorship programs — like the *Stand Up* conference — as well as education and teaching pursuits, social and youth services and extracurricular activities are most beneficial to the well-being of individuals if they also understand that it is not only their individual efforts that are responsible for their achievements, or lack thereof. Importantly, it is also how the social, economic and political structures — evidenced in legislation, policies, rules, regulations, procedures and related practices — operate to enable and allow their participation in society and the outcomes they seek. For racialized males, it is necessary to understand how patriarchy structures their masculine values, norms, customs and performance; learn ways to navigate the structures; read what is possible; construct aspirations; and develop an ethos of masculinity that resists the patriarchal system of marginalization and racialization. This means contesting the "truths" about maleness or the predisposition to a particular masculine performance (thinking, for example, that Black boys are troublemakers) with which individuals have lived for most of their lives and have been passed from generation to generation. These "truths," enshrined in laws, policies, rules, education and other sources, are passed on through significant others, authority figures and peers. Furthermore, immersed in prevailing neoliberal capitalist culture, it is often difficult to imagine or conceive of — or put in place — alternative constructs and possibilities of life in the society. Even in resisting the existing structures and racialization, we sometimes unwittingly replace existing ideas, values, norms and behaviours with others that, on the surface, might appear different but with closer examination are some version of that which we seek to change. This is so, in part, because the existing structure remains unaltered or untouched.

In the case of racialized youth, what is needed is ongoing reflection and learning processes by which individuals — males as well as females — come to terms with the complexities, relationalities, dynamism, variability and contextuality of culture, particularly the prevailing societal patriarchal culture of masculinity, which is equally as perilous to males as it is to females. The middle school male students at the conference — and all other young men grappling with similar situations, experiences and expectations in life as racialized individuals — need to know that it is not merely about the credentials, careers, occupations or social status of the "accomplished" men they encounter. Like us, their aspirations, achievements and exercise of agency are constantly mediated by the social, cultural, economic and political structures they encounter daily. In the face of these encounters, therefore, our work with young people is to help them develop ways in which they can hold onto their youthful optimism and hope while confronting the structural factors that so many of them frequently resist. And resist they must.

DISCUSSION QUESTIONS

1. What images come to mind when you hear the word masculinity with reference to racialized men — such as African Canadians, South Asians, Asians, Filipinos, Latino and others? How might these images inform the ways members of these groups are taken up or dealt with in the society?
2. To what extent can mentorship efforts, confidence in the promise of education, and political actions serve to address the situation of racialized men and youth and enable them to "make it" in Canadian society? What structures must be addressed or eliminated if racialized individuals are to "make it" in the society?
3. The word "visible minority" is a uniquely Canadian word. What are its limitations?

ACTION STEPS

1. Engage in conversations with the parents of racialized youth to gain a deeper understanding of the experiences of these youth in the education system.
2. Attend community events such as the annual *Stand Up* conference to get a stronger understanding of issues affecting racialized male students.

Supplemental Readings

Connell, R.W., and James W. Messerschmidt. 2005. "Hegemonic Masculinity: Rethinking the Concept." *Gender and Society,* 19, 6.
McCready, Lance. 2010. *Making Space for Diverse Masculinities: Difference, Intersectionality, and Engagement in an Urban High School.* New York: Peter Lang Publishing.
Wang, Athena. 2000. "Asian and White Boys' Competing Discourses about

Masculinity: Implications for Secondary Education." *Canadian Journal of Education,* 25, 2.

Additional Resources
100 Strong Foundation <100strong.ca/stand-up/>.
Canadian Civil Liberties Association <ccla.org/thinking-about-racial-profiling-and-carding-in-canada/>.

Notes
1. The focus on middle-school students, especially boys, has to do with the fact that students are increasingly being transferred, rather than promoted, from grade 8 to grade 9. And research shows that transferred students are more likely to drop out, underachieve and perform poorly in high school (Parekh and Brown 2013).
2. There were two police officers in uniform. One was the DJ playing music that might be familiar to the students on the big sound system.
3. Indeed, as Preston and Bhopal (2012: 214) write, "Many of us have been faced with the question 'What about class/gender/sexuality/disability/faith?' whereas rarely are speakers on these topics ever asked, 'What about "race?"'" A focus on 'race' in analysis is indicative, for some academics, as a sign of pathology or suspicion."

References
Bahdi, Reem. 2016. "Restricted Access, Limited Justice: Arab and Muslim Human Rights Claims Before the Canadian Human Rights Tribunals, 2002–2015." Racial Profiling Policy Dialogue, Ontario Human Right Commission. Toronto, ON: York University.

Connell, R.W., and James W. Messerschmidt. 2005. "Hegemonic Masculinity: Rethinking the Concept." *Gender and Society,* 19, 6.

Cui, Dan, and Jennifer Kelly. 2012. "Ruling through Discourse: The Experience of Chinese-Canadian Youth." In R.J. Gilmour, D. Bhandar, J. Heer and M.C.K. Ma (eds.), *"Too Asian?": Racism, Privilege, and Post-Secondary Education.* Toronto, ON: Between the Lines.

Dei, George J. Sefa, and Arlo Kempf. 2013. *New Perspectives on African-Centred Education in Canada.* Toronto, ON: Canadian Scholars' Press.

DiAngelo, Robin. 2011. "White Fragility." *International Journal of Critical Pedagogy,* 3, 3.

Frankenberg, Ruth. 1997. *Displacing Whiteness: Essays in Social and Cultural Criticism.* Durham, England, UK: Duke University Press.

Frost, Heather. 2010. "Being 'Brown' in a Canadian Suburb." *Journal of Immigrant and Refugee Studies,* 8, 2.

Gillborn, David. 2015. "Intersectionality, Critical Race Theory, and the Primacy of Racism: Race, Class, Gender, and Disability in Education." *Qualitative Inquiry,* 21, 3.

Groes-Green, Christian. 2009. "Hegemonic and Subordinated Masculinities: Class, Violence and Sexual Performance among Young Mozambican Men." *Nordic Journal of African Studies,* 18, 4.

Hope, Donna P. 2010. *Man Vibes: Masculinities in the Jamaican Dancehall.* Kingston. JA: Ian Randle Publishers.

Jackson, Carolyn, and Steven Dempster. 2009. "'I Sat Back on my Computer …
with a Bottle of Whisky Next to Me': Constructing 'Cool' Masculinity through
'Effortless' Achievement in Secondary and Higher Education." *Journal of Gender
Studies, Special Issue: Men and Masculinities*, 18, 4.

James, C.E. 2018. "Race, Racialization and Canadian Children of Immigrant Parents."
In S. Wilson-Forsberg and A. Robinson (eds.), *Immigrant Youth in Canada*.
Toronto, ON: Oxford University Press.

___. 2012a. "Troubling Role Models: Seeing Racialization in the Discourse Relating
to 'Corrective Agents' for Black Males." In Kenneth James Moffat (ed.), *Troubled
Masculinities: Reimagining Urban Men*. Toronto, ON: University of Toronto Press.

___. 2012b. "Students at Risk: Stereotyping and the Schooling of Black Boys." *Urban
Education*, 47, 2.

___. 2010. *Seeing Ourselves: Exploring Race, Ethnicity and Culture*. Toronto, ON:
Thompson Educational Publishing.

___. 2009. "Masculinity, Racialization and Schooling: The Making of Marginalized
Men." In W. Martino, W. Kehler and Marcus Weaver-Hightower (eds.), *The
Problem with Boys' Education: Beyond the Backlash*. New York: Routledge.

Jamil, Uzma. 2016. "Muslim Suspects: Racial Profiling and Securitization." Racial
Profiling Policy Dialogue, Ontario Human Right Commission. Toronto, ON:
York University.

Johal, Ravinder. 2014. "Contradictions and Challenges: Second Generation Sikh Males
in Canada." Unpublished PhD dissertation, Graduate Program in Education, York
University, Toronto, ON.

Kaur, Loveleen. 2014. "The Tear in the Fabric of Multiculturalism." *Sikh Formations:
Religion, Culture, Theory*, 10, 1.

Kimmel, Michael. 2008. *Guyland: The Perilous World Where Boys Become Men*. New
York: HarperCollins.

Leach, Mike. 1994. "The Politics of Masculinity: An Overview of Contemporary
Theory." *Social Alternatives*, 12, 4.

Leonardo, Zeuz. 2009. *Race, Whiteness, and Education*. New York: Routledge.

___. 2005. "Foreword." In Z. Leonardo (ed.), *Critical Pedagogy and Race*. Oxford,
UK: Blackwell.

Mac an Ghaill, Máirtín, and Chris Haywood. 2014. "Pakistani and Bangladeshi Young
Men: Re-Racialization, Class and Masculinity within the Neo-Liberal School."
British Journal of Sociology of Education, 35, 5.

Mahalingam, Ram. 2012. "Engendering Model Minority Myth and Psychological
Well-Being of Asian Americans." In E. Grigorinko (ed.), *Handbook of U.S.
Immigrant and Education*. New York: Springer.

McCready, Lance. 2010. *Making Space for Diverse Masculinities: Difference,
Intersectionality, and Engagement in an Urban High School*. New York: Peter
Lang Publishing.

Messerschmidt, James W. 2000. *Nine Lives: Adolescent Masculinities, the Body, and
Violence*. Boulder, CO: Westview Press.

Miles, Robert. 1989. *Racism*. New York: Routledge.

Parekh, Gillian, and Robert Brown. 2013. "Structured Pathways: An Exploration of
Programs of Study, School-Wide and In-School Programs, as well as Promotion
and Transference across Secondary Schools in the Toronto District School Board."
Research and Information Services, Toronto District School Board, Report No.
13/14-03.

Pon, Gordon. 2000. "Importing the Asian Model Minority Discourse into Canada: Implications for Social Work and Education." *Canadian Social Work Review,* 17, 2.

Preston, John, and Kalwant Bhopal. 2012. "Conclusion: Intersectional Theories and 'Race': From Toolkit to "Mash-Up." In K. Bhopal and J. Preston (eds.), *Intersectionality and "Race" in Education.* London, UK: Routedge.

Rockquemore, Kerry Ann, and Tracey Laszloffy. 2008. *The Black Academic's Guide to Winning Tenure without Losing Your Soul.* Boulder, CO: Lynne Rienner.

Sensoy, Ozlem, Raj Sanghera, Geetu Parmar, Nisha Parhar, Lianne Nosyk and Monica Anderson. 2010. "Moving Beyond Dance, Dress, and Dining in Multicultural Canada." *International Journal of Multicultural Education,* 12, 1.

Sumartojo, Widyarini. 2012. "'My Kind of Brown'; Indo-Canadian Youth Identity and Belonging in Greater." PhD dissertation, Department of Geography, Vancouver, BC: Simon Fraser University.

Tardiel, C. 2016. "Racial Profiling: The Unintended Outcome of Street Checks." Racial Profiling Policy Dialogue, Ontario Human Right Commission. Toronto, ON: York University.

Tecle, Samuel, and Carl E. James. 2014. "Refugee Students in Canadian Schools: Educational Issues and Challenges." In C.A. Brewer and M. McCabe (eds.), *Immigrant and Refugee Students in Canada.* Edmonton, AB: Brush Education Inc.

Theodore, Peter S., and Susan A. Basow. 2000. Heterosexual Masculinity and Homophobia: A Reaction to the Self. *Journal of Homosexuality,* 40, 2.

Ulysse, Gina Athena. 2015/17. "Pedagogies of Belonging." <huffingtonpost.com/gina-athena-ulysse/pedagogies-of-belonging_1_b_8693286.html>.

Vecchio, Ken Dolan-Del. 1998. "Dismantling White Male Privilege within Family Therapy." In M. McGoldrick (ed.), *Revisioning Family Therapy.* New York: New York University Press.

Wadham, Ben. 2004. "Differentiating Whiteness: White Australia, White Masculinities and Aboriginal Reconciliation." In Aileen Moreton-Robinson (ed.), *Whitening Race: Essays in Social and Cultural Criticism.* Canberry, ACT: Aboriginal Studies Press.

Wang, Athena. 2000. "Asian and White Boys' Competing Discourses about Masculinity: Implications for Secondary Education." *Canadian Journal of Education,* 25, 2.

7

RACISM IN CANADIAN EDUCATION

Hieu Van Ngo

Ethnoracial minority learners have transformed schools and communities across Canada. Among Canadian residents aged 24 years and under, approximately one in four (23 percent) is a member of an *ethnoracial minority* group, one in ten (10 percent) is born outside of Canada and about one in seven (15 percent) has a mother tongue other than English or French (Statistics Canada 2012, 2014). Though young Canadians are primarily affiliated with a Christian religion (61 percent), many identify themselves as Muslim (5 percent), Sikh (2 percent), Hindu (2 percent) and Buddhist (1 percent) (Statistics Canada 2013). The emergence of a young population with diverse cultural, linguistic and religious backgrounds has created an opportunity for Canadian schools to be leaders in promoting pluralism in education. Yet, community advocates have long voiced concerns about school responses to learners' linguistic, academic, psychosocial and economic challenges (see Watt and Roessingh 2001; Gunderson 2004; Ngo and Schleifer 2005; Ngo 2009; People for Education 2013; Di Cintio 2015). Critics have often questioned the role of the Canadian education system in perpetuating inequalities among racialized groups (Tator and Henry 1991; Kehoe 1994; Dei 1999; Kirk 2003; Braithwaite 2010).

This chapter examines Canadian schools as sites of complex, intergroup relations that involve intricate interplays of personal attitudes, interpersonal interactions and institutionalized structures, policies and practices, and in the context of power differentials, have resulted in the marginalization of ethnoracial minority learners. The chapter begins with a discussion of an anti-racist education framework. It then draws upon the existing body of knowledge and publicly available information to examine the experiences of ethnoracial minority learners in Canadian schools, school responses to the changing student population and the impact of racism on ethnoracial minority learners and Canadian society. The chapter concludes with recommended strategies to address educational inequities and to promote educational success for all learners.

The objectives of this chapter are to:

- gain theoretical understanding about anti-racist education;
- examine racism in Canadian schools at the interpersonal and institutional levels, as well as its impact on individual learners and Canadian society; and
- explore practical strategies to address racism in Canadian schools.

An Anti-Racist Education Approach

This chapter is informed by an *anti-racist education* approach. In Canada, anti-racist education has emerged as a critique of traditional multicultural education, which tends to maintain the status quo by focusing on cultural retention and intercultural harmony and often consists of short-term programs and supplemental curricular materials designed to facilitate attitudinal changes in individual students and teachers (Lund 2006a). Anti-racist education, on the other hand, explicitly recognizes the social and political significance of race and readily acknowledges and interrogates the existence of inequitable power relations in complex interactions at the interpersonal and institutional levels. It thus requires policymakers, administrators, teachers, students and parents to intentionally engage in ongoing reflection on their social, economic and political positions in society as related to race, ethnicity, religion, language, gender, class, sexuality, ability, age, geography, education and so forth, as well as the intersectionality of such social identities (Arnold et al. 1991; Kailin 2002). It calls for structural analyses of power and oppression, particularly historical and contemporary relations of domination and subordination among ethnoracial groups, cultural appropriation, institutional power and discretionary use by people in authority (Dei 1996; Lund 2006b). Anti-racist education, therefore, acknowledges the politics of difference, which often involve social rules, laws and institutional routines constraining particular social groups (Young 1990), and seeks to change the existing power structure within the education system (Dei 1999; Jakubowski 2001). It promotes racial equality through critical dialogue, personal transformation and collective action (Niemonen 2007).

In practice, anti-racist educators embrace their roles as change agents. They scrutinize underlying attitudes and beliefs that perpetuate stereotypes and prejudices against ethnoracial minorities. They recognize individual discrimination, such as racial slurs, harassment, violence and exclusion-ary acts. These educators examine institutional or systemic discrimination embedded in the portrayal of ethnoracial minorities, as well as the access of ethnoracial minorities to resources and decision-making processes. Proponents of anti-racist education identify and address biases in edu-cational policies, curriculum and learning materials, teacher training, personnel and practice (Tator and Henry 1991; Kehoe 1994; Lund 2006a). At the same time, they offer alternative pedagogical, curricular and organi-zational strategies to achieve racial equality (Arnold et al. 1991; Niemonen 2007). Informed by the theoretical lens of anti-racist education, the ensuing analysis examines how racism has been manifested at the interpersonal and institutional levels and how it has impacted individual learners and Canadian society.

Interpersonal Racism

Interpersonal racism encompasses prejudicial attitudes and discriminatory actions against people on the basis of race. Such discriminatory interactions can occur between individuals in their institutional roles or as public or private individuals (Krieger 1999). Prejudicial attitudes often involve biased opinions, or a false, generalized conception of an ethnoracial minority group. Discriminatory actions can be expressed as social avoidance, dif-ferential treatment and verbal and physical violence (Abrams, Hogg and Marques 2005). Contemporary media coverage has indeed reported inci-dents of interpersonal racism in Canadian schools, such as a school trustee sending racist tweets (cbc *News* 2013); teachers warning students to check their bags after a Black student went into a change room alone; teachers posting Islamophobic and racist tweets; elementary students using the N-word to address their peers; young teens committing racially motivated verbal and physical violence against a classmate (Javed and Rushowy 2016); and acts of harassment, vandalism and graffiti calling for violence against Syrians and mosques (Martin 2015; Ivanov 2016; Pilieci 2016).

Incidents of interpersonal racism cannot be dismissed as isolated inci-dents. Several studies show that Black students are often perceived by their teachers and peers as being academically inferior compared to students from other racial groups (Ryan 1999; Codjoe 2001). Carl James (2012) points out that Black males, in particular, are often designated as "at risk" and stereotyped as immigrants, fatherless youth, troublemakers, athletes and underachievers. He argues that those stereotypes serve to "categorize, essentialize and disenfranchise" Black male students, and together they construct Black masculinities that "are linked to fatherlessness, hopelessness, deviance, low expectations and poor academic performance" (James 2012: 484–85). In the post-9/11 period, students of Middle Eastern, African and South Asian backgrounds, particularly those of Muslim faith, have been implied to be radicalized, home-grown terrorists and many have been treated with fear and suspicion (Mueller 2006; Weine et al. 2009; Zhou 2014). At the other end of the spectrum, students of Asian descent are burdened with the "*model minority*" stereotype, which expects them to achieve higher success than other ethnoracial minority groups, especially in economic terms, academic performance, social achievement, family stability and law-abiding behaviours (Chou 2008). The model minority stereotype has been used to highlight the traits of self-determination, resourcefulness and polite conformity; to reinforce the belief that Canadian institutions — such as schools — are accommodating, fair and accessible to all those who work hard enough; and to pit Asian Canadians against other ethnoracial minority groups (Pon 2000; Ho 2014). The pressure of this stereotype has induced guilt, shame, psychological distress and negative attitudes toward seeking help among struggling individuals of Asian descent (Gupta, Szymanski and Leong 2011; Navaratnam 2011).

A number of Canadian studies and reports further describe the localized experiences of ethnoracial minority students in schools across the country. James Baker, Jonathan Price and Kenneth Walsh (2015) surveyed 850 junior and high school students in St. John's, Newfoundland. Their results show that half of the ethnoracial minority respondents (50 percent) had experienced racism at school, and that two-fifths of the ethnoracial minority respondents (40 percent) had experienced racism from their own peers. The same survey also highlighted that approximately two-fifths of all student respondents (42 percent) believed that racial prejudice exists in their schools. In another study conducted in New Brunswick, Cynthia Baker, Manju Varma and Connie Tanaka (2009) interviewed youth who have experienced racism. They provided detailed accounts of individual racism, including racial slurs, physical violence (or threats of it) and graffiti with hateful messages. Their findings also highlight that ethnoracial minority students perceive being singled out by teachers or feeling undermined by school personnel when they requested school intervention in dealing with racist incidents.

In Québec, the members of the Québec Human Rights Commission consulted with a wide range of community stakeholders and documented incidents of differential treatment of ethnoracial minority groups, especially young Blacks (see Eid, Magloire and Turenne 2011). They learned that ethnoracial minority youth had been disproportionately targeted for intense scrutiny and suspicion of delinquency by school personnel, and such scrutiny had occurred more frequently during extracurricular activities popular among Black students, such as basketball or hip-hop shows. They further learned that disciplinary measures had been too quickly applied against ethnoracial minority students. A survey of students with diverse ethnoracial minority backgrounds in Toronto had similar results. Martin Ruck and Scot Wortley (2002) found that ethnoracial minority students were much more likely than White students to perceive discrimination with respect to teacher treatment, school suspension, use of police assistance by school authorities and police treatment at school. Their analysis also showed that Black students perceived differential treatment most negatively, and that other social characteristics — including gender, socioeconomic status and age of immigration — predicted students' perception of differential treatment in school. Moreover, Black male students were approximately thirty-two times more likely than White students to perceive discrimination with respect to the use of police at school and twenty-seven times more likely to perceive that they would be treated worse by the police at school.

There is also evidence of racism experienced by ethnoracial minority youth in Western Canada. Hieu Van Ngo et al. (2017) documented incidents of racially motivated bullying against ethnoracial minority youth in Calgary, including racial segregation and hostility, frequent taunting with racial slurs by peers at school and acts of violence over a long period of time. This is exemplified in a youth's words:

> Getting called a Paki by itself made me upset, but it wasn't the main thing. It would come hand in hand with punching me or spitting on me or kicking me. Up until 10, I was bullied once a week. (Ngo et al. 2017: 71)

Ngo et al. also elaborate on students' perceived differential treatment on the basis of race from principals and teachers, particularly in applying disciplinary measures.

Henry Codjoe (2001) also examines the experience of Black students in Edmonton. Black students perceived low expectations from teachers, expressed in their unwillingness to recognize students' abilities and subsequent lack of encouragement and support for students to develop their potential — or surprised reactions to students' achievements. Black students had intense feelings of social deprivation and alienation in their schools. In British Columbia, Dan Cui (2011) and Brad Millington et al. (2008) note the struggles of Chinese Canadian students being subjected to racial slurs, taunting, stereotypes, exclusion from school projects and verbal and physical intimidation in physical education classes. Tan Phan (2003) interviewed young Vietnamese refugees in urban schools and documented their experience with racial conflict, harassment and unfair treatment from some teachers. Similarly, Dilek Kayaalp (2014) described the experience of Turkish immigrant youth with racism from teachers, including racist comments, hostile critiques of certain religious practices (such as wearing headscarves) or social distancing.

In contrast to the reported experience of ethnoracial minority students with racial prejudice and discrimination, school personnel are rarely willing to examine intergroup relations, and often adopt a non-critical or colourblind stance in approaching the issue of racism. For instance, James Ryan (2003) used both personal interviews and surveys to assess school administrators' perception of racism in thirty-two school districts across Canada. Many principals were reluctant to acknowledge occurrences of stereotyping and racist incidents in their schools, and those who did recognize racism tended to downplay its significance. In addition, principals primarily attributed incidents of individual racism to frustration and were not willing to examine school curriculum or the actions of educators. In some cases, principals dismissed complaints of alleged racist incidents. Tyler McCreary (2011) assessed teachers' constructions of racism and found that teachers consistently viewed racism as a phenomenon occurring outside of the school, and thus they attributed responsibility for addressing racism to other people. The author also found that teachers often dismissed complaints of alleged racist incidents from ethnoracial minority students and parents, and some counter-accused students and parents of "pull[ing] the race card" (McCreary 2011: 22).

The refusal of many administrators and teachers to meaningfully engage in critical dialogue on issues related to race relations and to respond to racism in schools does not mean that racism in schools does not exist. Rather, it accentuates the necessity of overcoming the "collective amnesia" in the education system to come to terms with and resolve a long history of discriminatory government and corporate policies and practices (Lund 2006b: 37). Refusal and avoidance of addressing educational inequities are indeed symptoms of institutional racism, which is the focus of the next section.

Institutional Racism

Institutional racism, in the education context, encompasses policies and practices that, regardless of intent, disadvantage ethnoracial minority learners directly or indirectly (Tator and Henry 2010). Racism has been embedded and reinforced in numerous systems, with individuals from the dominant group — who share dominant Eurocentric worldviews and values — making the decisions that impact racialized learners. The analysis of institutional racism in Canadian education addresses racial representation in governance, school administration, teaching, education policies, curriculum and responses to the unique needs of ethnoracial minority learners.

Racial Representation in Governance, School Administration and Teaching

The principle of *procedural social justice* raises questions about access of ethnoracial minority members to decision-making processes in school boards, school administration and teaching. With respect to boards, active engagement of ethnoracial minority community members in the electoral process at the school board level has influenced school responsiveness to ethnoracial diversity. For instance, school districts with a high percentage of ethnoracial minority board members have been linked to comparatively high numbers of ethnoracial minority members in school administrative and teaching positions (Stewart, England and Meier 1989; Polinard, Wrinkle and Longoria 1990; Leal, Martinez-Ebers and Meier 2004). Further, representation of ethnoracial minority members on school boards has been associated with reduced discrimination in schools, more funding for bilingual education, favourable school ratings and positive educational outcomes for ethnoracial minority students (Meier and Stewart 1991; Leal and Hess 2000; Spring 2000; Marschall 2005; National School Boards Association 2008). Conversely, the absence of ethnoracial minority members on school boards has been associated with the likelihood of ethnoracial minority students experiencing suspension and expulsion, underrepresentation in gifted classes, overrepresentation in special education classes and poor student achievement (Meier and Stewart 1991).

Ethnoracial learners have also benefited from reflective ethnoracial representation among school administrators and teachers. Quite often, ethnoracial diversity among school administrators also translates into a comparatively high presence of ethnoracial minority teachers in schools (Ross, Rousse and Bratton 2010). Ethnoracial representation among administrators has also been associated with decreased dropout rates, better academic performance, less placement in special needs classes and stronger presence in gifted classes among ethnoracial minority students (Meier and Stewart 1992; Pitts 2005). Similarly, ethnoracial minority representation among teachers has been linked to better test-score performance among all students, lower levels of discrimination in schools, less frequent use of punitive disciplinary practices such as expulsion and out-of-school suspension, increased rehabilitative disciplinary practices, fewer ethnoracial minority students assigned to special needs classes and stronger ethnoracial diversity in gifted classes (Meier and Stewart 1992; Pitts 2005; Rocha and Hawes 2009; Roch, Pitts and Navarro 2010).

In spite of the known benefits of having ethnoracial diversity in schools, ethnoracial minority members have been underrepresented in school board governance, administration and teaching across Canada. A review of the compositions of the board of trustees in the top ten Canadian metropolitan centres in 2016 showed that ethnoracial minority community members accounted for 11 percent of all trustee positions (compared to the ethnoracial minority population at about 19 percent) (table 7.1). Out of the ten school boards, five had no ethnoracial minority members and four had only one ethnoracial minority representative. The Toronto School District Board had the highest ethnoracial minority representation at 38 percent (eight of twenty-one trustees), but still about 9 percent behind the ethnoracial minority population in Toronto (about 47 percent according to the 2011 National Household Survey).

With respect to ethnoracial representation in school administration and teachers, Canadian schools are not in sync with the changing ethnoracial demographics in their communities. In a survey of principals across the country, James Ryan, Katina Pollock and Fab Antonelli (2007) found that only 4 percent of them identified themselves as visible minorities. Moreover, according to Ryan, Pollock and Antonelli (2009), ethnoracial minority members accounted for 7 percent of all teaching positions in Canadian elementary and secondary schools (the visible minority population in 2006 was 16 percent). All the major metropolitan centres included in the study, namely Vancouver, Toronto and Montréal, showed significant discrepancies between representation of ethnoracial minority members in the general populations and the teacher labour force. For instance, ethnoracial minority members are 49 percent and 42 percent of the general population in Vancouver and Toronto in 2006. Yet, they respectively accounted for only 20 and 19 percent of the teaching workforces in the two cities. Ryan,

Table 7.1: Ethnoracial Minority Representation in Major Canadian School Boards, 2016

School Board	Population %Visible Minorities	Total Board Members	#Visible Minority	%Visible Minority
Toronto School District Board	47.0	21	8	38.1
Montréal School Board	20.3	11	0	0.0
Vancouver School Board	45.2	9	1	11.1
Calgary Board of Education	28.1	7	1	14.3
Edmonton Public School Board	22.4	9	1	11.1
Ottawa-Carleton District School Board	19.2	12	0	0.0
Central Québec School Board	3.1	13	0	0.0
Winnipeg School Board	19.7	9	0	0.0
Hamilton-Wentworth District School Board	14.3	11	0	0.0
Waterloo Region District School Board	16.2	11	1	9.1
Total		113	12	10.6

Sources: Data related to trustees was extracted from public information available on school board websites. Visible minority data came from the 2011 National Household Survey (Statistics Canada 2014).

Pollock and Antonelli (2009) further note a decline of ethnoracial minority members in the teacher workforce between 2001 and 2006. They raise two key systemic issues contributing to underrepresentation of ethnoracial minority members in the teaching profession. First, inequitable schooling practices contribute to uneven achievement of ethnoracial minority students in Canadian schools and thus limit their chances of entering teacher education in Canadian universities. Second, discriminatory licensing and hiring practices exclude those who have completed their teacher education programs.

Anti-Racist Education in School Policies and Regulations

Over the years, school boards have demonstrated varying efforts to address the issues of race and racial inequity. According to a recent review of the existing policies and regulations among the major public-school boards in Canada, most school boards have addressed human rights, diversity, multiculturalism and discrimination (table 7.2). However, only four school boards, namely Vancouver School Board, Toronto School District Board, Ottawa-Carleton District School Board and Montréal School Board, have incorporated the principles of anti-racist education in their policy documents and acknowledged the various levels of racism. Other school boards have reinforced *multicultural education*, which encourages respect for diverse cultural norms, values and traditions but does not adequately deal with biased attitudes and discriminatory behaviours at the individual level and racial inequities at the structural level.

Patrick Solomon and Cynthia Levine-Rasky (2003) reviewed the policies, task force reports and action plans of five school boards in British Columbia, Manitoba, Nova Scotia and Ontario. Their findings suggest that school boards have developed policies on equity and diversity grounded in the principles of multicultural education, and they primarily articulate their commitments to the production of bias-free curriculum materials; the development of culturally appropriate assessment; staff development to strengthen cross-cultural competency; employment equities related to race, culture and ethnicity; and involvement of parents, school and community partners in the schooling process. Their interviews with school administrators and educators on their responses to equity and diversity policies, however, points out a lack of awareness of equity and diversity policies, reluctance and discomfort in dealing with issues of race and racism, and resistance to anti-racist education principles. Similarly, Paul Carr and Darren Lund (2008) observe that anti-racism policies are often fraught with the very issues that they are intended to dismantle, namely systemic discrimination, passive resistance and marginalized status in a traditional curriculum.

Eurocentric Curriculum

Curriculum encompasses philosophical approach, learning objectives, academic content, instructional strategies and learning experiences (Lunenburg 2011). In Canadian education, the dominance of Eurocentrism in the school curriculum manifests, reinforces and defends institutional racism. James Joseph Scheurich and Michelle Young (1997) speak of "*epistemological*

Table 7.2: Policies Related to Anti-Racism Education in Selective Canadian School Boards

School Board	Policy/Regulation
Toronto School District Board	Human Rights; Bullying Prevention and Intervention
Montréal School Board	Multicultural/Multiracial Education; Racial Incidents
Vancouver School Board	Multiculturalism and Anti-racism; Non-discrimination; Procedures for Dealing with Racial, Ethno-Cultural and/or Religious Harassment
Calgary Board of Education	Harassment, Sexual Harassment and Discrimination
Edmonton Public Schools	Multicultural Education
Ottawa-Carleton District School Board	Equity and Inclusive Education; Anti-racism and Ethnocultural Equity
Winnipeg School Board	Human Rights; Diversity and Equity Education
Waterloo Region District School Board	Racial, Religious and Ethnocultural Harassment; Faith and Religious Accommodation

Sources: Data related to trustees was extracted from public information available on school board website.

racism" to question Eurocentric assumptions about the nature of reality, the ways of knowing that reality and the embedded values and ethical/moral judgements in the education system. Sharing their view, Carol Tator and Frances Henry (2010) maintain that the dominant Eurocentric ways of knowing have readily been asserted in books, music and art and have constructed a particular brand of universal truth to be found only in the great works of the Western-based canon of knowledge. They point out that the dominant ideologies and discourses often focus on universalism, colourblindness, objectivity, neutrality, merit, standards and equal opportunity, which undermine racial inequality and instead attribute individual struggles to their lack of capacity, poor work ethics or life choices. Celine-Marie Pascale (2011) contends that the Cartesian framework, which views events and phenomena as singular, external and objective realities that can be more or less accurately studied, has shaped the pervasive epistemology of education in North America and rejected the notion of cultural relativity in knowledge production. John Stanfield (1985) points out that the dominant epistemology has been reinforced for hundreds of years and has become so intricately embedded in society that it is deemed to be natural rather than socially constructed throughout history.

Policymakers, school administrators and educators live and function within the historical, social, political and economic contexts that consistently privilege White people and legitimize the dominant Eurocentric epistemology. They have internalized "border thinking," which, on the one hand, has routinely informed their making sense of the world and the development and implementation of school curriculum through the dominant epistemological lens and, on the other hand, has enabled them to discount or doubt other ways of knowing and perspectives (Bernasconi 1997; Mignolo 2002: 71). This doubly blind dynamic perpetuates the dominance of a Eurocentric worldview and the exclusion and subjugation of epistemologies of "Others" in the school curriculum (see Almeida 2015).

Contemporary Canadian education has been plagued with non-recognition and misrecognition of the contribution of ethnoracial minority people (Ghosh 2010). Black students, for example, complain about the curriculum and texts' lack of relevancy to their lives, the invisibility of Black/African studies, a lack of acknowledgement of African Canadians' contribution to the evolution of Canada as a nation and negative references to African Canadians (Codjoe 2001). Allison Skerrett (2010) points out the dominance of works of Anglo or European origin in the secondary English literacy curriculum; policy documents have used codified words and phrases such as "traditional," "challenging," "significant," "major," "university" and "analytical reading" to describe Eurocentric literary work and words and phrases such as "contemporary," "key reading" and "world literature" to describe selective texts in ELL, elective and applied stream curricula. Such framing reinforces the dominant Eurocentric curriculum and a compromised commitment to include diverse ethnoracial minority perspectives. Similarly, Ken Montgomery (2005) identifies in Canadian history textbooks the entrenched encapsulation of racism, which acknowledges racism in Canada but often characterizes it as a series of isolated occurrences confined to exceptionally flawed individuals or unusual times. While such an approach recognizes the suffering of certain groups of people, particularly those identified as Chinese, Japanese, Sikh and Black, it offers no analysis of the historical power and privilege of the dominant White group. Montgomery (2005: 439) implored:

> This depiction of Canada as a space of vanquished and managed racism or, indeed, as a space of antiracist achievement, perpetuates

mythologies of white settler benevolence while it at once obscures the banal racisms upon and through which the nation state is built and rebuilt.

It is important to stress that racism has existed prior to and after Canada became a nation-state in 1867.

There is also evidence of Eurocentric curriculum in other content areas, such as physical education and sex education. Physical education primarily privileges Eurocentric sports and values (such as embodied strength, competitiveness and aggression), and ethnoracial minority students have experienced routine harassment both through language and physical intimidation in physical education classes (Millington et al. 2008). Amanda Whitten and Christabelle Sethna (2014) criticized the tendency of school boards and schools to neutralize sex education by avoiding explicit examination of how racism, classism and gender inequities have influenced sexuality, sexual health and access to sexual health services. They objected to the depiction of diverse opinions about the content and pedagogical approach to sex education as synonymous with opposition to teaching of and learning about sex education. Such framing reinforces the assumption that membership in a cultural, racial, ethnic or religious minority group is not compatible with sex education and perpetuates the biased view of refusal or failure on the part of ethnoracial minority members to assimilate into the normative values of the country.

School Responses to the Need for English Language Instruction

One of the persistent systemic issues facing ethnoracial minority students with English as a second language is the lack of English language instruction. In urban K–12 school jurisdictions, the number of students requiring English language instruction has grown exponentially. In fact, English language learners (ELLs) make up between 20 and 57 percent of students in the major school boards (see Calgary Board of Education 2016; Toronto District School Board 2016; Vancouver School Board 2016). Depending on their age, previous learning, socioeconomic status, migration experience, parents' education level and individual student factors, ELL students require three to seven years of explicit English language instruction to develop academic language proficiency (Collier 1989; Hakuta, Butler and Witt 2000; Moore and Zainuddin 2003). In most school boards, ELL students generate additional funding for English language instruction on top of the base instruction funding available for all students. For example, ELL students brought over $300 million in funding for base instruction and English language instruction into school boards across Alberta in 2008 (Ngo 2009). The Ministry of Education in Ontario provided school boards with about $225 million for English language instruction in 2005 (Office of the Auditor General of Ontario 2005).

Yet, the funding meant to support ELL students to acquire academic language proficiency has not always followed them into their classrooms. In fact, there has been widening incongruence between the complex needs of ELL students and the availability of ELL services in schools (see People for Education 2007; Ngo 2009; Di Cintio 2015). Many ELL students have not received explicit English language instruction at all, and schools with English language instruction have reported a ratio of between 42 and 115 ELL students per ELL teacher (Ngo 2001; Howard Research and Management Consulting 2006; People for Education 2007, 2015). The experience of ELL students in Canadian schools reveals a lack of formal standards and procedures for English language instruction, particularly in resource allocation, identification and assessment of linguistic needs, explicit instruction and tracking the progress of English language development (Ngo 2009). Provincial ministries of education have not put in place the appropriately rigorous reporting measures, and school boards have persistently shown a lack of accountability for English language instruction funding. School board trustees and school principals have been reported to dip into funding for English language instruction to finance library services, teachers' salaries and heat and light for school buildings (Duffy 2003; Rushowy 2007). Inadequate English language instruction and the lack of accountability for related funding have laid bare the undermining by decision makers and administrators in school boards of the very linguistic foundation that is crucial for academic success and social integration of ELL students in Canadian society.

Impact of Racism

Racism in the Canadian education system has contributed a negative educational, physical, psychological and social impact on ethnoracial minority youth. With respect to academic consequences, students who have experienced or perceived racial discrimination in schools are likely to have poor academic performance, be more likely to drop out, undervalue the importance of schooling, find school unenjoyable and struggle with adjustment to school practices and expectations (Brown 2015). Particularly, students from African, Latin American and Middle Eastern backgrounds have lower graduation rates (Toronto District School Board 2012). Those from a Caribbean background have a high dropout rate — up to 40 percent (Anisef et al. 2010). The dropout rates among ethnoracial minority students with English as a second language have also been significantly high, ranging between 40 and 74 percent (Alberta Education 1992; Derwing, DeCorby, Ichikawa and Jamieson 1999; Watt and Roessingh 2001; Gunderson 2004; Toohey and Derwing 2008).

Furthermore, recurring experience with racism has been definitively linked to poor physiological and mental health (Williams and Williams-Morris 2000; Paradies et al. 2015). Ethnoracial minority youth subjected to racial discrimination have exhibited symptoms of depression, anxiety, hopelessness and post-traumatic stress, as well as health-risk behaviours and anti-social behaviours (Kasper and Noh 2000; Nyborg and Curry 2003; Ellis et al. 2010; Flores et al. 2010; Rivera et al. 2011). Experience with racism is associated with physiological issues, such as high output of cortisol (the hormone released in response to stress), obesity, high blood pressure and hypertension (Brondolo, Lackey and Love 2011; Zeiders, Doane and Roosa 2012; Dolezsar, McGrath, Herzig and Miller 2014). Youth have struggled to develop positive identities, particularly self-concept, self-esteem, ethnic identity and a sense of citizenship (Williams-Morris 1996; Kasper and Noh 2001; Kroger 2007; Reitz and Banerjee 2007; Ngo et al. 2017).

Some have internalized racism and developed self-hatred (Bryan 2009; Ngo et al. 2017). For instance, after years of coping with racism in school and in the community, a Sudanese youth described how he saw himself:

> I was looking at the mirror … I just wanted to, feel like, spitting at myself, you know, spit on my skin or something. I just hated it, you know, disliked it … I just felt like, people look at me and call me the N-word, you know. That's why I hated myself, even if I was a little bit lighter than this. You see, (gesturing vertical hierarchy) there's Black, and then there is light, and then there is a little bit Black, and then there is mulatto, and then all the way down here is where tar is, you know. And I'm like there (pointing to the bottom), that's what I feel like, you know. (Ngo et al. 2017)

It has been suggested that persistent experiences with interpersonal and institutional racism have alienated ethnoracial minority youth and pushed some youth toward behaviour that involves them with the criminal justice system (see Salole and Abdulle 2015; Ngo et al. 2017).

Beyond the negative educational, psychological, physiological and social impacts on ethnoracial youth, racism in Canadian education has incurred societal costs. The Ontario Human Rights Commission (2003) warned that racial discrimination has compromised the well-being and prosperity of all citizens, brought into question Canada's commitment to the internationally recognized right of young people to education, eroded public trust in Canadian institutions and challenged social cohesion. Canada can take warning from estimates of the economic costs of racism in Australia and the United States, at AUD 45 billion and USD 2 trillion a year in the forms of lost incomes, unrealized productivity, loss of corporate profits, lost tax revenues, income support and costs to address issues related to racial inequities in education, health, housing, social service and justice (Elias 2015; Turner 2016). In education, McKinsey and Company (2009) suggest that the education gap between ethnoracial minority students and White students in the United States cost the country between USD 310 billion and USD 525 billion in lost economic productivity, or 2 to 4 percent of the GDP, in 2008.

Educational Equity by Design

Interpersonal and institutional racism in Canadian schools has a significant impact on ethnoracial minority learners and all of society. The identified points of tension, particularly in interracial interactions among students, teachers, school administrators and decision makers; racial representation in governance, administration and teaching workforce; school policies and regulations; curricula; and school responses to ethnoracial students' learning needs, call for policymakers, administrators and educators to demonstrate individual and collective commitment to address racial inequalities and inequities in Canadian schools. That is, they need to institute a by-design approach to transform the Canadian education system through intentional, coordinated, system-wide efforts to integrate anti-racist education into all educational policies, organizational structures and practices.

Anti-racist education by design would first require willingness on the part of each policymaker, decision maker, administrator and educator to examine their social locations/privilege, worldviews and life experiences; welcome critical conversations about race and race relations; be able to analyze power, oppression and privilege at the personal, institutional and cultural levels; and explore their roles as critics, advocates, allies, champions and change agents in addressing racial inequities. Opportunities for anti-racist training should be readily available in pre-service teacher training and educational leadership programs, as well as in ongoing professional development programs in education ministries, school boards and schools.

At the policy level, provincial ministries of education and school boards could integrate anti-racist education principles and practice into educational policies, regulations, operational guidelines and procedures. For example, in the 1990s, Ontario formally mandated school boards to develop anti-racist and ethnocultural equity policies that addressed ten key areas: board policies, guidelines and practice; leadership; community-school partnership; curriculum; student languages; student evaluation, assessment and placement; guidance and counselling; racial and ethnocultural harassment; employment practices; and staff development (Ontario Ministry of Education 1993). At the same time, policymakers can draw upon contemporary lessons from across the globe. For instance, the New South Wales Department of Education (2005) has developed an explicit anti-racism policy that commits the department to eliminate all forms of racial discrimination in schools and requires all schools to address racial equities in school practices. Anti-racist education policies ought to address the issues of school representation, teacher training and certification, curriculum, teaching pedagogy, equity-based resource allocation, funding accountability, equitable educational outcomes for ethnoracial minority youth and collection and use of race-related data. In other words, anti-racism should be integrated into all structures and functions in Canadian schools. Education ministries and school boards also need to ensure adequate guidelines, accountability measures and support for policy implementation.

At the practical level, anti-racist education needs to be operationalized in all aspects of schooling experience. Schools could adopt a participatory, action-oriented approach to involve school administrators, teachers, students, parents and community partners in examining and taking action to achieve an inclusive school environment. There should also be equitable ethnoracial minority representation, anti-racist school practices (e.g., methods of teaching, topics in curriculum, school support services, selection of textbooks, planning of extracurricular activities), diversity competence of school personnel, respectful interactions and collaboration with ethnoracial minority students and parents, and respectful and mutually beneficial collaboration with ethnoracial minority communities (see Ngo 2012). School leaders can foster a school culture open to critical, transformative dialogue on issues of race and race relations. They can ensure adequate support, including ongoing training and professional development opportunities, to help school administrators, educators and other school personnel to develop knowledge and skills for anti-racist education practice.

Finally, ethnoracial minority community members across the country have asked policymakers, school administrators and educators to return to, strengthen and operationalize their commitment to social justice in public education (see Carr and Lund 2008; Ngo 2009; Baker Price and Walsh 2015; People for Education 2013, 2015). Principles of *distributive social justice*, concerned with access of community members to resources that develop their human capacities, could inform decisions for equitable allocation of funding and support to ensure the academic success of all ethnoracial minority learners. Adherence to procedural social justice would ensure access of ethnoracial minority learners, parents and community members to decision-making processes that influence educational experiences and outcomes for ethnoracial minority children and youth (see Guo 2010).

Signalling individual and collective empowerment, ethnoracial minority members are changing the electoral landscapes in various political jurisdictions by assuming leadership roles, supporting progressive candidates and asking critical questions about race relations. Ethnoracial minority groups have also offered leadership training to youth and parents to strengthen their knowledge and skills in working with decision makers as advocates and partners. Education ministries, school boards and schools can readily tap into the expertise from within ethnocultural communities to lead, guide, develop and support the implementation of anti-racist education initiatives.

DISCUSSION QUESTIONS

1. Reflecting on your K–12 education experience, how did your schools address ethnoracial diversity? How did the issues of race and racism play out in interpersonal interactions and school policies and practice?

2. How is anti-racist education different from multicultural education? What are the critiques of the two approaches? What is your stand on the debate?

3. What are some of the key areas of education policy and practice outlined in this chapter? What strategies would you suggest to contribute to positive changes in the identified areas? How would you see your role in change efforts?

ACTION STEPS

1. Engage a trustee, principal, educator or peer in a respectful, critical conversation about ethnoracial diversity, racism and anti-racist education.
2. Examine an educational policy or school curriculum through the anti-racist lens, and prepare and present to decision makers a policy brief that offers an analysis and recommended strategies for change.

Supplemental Readings

Arnold, Rick, Bev Burke, Carl James, D'Arcy Martin and Barb Thomas. 1991. *Educating for a Change.* Toronto: Between the Lines.
Arthur, James, Ian Davies and Carole Hahn. 2008. *The Sage Handbook of Education for Citizenship and Democracy.* London: Sage.
Lea, Virginia, and Judy Helfand. 2004. *Identifying Race and Transforming Whiteness in the Classroom.* New York: Peter Lang Publishing.

Additional Resources

Calgary Antiracism Education <ucalgary.ca/cared/>
Canadian Antiracism Education and Research Society
Coalition for Equal Access to Education
People for Education

References

Abrams, Dominic, Michael A. Hogg and Jose M. Marques. 2005. "A Social Psychological Framework for Understanding Social Inclusion and Exclusion." In D. Abrams, M.A. Hogg and J.M. Marques (eds.), *The Social Psychology of Inclusion and Exclusion.* New York: Psychology Press.
Alberta Education. 1992. "Review of Transcripts of Selected Immigrant Learners Who Received ESL Funding." Edmonton, AB: Author.
Almeida, Shana. 2015. "Race-Based Epistemologies: The Role of Race and Dominance in Knowledge Production." *Wagadu, A Journal of Transnational Women's and Gender Studies,* 13 (Summer).
Anisef, Paul, Robert S. Brown, Kelli Phythian, Robert Sweet, and David Walters. 2010. "Early School Leaving among Immigrants in Toronto Secondary Schools." *Canadian Review of Sociology,* 47, 2.
Arnold, Rick, Bev Burke, Carl James, D'Arcy Martin and Barb Thomas. 1991. *Educating for a Change.* Toronto, ON: Between the Lines.
Baker, Cynthia, Manju Varma and Connie Tanaka. 2009. "Sticks and Stones: Racism as Experienced by Adolescents in New Brunswick." *Canadian Journal of Nursing Research,* 41, 1.
Baker, James, Jonathan Price and Kenneth Walsh. 2015. "Unwelcoming Communities: Youth Observations of Racism in St. John's, Newfoundland and Labrador, Canada." *Journal of Youth Studies,* 19, 1.
Bernasconi, Robert. 1997. "African Philosophy's Challenge to Continental Philosophy." In E.C. Eze (ed.), *Postcolonial African Philosophy: A Critical Reader.*

Oxford: Wiley-Blackwell.

Brathwaite, Oscar. 2010. "The Role of the School Curriculum to Obliterate Anti-Black Racism." *Our Schools, Our Selves*, 19, 3.

Brondolo, Elizabeth, Shonda Lackey and Erica Love. 2011. "Race, Racism and Health: Evaluating Racial Disparities in Hypertension to Understand the Links Between Racism and Health Status." In A. Baum, T.A. Revenson and J.E. Singer (eds.), *Handbook of Health Psychology*, second edition. New York: Psychology Press.

Brown, Christia Spears. 2015. "The Educational, Psychological, and Social Impact of Discrimination on the Immigrant Child." Washington, DC: Migration Policy Institute.

Bryan, Audrey. 2009. "The Intersectionality of Nationalism and Multiculturalism in the Irish Curriculum: Teaching against Racism." *Race, Ethnicity and Education*, 12, 3.

Calgary Board of Education. 2016. "Community Report." <cbe.ab.ca/FormsManuals/Community-Report-2014-15.pdf >.

Carr, Paul R., and Darren Lund. 2008. "Antiracist Education." In F.E. Provenzo (ed.), *Encyclopedia of the Social and Cultural Foundations of Education*. Thousand Oaks, CA: Sage Publications.

CBC *News Online*. 2013. "Central Alberta School Trustee Accused of Racist, Homophobic Tweets." November 6. <cbc.ca/news/canada/edmonton/central-alberta-school-trustee-accused-of-racist-homophobic-tweets-1.2417190>.

Chou, Chih-Chou. 2008. "Critique on the Notion of Model Minority: An Alternative Racism to Asian American?" *Asian Ethnicity*, 9, 3.

Codjoe, Henry M. 2001. "Fighting a 'Public Enemy' of Black Academic Achievement — the Persistence of Racism and the Schooling Experiences of Black Students in Canada." *Race Ethnicity and Education*, 4, 4.

Collier, Virginia P. 1989. "How Long? A Synthesis of Research on Academic Achievement in a Second Language." TESOL *Quarterly*, 23.

Cui, Dan. 2011. "Two Multicultural Debates and the Lived Experiences of Chinese Canadian Youth." *Canadian Ethnic Studies*, 43, 3.

Dei, George J. Sefa. 1999. "Knowledge and Politics of Social Change: The Implications of Anti-racism." *British Journal of Sociology of Education*, 20, 3.

___. 1996. *Anti-Racism Education: Theory and Practice*. Halifax, NS: Fernwood Publishing.

Derwing, Tracey M., Emilie DeCorby, Julia Ichikawa and Kama Jamieson. 1999. "Some Factors that Affect the Success of ESL High School Students." *Canadian Modern Language Review*, 55, 4.

Di Cintio, Marcello. 2015. "Language Limbo: The Urgent Need for More ESL Instruction in School." *Alberta View*. <albertaviews.ab.ca/2015/08/18/language-limbo/>.

Dolezsar, Cynthia M., Jennifer J. McGrath, Alyssa J.M. Herzig and Sydney B. Miller. 2014. "Perceived Racial Discrimination and Hypertension: A Comprehensive Systematic Review." *Health Psychology*, 33, 1.

Duffy, Andrew. 2003. "Class Struggles: Public Education and the New Canadian." Toronto: Atkinson Foundation. <cmef.ca/downloads/ClassStrugglesPublicEducationandtheNewCanadian.pdf>.

Eid, Paul, Johanne Magloir and Michèle Turenne. 2011. "Racial Profiling and Systemic Discrimination of Racialized Youth." Montreal, QC: Commission des Droits de la Personne et des Rroits de la Jeunesse. <cdpdj.qc.ca/publications/Profiling_final_EN.pdf>.

Elias, Amanuel. 2015. "Measuring the Economic Consequences of Racial Discrimination in Australia." Unpublished dissertation, Deakin University, Melbourne, Australia.

Ellis, B. Heidi, Helen Z. MacDonald, Julie Klunk-Gillis, Alisa Lincoln, Lee Strunin and Howard J. Cabral. 2010. "Discrimination and Mental Health Among Somali Refugee Adolescents: The Role of Acculturation and Gender." *American Journal of Orthopsychiatry*, 80, 4.

Flores, Elena, Jeanne M. Tschann, Juanita M. Dimas, Lauri A. Pasch and Cynthia L. de Groat. 2010. "Perceived Racial/Ethnic Discrimination, Posttraumatic Stress Symptoms, and Health Risk Behaviours among Mexican American Adolescents." *Journal of Counseling Psychology*, 57, 3.

Ghosh, Ratna. 2010. "Racism: A Hidden Curriculum." *Education Canada*, 48, 4. <cea-ace.ca/sites/cea-ace.ca/files/EdCan-2008-v48-n4-Ghosh.pdf>.

Gunderson, Lee. 2004. "The Language, Literacy, Achievement, and Social Consequences of English-Only Programs for Immigrant Learners." In J. Hoffman (ed.), *The Fity-Third Annual Yearbook of the National Reading Conference*. Milwaukee, WI: National Reading Conference.

Guo, Shibao. 2010. "Toward Recognitive Justice: Emerging Trends and Challenges in Transnational Migration and Lifelong Learning." *International Journal of Lifelong Education*, 29, 2.

Gupta, Arpana, Dawn M. Szymanski and Frederick T.L. Leong. 2011. "The Model Minority Myth: Internalized Racialism of Positive Stereotypes as Correlates of Psychological Distress, and Attitudes Toward Help Seeking." *Asian American Journal of Psychology*, 2, 2.

Hakuta, Kenji, Yuko Goto Butler and Daria Witt. 2000. "How Long Does It Take English Learners to Attain Proficiency?" Berkeley, CA: University of California Linguistic Minority Research Institute.

Ho, Rob. 2014. "Do All Asians Look Alike? Asian Canadians as Model Minorities." *Studies on Asia*, 4, 2.

Howard Research and Management Consulting. 2006. *Review of ESL K–12 Program Implementation in Alberta: Final Report*. Edmonton, AB: Alberta Education.

Ivanov, Jennifer. 2016. "Prime Minister Trudeau Responds to Racist, Hateful Graffiti Sprayed on Calgary School." *Global News*, February 14. <globalnews.ca/news/2517545/racist-graffiti-sprayed-on-calgary-school/>.

Jakubowski, Lisa M. 2001. "Teaching Uncomfortable Topics: An Action-Oriented Strategy for Addressing Racism and Related Forms of Difference." *Teaching Sociology*, 29, 1.

James, Carl E. 2012. "Student 'At Risk' Stereotypes and the School of Black Boys." *Urban Education*, 47, 2.

Javed, Noor, and Kristin Rushowy. 2016. "Racist Incidents Ignored by York Region School Board, Families Say." *Toronto Star*, February 25. <thestar.com/yourtoronto/education/2016/02/23/racial-incidents-ignored-by-york-board-families-say.html>.

Kailin, Julie. 2002. *Antiracist Education: From Theory to Practice*. Lanham, MD: Rowman and Littlefield Publishers.

Kaspar, Violet, and Samuel Noh. 2001. "Discrimination and Identity: An Overview of Theoretical and Empirical Research." Halifax, NS: Canadian Heritage.

___. 2000. "Adolescent Coping with Discrimination-Related Stress: An Analysis of the Stress-Buffering Effect on Depression in Youth." Paper presented at the Fourth

National Metropolis Conference, Toronto, ON.

Kayaalp, Dilek. 2014. "Educational Inclusion/Exclusion of Turkish Immigrant Youth in Vancouver, Canada: A Critical Analysis." *International Journal of Inclusive Education,* 18, 7.

Kehoe, John W. 1994. "Multicultural Education vs. Anti-racist Education: The Debate and the Research in Canada." *Social Education,* 58, 6.

Kirk, Mark. 2003. "An Argument for Anti-racism Education for School Personnel." *Orbit,* 33, 3.

Krieger, Nancy. 1999. "Embodying Inequality: A Review of Concepts, Measures, and Methods for Studying Health Consequences of Discrimination." *International Journal of Health Services,* 29, 2.

Kroger, Jane. 2007. *Identity Development: Adolescence through Adulthood.* Thousand Oaks, CA: Sage.

Leal, David L., and Frederick M. Hess. 2000. "The Politics of Bilingual Education Expenditures in Urban School Districts." *Social Science Quarterly,* 81, 4.

Leal, David L., Valerie Martinez-Ebers and Kenneth J. Meier. 2004. "The Politics of Latino Education: The Biases of At-large Elections." *Journal of Politics,* 66, 4.

Lund, Darren E. 2006a. "Rocking the Racism Boat: School-Based Activists Speak Out on Denial and Avoidance." *Race Ethnicity and Education,* 9, 2.

___. 2006b. "Waking Up the Neighbors: Surveying Multicultural and Antiracist Education in Canada, the United Kingdom, and the United States. *Multicultural Perspectives,* 8, 1.

Lunenburg, Fred C. 2011. "Theorizing about Curriculum: Conceptions and Definitions." *International Journal of Scholarly Academic Intellectual Diversity,* 13, 1.

Marschall, Melissa J. 2005. "Minority Incorporation and Local School Boards." In W. Howell (ed.), *Besieged: School Boards and the Future of Education Politics.* Washington, DC: Brookings Institution Press.

Martin, Nick. 2015. "Racism towards Syrian Students Tears through Winnipeg School Division." *Winnipeg Free Press,* July 12. <winnipegfreepress.com/breakingnews/ Racism-towards-Syrian-students-runs-rampant-on-social-media-360874551. html>.

McCreary, Tyler. 2011. Colour-Blind: Discursive Repertoires Teachers Used to Story Racism and Aboriginality in Urban Prairie Schools. *Brock Education,* 21, 1.

McKinsey and Company. 2009. "The Economic Impact of the Achievement Gap in America's School." <mckinseyonsociety.com/downloads/reports/Education/ achievement_gap_report.pdf>.

Meier, Kenneth J., and Joseph Stewart. 1992. The Impact of Representative Bureaucracies: Educational Systems and Public Policies. *The American Review of Public Administration,* 22, 3.

___. 1991. *The Politics of Hispanic Education.* Albany: State University of New York Press.

Mignolo, Walter D. 2002. "The Geopolitics of Knowledge and the Colonial Difference." *South Atlantic Quarterly,* 101, 1.

Millington, Brad, Patricia Vertinsky, Ellexis Boyle and Brian Wilson. 2008. "Making Chinese-Canadian Masculinities in Vancouver's Physical Education Curriculum." *Sport, Education and Society,* 13, 2.

Montgomery, Ken. 2005. "Imagining the Antiracist State: Representation of Racism in Canadian History Textbooks." *Discourse: Studies in the Cultural Politics of Education,* 26, 4.

Moore, Rashid A., and Hanizah Zainuddin. 2003. "ESL Learners, Writing and the Acquisition of Academic Language." ERIC No. ED475746. Washington, DC: Educational Resources Information Center.

Mueller, Robert S. 2006. "Homegrown Terrorism and the Radicalization Process." *Vital Speeches of the Day*, 72, 20/21.

National School Boards Association. 2008. "A Question of Representation: Diversity and 21st Century School Boards." *Leadership Insider*. <nsba.org/sites/default/files/reports/1008Insider.pdf>.

Navaratnam, Sangeetha. 2011. "Guilt, Shame and Model Minorities: How South Asian Youth in Toronto Navigate the Canadian Educational System." Unpublished Master of Arts thesis, Sociology and Equity Studies in Education. Toronto, ON: Ontario Institute for Studies in Education.

New South Wales Department of Education. 2005. "Antiracism Policy." <education.nsw.gov.au/policy-library/policies/anti-racism-policy>.

Ngo, Hieu Van. 2012. "Cultural Competence in Alberta Cchools. TESL *Canada Journal*, 29, 6.

___. 2009. "Evaluation of ESL Education in Alberta: Perceptions of ESL Students in Four Major School Boards." Calgary, AB: Coalition for Equal Access to Education.

___. 2001. "English as a Second Language Education: Context, Current Responses and Recommendations for New Directions." Calgary, AB: Coalition for Equal Access to Education.

Ngo, Hieu Van, Avery Calhoun, Catherine Worthington, Tim Pyrch and David Este. 2017. "The Unravelling of Identities and Belonging: Criminal Gang Involvement of Youth from Immigrant Families." *International Journal of Immigration and Integration*, 18.

Ngo, Hieu Van, and Barbara Schleifer. 2005. "Immigrant Children in Focus." *Canadian Issues*, Spring.

Niemonen, Jack. 2007. "Antiracist Education in Theory and Practice: A Critical Assessment." *The American Sociologist*, 38, 2.

Nyborg, Vanessa M., and John F. Curry. 2003. "The Impact of Perceived Racism: Psychological Symptoms among African American Boys." *Journal of Clinical Child and Adolescent Psychology*, 32, 2.

Office of the Auditor General of Ontario. 2005. *2005 Annual Report*. Toronto, ON: Author. <poltext.org/sites/poltext.org/files/rapportsVerificateurGeneral/Ontario/ON%202005.pdf>.

Ontario Human Rights Commission. 2003. "Paying the Price: The Human Cost of Racial Profiling." Toronto, ON: Author.

Ontario Ministry of Education. 1993. *Antiracism and Ethnocultural Equity in School Boards: Guidelines for Policy Development and Implementation*. Toronto: Queen's Printer.

Paradies, Yin, Jehonathan Ben, Nida Denson, Amanuel Elias, Naomi Priest, Alex Pieterse, Arpana Gupta, Margaret Kelaher and Gilbert Gee. 2015. "Racism as Determinants of Health: A Systematic Review and Meta-Analysis." PLoS ONE 10, 9.

Pascale, Celine-Marie. 2011. "Epistemology and the Politics of Knowledge." *Sociological Review*, 58, 2.

People for Education. 2015. "Ontario's Schools: The Gap between Policy and Reality." Annual report on Ontario's Publicly Funded Schools 2015. Toronto: People for Education.

___. 2013. "Mind the Gap: Inequality in Ontario's Schools." Toronto: People for Education.

___. 2007. "Annual Report on Ontario Schools." Toronto: People for Education.

Phan, Tan. 2003. "Life in School: Narratives of Resiliency among Vietnamese-Canadian Youths." *Adolescence*, 38, 151.

Pilieci, Vito. 2016. "'Not the Vanier We Call Home': Tolerance, Acceptance Touted at School Targeted by Racist Graffiti." *Ottawa Citizen*, April 18. <ottawacitizen.com/news/local-news/city-councillor-holds-event-at-school-targeted-by-racist-graffiti>.

Pitts, David W. 2005. "Diversity, Representation, and Performance: Evidence about Race and Ethnicity in Public Organizations." *Journal of Public Administration Research and Theory: J-PART,* 15, 4.

Polinard, J.L., Robert D. Wrinkle and Tomas Longoria. 1990. "Education and Governance: Representational Links to Second Generation Discrimination." *Western Political Quarterly,* 43.

Pon, Gordon. 2000. "Importing the Asian Model Minority Discourse into Canada: Implications for Social Work and Education." *Canadian Social Work Review,* 17, 2.

Reitz, Jeffrey G., and Rupa Banerjee. 2007. "Racial Inequality, Social Cohesion, and Policy Issues in Canada." In K.G. Banting, T.J. Courchene and L.F. Seidle (eds.), *Belonging? Diversity, Recognition and Shared Citizenship in Canada.* Montreal: Institute for Research on Public Policy.

Rivera, Fernando, Irene Lopez, Peter Gurnaccia, Glorisa Camino and Hector Bird. 2011. "Perceived Discrimination and Antisocial Behavior in Puerto Rican Children." *Journal of Immigrant and Minority Health,* 13, 3.

Roch, Christine H., David W. Pitts and Ignacio Navarro. 2010. "Representative Bureaucracy and Policy Tools: Ethnicity, Student Discipline, and Representation in Public Schools." *Administration and Society,* 42, 1.

Rocha, Rene R., and Daniel P. Hawes. 2009. "Racial Diversity, Representative Bureaucracy, and Equity in Multiracial School Districts." *Social Science Quarterly,* 90, 2.

Ross, Ashley D., Stella M. Rouse and Kathleen A. Bratton. 2010. "Latino Representation and Education: Pathways to Latino Student Performance." *State Politics and Policy Quarterly,* 10, 1.

Ruck, Martin D., and Scot Wortley. 2002. "Racial and Ethnic Minority High School Students' Perceptions of School Disciplinary Practices: A Look at Some Canadian Findings." *Journal of Youth and Adolescence,* 31, 3.

Rushowy, Kristin. 2007. "ESL Funds Used to Heat Schools." *Toronto Star,* June 13. <thestar.com/news/2007/06/13/esl_funds_used_to_heat_schools.html>.

Ryan, James. 2003. "Educational Administrators' Perceptions of Racism in Diverse School Contexts." *Race Ethnicity and Education,* 6, 2.

___. 1999. *Race and Ethnicity in Multiethnic Schools.* Clevedon, UK: Multicultural Matters.

Ryan, James, Katina Pollock and Fab Antonelli. 2009. "Teacher Diversity in Canada: Leaky Pipelines, Bottlenecks, and Glass Ceilings." *Canadian Journal of Education,* 32, 3.

___. 2007. "Teacher and Administrator Diversity in Canada: Leaky Pipelines, Bottlenecks, and Glass Ceilings." Paper presented at the Annual Conference of the Society for the Study of Education, Saskatoon.

Salole, Abigail T., and Zakaria Abdulle. 2015. "Quick to Punish: An Examination of the School to Prison Pipeline for Marginalized Youth." *Canadian Review of*

Social Policy, 72/73.

Scheurich, James Joseph, and Michelle D. Young. 1997. "Coloring Epistemologies: Are Our Research Epistemologies Racially Biased?" *Educational Researcher,* 26, 4.

Skerrett, Allison. 2010. "Of Literacy Import: A Case of Cross-National Similarities in the Secondary English Curriculum in the United States and Canada." *Research in the Teaching of English,* 45, 1.

Solomon, Patrick R., and Cynthia Levine-Rasky. 2003. *Teaching for Equity and Diversity: Research to Practice.* Toronto, ON: Canadian Scholars' Press and Women's Press.

Spring, Joel. 2000. *American Education,* ninth edition. Boston: McGraw-Hill.

Stanfield, John H. 1985. "The Ethnocentric Basis of Social Science Knowledge Production." *Review of Research in Education,* 12.

Statistics Canada. 2014. "2011 National Household Survey: Immigration and Ethnocultural Diversity." [Catalogue numbers 99-010-X]. <www12.statcan.gc.ca/nhs-enm/2011/dp-pd/dt-td/Index-eng.cfm>.

___. 2013. "2011 National Household Survey: Data Tables." [Catalogue number 99-010-X2011032]. <www12.statcan.gc.ca/nhs-enm/2011/dp-pd/pol-plo/Index-eng.cfm>.

___. 2012. "2011 Census of Canada: Topic-Based Tabulations: Mother Tongue, Age Groups and Sex for the Population of Canada." [Catalogue number 98-314-XCB2011022]. Ottawa: Statistics Canada. <www12.statcan.gc.ca/nhs-enm/2011/dp-pd/pol-plo/Index-eng.cfm>.

Stewart, Joseph, Robert E. England and Kenneth J. Meier. 1989. "Black Representation in Urban School Districts: From School Board to Office to Classroom." *Western Political Quarterly,* 42, 2.

Tator, Carol, and Frances Henry. 2010. "The Struggle for Anti-Racism, Inclusion, and Equity in the Canadian Academy: Representation Is Not Enough." *Our Schools, Our Selves,* 19, 3.

___. 1991. *Multicultural Education: Translating Policy into Practice.* Ottawa: Multiculturalism and Citizenship Canada.

Toohey, Kelleen, and Tracey M. Derwing. 2008. "Hidden Losses: How Demographics Can Encourage Incorrect Assumptions about ESL High School Students' Success." *Alberta Journal of Educational Research,* 54, 2.

Toronto District School Board. 2016. "The 2013–2014 Environmental Scan of the Toronto District School Board." <tdsb.on.ca/Portals/0/AboutUs/Research/2013-2014TDSBEnvironmentalScan.pdf>.

___. 2012. "The TDSB Grade 9 Cohort 2006–2011. Trend data: Fact sheet No.1." <tdsb.on.ca/Portals/0/Community/Community%20Advisory%20committees/ICAC/research/September%202012%20Cohort%20dataAcrobat%20Document.pdf>.

Turner, Ani. 2016. "The Business Case for Racial Equity." *National Civic Review,* 105, 1.

Vancouver School Board. 2016. "District Plan for Student Learning 2014/2015." <vsb.bc.ca/sites/default/files/DLP%20VBE%202014-2015%28with%20Cover%29.pdf>.

Watt, David, and Hetty Roessingh. 2001. "The Dynamics of ESL Drop-out: Plus Ça Change…" *Canadian Modern Language Review,* 58, 2.

Weine, Stevan, John Horgan, Cheryl Robertson, Sana Loue, Amin Mohamed and Sahra Noor. 2009. "Community and Family Approaches to Combating the Radicalization and Recruitment of Somali-American Youth and Young Adults: A Psychosocial Perspective." *Dynamics of Asymmetric Conflict,* 2, 3.

Whitten, Amanda, and Christabelle Sethna. 2014. "What's Missing? Anti-Racist Sex

Education!" *Sex Education,* 14, 4.

Williams, David R., and Ruth Williams-Morris. 2000. "Racism and Mental Health: The African American Experience." *Ethnicity and Health,* 5, 3/4.

Williams-Morris, R.S. 1996. "Racism and Children's Health: Issues in Development." *Ethnicity and Disease,* 6, 1–2.

Young, Iris. 1990. *Justice and the Politics of Difference.* Princeton, NJ: Princeton University Press.

Zeiders, Katharine H., Leah D. Doane and Mark W. Roosa. 2012. "Perceived Discrimination and Diurnal Cortisol: Examining Relations among Mexican American Adolescents." *Hormones and Behaviour,* 61, 4.

Zhou, Steven. 2014. "Canada's Muslims: From Detoxing Radicalization to Citizenship." *Aljazeera,* February 3. <aljazeera.com/indepth/opinion/2014/01/canada-muslimsfrom-detoxing-radi-20141309549990632.html>.

8

SEXUAL AND GENDER DIVERSITY

Resituating within the Frame of Anti-Racism and Anti-Colonialism

Edward Ou Jin Lee

Over the past decade, Canada has asserted itself as a global leader in *lesbian, gay, bisexual, trans, queer and intersex* (LGBTQI) human rights advocacy by claiming its recognition of same-sex marriage, anti-discrimination laws and general social acceptance of LGBTQI people and its status as a *"safe haven"* for those fleeing homophobic and transphobic violence abroad (Jenicek, Lee and Wong 2009; Gamble et al. 2015; Murray 2016a; Lee, Hafford-Letchfield, Pullen Sansfaçon, Kamgain and Gleeson 2017). This message is echoed in a documentary about lesbian, gay, bisexual and trans (LGBT) refugees produced by the National Film Board titled *Last Chance* (d'Entremont 2013). The documentary includes the voices of LGBT refugee claimants and their family members, along with some leading Canadian refugee advocates. Along with sharing disturbing experiences of homophobic and transphobic violence in their countries of origin, the refugee claimants describe Canada as a land free of discrimination, and the trailer concludes with a leading refugee advocate exclaiming, "if Canada cannot offer this kind of generosity, what country possibly can?" (d'Entremont 2013).

This media representation of Canada as a "safe haven" for LGBTQI refugees recycles a particular narrative about the state of LGBTQI human rights in Canada. This prevailing story of LGBTQI migration as a simple movement from repression to liberation suggests that other countries, particularly in the Global South, are unimaginably *homophobic* and *transphobic*, whereas Canadian society is affirmed as an exemplary model of LGBTQI human rights (Jenicek, Lee and Wong 2009; Murray 2016a). This perception is further entrenched, at both domestic and international levels, by the story of Canada as a discrimination-free nation, not only for LGBTQI migrants but all migrants (Thobani 2007). However, a closer examination of the everyday realities of queer and trans people living in Canada (Namaste 2000; Mulé 2009), especially those who are racialized and/or migrants (Lee 2012; El-Hage and Lee 2016; Murray 2016a), reveals different stories that bump up against the story of Canada as a global leader of LGBTQI human rights and a country free of discrimination.

As a scholar-activist who organizes with *queer and trans people of colour* communities and who is personally part of them, I have repeatedly encountered the "safe haven" story. Certainly, there has been historical progress of LGBTQI rights in Canada (see Lee and Brotman 2015: 265) that includes the partial decriminalization of same-sex sexuality (Kinsman 1998) along with laws and refugee protection based on sexual orientation and gender identity discrimination. Affirmed by some research and repeated by citizens and migrants alike, this story is not without merit (d'Entremont 2013; Murray 2016a). And yet, my experiences of supporting queer and trans migrants locked in detention centres, fighting deportation orders and/or living undocumented tear apart the story of LGBTQI migration as a simple path from repression to liberation. These experiences necessitate more complex explanations and demand alternative stories. My longstanding scholarly and activist pursuits have led me to ask critical questions about how and why Canada may be free for some but not for others — how and why it may be a "safe haven" for some and not for others. The multitude of ways in which queer and trans people of colour must navigate both structural and interpersonal violence nuance and challenge the dominant narratives of Canada as a liberal, multicultural nation free of discrimination and, in particular, a "safe haven" for LGBTQI people (see Dryden and Lenon 2016; Murray 2016b).

Keguro Macharia (2010), drawing from the words of Chimamanda Ngozi Adichie (2009), cautions against reproducing single stories about the origins of homophobia in Africa that erase the complexities of individual and collective histories along with contemporary realities. Similarly, the disruption of the single story, or ideological account, of Canada as an LGBTQI "safe haven" requires the denaturalization of prevailing assumptions related to queer and trans people of colour living here. Mapping out the histories, social relations and conditions that organize the contemporary realities of queer and trans people of colour reveal power relations that "shape what can be known, thought and said ... calculating not only who can speak and how they are likely to be heard, but also how we know what we know and the interest we protect through our knowing" (Razack 1998: 10). Reframing how we know, think and talk about the lives and bodies of queer and trans people of colour may transform how we engage in activism against racism.

In this chapter, I trace the historical, material and transnational conditions for homophobic and transphobic violence both globally and within Canada. I map out current tensions in relation to the ways in which sexual and gender diversity is taken up within reflexive and multi-dimensional ways of knowing. This mapping includes how the erasure of histories of colonial violence have shaped the present-day dominant framing of LGBTQI human rights in Canada. These historical and intergenerational forces shape the kinds of structural and interpersonal violence experienced by queer and trans people of colour, especially those who are women, poor or working class and disabled. I also highlight the ways in which queer and trans people of colour survive, thrive and resist multiple oppressions both individually and collectively. Finally, I consider the possibilities and tensions in shifting toward an anti-racist and anti-colonial politics that centres the lives of queer and trans people of colour; I also present key principles and action steps to affirm multiple identities while also working toward dismantling racism and colonialism in Canada.

The objectives of this chapter are to:

- reframe "sexual and gender diversity" within overlapping global and Canadian historical contexts of colonialism and imperialism;
- better understand the lived realities of queer and trans people of colour living in Canada through an intersectional lens; and
- explore the possibilities and tensions of moving toward an anti-racist and anti-colonial politics that places queer and trans people of colour at the centre of strategies to eliminate racism in Canada.

Sexual and Gender Diversity through Identities, Theories and Politics

Although the terms "people of colour" and "racialized" are used often, here and elsewhere, there are important debates related to their usage. There has been a shift, for example, from the use of "people of colour" to "Black, Indigenous and other people of colour" to avoid erasing the particularities of Black and Indigenous experiences (Cook-Lynn 2007; Sexton 2010). Moreover, "people of colour" has its origins within the US (Vidal-Ortiz

2008; Ross 2015) and thus does not always translate neatly into the Canadian context. These debates are important to acknowledge. I thus engage with both terms not only to identify groups but also to make visible the social processes through which people become racialized (Miles 2003) as well as the political character of the term "people of colour." However, I also use the terms Black, Indigenous, Arab and Asian to highlight the particularities related to anti-Black, anti-Indigenous, anti-Arab and anti-Asian racisms.

Over the past few decades, particularly within the Anglo-Canadian and US contexts, the term "*queer*" has shifted from its use as discriminatory label to one of empowerment (Lee and Brotman 2015). By reclaiming this label, some identify queer as an umbrella term that includes people of diverse sexual and gender identities (Carlin and DiGrazia 2003; Lee and Brotman 2015). Although using queer as an umbrella term includes the term "*trans*," some have pushed back against this inclusion by asserting that trans identities have and continue to be subsumed and obscured by sexual identities (lesbian, gay, bisexual, etc.) (Namaste 2000; Stryker 2008). Instead, the terms "*transgender*" or "*trans*" have been suggested as an umbrella term that includes the full range of gender identities and expressions (Stryker 2008). However, Viviane Namaste (2000) critiques the use of transgender as an umbrella term, instead suggesting that the term's emergence from the US context reinforces Anglo-imperialism, as English language terms cannot fully represent how everyone understands gender.

Some scholars have extended the meaning of sexual and gender identity categories by calling for the flourishing of queer theories and politics (Warner 1993; Cohen 1997, 2003; Carlin and DiGrazia 2003; De Genova 2010). These scholars have called upon the "queer-ing" and "trans-ing" of critical theories. Some have also suggested that a queer and trans politics includes challenging not only normative sexual practices, trans erasure and the gender binary but also mainstream politics related to issues such as immigration reform (De Genova 2010). The "*intersex*" category (when an individual has a combination of gender characteristics that don't conform to medically defined male- or female-gendered bodies) has also been examined through a critical lens to unpack how intersex people are pathologized through medical discourse in ways that overlap with, and yet are distinct from, queer and trans identities (Bastien-Charlebois 2011; Bastien-Charlebois and Guillot 2014). The re-configuration of queer and trans as particular modes of analysis suggest the importance of examining how heteronormativity and cisnormativity operate as dominant societal norms (Warner 1993; Cohen 1997; Stryker 2008).

Table 8.1: Key Definitions

Cis	Cis is used for people whose gender identity has always been concordant with their gender assigned at birth (Serano 2007; Bauer et al. 2009).
Cisnormativity	Cisnormativity describes the ways in which social institutions and practices reproduce the gender binary as a societal norm, along with the erasure of trans people (Serano 2007; Bauer et al. 2009).
Heteronormativity	Heteronormativity is described as "the practices and institutions that legitimize and privilege heterosexuality and heterosexual relationships as fundamental and 'natural' within society" (Cohen 1997: 40).
Heterocisnormativity	Heterocisnormativity is when heteronormative and cisnormative processes are interconnected.

However, queer and trans theories and politics have been criticized for reinscribing White dominance by failing to contend with the ways in which sexuality and gender have been historically and are presently experienced by queer and trans people of colour (Perez 2005; Eng 2010; Smith 2010; Bhanji 2012; Haritaworn 2012). These scholars suggest that the "subject-less" critique of heteronormativity or cisnormativity (a critical theory that focuses on social processes versus sexual and gender identities) in fact reproduces the White, cis, gay, male gaze. Joseph Massad (2007) suggests that even the term "*sexuality*" was socially constructed as part of Western European colonial thought, erasing alternative modes of conceptualizing and organizing various forms of social expressions, behaviours and intimacies. Rather than reproduce colonial and imperial modes of knowledge, these scholars suggest engaging in *queer of colour critique* (Munoz 1999; Ferguson 2004), *queer Indigenous critique* (Driskill 2010; Driskill, Finley, Gilley and Morgensen 2011) and *queer diasporic critique* (Puar 1996; Eng 1997; Gopinath 1996) by recognizing the ways in which many contemporary sexual and gender identity categories were "historically formed through specific epistemologies and social relationships that upheld colonialist, xenophobic, racist and sexist regimes" (Luibheid 2005: xi).

I thus use these terms while also recognizing the limitations of existing identity categories in capturing the actualities and complexities of how queer and trans people, particularly those who are racialized, navigate and express their sexualities and genders. Instead of viewing these varying conceptions of queer and trans as irreconcilable, I engage with their multiple meanings in context-specific ways. I also draw from queer Indigenous, diasporic and of colour critique to reveal the intimate relationship between heterocisnormative processes and global histories of *colonialism* and *imperialism*. In doing so, I suggest that a liberatory queer and trans politics is intertwined with *anti-racist* and *anti-colonial* politics — and that social movements working toward ending racism cannot have one type of politics without the other.

Toward Reflexive Ways of Knowing

The following sections make explicit the epistemological terrain that grounds my claims and introduces key debates that frame the multiple identities, theories and politics related to *"sexual and gender diversity"* in Canada. Rather than strive to present "objective" knowledge, I engage with *reflexive ways of knowing* that recognize the power relations that are embedded within the knowledge-making process and organize what is accepted as valid knowledge (Smith 1990, 2005; Naples 1996; Collins 2000). To foster reflexive ways of knowing, I engage with a *multi-dimensional standpoint framework* (Naples 2003; Cantu 2009) that integrates key features of *materialist feminist* (Smith 1990, 2005) and *Black feminist standpoints* (Collins 2000).

This framework encourages me to both recognize the material realities that shape queer and trans people of colour's lives as well as how my history, social location and activism inform the ways that I build knowledge. My knowledge-building process rests on my own history and social location as a queer and gender non-conforming person of colour who was born in Seoul, South Korea, and grew up in the 1980s as a migrant-turned-citizen/settler in Bearspaw, Chiniki, Blood, Piikani, Siksika, Tsuu T'ina and Wesley First Nations (Treaty 7) territories (also known as Calgary, Alberta). I am now living in Mohawk/Kanien'kehá:ka territories (also known as Montréal, Québec). My analysis is equally informed by over a decade of community building and organizing with queer and trans people of colour and as a student at Anglophone universities and in my present academic position as an assistant professor at a Francophone university.

My reflexive stance is further grounded by a Black feminist standpoint through an ethics of caring and accountability, particularly vis-à-vis queer and trans people of colour communities (Collins 2000). My knowledge-building practices are guided by critical, community-based and participatory methodologies. This means that my knowledge claims are grounded in the relationships that I have built with queer and trans people of colour. These relationships involve expressiveness and emotions — they are connected to dialogue and, thus, reflect an ethics of caring (Collins 2000). Finally, my knowledge-building practices are based on an ethics of accountability. This ethics includes being transparent about my social location and access to (and limits of) institutional power, as well as the importance of engaging in dialogue about my knowledge claims with queer and trans people of colour, especially those who are gender non-conforming, women, trans, poor, working class, disabled and migrants.

My hope in being explicit about the epistemology that informs this chapter is to encourage students, activists and scholars to develop their own strategies to reflect upon their relationship to their knowledge-building practices with directly affected communities. Although it is not possible to be this transparent in every context, it is crucial to understand, at least for yourselves, how your history and social location shape your analysis and activism.

Global and Canadian Historical Context

The contemporary global human rights landscape is marked by uneven levels of societal acceptance of and violence against LGBTQI people. This is a hotly contested terrain. A global survey published annually by the International Lesbian, Gay, Bisexual, Trans and Intersex Association shows that there has been an increase over the past few years in United Nations member states that allow same-gender marriage (nine) and prohibit discrimination based on sexual orientation (fifty-two) and/or gender identity (nineteen), mostly within the Global North. There remain seventy-eight countries, mostly in the Global South, that have laws that define promoting or engaging in same-gender sexuality as illegal, resulting in imprisonment and in some cases, the death penalty (Carroll and Ramon Mendos 2017). Certainly, state legislation criminalizing same-sex sexuality shapes interpersonal and state violence against LGBTQI people, which includes harassment, torture, arrest, threats, imprisonment, rape and murder.

At first glance, this pattern of LGBTQI human rights reinforces the prevailing narrative of the West (Europe, US, Canada, etc.) as LGBTQI human rights leaders, compared to the homophobic and transphobic Global South. A closer examination of the everyday realities of LGBTQI people in the Global South reveals more complicated stories (Agrawal 1997; Wieringa and Blackwood 1999; Atluri 2012; Dutta 2012; Mwikya 2013; Ndashe 2013; Nicol, Gates-Gasse and Mulé 2014). As such, the single story of "homophobia in Africa" should be challenged, since "African homophobia does not exist, nor does European homophobia, Asian homophobia or South American homophobia. Acts of homophobia occur in each of these spaces … within their specific local histories as these intersect with broader global histories" (Macharia 2010: para 3).

The Recovery of Forgotten Colonial and Imperial Histories

To reframe *homophobic/transphobic violence* as a truly global phenomenon, we can use the *"politics of lacking knowledge"* (Lowe 2006: 206). Our lack of knowledge about colonial and imperial violence can be traced back to the nineteenth-century emergence of the Western European liberal philosophy of modern humanism (Lowe 2006). Western Europe's supposed "universal" vision of full personhood achieved through state citizenship, wage labour, the exchange market, property rights and a civil and secular society occurred at the same time as African enslavement, Indigenous genocide in the Americas and indentured labour of Asians (Lowe 2006; Mills 2008). It is the purposeful forgetting of this global racialized conflict between colonial rulers and colonized peoples that has ultimately shaped what we "know" and what we don't know about the origins and causes of homophobic/transphobic violence today.

During the nineteenth and twentieth centuries, White/Western colonial powers were consumed by the desire to regulate *"carnal knowledge"* in the colonies, which included anything related to bodily contact (including sexual contact) within the overlapping realms of social mores, education, health and family (Stoler 2006). The regulation of "carnal knowledge" between and among the colonizers and the colonized served to consolidate colonial power (Stoler 2006: 4). Moreover, management of sexuality and gender in the colonies was intimately tied to the growing working and middle class in Europe. Across the British Empire the owning class developed and imposed the norm of the nuclear (White) family, with the husband as breadwinner and his inferior wife, whose role was restricted to the domestic sphere (Davidoff 1995).

The home thus served as a site that regulated the desire for respectable, White, middle-class domesticity (Mosse 1995; Fellows and Razack 1998). Within Western Canada, affluent settlers explicitly promoted the central place of a "White life for two" in Canadian nation building — a Christian, monogamous and lifelong marriage between a (hetero and cis) man and woman (Carter 2008: 8). This patriarchal and heterocisnormative form of marriage replaced more flexible forms of Indigenous marriage, which

included same-gender marriage, accepted within many Indigenous societies (Carter 2008). Indeed, White settlers "were shocked by the position
Indigenous womyn had in their communities ... if they wanted to take over
the land, especially the people, they would have to dismantle the power of
womyn" (Metallic 2013: 5).

The Eugenic Discourses of Respectability:
Degeneracy and Homosexuality

A key pathway to achieve this respectable White domesticity was through
the *eugenic discourse* of scientific racism, which circulated throughout the
British Empire, including the White settler colony of Canada (McClintock
1995; Valverde 2008; Vidal-Ortiz, 2008). Considered mainstream "scientific
knowledge," medical professionals began to classify phenotypical differences (e.g. size of nose, head, etc.) by marking racialized bodies as inferior
to White bodies (McClintock 1995; Somerville 1996, 2000). This marking
of racialized bodies was simultaneously gendered, as racial difference was
located differently between racialized men and women (Somerville 2000).
Alongside these racialized and gendered hierarchies, this classification
enforced a rigid gender binary — male and female — with any variation
being deemed outside the "normal" workings of human biology (Fausto-
Sterling 2000). The normative power of respectable, White, middle-class,
heterocisnormative domesticity was thus reinforced by eugenic discourses
that scientifically labelled certain bodies as degenerate.

The emergence in Britain of a regime of sexual categories, otherwise
known as the "*sexual sciences*," resulted in the pathologizing of diverse
gender expressions and same-gender sexuality (Kinsman 1996). Same-
gender sexuality transitioned from being considered as perverse sexual
acts — sodomy — into a pathological condition inherent in individuals
— homosexuality (D'Emilio 1983; Bleys 1995; Ferguson 2004). This shift
was also shaped by industrial capitalism, since the "*homosexual*" identity
only became possible due to the emergence of wage labour in urban areas
and the partial dismantling of interdependent family units (D'Emilio
1993/1998: 242).

The pathological condition of homosexuality was part of a broader
knowledge system of the "sexual sciences" that strengthened eugenic
discourses of who and what was respectable. *Degeneracy* was deployed by
the Victorian elite to separate White respectability from those identified
as "dangerous" and "deviant," such as homosexuals, the poor or working
class, Jewish people, feminists, prostitutes, the "insane" and criminals

(McClintock 1995). These eugenic discourses were intimately tied to imperial and colonial exploits, which served to consolidate racial, economic and
political power through notions of sexual purity, public hygiene and moral
sanitation (McClintock 1995). These grand narratives of social, moral and
racial purity were institutionalized by criminalizing a host of activities
such as prostitution, sodomy and vagrancy across the British Empire. This
discourse also circulated across Europe and the colonies through White/
Western men who spoke of the deviance of colonized people they met
during their imperial exploits. They classified people as "*eunuchs*"[1] and
"hermaphrodites," along with denouncing perverse sexual acts such as
"sodomy" or "buggery."

Within the Canadian context, these eugenic discourses related to sexual
deviancy were interwoven into key political and social institutions. For
example, the Canadian *Immigration Act* of 1906 included the term "moral
turpitude" (behaviour deemed vile and against established social mores)
as a category of exclusion; in 1927 the Act added "deviants" and in 1952
"homosexuals" as categories of exclusion. These discourses surfaced and
changed over time to exclude specific groups of potential migrants who were
deemed to transgress prevailing sexual and gender norms, as articulated
by the ruling Canadian White settler elite (Lee 2015).

The Criminalization of Sexual and Gender
Transgressions as a Colonial Tool of Domination

As nineteenth- and twentieth-century eugenic discourses of respectability–degeneracy reorganized the colonial management of sexual relations
through laws related to concubinage,[2] marriage and prostitution (Stoler
1989, 2002), colonial rulers simultaneously criminalized and policed sexual
and gender transgressions (Bleys 1995; Aldrich 2003; Gupta 2008; Finley,
2011; Gannon 2011; Mogul, Ritchie and Whitlock 2011). Inspired by the
British legislation *Offences against the Person Act* in 1837 and the *Vagrancy
Act* in 1824, the policing of sexual and gender transgressions in the colonies
can be traced back to British India and the passing of section 377 of the
Indian Penal Code (IPC) in 1860 and the *Act for the Registration of Criminal
Tribes and Eunuchs* (ARCTE) in 1897 (Gupta 2008). Although French and
Dutch colonies also had laws that criminalized sexual and gender trans-
gressions, section 377 would become "the model for British colonies' legal
systems throughout most of Asia and Africa" (Gupta 2008: 21).

Section 377 was applied to criminalize colonized people who practised "sodomy" in addition to deterring White/Western men, particularly

soldiers, from this type of "deviancy," thus bolstering the political and military strength of the British Empire though the "manpower" of White, heterosexual, masculine men (Gupta 2008; Stoler 1989, 2002). On the other hand, the ARCTE was designed to target individuals who transgressed gender norms, labelling them as "eunuchs," and denied them the rights to have a will or dress or dance "like a woman," and taking away their traditional village rights to the land. Not only were "eunuchs" criminalized for their gender expression and sexual behaviour, they lost their social role/status within their particular village; this law thereby impacted entire Indigenous communities in India.

Through IPC and the ARCTE, sexual and gender transgressions were shorn of any material, social and spiritual relations. This extended beyond the British colony of India, as the criminalization of Indigenous sexual and gender expressions served as a key mechanism through which many Indigenous societies were reorganized (Gupta 2008; Driskill et al. 2011; Mogul, Ritchie and Whitlock 2011). These laws set the boundaries of heterocisnormative intimacies that hierarchically marked sexualized and gendered bodies for life or death. Indigenous social organization was replaced by colonial constructions of sex and sexuality. By separating groups of people from their communities and land base, "imperialist interventions in sexuality could also enforce local patriarchies, stigmatize alternative sexualities, and serve as instruments of imperial control over colonized peoples" (Sreenivas 2014: 76).

By extension, the colonial laws related to sodomy, "eunuchs" and vagrancy also operated as a colonial tool of domination. These colonial laws about sexual relations served to reorganize and contain Indigenous socie-ties, "to place not just behaviours, but classes of people under surveillance and control" (Gupta 2008: 30). Sodomy laws had a wide reach and were imposed on a global scale across much of the British (and other European) empires, serving to consolidate the colonial relation of the civilized and respectable (heterosexual/cissexual, White/Western) versus the uncivilized and degenerate "Others."

Within Canada, the criminalization of "perverse" sexual and gender behaviour was part of a broader set of sexualized and gendered violence designed to destroy Indigenous ways of life, including the central and spir-itual place of those targeted by White settlers. These Indigenous people often occupied valued social positions within their respective Indigenous Nations, as each Nation had their own, and often multiple, terms to signify a group's particular sexual and/or gender expressions that were intricately tied to the

Nation's social organization (Meyer-Cook and Labelle 2004; Meyer-Cook 2008; Morgensen 2011; Metallic 2013). From early imperial and colonial excursions through to the implementation of Indian residential schools, Indigenous people who transgressed sexual and gender norms were killed, abused and separated from their communities. For Indigenous people, and especially those who now identify as "*two-spirited*," the criminalization of sexual and gender transgressions was used as a colonial tool of genocide.

The criminalization of sexual and gender transgressions operated differently for Asian migrants. Their arrival to Canada at the turn of the twentieth century was hotly contested by White settlers and the political elite (Dua 2007; Shah 2011). Various sodomy, public indecency and vagrancy laws, which included provisions against cross-dressing, were systematically used to contain and control South Asian migrant men. According to Gorden Brent Ingram (2003: 91), "the South Asian population in British Columbia numbered only in the thousands. Yet Sikh males were defendants in scores of 'oriental cases' and in British Columbia's first legal attacks on group and public homosexuality." South Asian migrant men were thus racially profiled and targeted through laws that criminalized same-gender relations. The prosecution of sodomy, public indecency and vagrancy worked in concert with a deportation regime targeting racialized migrant men to operate as a colonial tool of domination.

The Erasure of Social Violence and Contemporary Implications

Historical Shifts and Continuities

Over the course of the twenty-first century, the British colonial laws that criminalized sexual and gender transgressions continued to expand, albeit unevenly, across most of the Global South (Bleys 1995; Gupta 2008). From the 1940s to the 1970s, anti-colonial uprisings overturned British and French colonial rule, as some regions transitioned into nation-states (Alexander and Mohanty 1997). However, as former colonies gained "independence," there remained neo-colonial continuities in how mostly White/Western economic interests guided the political decisions of emerging militarized dictatorships across the Global South (Alexander and Mohanty 1997; Ekine 2013). These White/Western-driven, capitalist processes of recolonization included the making of loyal heterosexual (and cissexual) citizens (Alexander 2005).

As the local elite occupied political power, the criminalization of sexual and gender transgressions, born mostly out of White/Western colonial morality, was reframed as integral to local cultural values (Bleys 1995; Alexander 2005; Alexander and Mohanty 1997; Walcott 2006; Gupta 2008; Awondo 2010; Awondo, Geschiere and Reid 2012; El-Menyawi 2012; Blake and Dayle 2013). Thus, central to post-independence nation building was the maintenance of a patriarchical and heterocisnormative social order. This was achieved through the circulation of discourses related to "family values," the promotion of monogamous marriage and the continued criminalization of sexual and gender transgressions, which actually expanded in some states to include sexual activity between two women (Alexander 2005; Gupta 2008). With this shift, the extended history of the colonial management of sexual relations, along with the social violence required to impose heterocisnormative intimacies of empire, was erased.

Uncovering the colonial legacies of the criminalization of sexual and gender transgressions reveals the often purposefully forgotten histories of social violence. This historical recovery reframes knowledge about the origins of homophobic/transphobic violence and reframes what we know and how we think about contemporary sexual and gender identity categories. The historical underpinning of contemporary "homophobic acts" across the Global South should thus be framed within broader heterocisnormative processes that are interwoven into colonial legacies, post-colonial nationalisms and an uneven global political economic order.

Historical Displacement and Intergenerational Trauma

Shaped by this historical social violence, queer and trans people of colour living in Canada today must often differently and differentially contend with the effects of historical displacement and intergenerational trauma (Lee 2012). For many Indigenous Peoples, as well as Black and Asian peoples whose ancestry can be traced back in Canada for generations, experiences of homophobia and/or transphobia cannot be untied from historical and ongoing colonial policies related to the taking of land, the reserve system and residential schools (LGBTQI Indigenous and Two-Spirit people), slavery and lynching (queer/trans Black people), indentured labour practices (Chinese head tax, continuous journey law, etc.) and racial segregation.

Recovering and unpacking these almost entirely forgotten histories is often difficult and deeply painful. As Grace Cho (2008: 53) says, "unspeakable trauma does not die out with the person who first experienced it. Rather, it takes on a life of its own, emerging from the spaces where secrets are concealed." These intergenerational histories of genocide, slavery and exploitation are, on both individual and collective levels, interlinked with various mental health consequences such as anxiety, depression and suicide.

This historical recovery equally suggests a need to reframe how we understand contemporary social movements across the Global South against the criminalization of sexual and gender transgressions as part of, and even integral to, the legacies of Indigenous Peoples' resistance against colonial and imperial regimes. Within the Canadian context, we need to resituate the role of queer and trans people of colour within Indigenous, racial and migrant justice movement building and organizing. Indeed, retracing historical continuities of resistance, alongside violence, may open alternative pathways and strategies for ending racism in Canada that centre the voices and experiences of queer and trans people of colour.

Resituating Structural Violence, Heterocisnormative Processes and Racialized Bodies

Understanding how racism operates in Canada requires seeing it as a form of *structural violence* shaped by colonial and White supremacist histories. Some forms of contemporary structural violence include missing and murdered Indigenous women, the intergenerational effects of residential schools and slavery, the overrepresentation of Black and Indigenous people in prisons, and systemic barriers and discrimination in relation to the labour market, employment, citizenship and immigration policies, migrant labour policies, racial profiling and educational institutions. Many of these issues are discussed in depth elsewhere in this book. These forms of structural violence have either directly impacted queer and trans people of colour or their biological and/or chosen family members. Queer and trans people of colour realities are inextricably shaped by these historical, material and social contexts.

That is, racialized realities should not be presumed to be solely heterosexual and/or cissexual. Heteronormative and cisnormative processes are intertwined with various forms of structural violence and thus impact all racialized people — albeit differently. For example, in chapter 6, Carl James addresses how heteronormative processes integral to White supremacy impact racialized men and shape violence against, in particular, racialized women.

Intersectional Structural Violence

Along with the structural violence faced by all racialized people, queer and trans people of colour face particular forms of structural violence because of their multiple identities. Kimberlé Crenshaw (1991) was one of the first, among other critical race and Black feminist scholars, to develop an analysis of intersectional forms of structural violence. Structural intersectionality is not due to intentional institutional practices but is, rather, "a consequence of the imposition of one burden interacting with predisposing vulnerabilities to create yet another dimension of disempowerment" (Crenshaw 1996: 359).

Avenues through which queer and trans people experience intersectional structural violence include barriers to accessing health care and social services (Lee 2012; Ristock, Zoccole and Passante 2010; El-Hage and Lee 2016). For LGBTQI Indigenous and Two-Spirit individuals, historical trauma related to colonization interacts with heterocisnormative health care and social services resulting in particular barriers to care (Ristock, Zoccole and Passante 2010). These barriers include a lack of residential transition services (for those migrating from their Indigenous community to an urban area), service providers who do not understand the complex links between sexuality/gender and colonialism and a lack of specialized services (Ristock, Zoccole and Passante 2010). Queer and trans people of colour also experience particular structural barriers to accessing care when the multiple oppressions they encounter are not addressed in a holistic manner (Lee 2012; El-Hage and Lee 2016). Health care providers and therapists do not assess the degree to which race, gender, class, sexuality, religion, disability, etc. intersect and mediate the everyday lives of queer and trans people of colour service users, along with their physical and mental health (Lee 2012).

For queer and trans migrants with precarious status (visitors, international students, temporary workers, refugee claimants, protected persons, along with those detained and undocumented), their migrant status results in particular forms of intersectional structural violence (Lee and Brotman 2013). Cisnormativity and heteronormativity have particular impacts on (mostly) racialized migrants who have to navigate the Canadian immigration regime. For example, throughout the refugee process, to access various educational, employment and health care institutions LGBTQI refugee claimants are compelled to "out" their sexual orientation and/or gender identity. This forced "coming out" to service providers and immigration agents makes LGBTQI refugee claimants systematically more vulnerable to homophobia and transphobia than LGBTQI citizens. Trans refugee claimants are particularly impacted "if their gender expressions do not correspond with their legal names, which they are required to use in order to make their claims" (Lee and Brotman 2013: 166). Moreover, trans migrants in Québec are presently not able to legally change their gender marker or name until they become a citizen, resulting in increased exposure to cisnormative practices and transphobic violence (Tourki 2016). Queer and trans migrants with precarious status who are detained also navigate heteronormative and cisnormative detention policies and practices, such as a gay or lesbian couple not being recognized as a family or a trans person being held in isolation due to having a gender expression that does not match their legal name and gender marker (Lee 2015).

Intersectional marginalization often interacts with the various kinds of intersectional structural violence experienced by racialized people. For example, due to structural violence perpetuated by the state (i.e., police, judges, immigration agents, social workers, etc.), queer and trans people of colour may be reticent to seek state protection. If an undocumented queer Muslim woman of colour was sexually harassed by a stranger, an acquaintance, fellow community organizer or partner who is a citizen, she would be vulnerable to being detained and/or deported if she filed a police report. Moreover, this person may have limited support from her communities, especially if she has experienced racism within the LGBTQI community and homophobia within the racialized/migrant community. In contrast, a queer Black man who encounters racial profiling by the police may also experience anti-Black racism within LGBTQI communities and homophobia within Black communities.

Queer and trans people of colour experience intersectional marginalization and structural violence in many varied settings (Lee 2012). They can experience interpersonal discrimination and violence in public, community and activist spaces. For queer and trans women of colour, simply walking down the street may elicit sexual harassment and violence (SAWCC 2012). Sexual harassment and violence against queer and trans women of colour may also be reproduced within various activist/organizing organizations (e.g., Indigenous sovereignty, Black liberation, migrant justice, LGBTQI rights, student activism, etc.). This form of intersectional marginalization often centres cis men within community and activist spaces while queer and trans feminine bodies are pushed aside.

Queer and trans people of colour are also vulnerable to intersectional marginalization within various community and group spaces. A Latina transwoman may experience racism and sexism within LGBTQI communities, while also experiencing transphobia and sexism within the Latinx communities. Various forms of oppression may also be reproduced within intentional queer and trans people of colour spaces and organizing, such as anti-Black racism, sexism and ableism.

Individual and Collective Survival and Resistance

Historical displacement, intergenerational trauma, intersectional structural violence and marginalizing experiences often have consequences for queer and trans people of colour. These consequences include social isolation, material deprivation, negative health outcomes (physical ailments, depression, etc.), suicide and premature death (Lee 2012). However, many queer and trans people of colour continue to survive, thrive and resist. Sometimes, individual survival occurs from simply affirming multiple identities, maintaining familial and community ties and waking up every day refusing to succumb to oppression.

In some cases, queer and trans people of colour navigate dominant health care, social service, educational and political institutions as service users, students, practitioners, teachers or politicians, disrupting and challenging normative practices. By doing so, short- and long-term institutional spaces are built that make the lives of queer and trans people of colour legible and recognizable. For example, queer and trans people of colour may be community members and organizational workers, pushing community organizations to respond to the multiple oppressions that shape their everyday lives. Community organizations like the 2-Spirited People of the 1st Nations[3] (2-Spirits), and the Black Queer Youth (BQY) Initiative[4] are at the forefront of providing community resources by and for queer and trans Indigenous and Black people.

In some cases, queer and trans people of colour are involved within broader Indigenous, racial and migrant justice organizing, pushing these spaces to centre queer and trans Indigenous, Black and people of colour lives. For example, the Native Youth Sexual Health Network[5] aims to build sexual and reproductive health within and across Indigenous communities, while also advocating for Indigenous sovereignty. Almassir[6] is an LGBTQI and feminist collective in Montréal that organizes not only against sexism and homophobia but also anti-Arab sentiment, Islamophobia, migrant justice and for Indigenous rights, including those of Palestinians. The Third Eye Collective[7] applies a transformative justice approach to addressing structural and interpersonal violence against Black communities and, in particular, sexual violence against Black women. Queer and trans people of colour are also building transformative queer and trans diasporic spaces through arts-based organizing such as the Asian Arts Freedom School,[8] the People Project[9] and Qouleur.[10] Many are at the forefront of social movements and in leadership roles in building various types of identity-based and coalitional politics that disrupt and confront mainstream activism and community organizing strategies (Wong 2013).

Table 8.2 Queer and Trans People of Colour Cultural Workers and Community Leaders (Canada)

Kimura Byol <starkimproject.com>
Kim Katrin Milan <kimkatrinmilan.com>
Kama La Mackerel <lamackerel.net>
Lindsay Nixon <aabitagiizhig.com>
Kai Cheng Thom <ladysintrayda.wordpress.com>
Jack Saddleback <@JackSaddleback>

Queer and trans people of colour across Turtle Island are building identities, theories and politics within formal institutional/organizational settings and/or informal community/public spaces that challenge and reconfigure the what, why and how of organizing and activism against various racisms and colonialisms. Indeed, there is a longstanding history of queer and trans of colour individuals, collectives and initiatives who have actively contributed to ending racism, paying particular attention to how it is integrated into colonialism, imperialism, patriarchy, ableism, classism and homophobia/transphobia. In the following section, I propose three overarching principles that should be integrated into any community, organizational or institutional context with individuals and collectives that include an anti-racist and/or anti-colonial mandate. These principles reframe how we understand the inextricable relationship between racism and "sexual and gender diversity," as well as point to concrete ways to improve the living conditions of the most marginalized queer and trans people of colour.

Key Principles and Action Steps

Starting with the Recovery of Histories of Social Violence

Recovering or at least acknowledging erased colonial and imperial histories helps us trace how the colonial regulation of sexual and gender transgressions was central to making of White/Western personhood built on a racialized global division of labour. Heterocisnormative processes were central to White/Western empire building, both globally and within Canada. Erasing these complex histories of structural violence allows for the current articulations of Canada as discrimination-free and a "safe haven" for LGBTQI refugees to go uncontested. It is this sort of haunted "freedom" that makes it possible for Canada to laud itself for its legalization of same-sex marriage in 2006, while violently forgetting the ways in which Indigenous family laws within many First Nations celebrated and honoured same-gender marriages for centuries.

One strategy for recovering these forgotten histories is to recognize that we are born into a set of social circumstances that condition how we can know, think and talk about racism and oppression in Canada. Poet and professor Lillian Allen suggests that we learn to listen to "what we don't know we don't know."[11] By constantly asking ourselves what it is that we do not know we do not know about the histories of racialized communities in Canada, we can foster openness toward learning more forgotten histories. This openness can then allow us to reframe how we situate ourselves within the history of Canada and shift how we see ourselves within our own intergenerational histories. As Black/Brown trans femme artist and movement builder Kama La Mackerel (2016) reflects on intergenerational family trauma, she eloquently states,

> the repercussions of colonial violence are still too close to our homes, too close to our hearts, they are in our homes, they are in our hearts (I wonder where the healing lies? Where justice lies? How many more generations until this is undone?).[12]

The internalization of colonial logics, over generations, have thus contributed to the ways in which queer and trans people of colour experience intersectional forms of violence today.

Developing Strategies That Address Both
Intersectional Structural and Interpersonal Violence

Queer and trans people of colour must navigate both structural and interpersonal forms of violence faced by all racialized people, in addition to intersectional forms of violence also shaped by their sexuality and/or gender. A key challenge becomes untangling the structural from the interpersonal and developing multi-level strategies of resistance.

On one hand, an over-emphasis on structural violence obscures interpersonal experiences. For example, an individual or a group might be accused of reinforcing structural racism if they bring up misogyny perpetuated by a hetero and cis man of colour within a migrant justice organizing space (or, as another example, transphobic behaviours within a queer and trans people of colour collective) and attempt to hold people accountable to oppressive behaviours by excluding abusive people from organizing spaces. Attempts to hold individuals accountable to *interpersonal violence* (shaped by broader social forces) can also get framed as enacting harmful "identity politics" or "dividing" the movement.

On the other hand, a focus solely on interpersonal violence often reproduces individualist and culturalist explanations for violence (it's *that* person's fault or *that* culture's fault) and thus erases the historical, intergenerational and structural conditions for oppression. Structural violence is often reproduced through its non-acknowledgement. For example, reducing alcohol addiction and domestic violence to an individual concern justifies taking Indigenous and Black children from their families for their safety but does not recognize the intergenerational effects of colonial and structural violence related to genocide, slavery, residential schools and racial segregation. This allows dominant groups, especially those in positions of authority (police, immigration agents, social workers) and political decision making (politicians, policymakers) to evade accountability for the historical and contemporary reproduction of White supremacist and colonial violence.

To improve the living conditions and/or foster social transformation for all racialized communities, and especially queer and trans racialized people, it is crucial to take into account both structural and interpersonal forms of violence. This is, unfortunately, easier said than done. Developing strategies that address both simultaneously can feel overwhelming and seemingly impossible. People often end up addressing one or the other, either in silos or by simply ignoring one over the other.

One strategy is to focus on the process of organizing rather than just the outcome. Being process-oriented helps to attend to the micro-practices of organizing by reflecting on: Who is talking? Who is taking up space? Who is not? It can also include the use of consensus-based decision making. Paying attention to the micro-practices of how you organize may reveal concrete, day-to-day strategies. My own involvement in anti-deportation campaigns with queer and trans migrants has taught me how being process-oriented helps to incrementally build space for directly affected people to have some type of control over their everyday lives. When people have space to understand and reflect upon their options, even if the available options are limited, and then use their power to make a decision, it can cultivate kernels of hope and resistance that can grow over time.

Another strategy is to begin with the issue that an individual or collective is most directly affected describes as the most pressing, regardless of whether it's articulated as structural or interpersonal violence. Within activist and community organizing settings, beginning with addressing the immediate needs of directly affected community members becomes a crucial starting point for collective mobilization. Although this type of strategy can begin with supporting one or two people, its scope can widen as more people get involved. Campaign or support goals and actions are often tied to demands to change or apply laws and policies (e.g., stopping a deportation by providing someone with a humanitarian and compassionate grounds permit), which serve to also highlight major systemic flaws (e.g., in immigration policy). For example, there was a campaign initiated and led by trans migrants during summer 2017 that demanded that the Québec provincial government change the law so that trans migrants would be able to change their gender marker and name.[13]

If you are a worker within an organizational or institutional context with a social justice mandate, it would be helpful to reflect upon how you may first encounter the directly affected person. For example, if you are a social worker in a health clinic, it may be helpful to assess the degree to which your clinic reinforces or pushes back against structural violence. How you might support a queer Muslim migrant or trans woman of colour sex worker will depend on how your organization or institution responds to the parts of immigration and criminal law that make queer and trans people of colour vulnerable to intersectional structural violence. If you have decision-making power within a particular organization, reflect upon how you can contribute to fostering or building spaces that affirm queer and trans racialized identities and lives. Finally, validate and affirm the experiences of directly impacted people through the use of active listening.

Table 8.3: Strategies to Foster Intersectional Organizing Spaces

- Respect (and do not assume) how people self-identify their sexual and/or gender identity.
- Recognize that some people may not identify with Western identity labels (lesbian, gay, bisexual, trans, queer, etc.).
- Remember that how people self-identify their sexual and/or gender identity may change over time.
- Reflect upon the level of awareness within your organizing space about how the terms "queer" and "trans" signify identities, versus theories and/or politics.
- Reflect upon the degree to which queer and trans identities, theories and politics may be situated within the frame of colonialism and imperialism.
- Raise awareness of homophobia and transphobia within your organizing space.
- Assess the degree to which your organizing space reproduces heteronormativity and cisnormativity.
- Engage in critical self-reflection about your own relationship to heteronormative and cisnormative processes.
- Collaborate with queer and trans people of colour who are involved in your space to develop context-specific strategies to address intersecting forms of racism, sexism, classism, ableism or homophobia/transphobia within your organizing or activist space.
- Ask yourself ongoing reflexive questions about your organizing or activist space: Who are in leadership positions? Who are on the margins? How do we affirm multiple identities? How do we work across difference? Are there ways that we are reproducing various oppressions?

Recognize All Community and Organizing Spaces as Intersectional

A key principle when engaging in any type of anti-colonial and/or anti-racist activism is to be aware that all community and organizing spaces are intersectional. Organizing spaces are already and always racialized, gendered, sexualized, able-ized, etc. Whether it is the fight for Indigenous sovereignty, Black liberation, or immigration rights, organizing efforts need to implement concrete strategies that foster the participation and leadership of women, queer and trans, poor or working class and disabled people of colour. Efforts need to include recognizing identity politics; however, this inclusion should not be reduced to an issue of "identity politics," nor should this be viewed as further dividing movement building efforts. For example, a queer and/or trans person of colour might be hired within a social justice organization simply because of their social location, without consideration of how this person's skills and analysis may contribute to the organization or serious internal analysis of how the current organizational culture engages with intersectionality and issues of racism, sexism and homophobia/transphobia. This type of tokenistic hiring can result in placing burdens on this person because, as the "expert" on the lives of queer and trans people of colour, they are required to know everything about this "topic." But if this person brings up this dynamic to the organization, they can quickly become identified as the "troublemaker" who is trying to use their identity to blame people or the organization.

Centring the lives and bodies of multiply marginalized, racialized people across social movements directly challenges White supremacist and colonial logics that have operated for centuries on a global scale to disintegrate collective and feminine power, and eliminate queer, trans and disabled bodies. This may lead us to recalling various forms of Indigenous social organization that were nearly erased from our collective memories. Recognizing these histories and bodies that were, in some cases, almost entirely erased, point us to how we may build alternatives to the present global capitalist colonial social order. The ways in which both LGBTQI people in India, Pakistan and Bangladesh and LGBTQI Indigenous and Two-Spirit people in Canada have organized to create resurgent spaces that affirm Indigenous identities and social organization point us to powerful alternative ways of moving and living. This also helps us to honour how queer and trans people of colour have resisted colonialism and imperialism for centuries on a global scale. Table 8.3 includes some suggestions to foster intersectional organizing spaces.

DISCUSSION QUESTIONS
1. What did you not know that you did not know about the erasure of histories of social violence described in this chapter?
2. How does heteronormativity and cisnormativity affect your everyday life, based on your particular social location?
3. How might you address intersectionality within your activist or organizing space?

ACTION STEPS
1. Collaborate with queer and trans people of colour to develop context-specific strategies to address intersecting forms of racism, sexism, classism, ableism, homophobia and transphobia.
2. Pay attention to whose agenda is being prioritized and whose voices are being heard when doing anti-oppressive community organizing. Queer and trans people of colour who are directly affected by an issue of oppression should name and prioritize the action agenda.
3. Validate and affirm the experiences of people who are directly impacted by oppression through the use of active listening; focus on

the process of organizing from a place of solidarity, rather than just the outcome of a project or community initiative.

Supplemental Readings

Lee, Edward Ou Jin, and Shari Brotman. 2013. "Speak Out! Structural Intersectionality and Anti-Oppressive Practice with LGBTQ Refugees in Canada." *Canadian Social Work Review*, 30, 2: 157–183.

Meyer-Cook, Fiona, and Diane Labelle. 2004. "Namaji: Two-Spirit Organizing in Montreal, Canada." *Journal of Gay and Lesbian Social Services,* 16, 1.

Rwigema, Marie-Jolie, Onyinyechukwu Udegbe and David Lewis-Peart. 2016. "'We Are Expected to Work As If We Are Not Who We Are': Reflections on Working with Queer Black Youth." In Brian J. O'Neill, Tracy A. Swan and Nick J. Mulé (eds.), LGBTQ *People and Social Work: Intersectional Perspectives.* Toronto: Canadian Scholars' Press.

Additional Resources

Asian Freedom School <facebook.com/groups/asianartsfreedomschool>.

The People Proejct <thepeopleproject.ca>.

Qouleur <qouleur.ca>.

Lilian Allen: Learning to Listen to What We Don't Know We Don't Know <youtube.com/watch?v=afS4ROxdXFM>.

Kama La Mackerel <kama-la-mackerel.tumblr.com/post/136938040457/forgiveness>.

Notes

1. The term "eunuch" can be traced back to the time period of antiquity across Europe and Asia and was commonly understood as a castrated and/or celibate male who occupied a particular social role within their society (Tougher 2009).
2. Laura Ann Stoler (1989: 637) describes concubinage in the colonies as domestic arrangements outside marriage between colonizer (White) men and colonized women, "which included sexual access to a non-European woman as well as demands on her labor and legal rights to the children she bore" (citing Pollman 1986 and Lucas 1986).
3. <2spirits.com/index.html>.
4. <soytoronto.org/current/bqy.html>.
5. <nativeyouthsexualhealth.com/whatwedo.html>.
6. <facebook.com/pg/almassir.montreal/about/?tab=page_info>.
7. <thirdeyemontreal.com/>.
8. <facebook.com/groups/asianartsfreedomschool/>.
9. <thepeopleproject.ca>.
10. <qouleur.ca>.
11. <youtube.com/watch?v=afS4ROxdXFM>.
12. <kama-la-mackerel.tumblr.com/post/136938040457/forgiveness>.
13. For more about the campaign, please see <change.org/p/ministre-justice-gouv-qc-ca-justice-for-trans-migrants-in-quebec-pass-bill-895>.

References

Adichie, Chimamanda Ngozi. 2009. "The Danger of a Single Story." <ted.com/talks/chimamanda_adichie_the_danger_of_a_single_story/transcript?language=en>

Agrawal, Anuja. 1997. "Gendered Bodies: The Case of the Third Gender in India." *Contributions to Indian Sociology,* 3, 2.

Aldrich, Robert. 2003. *Colonialism and Sexuality.* New York: Routledge.

Alexander, M. Jacqui. 2005. *Pedagogies of Crossing: Meditations on Feminism, Sexual Politics, Memory and the Sacred.* Durham and London: Duke University Press.

Alexander, M. Jacqui, and Chandra Talpade Mohanty. 1997. *Feminist Genealogies, Colonial Legacies, Democratic Futures.* New York: Routledge.

Atluri, Tara. 2012. "The Prerogative of the Brave: Hijras and Sexual Citizenship after Orientalism." *Citizenship Studies,* 16, 5–6.

Awondo, Patrick. 2010. "The Politicisation of Sexuality and Rise of Homosexual Movements in Post-Colonial Cameroon." *Review of African Political Economy,* 37, 125.

Awondo, Patrick, Peter Geschiere and Graeme Reid. 2012. "Homophobic Africa? Toward a More Nuanced View." *African Studies Review,* 55, 3.

Bastien-Charlebois, Janik. 2011. « Pour une Sensibilité Intersexe ». Forum Genre et Sexualité. *Revue Canadienne de Service Social,* 28, 1.

Bastien-Charlebois, Janik, et Vincent Guillot. 2014. « Les Résistances Médicales aux Critiques d'Activistes Intersexes : Quelques Opérations sur le Front de la Crédibilité ». *La Normativité de Genre et ses Effets sur l'Enfance et l'Adolescence.* Congrès Scientifique International.

Bauer, Greta R., Rebecca Hammond, Robb Travers, Matthias Kaay, Karin M. Hohenadel and Michelle Boyce. 2009. "'I Don't Think This Is Theoretical; This Is Our Lives': How Erasure Impacts Health Care for Transgender People." *Journal of the Association of Nurses in AIDS Care,* 20, 5.

Bhanji, Nael. 2012. "Trans/Scriptions: Homing Desires, (Trans)Sexual Citizenship and Racialized Bodies." In Trystan T. Cotton (ed.), *Transgender Migrations: The Bodies, Borders, and Politics of Transition.* New York: Routledge.

Blake, Conway, and Philip Dayle. 2013. "Beyond Cross-Cultural Sensitivities: International Human Rights Advocacy and Sexuality in Jamaica." In Corinne Lennox and Matthew Waites (eds.), *Human Rights, Sexual Orientation and Gender Identity in the Commonwealth: Struggles for Decriminalisation and Change.* London, UK: University of London Press.

Bleys, Rudi. 1995. *The Geography of Perversion: Male-to-Male Sexual Behaviour Outside the West and the Ethnographic Imagination, 1750–1918.* New York: New York University Press.

Cantu, Lionel. 2009. *The Sexuality of Migration: Border Crossings and Mexican Immigrant Men.* New York: New York University Press.

Carlin, Deborah, and Jennifer DiGrazia. 2003. *Queer Cultures.* New Jersey: Prentice Hall.

Carroll, Aengus, and Lucas Ramon Mendos. 2017. *State-Sponsored Homophobia: A World Survey of Sexual Orientation Laws: Criminalisation, Protection and Recognition.* Geneva: ILGA.

Carter, Sarah. 2008. *The Importance of Being Monogamous: Marriage and Nation Building in Western Canada to 1915.* Edmonton, AB: University of Alberta Press.

Cho, Grace M. 2008. *Haunting the Korean Diaspora: Shame, Secrecy and the Forgotten*

War. Minneapolis, MN: University of Minnesota Press.

Cohen, Cathy J. 2003. "Contested Membership: Black Gay Identities and the Politics of AIDS." In Robert J. Corber and Stephen Valocchi (eds.), *Queer Studies: An Interdisciplinary Reader.* Malden: Blackwell Publishing.

____. 1997. "Punks, Bulldaggers and Welfare Queens: The Radical Potential of Queer Politics?" *Feminist Theory,* 4, 3.

Collins, Patricia Hill. 2000. *Black Feminist Thought: Knowledge, Consciousness and the Politics of Empowerment.* New York: Routledge.

Cook-Lynn, Elizabeth. 2007. "Scandal." *Wicazo Sa Review,* 22, 1.

Crenshaw, Kimberle. 1996. "Mapping the Margins: Intersectionality, Identity Politics, and Violence against Women of Color." In Kimberlé Crenshaw, Neil Gotanda, Garry Peller and Kendall Thomas (eds.), *Critical Race Theory: The Key Writings that Formed the Movement.* New York: New Press.

1991. "Mapping the Margins: Intersectionality, Identity Politics and Violence against Women of Colour." *Stanford Law Review,* 43, 6.

D'Emilio, John. 1993/1998. "Capitalism and Gay Identity." In William B. Rubenstein, Carlos A. Ball and Jane S. Schacter, *Cases and Materials on Sexual Orientation and the Law: Lesbians, Gay Men and the Law.* New York: New Press.

____. 1983. *Sexual Politics, Sexual Communities: The Making of the Homosexual Minority in the United States, 1940–1970.* London: University of Chicago Press.

d'Entremont, Paul Émile. 2013. *Last Chance.* National Film Board. <nfb.ca/film/last-chance/>.

Davidoff, Leonore. 1995. *Worlds Between: Historical Perspectives on Gender and Class.* Cambridge: Polity Press.

De Genova, Nicholas. 2010. "The Queer Politics of Migration: Reflections on 'Illegality' and Incorrigibility." *Studies in Social Justice,* 4, 2.

Driskill, Qwo-Li. 2010. "Doubleweaving Two-Spirit Critiques: Building Alliances between Native and Queer Studies." GLQ, 16, 1–2.

Driskill, Qwo-Li, Chris Finley, Brian Joseph Gilley, and Scott Lauria Morgensen (eds.). 2011. *Queer Indigenous Studies: Critical Interventions in Theory, Politics and Literature.* Tucson, AZ: University of Arizona Press.

Dryden, OmiSoore H., and Suzanne Lenon. 2016. *Disrupting Queer Inclusion: Canadian Homonationalisms and the Politics of Belonging.* Vancouver, BC: UBC Press.

Dua, Enakshi. 2007. "Exclusion through Inclusion: Female Asian Migration in the Making of Canada as a White Settler Nation." *Gender, Place and Culture,* 14, 4.

Dutta, Aniruddha. 2012. "An Epistemology of Collusion: Hijras, Kothis and the Historical (Dis)continuity of Gender/Sexual Identities in Eastern India." *Gender and History,* 24.

Ekine, Sokari. 2013. "Contesting Narratives of Queer Africa." In Sokari Ekine and Hakima Abbas (eds.), *Queer African Reader.* Dakar: Pambazuka Press.

El-Hage, Habib and Edward Ou Jin Lee. 2016. "LGBTQ Racisés: Frontières Identitaires et Barrières Structurelles." *Alterstice: Revue Internationale de la Recherche Interculturelle,* 6, 2.

El-Menyawi, Hassan. 2012. "The Great Reversal: How Nations in the Muslim World Went from Tolerating Same-Sex Practices to Repressing LGB People, 1750–2010."

Eng, David L. 2010. *The Feeling of Kinship: Queer Liberalism and the Racialization of Intimacy.* Durham and London: Duke University Press.

____. 1997. "Out Here and Over There: Queerness and Diaspora in Asian American

Studies." *Social Text,* 52/53 (Autumn–Winter).

Fausto-Sterling, Anne. 2000. *Sexing the Body: Gender Politics and the Construction of Sexuality.* New York: Basic Books.

Fellows, Mary Louise, and Sherene Razack. 1998. "The Race to Innocence: Confronting Hierarchical Relations among Women." *Gender, Race and Justice,* 1.

Ferguson, Roderick A. 2004. *Aberrations in Black: Toward a Queer of Colour Critique.* Minneapolis, MN: University of Minnesota Press.

Finley, Chris. 2011. "Decolonizing the Queer Native Body (and Recovering the Native Bull-Dyke): Bringing 'Sexy Back' and Out of Native Studies' Closet." In Qwo-Li Driskill, Chris Finley, Brian Joseph Gilley and Scott Lauria Morgensen (eds.), *Queer Indigenous Studies: Critical Interventions in Theory, Politics and Literature.* Tucson, AZ: University of Arizona Press.

Gamble, Kathleen, Nick Mulé, Nancy Nicol, Phyllis Waugh and Sharalyn Jordan. 2015. *Envisioning LGBT Refugee Rights in Canada: Is Canada a Safe Haven?* Toronto, ON: York University.

Gannon, Shane. 2011. "Exclusion as Language and the Language of Exclusion: Tracing Regimes of Gender through Linguistic Representations of the 'Eunuch.'" *Journal of the History of Sexuality,* 20, 1.

Gopinath, Gayatri. 1996. "Nostalgia, Desire, Disapora: South Asian Sexualities in Motion." In *Russell Leong* (ed.), *Asian American Sexualities: Dimensions of the Gay and Lesbian Experience.* New York: Routledge.

Gupta, Alok. 2008. *This Alien Legacy: The Origins of "Sodomy" Laws in British Colonialism.* New York: Human Rights Watch.

Haritaworn, Jin. 2012. "Colorful Bodies in the Multikulti Metropolis: Vitality, Victimology and Transgressive Citizenship in Berlin." In Trystan T. Cotton (ed.), *Transgender Migrations: The Bodies, Borders, and Politics of Transition.* New York: Routledge.

Ingram, Gorden Brent. 2003. "Returning to the Scene of the Crime: Uses of Trial Dossiers on Consensual Male Homosexuality for Urban Research, with Examples from Twentieth-Century British Columbia." *GLQ: A Journal of Lesbian and Gay Studies,* 10, 1.

Jenicek, Ainsley, Edward Ou Jin Lee and Alan D. Wong. 2009. "Dangerous Shortcuts: Media Representations of Sexual Minority Refugees in the post-9/11 Canadian Press." *Canadian Journal of Communications,* 34, 4.

Kinsman, Gary. 1998. "Constructing Sexual Problems: These Things May Lead to the Tragedy of Our Species." In Wayne Antony and Les Samuelson (eds.), *Power and Resistance: Critical Thinking about Canadian Social Issues,* second edition. Halifax: Fernwood Publishing.

___. 1996. *The Regulation of Desire: Homo and Hetero Sexualities.* Montréal: Black Rose Books.

La Mackerel, Kama. 2016. "On Forgiveness and Geographical Spaces of the Heart." January 9. <kama-la-mackerel.tumblr.com/post/136938040457/forgiveness>.

Lee, Edward Ou. 2015. "The Social Organization of Queer/Trans Migrations: The Everyday Ways in which Queer and Trans Migrants with Precarious Status." *International Journal of Child, Youth and Family Studies.*

___. 2012. "Escape, Retreat, Revolt: Queer People of Colour Living in Montreal: Using Photovoice as a Tool for Community Organizing." In Aziz Choudry, Jill Hanley and Eric Shragge (eds.), *Organize! Building from the Local for Global Justice.* Oakland, CA: PM Press.

Lee, Edward Ou, and Shari Brotman. 2015. "Social Work and Sexual and Gender Diversity." In Nicole Ives, Myriam Denov and Tamara Sussman (eds.), *Social Work Histories, Contexts and Practices: A Canadian Perspective.* Don Mills, ON: Oxford University Press.

___. 2013. "Speak Out! Structural Intersectionality and Anti-Oppressive Practice with Sexual Minority Refugees in Canada." *Canadian Social Work Review,* 30, 2.

Lee, Edward Ou, Trish Hafford-Letchfield, Annie Pullen Sansfaçon, Olivia Kamgain and Helen Gleeson. 2017. *The State of Knowledge about LGBTQI Migrants Living in Canada in Relation to the Global LGBTQI Rights Agenda.* Montréal, QC: Université de Montréal.

Lowe, Lisa. 2006. "The Intimacies of Four Continents." In Laura Ann Stoler (ed.), *Haunted by Empire: Geographies of Intimacy in North American Intimacy.* Durham & London: Duke University Press.

Luibheid, Etithne. 2005. "Introduction: Queering Migration and Citizenship." In Eithne Luibhed and Lionel Cantu Jr. (eds.), *Queer Migrations: Sexuality, US Citizenship, and Border Crossings.* Minneapolis, MN: University of Minnesota Press.

Macharia, Keguro. 2010. "Homophobia in Africa Is Not a Single Story." *The Guardian,* May 26. <theguardian.com/commentisfree/2010/may/26/homophobia-africa-not-single-story>.

Massad, Joseph A. 2007. *Desiring Arabs.* Chicago and London: University of Chicago Press.

McClintock, Anne. 1995. *Imperial Leather: Race, Gender and Sexuality in the Colonial Context.* New York: Routledge.

Metallic, G. 2013. "Finding Two-Spirit Identity: An Autoethnography." Master of Social Work research report, McGill University, Montréal, QC.

Meyer-Cook, Fiona. 2008. "Two-Spirit People: Traditional Pluralism and Human Rights." In Shari Brotman and Joseph J. Levy (eds.), *Homosexualités: Variations Linguistiques et Culturelles.* Québec: Presses de l'Université du Québec, Coll., Santé et Société.

Meyer-Cook, Fiona, and Diane Labelle. 2004. "Namaji: Two-Spirit Organizing in Montreal, Canada." *Journal of Gay and Lesbian Social Services,* 16, 1.

Miles, Robert. 2003. *Racism. Key Ideas,* second edition. London and New York: Routledge.

Mills, Charles W. 2008. "Racial Liberalism." PMLA, 123, 5.

Mogul, Joey L., Andrea J. Ritchie and Kay Whitlock. 2011. *Queer (In)Justice: The Criminalization of LGBT People in the United States.* Boston, MA: Beacon Press.

Morgensen, Scott Lauria. 2011. *Spaces Between Us: Queer Settler Colonialism and Indigenous Decolonization.* Minneapolis, MN: University of Minnesota Press.

Mosse, George. 1995. *Nationalism and Sexuality: Respectability and Abnormal Sexuality in Modern Europe.* New York: Howard Fertig.

Mulé, Nick J. 2009. "Demarcating Gender and Sexual Diversity on the Structural Landscape of Social Work." *Critical Social Work,* 9, 1.

Munoz, Jose Esteban. 1999. *Disidentifications: Queers of Color and the Performance of Politics.* Minneapolis, MN: University of Minnesota Press.

Murray, David A.B. 2016a. "Real Queer: 'Authentic' LGBT Refugee Claimants and Homonationalism in the Canadian Refugee System." *Anthropologica,* 56, 1.

___. 2016b. *Real Queer? Sexual Orientation and Gender Identity in the Canadian Refugee Apparatus.* London, UK: Rowman and Littlefield.

Mwikya, Kenne. 2013. "The Media, the Tabloid and the Uganda Homophobia Spectacle." In Sokari Ekine and Hakima Abbas (eds.), *Queer African Reader*. Dakar: Pambazuka Press.

Namaste, Viviane. 2000. *Invisible Lives: The Erasure of Transsexual and Transgendered People*. Chicago, IL: University of Chicago Press.

Naples, Nancy. 2003. *Feminism and Method: Ethnography, Discourse Analysis and Activist Research*. New York: Routledge.

___. 1996. "A Feminist Revisiting of the Insider/Outsider Debate: The 'Outsider Phenomenon' in Rural Iowa." *Qualitative Sociology*, 19, 1.

Ndashe, Sibongile. 2013. "The Single Story of 'African Homophobia' Is Dangerous for LGBTI Activism." In Sokari Ekine and Hakima Abbas (eds.), *Queer African Reader*. Dakar: Pambazuka Press.

Nicol, Nancy, Erika Gates-Gasse and Nick Mulé. 2014. "Envisioning Global LGBT Human Rights: Strategic Alliances to Advance Knowledge and Social Change." *Scholarly and Research Communication*, 5, 3.

Perez, Hiram. 2005. "You Can Have My Brown Body and Eat It Too!" *Social Text*, 23, 3–4 (84–85).

___. 1996. "Transnational Sexualities: South Asian (Trans)nation(alism)s and Queer Disaporas." In Russell Leong (ed.), *Asian American Sexualities: Dimensions of the Gay and Lesbian Experience*. New York: Routledge.

Razack, Shirene H. 1998. *Looking White People in the Eye: Gender, Race, and Culture in Courtrooms and Classrooms*. Toronto, ON: University of Toronto Press.

Ristock, Janice, Art Zoccole and Lisa Passante. 2010. "Aboriginal Two-Spirit and LGBTQ Migration, Mobility and Health Research Project: Winnipeg, Final Report, November 2010." Winnipeg, MB.

Ross, Loretta. 2015. "Here's a Much-Needed History Lesson on the Origins of the Term 'Women of Color.'" *Everyday Feminism*, March 10. <everydayfeminism. com/2015/03/origin-of-term-woc/>.

SAWCC (South Asian Women's Community Centre). 2012. "Bulletin August 2012." Montreal, QC.

Serano, Julia. 2007. *Whipping Girl: A Transsexual Woman on Sexism and the Scapegoating of Femininity*. Emeryville, CA: Seal.

Sexton, Jared. 2010. "People-of-Color-Blindness: Notes on the Afterlife of Slavery." *Social Text*, 28, 2 (103).

Shah, Nayan. 2011. *Stranger Intimacy: Contesting Race, Sexuality and the Law in the North American West*. Berkeley, CA: University of California Press.

Smith, Andrea. 2010. "Queer Theory and Native Studies: The Heteronormativity of Settler Colonialism." GLQ, 16, 1–2.

Smith, Dorthy E. 2005. *Institutional Ethnography: A Sociology for People*. Lanham, MD: Altamira Press.

___. 1990. *The Conceptual Practices of Power: A Feminist Sociology of Knowledge*. Toronto, ON: University of Toronto Press.

Somerville, Siobhan. 2000. *Queering the Color Line: Race and the Invention of Homosexuality in American Culture*. Durham & London: Duke University Press.

___. 1996. "Scientific Racism and the Invention of the Homosexual Body." In Brett Beemyn and Michele Eliason (eds.), *Queer Studies: A Lesbian, Gay, Bisexual and Transgender Anthology*. New York: New York University Press.

Sreenivas, Mytheli. 2014. "Sexuality and Modern Imperialism." In Robert M. Buffington, Eithne Luibheid and Donna J. Guy (eds.), *A Global History of Sexuality:*

The Modern Era. Oxford: Wiley Blackwell.

Stoler, Anne L. 2006. "Intimidations of Empire: Predicaments of the Tactile and Unseen." In Anne L. Stoler (ed.), *Haunted by Empire: Geographies of Intimacy in North American Intimacy.* Durham & London: Duke University Press.

___. 2002. *Carnal Knowledge and Imperial Power: Race and the Intimate in Colonial Rule.* London: University of California Press.

___. 1989. "Making Empire Respectable: The Politics of Race and Sexual Morality in 20th Century Colonial Cultures." *American Ethnologist,* 16, 4.

Stryker, Susan. 2008. *Transgender History.* Berkeley, CA: Seal Press.

Thobani, Sunera. 2007. *Exalted Subjects: Studies in the Making of Race and Nation in Canada.* Toronto, ON: University of Toronto Press.

Tourki, Dalia. 2016. "I'm an Arab Trans Woman, Struggling to Find Myself in Language." *Huffington Post,* October 28. <huffingtonpost.com/entry/im-an-arab-trans-woman-struggling-to-find-myself_us_5813cff6e4b096e870696596>.

Valverde, Mariana. 2008. *The Age of Light, Soap and Water: Moral Reform in English Canada, 1995–1925.* Toronto, ON: University of Toronto Press.

Vidal-Ortiz, Salvador. 2008. "People of Color." *Encyclopedia of Race, Ethnicity, and Society,* 1.

Walcott, Rinaldo. 2006. "Black Men in Frocks: Sexing Race in a Gay Ghetto (Toronto)." In Cheryl Teelucksingh (ed.), *Claiming Space.* Waterloo, ON: Wilfrid Laurier University Press.

Warner, Michael (ed.). 1993. *Fear of a Queer Planet: Queer Politics and Social Theory.* Minneapolis, MN: University of Minnesota Press.

Wieringa, Saskia, and Evelyn Blackwood. 1999. "Introduction." In Evelyn Blackwood and Saskia Wieringa (eds.), *Female Desires: Same-Sex Relations and Transgender Practices across Cultures.* New York: Columbia University Press.

Wong, Alan. 2013. "'Between Rage and Love': Disidentifications among Racialized, Ethnicized and Colonized Allosexual Activists in Montreal." PhD Dissertation, Concordia University, Montreal.

9

DISMANTLING RACISM IN THE CANADIAN CRIMINAL JUSTICE SYSTEM

Wendy Chan

Even though the crime rate in Canada has fallen steadily in the past two decades, the legacy of Harper's Conservative government policy to promote a *"tough on crime"* agenda (CBC *News* 2011) continues to shape criminal justice outcomes. Policies such as mandatory minimum sentences and delays in granting parole to prisoners are examples of how crime remains heavily politicized (Ha-Redeye 2015). The situation has been compounded by a ballooning prison population in many provinces, fuelled to a large extent by an increased use of detention for individuals who are awaiting trial or are unable to pay their bail fee (Parkes and Deshman 2014). Although neither group is considered a threat to public safety, as violent crime rates have been steadily declining, a politics of fear combined with increased criminalization of administrative violations (such as violating bail conditions) has led to overcrowding in prisons and detention centres.

These aggressive crime policies and practices are unevenly distributed, leading to a disproportionate effect on racialized and/or poor individuals and communities, as they are more vulnerable to being criminalized for their actions and behaviours. Recent controversies over the issue of *carding* by the Toronto Police Service highlights the tensions that already exist between racialized communities and law enforcement (Decoste 2015). Furthermore, the ongoing campaigns to raise awareness of *missing and murdered Indigenous women* across Canada, along with the launch of a national inquiry into this matter in 2016, reinforce the perception that racial bias operates throughout the criminal justice system (CBC *News* 2015d, 2016). These are just a few of the many examples that suggest there is still an uneasy relationship between racialized groups and the *criminal justice system* in Canada.

Despite these important issues, there is a popular perception, propagated by the mainstream media and politicians, that we now live in a *post-racial* society. Racial exclusion and discrimination are seen as battles that have been resolved either because racial equality has been achieved or because racism is no longer a political priority. When racism occurs, it is compartmentalized as an isolated incident rather than the result of systemic and institutional arrangements, or complaints about it are dismissed altogether as "*political correctness*" (Lentin 2014: 1269). In Canada, this was exemplified in debates around the niqab being worn during citizenship ceremonies. Where once there was strong support for the preservation of minority cultural customs, this support has faded as defenders of the niqab are increasingly perceived as demanding special privileges not enjoyed by other Canadians. In a poll on the subject, more than 60 percent of Canadians supported a dress code for citizenship ceremonies that excludes wearing the niqab (*CBC News* 2015a). In his support for a ban, former Canadian prime minister Stephen Harper stated that Canada is "a society that is transparent, open and where people are equal" (*CBC News* 2015b). Paradoxically, policies denying cultural differences legitimate the exclusion of racialized minorities and reinforce racial inequalities rather than overcome them.

Given this current political and social context, it is not surprising to find that efforts to highlight the experiences of racialized groups in the criminal justice system have been downplayed or dismissed altogether. Yet, issues of racism in the criminal justice system are far from resolved and new problems continue to emerge. The starting point for the discussion in this chapter is that racism continues to shape criminal justice attitudes, treatment and outcomes. *Racial bias* has contributed to the over-incarceration of Indigenous people while minimizing their criminal victimization (Balfour 2012). It has also led to the belief that migrants to Canada are either terrorists or criminals, and it has legitimated the use of racial profiling by law enforcement agencies. As David Tanovich (2006) reminds us, to be non-White in the Canadian justice system is to be more likely viewed as a crime suspect rather than a crime victim, to experience higher levels of policing and surveillance and to receive harsher penalties for criminal violations. *Criminal justice* issues in Canada illustrate how we are not yet a post-racial society. From the "war on drugs" to the "war on terrorism," definitions of crime and criminal behaviour remain heavily racialized. Ideologies of race are deeply embedded in the criminal justice system and other Canadian social institutions, and these ideologies structure the policies and practices that have a deep and lasting impact on racialized communities.

This chapter begins with a brief overview of debates on race and crime in Canada. There is a rich and diverse body of critical research that helps us understand the role that race and racism has played in shaping criminal justice decisions (e.g., Gill 2000; Comack 2012; Razack 2012; Chan and Chunn 2014). How racialized individuals are perceived and constructed has influenced the laws and policies that seek to govern them. The second part of this chapter examines the racialization of crime — the perception that crime is the peculiar activity of racialized individuals and groups. *Racial stereotypes* continue to shape criminal justice responses, often with tragic consequences, as in the case of Frank Paul, an Indigenous man who died in police custody in Vancouver (*CBC News* 2009a). This second section explores the various ways in which myths about racialized groups, along with broader social inequalities, contribute to the *racialization of crime* in Canada. In the third part of this chapter, I document how racialized perceptions of crime have resulted in higher rates of criminalization and punishment for peoples of colour. Whether it is racialized youth, immigrants and refugees, or Indigenous people, there is a long and distinct pattern of punitive treatment toward these groups in the criminal justice system. This has led some scholars to suggest that the criminal justice system is being used to establish and reinforce a racial caste system in society (Marable 2007). Others (Tanovich 2006; Crichlow 2014) contend that criminal justice policies and procedures are a means of socially controlling racialized populations. I examine these patterns of punishment and the harms individuals and groups have suffered by virtue of their race/ethnicity. This chapter concludes with a discussion of how we might imagine an *anti-racist* criminal justice system in Canada. A key aspect of such a project is the need to enhance, identify and contest our understanding of racism so that we can take these insights into the activist arena in the promotion of social change.

Throughout this chapter, the term *race* is understood to be a socially constructed category of differentiation that is subject to change and contestation over time. Ideas about race are not static and there is significant disagreement over its definition (Miles 1989; Banton 1998). However, rather than reject the concept of race, given that we continue to live in a society where racial differences shape contemporary social relations, particularly in the context of criminal justice, I believe the term is still analytically relevant for highlighting the power differentials between different groups. The concept of *racialization* — the process by which individuals and groups are marked as racially different — is also employed in this chapter, as it is helpful for capturing the many different ways in which racial groups are denigrated and seen as inferior (Murjui and Solomos 2005). Racialization also allows for intersectional understandings because, as a dynamic concept, it is able to incorporate the idea that there are multiple axes of differentiation (gender, class, sexuality and nation) that are irreducible to a discrete category or experience. Where appropriate, this chapter adopts an *intersectional approach* that takes into account the multiple locations of racialized Canadians to illustrate the complexity of their lives. For example, immigrant battered women may not seek police help for fear that they, or other family members, may be deported. Their responses differ from battered Indigenous women, who often do not call the police because they do not want to further criminalize male Indigenous members in their community. Race, along with gender, class and nationality converge in different ways for different racialized groups. By taking an intersectional approach to examining race and crime, my aim is to capture some of the nuances of these convergences for understanding criminal justice policy and practices.

The objectives of this chapter are to:
- demonstrate how racism continues to shape criminal justice outcomes in Canada; and
- understand the relationship between racism and crime.

Race in the Canadian Criminal Justice System

Research on race and crime in Canada is empirically diverse and theoretically sophisticated, with attention being drawn to the many ways in which racial bias informs the administration of criminal justice. A broad range of studies examining historical and contemporary issues demonstrates how differential enforcement, adjudication and punishment are based on stereotypes and assumptions about racialized groups (Mosher 1998; Backhouse 1999; Hylton 2002; Mirchandani and Chan 2007). Racial bias has been, and continues to be, a common phenomenon in shaping criminal justice policy and practice, and these disparities are well documented.

Race and Crime in Canadian History

Historical studies highlight the legacy of racism that has evolved within the criminal justice system, demonstrating that patterns of racialized minority *overrepresentation* and discrimination are not a contemporary phenomenon. They document the historical antecedents of *systemic racism* in Canada's criminal justice system and draw important connections between earlier colonial periods and the contemporary context. Clayton

Mosher's (1998) study of Canada's legal and criminal justice system between 1892 to 1961 uses extensive evidence to show how discrimination against Asians and Blacks in Canada during this period was pervasive. Widespread racism, such as the disproportionate police focus on Black offenders, meant that these groups experienced racial inequality and disadvantage in virtually all spheres of social, legal and criminal justice systems. The negative treatment they experienced was the product of racist practices such as restrictive immigration legislation, but it was also due to the silence and complicity of officials unwilling to address problems of racism (Mosher 1998). Negative stereotypes flourished and gave way to the perception of racialized groups as a threat to the broader society. Jeffrey Monaghan's (2013) examination of *racialized surveillance* in Canada's North-West in the mid-1880s demonstrates how Indigenous opposition to colonialism was stifled by constructing Indigenous Peoples as dangerous, abnormal and deviant. This made it possible to impose regulations that would subject the Indigenous population to greater forms of control (Monaghan 2013). For example, Indigenous people who refused to work on agricultural projects were arrested as "bad Indians" (Monaghan 2013: 502). Similarly, Augustin Brannigan and Zhiqiu Lin's (1999) study of policing in the late nineteenth century notes how public order offences were used to enforce the assimilation of "dangerous foreigners" from southern and eastern Europe. These studies illustrate how official discourses focused on the need to protect the White, settler communities from the threatening, racialized "Other" as a means for justifying various law-and-order campaigns throughout the late nineteenth and early twentieth centuries against racialized groups, often with devastating effects on those who were targeted. Being aware of this historical *legacy of colonialism* is vital, Joyce Green (2006: 512) argues, for recognizing how the unequal distribution of power is a consequence of racism.

Race and Crime in Our Time

Contemporary research on race and crime in Canada continues to document how racism occupies a significant role in criminal justice proceedings while also expanding its lens to incorporate the role of broader social issues, such as poverty, mental health and immigration, in analyses of crime and victimization. A range of empirical studies highlights the entrenched patterns of racial disparities by focusing on policing practices, sentencing and incarceration rates, the treatment of crime victims in racialized communities and the impact of criminal justice policy development and reform for racialized groups (Wortley and Owusu-Bempah 2011; Kitossa 2012; Wane 2013). One of the key themes to emerge from this body of scholarship is how crime and justice are racially constructed insofar as definitions of what is a crime and who is a victim are shaped by stereotypical ideologies of racial groups in Canada (Comack 2012; Warde 2012; Khenti 2014). For example, young Black men are typically regarded as the classic figure of the criminal and, as a result, they are more likely to be *over-policed*, leading to the perception of higher crime rates among this group. This creates a vicious cycle where, due to a panic about high rates of crime by young Black men, police surveillance increases in Black communities, resulting in more control and regulation of this "problem" population. Crime control policies have expanded rapidly, in part due to a racialized fear of crime that has governed how particular populations are constructed and configured by the state as a category of concern. The preoccupation with terrorism and fears of radicalized Arab and Muslim people are two recent examples of how a *culture of fear and control* dominate current criminal justice decision making. Various scholars have sought to illustrate how race-based narratives about crime and disorder are directly linked to punitive legislation that disproportionately impacts and targets racialized groups (Thornhill 2008; Williams 2015).

The systemic, unequal treatment of racialized people in Canada is illustrated in several key issues that have punctuated the discussion about race and crime in Canada over the last two decades. First, during the mid-1990s, there was a lively debate over whether or not the government should collect statistics on race and crime. There has never been a systematic collection of *race-based data* in the criminal justice system due to concerns that this type of information would perpetuate racism or that the information would not be properly collected (Johnston 1994). Others argued that the public should not be denied access to such information (Gabor 1994) and, increasingly, racialized groups have been calling for more access to race-based crime statistics to counter and challenge racial inequalities. The federal government's continued unwillingness to collect this data has been perceived by some as a way to hide the differential criminal justice treatment of racialized groups (Owusu-Bempah and Millar 2010). Second, there have been ongoing discussions in Ontario over carding and racial profiling, which is understood as the differential treatment of individuals by law enforcement agents, based on stereotypes about race or ethnicity, for reasons of safety, security or public protection (Ontario Human Rights Commission 2003). Since the early 2000s, when the *Toronto Star* newspaper published a series of articles on racial profiling in Kingston, there has been significant scholarly attention given to this issue (Tanovich 2003–04; Meng, Giwa and Anucha 2015). Efforts to document the extent to which some communities are racially profiled more than others, along with debates about whether or not this is an acceptable practice and how to prevent such practices from occurring, have shaped the discussions. Last, the longstanding racialized injustices experienced by Indigenous people involved in the criminal justice system remains an important site of investigation. The high rates of Indigenous *criminal victimization* (Perreault 2009), the lack of justice for violence against Indigenous women (Cannon 2014) and the challenges of keeping Indigenous youth out of the criminal justice system (Kroes 2008) are some of the main issues of concern. One of the most disturbing criminal justice issues for Indigenous communities has been the freezing deaths of Indigenous men in the Prairie provinces. Known as *"starlight tours,"* this practice involves police officers picking up "troublesome" people — including the homeless, the addicted and the mentally distressed — driving them to the outskirts of town and leaving them there to walk back, often without adequate clothing against the harsh winter weather (Comack 2012). To date, three Indigenous men have been found frozen to death as a result of these police practices. Despite several inquests and inquiries into the freezing deaths, which found that Indigenous people were routinely treated by the criminal justice system in a dehumanizing way, there has been mostly denial and obfuscation by the police over their responsibility for these deaths (Green 2006).

The picture that emerges in Canada is one where deeply entrenched beliefs enshrined in law and policy about racialized groups has resulted in their differential treatment. Most critical scholars accept that *racial discrimination* in criminal justice processing is an empirical fact, even though political interest and efforts at reform have waxed and waned over time. Drawing on extensive evidence, critical scholars have argued that "White" is the norm against which racialized minorities have been judged and, consequently, systemic racism is commonplace in Canada and in many other Western criminal justice systems (Phillips and Bowling 2003). For example, in a report by the Correctional Investigator of Canada (2013), Howard Sapers concluded that covert racism, discrimination and cultural bias was evident in Canada's federal prisons. The disproportionate representation of Indigenous people and racial minorities in prison suggests that Canada's commitment to social inclusion, equity and equality may be lagging (Correctional Investigator of Canada 2013). A legacy of colonial and racist assumptions has contributed to common-sense ideas about "good" and "bad" women and men and how "normal" women and men think and behave. Despite claims that racial (and gender) equality has been achieved, it is the maleness and Whiteness of Canadian criminal justice that makes it possible to view Black men as more naturally propelled toward sexual deviance and Black or Indigenous women as unrapeable because they are sexually available and inherently promiscuous (Gotell 2008; Razack 2000).

Race and Victimization

While the relationship between race and crime has received significant attention, much less is known about the criminal victimization of racialized individuals and groups. There is much less research and information available on this topic, leading to criticisms that racialized individuals are invisible as crime victims even though, as Jo Goodey (2005: 1) observes, "most of us do not experience crime as criminals but as victims." Feminists have long argued that the criminal victimization of racialized women, particularly in the area of family violence, receives virtually no attention (Meloy and Miller 2011), while other scholars have claimed that the victimization of new immigrants has also largely been ignored (Janhevich, Bania and Hastings 2008). Furthermore, when race intersects with age, class and sexual orientation, problems such as bullying among immigrant youth (McKenney, Pepler, Craig and Connolly 2006); the sexual exploitation, harassment and violence experienced by homeless women, many of whom are racialized (Huey and Quirouette 2010); and the sexual assault, robbery and physical assault of racialized gays, lesbians and bisexuals (Beauchamp 2004) have remained largely hidden from public view. Criticism about the delays in establishing a national inquiry into the many missing and murdered women in Canada, many of whom are Indigenous, lends credence to the claim that there is a racialized hierarchy of concern when it comes to determining whose victimization is worthy of protection (*Toronto Star* 2016). The presence of these disparities has led to greater calls for acknowledging how racialized perceptions and bias have influenced criminal justice approaches to crime and victimization.

When racialized men and women do report their criminal victimization to authorities, they often encounter a situation where they are less likely to be viewed as "real victims" of crime when compared to their White counterparts (Comack 2012). For racialized women, their criminal victimization is complicated by gender, race and class — factors that can influence their risk of victimization and how the state responds to the violence they experience. In the context of domestic violence, for example, feminists point out how cultural differences shape state interpretations of what constitutes domestic violence, the likelihood of disclosure to authorities and the behaviour of men and women in racialized communities (Gill 2004). It is not unusual for police and the criminal justice system to see violence in racialized communities as normal, leaving vulnerable members of these communities to fend for themselves or to be blamed for their victimization. In cases of sexual violence, "legitimate" victims are often stereotyped as "good" women who are worthy and deserving of state protection, while those who act outside the bounds of acceptable femininity by engaging in "risky" behaviour are deemed less worthy. In a society characterized by racism, racialized and Indigenous women often do not fit the role of the ideal or authentic victim, typically understood by the courts as someone who is passive, does not fight back, is not promiscuous and does not use drugs or alcohol (Randall 2010). Racial stereotypes about racialized and Indigenous women construct them as less credible and, consequently, they are less likely to be believed when giving testimony and their perpetrators are more likely to receive lenient sentences (Crenshaw 1991). Documented statements of trial court judges making disparaging comments about racialized female complainants, particularly Indigenous women, in sexual assault cases demonstrates how the problem of racism is pervasive and systemic. Societal discourses about victimization shape how authorities interpret and respond to the harms suffered, and this has often resulted in racialized victims having their harms trivialized or dismissed altogether (Adelman, Erez and Shalhoub-Kevorkian 2003). Barbara Hudson (2006: 31) claims that, for racial and ethnic minorities to receive the same treatment as White men or women, they have to prove that they are the "same as" White men or women. Yet, equal treatment is also problematic because it cannot take into account inequities that stem from historical, political, social and economic differences.

Not surprisingly, public trust in the criminal justice system is significantly lower in some racialized communities. A report on community satisfaction with policing among racialized and non-racialized groups found widespread dissatisfaction with the way Toronto police interacted with community members (Logical Outcomes 2014). Overall, the study found that public trust in the police was low, the perception that police officers abused their powers was high and approximately 40 percent of respondents in the study stated that police–community relations were poor (Logical Outcomes 2014).

Scot Wortley and Akwasi Owusu-Bempah's (2009) study also found racial differences in perceptions of the justice system. In Toronto, there were higher rates of unfavourable attitudes toward the criminal justice system in Black and Chinese Canadians compared to White Canadians. They note, however, that less favourable attitudes tend to develop the longer a person has resided in Canada and that, generally, new immigrants had a mostly positive attitude toward the justice system (Wortley and Owusu-Bempah 2009). Jane Sprott and Anthony Doob's (2014) and Liqun Cao's (2014) studies of confidence in the police across Canada had similar conclusions. Black Canadians, Chinese Canadians and Indigenous people were more likely to rate the police negatively (Cao 2014; Sprott and Doob 2014). The belief among these groups that they are less likely to receive fair and impartial treatment in the criminal justice system can produce a wide range of adverse effects, not least because social cohesion and stability depend upon the public having confidence in the justice system. The racial tensions in the United States, where riots have erupted over police shootings of African Americans, serve as an important reminder of the need to combat racial inequalities.

Racializing Crime

Racialization is used to describe the processes that allows racial meanings to be attached to particular social problems, whereby race is a key factor in defining and understanding the problem (Murji and Solomos 2005: 3). It is also the process of racial categorization by which people are selected, sorted, given attributes and assigned particular actions (Ontario Human Rights Commission 1995). Michael Banton (1998: 35) states, "to say that the differences [between people] were racialized is to say that [these differences] were interpreted in the light of prevailing racial theories, without entering into any debate about the validity of these theories." Racialization focuses on how racial differences — the specific characteristics ascribed to human beings based on particular biological features — are deployed in the construction of racial identities and meanings (Miles 1989). While the term can be traced back to nineteenth-century writings, the contemporary usage of racialization began in the late 1970s and the early 80s when scholars sought to bring greater conceptual clarity to the study of racial discrimination, to avoid reifying race and to better understand racial formations and the persistence of racial hierarchies (Barot and Bird 2001). By exposing the ways in which social relations are structured by biological differences based on race, scholars sought to demonstrate how racism is reproduced over time.

For many scholars, racialization is preferred over the concept of "race," as the latter has come to be regarded by many as a concept that signifies nothing (Miles 1989) or an empty signifier that is dangerous because of its emptiness (Rustin 1991). This is because racial classification schemes based on biological differences have been scientifically proven to be false; it is not possible to classify humans based on physical differences such as skin colour, facial features and hair colour. Others add that the concept of "race" is analytically useless (Miles 1989) and it cannot overcome the notion that racial categories are not fixed and natural, but always in a state of flux. Robert Miles (2000: 192) concurs: "race is an idea created by human beings in certain historical and material conditions and is used to represent the world in certain ways, under certain historical conditions and for certain political interests." Racialization is better able to explain how racist ideology becomes embedded in the representation and treatment of groups and how this is dependent on specific historical contexts. It also helps us think about race and racism by pointing to both the continuity and change in racialization processes.

The process of racializing crime involves many different strategies, with the two most common practices being the overemphasis on crimes committed by people of colour, leading to their overrepresentation in the justice system, and the use of specific terms and categories in discourses about racialized groups and crime. Within the criminal justice system, there is a long legacy of using racial meanings to define particular populations and justify their ill treatment. Throughout Canadian history, groups were routinely racialized and treated differently based on how they were defined by the dominant group. For example, Ukrainians were stigmatized as "dangerous" because they were seen as communist sympathizers (Avery 1979) while Indigenous Peoples were deemed uncivilized by colonial powers and required forced assimilation. Various non-White immigrant groups (Chinese, Japanese, Eastern Europeans) were routinely excluded from entry into Canada because they were seen as "undesirable" and a poor fit for Canada's nation-building communities except as a form of cheap labour. There was also a general distrust of non-White immigrants based on racialized beliefs that strong links exist between immigrants and crime (Sayad 2004). Of particular note is Mosher's (1996) historical study of Ontario between 1892 and 1930, which found that racist criminal justice practices were commonplace. Black offenders were given disproportionate police attention and racialized minority offenders had higher rates of conviction and lengthier sentences for these offences (Mosher 1996). Indigenous offenders were also harshly treated by colonial authorities in the justice system. Historians have traced back the problem of over-policing in Indigenous communities to over a century ago (Backhouse 1999; Hylton 2002).

For many of these groups, the passage of time has not changed the type of treatment they have received. The overrepresentation of Indigenous people at all levels of the criminal justice system persists, with the Supreme Court of Canada labelling the situation as "a crisis in the Canadian justice system" while the Royal Commission on Aboriginal Peoples described the problem as "injustice personified" (Rudin 1996). Black and African Canadians continue to be heavily targeted by law enforcement and they remain intensely distrustful of the law and legal system (Thornhill 2008). Since September 11, 2001, Arab and Muslim groups now find themselves subjected to racial profiling and harassment due to concerns that they may be terrorist threats. The treatment of Omar Khadr, a racialized Canadian citizen and former child soldier, demonstrates how fears about terrorism can easily override citizenship rights and justify the use of torture and ill treatment. At fifteen, Khadr was imprisoned at Guantanamo for a decade, where he was repeatedly abused and tortured and forced to confess to crimes in exchange for the possibility of a shorter sentence and repatriation to Canada (*Globe and Mail* 2015). The Supreme Court of Canada ruled in 2010 that Khadr's human rights had been violated, yet it would be another two years before Harper's government reluctantly agreed to repatriate him (Mackay 2016).

The use of encoded terms when speaking about specific racial groups is a common strategy of *racialized exclusion*. Peter Li argues that using such terms makes it possible to reference race in the political arena without suggesting that race is socially significant (Li 2007: 44). For example, in immigration debates, coded terms like "non-traditional" have been used to describe immigrants coming from "non-White" countries of origin (Li 2007: 44). Similarly, economic migrants, many of whom are racialized, have been vilified by the government and the mainstream media for seeking better opportunities for themselves and their families. They have been repeatedly branded as "bogus" by successive immigration ministers and, if they arrive by boat, they are now automatically held in indefinite detention despite the fact that irregular immigration is not a criminal offence (Hesson 2012). Within the criminal justice system, the term "*gang*" is a well-known descriptor that is routinely used by police officers in reference to groups composed of racialized youth even though the term is applicable to all racial groups (Symons 2002). As a result of this labelling process, racialized groups have experienced a range of injustices as criminal identities become fused with racial identities in the justice system. Racial bias makes it possible to assume that these groups are not entitled to the presumption of innocence, nor are they entitled to due process and fair treatment.

Critical criminologists have long argued that what is understood to be a crime is less about the behaviour in question and more about the characteristics of who has broken the law. Compare, for example, the treatment of *white-collar criminals* to those who commit property crimes or welfare fraud. There are numerous Canadian cases involving companies violating laws and regulations that have resulted in workers dying or the public being harmed. One example is the Westray Mine disaster in Nova Scotia in 1992. Twenty-six miners were killed when methane gas exploded underground (Snider 2000: 177). The owners of the mine had not taken proper precautions and repairs to the mines had not been completed. All criminal charges against the mine owners were eventually dropped (Cox 1999). Similarly, Conrad Black, a convicted criminal in the US, wanted to return to Canada after serving his prison sentence. Black had renounced his Canadian citizenship in 2001 to accept a British peerage and, even though Canadian immigration rules state that a foreigner with a criminal record is inadmissible to Canada, Black was allowed to return to Canada (*CBC News* 2012). Critics argued a double standard exists because many other foreigners with criminal convictions have not been allowed into Canada (Davis, Kennedy Jason Fekete 2012).

These situations stand in stark contrast to the intensity with which crimes committed by poor, often racialized people are policed. Aiyanas Ormond's (2013) study highlights how poor, often racialized people are targeted for criminalization and mass incarceration across many Canadian cities. Homelessness, panhandling, squeegeeing, gathering returnables for recycling and jaywalking are just a few of the activities poor people engage in that are now considered illegal under many city bylaws, leading to thousands of tickets being issued to people who are often unable to pay the fines (Ormond 2013). As a result, incarceration rates for white-collar and corporate crimes are significantly lower than for street crimes, another key indicator of how criminal justice resources are funnelled to target crimes that are committed by the poor and people of colour rather than by wealthy White offenders. Recent legislative changes to the Criminal Code, encompassed in the omnibus crime bill, Bill C-10 — such as increased mandatory minimum sentences, tougher penalties for youth and the creation of new offences — will only exacerbate the overrepresentation of racialized communities in the criminal justice system. These examples highlight how differential treatment of racialized groups is a result of structural racism rather than simply the work of a "few bad apples." As Lisa Cacho (2012: 37) reminds us, "certain bodies and behaviors are made transparently criminal while privileged bodies and their brutal crimes are rendered unrecognizable as criminal or even as violent."

Media representations of crime issues have also contributed to perceptions that racialized communities are more deviant, lawless, violent and threatening. The racialization of crime in the media has fuelled many moral panics about violent "gangs," criminal immigrants or situations where the suspect is a racialized man and the victim is a White woman (Lawson 2014; D'Arcy 2007). In the mid-1990s, a robbery and shooting of a White female victim by three racialized men at a downtown Toronto café resulted in a "state of intense and escalating anxiety as fears spread about violence, crime and a perceived decline in the safety of Toronto's streets" (D'Arcy 2007: 242). The city whipped the population into panic by drawing a hard line between an innocent White woman, who happened to be at the wrong place at the wrong time, and the "Jamaican criminals," who shot indiscriminately because they did not respect Canadian values (D'Arcy 2007: 248–50; Zerbisias 1994). The men, who were awaiting deportation to Jamaica when they committed their crime, prompted the state to enact reforms that would expedite the deportation process (Chan 2005). In the years that followed these changes, a disproportionate number of Jamaican immigrants were deported relative to their population in Toronto (Chan 2005). Bernard Schissel (2006) notes how media constructions of racialized individuals as un-Canadian and threatening can easily lead to the implementation of "get tough" campaigns and the call for more "*law and order.*" It should be noted that the depiction of racialized individuals as "*criminal Others*" is not confined to news media outlets, as these themes are also very commonplace in entertainment programming.

As a result of the overrepresentation of racialized minorities in the justice system, racialized communities have been stereotyped as being more criminogenic (i.e., prone to crime) than others or as having flawed cultural and moral values. These attitudes have been endorsed by right-wing politicians and researchers. Yet, when the issues of race and crime are properly contextualized, we see that a history of colonization and racial discrimination in Canada has significantly shaped contemporary criminal justice processes. Differential power relations have resulted in a racial hierarchy where privilege and superiority are conferred onto White groups while disadvantage and discrimination are more common among non-White groups (Chan and Chunn 2014). Hudson (2006: 30) notes that, within criminology and legal studies in Western societies, it is no longer controversial to claim that "criminal justice is 'white man's justice'" as it has been sufficiently well established. She notes that the law treats racialized minorities and women the same way that dominant society treats them and, until these harms are socially recognized, legal remedies will fail to address the injustices.

The difficulties that racialized communities have in challenging and contesting how they are constructed by the criminal justice system, politicians and the mainstream media is indicative of their lack of power to fundamentally alter dominant definitions of who they are. The conflation of dangerousness and criminality with racialized communities was seen in the police shooting death of Andrew Loku — a man from Sudan who had mental health issues and was wielding a hammer in his Toronto apartment when he was fatally shot (Gillis 2015). This case highlights how racial differences continue to have significant consequences for racialized groups and individuals.

Criminalizing and Punishing Racialized Populations

Over the last several decades, a punitive crime agenda has taken hold despite continuous declines in the rate of crime across most regions in Canada. David Garland traces the development of populist punitiveness and the risk management of dangerous populations that characterized criminal justice reform to the 1980s (Garland 2001). The *politicization of crime* combined with the failure of the rehabilitative approach meant that new strategies were needed to respond to the general public's fear of crime. Tough-on-crime talk by politicians led to a significant expansion of the criminal law in many Western, industrialized countries, with punitive "law and order" policies as the centrepiece of these reforms (Garland 2001; Simon 2007). The result was an increased use of surveillance in all areas of social life (e.g., cctv), harsher treatment toward groups identified as dangerous or threatening (e.g., terrorists, homeless people, people with mental illnesses, migrants), an expansion of prisons and detention centres and the widening of the social control net as seen in the rise of private security companies. These trends did not affect everyone equally as racialized and gendered ideas of crime and deviancy shaped how, for example, fear of crime was strongly equated with fear of racialized men (Patel and Tyrer 2011).

Efforts to reform criminal law, as seen most recently in the passage of Bill C-10 and the *Truth in Sentencing Act*, are felt most intensely by people who are already highly vulnerable and multiply marginalized (Comack 2015). When racist assumptions about crime and deviance are added to the mix, we can see how what is deemed to be a crime becomes strongly associated with particular racial groups, leading to people of colour receiving more criminal justice attention and control but not protection from criminal victimization. Their treatment in the criminal justice system has been, and continues to be, overwhelmingly negative, particularly when punitive crime policies and demands for greater efficiency in criminal justice processing trump humane treatment. A parallel trend to the racialization of crime is the increased criminalization of racial groups. *Criminalization* refers to an "institutional process through which certain acts and behaviours are selected and labelled as 'crimes' and through which particular individuals and groups are subsequently selectively identified and differentially policed and disciplined" (Fergusson and Muncie 2008: 103). To be criminalized, as Cacho (2012: 4–5) notes, is to be "prevented from being law-abiding," to be presumed guilty rather than innocent, to be "excluded from law's protection," but "not excluded from law's discipline, punishment and regulation."

Criminalization is a particular process of "Othering" — of attaching negatively evaluated attributes such as "criminality," "deviancy" or "inferiority" onto individuals and groups targeted for discrimination and exclusion (Webster 2007; Williams 2015). The conflation of race and crime is most widely evident in the perception of Black people as more threatening thanmembers of other social groups, leading to anxieties and concerns about "*Black criminality*." In many Western countries, Black communities are portrayed as deviant, fragmented and unable to properly socialize their children to be law-abiding (Smith 2008). As noted earlier, overreaction to crimes committed by Black youth in particular led to panic and fear among the general public, followed by demands that the state implement punitive responses to the crime problem (Garland 2001). The classic study of this is Stuart Hall, Charles Critcher, Tony Jefferson, John Clarke and Brian Roberts' (1978) research on "mugging" in the UK, where they demonstrate how the media, believing that society had become too permissive on crime and criminals, mobilized the public to believe there was a significant problem with Black youth robbing and beating (i.e., mugging) people. The authors show how the media manufactured the problem of mugging by creating a moral panic about Black youth, who were constructed as inherently dangerous because they were unemployed and therefore warranted greater policing and more criminalization (Hall et al. 1978). Mugging had not increased and the phenomenon was not new, but by attaching a new label onto the crime of robbery, new and different meanings could be attached to the event. Crime became a symbol for other social anxieties, and criminal justice policy changes were less about reducing crime than they were a reflection of particular political decisions. Hall et al. (1978) argue that mugging, and crime more generally, was a political strategy used to manage economic problems, especially among racialized populations. Importantly, it was not just the media that constructed the problem of mugging, but the police and the courts were also an integral part of the construction process. After all, they get to decide which crime issues are given attention, how crime statistics are interpreted, where resources are allocated and how this is all related to the wider societal context.

The harshest reactions to fears of "Black criminality" can be found in the United States, where myths about Black crime have led to a massive over-incarceration of African Americans for many decades. In many criminal justice systems across the United States, colour was used as a proxy for dangerousness, and being Black, young and male was routinely equated with "probable cause" (Kennedy 1997; Gaynes 1993). Vesla Weaver (2007: 230) contends that, by linking crime to anxieties about racial disorder, policies related to crime were racialized and crime became a racial code word for Black criminality. Bruce Western (2006: 5) adds, "the prison boom was a political project that arose partly because of rising crime but also in response to an upheaval in American race relations in the 1960s."

Unlike the US and UK, the racial framing of crime in Canada involves more than just one racialized group. Although the iconic image of criminality is strongly associated with Black communities in Southern Ontario and various parts of the Atlantic provinces, in the Prairie provinces, Indigenous people are more likely to be over-policed and suffer mistreatment, while in BC, South Asian and Vietnamese people are routinely linked to gang problems, the drug trade and related offences (Chan and Chunn 2014: 17). Among these groups, widespread allegations of over-policing, unfair sentencing and mistreatment in the criminal justice system are not new. Significant disparities exist at all stages of the criminal justice system due to "common-sense" assumptions held by police, prosecutors, judges and correctional personnel about who are most likely "criminals" and victims of crime. Studies conducted of criminal justice professionals have found that they rely on ideas of cultural difference to understand why some racialized communities are overrepresented in the justice system (Denney, Ellis and

Barn 2006). Despite the presence of much anti-discrimination legislation (e.g., *Bill of Rights, Charter of Rights and Freedoms*), these professionals rarely entertain the notion that colonialism or differential power relations stemming from socioeconomic disadvantage may be the cause of Black or Indigenous overrepresentation, preferring instead to fall back on racial stereotypes.

One of the most devastating consequences to emerge from this way of *"race thinking"* is when police officers use excessive force to contain a situation. In the Criminal Code, the use of deadly force by law enforcement is permitted under certain circumstances, although what constitutes "reasonable grounds" and "necessary" force is subject to dispute. There is currently significant public attention on this issue due to a cluster of police shootings in the United States, giving rise to the social media campaign #blacklivesmatter. In Canada, the fatal shooting of Andrew Loku in Toronto has also sparked criticism that the police overreacted and that Loku, a Black man suffering from mental health issues, was not a threat and, given time, he would have calmed down (*CBC News* 2015c). While the use of lethal force in Canada is rare when compared to the United States, the police have not escaped charges that there is an epidemic of *police brutality* (Hodgson 2001). Wortley's (2006) study of police use of force found that, when deadly force is used, African Canadian men and Indigenous men are "grossly overrepresented" in police use of force and police officers are rarely charged for using excessive force regardless of the racial status of the victims (Wortley 2006). One recent reform to police use of lethal force has been the introduction of the taser or stun gun in 2001 (*CBC News* 2009b). The intent of the taser is for the police to incapacitate suspects with less-than-lethal use of force and, by 2010, at least 129 law enforcement agencies were using them (Murphy 2012). Yet, the case of Robert Dziekański — a newly arrived immigrant who died after being tasered five times by RCMP officers at Vancouver International Airport — demonstrates that the police are still required to exercise appropriate judgment when using a weapon, and the Braidwood Comission's inquiry into his death concluded that the police were not justified in using a taser against him (Braidwood 2010).

As the use of criminalization strategies intensify and spread to other social institutions, the criminalization of racial groups can be seen also in the policing of welfare and in immigration enforcement. Rates of poverty in Canada are unevenly distributed, with recent immigrants (34 percent), single mothers (33 percent) and Indigenous people (25 percent) experiencing high levels of poverty and therefore, more likely to be using the welfare system for support (Citizens for Public Justice 2014). Various studies have shown how racism pervades the Canadian welfare system, where claims of excessive surveillance and policing of racialized welfare recipients are commonplace (Mirchandani and Chan 2007; Maki 2011; O'Grady, Gaetz and Buccieri 2013). The belief that people of colour on welfare are irresponsible and deviant is central to the *"culture of poverty"* thesis, which views poor people as different from mainstream society insofar as they are said to lack a work ethic, have an ethic of dependency, and hold improper family values via sexual activity outside of marriage and single parenthood (Jones and Luo 1999). In the United States, these ideas have been strongly attached to African American welfare recipients, who are deemed undeserving of state support because they prefer to live a state-dependent lifestyle. Indeed, the racial stereotype of the "welfare queen" was borne out of the myth that African American women are having more babies so that they can collect welfare support from the state (Bezusko 2013: 48). These attitudes, evident in many Western welfare systems, were influential in shaping state responses to welfare reform that included significant cuts to support and benefits and greater surveillance and demonization of welfare recipients.

In a similar trend, immigration systems across many Western states have also adopted more hostile attitudes toward immigrants and refugees. As global migration increases, developed nations have taken to securing their borders, increasing the use of immigration detention and deportation and dehumanizing "undesirable" immigrants and refugees by framing them as "illegal immigrants" or "queue-jumpers." In Canada, there has been a plethora of immigration policy reforms within the last decade aimed at making it more difficult for immigrants to enter Canada and for refugees to find protection. The use of biometric technology in the form of e-passports, fingerprinting databases and permanent resident cards are examples of government efforts to screen out high-risk travellers while improving efficiency and security (Lyon 2008). Although these technologies are hailed as a significant advancement for reducing global risks, critics cite many concerns regarding the potential for abuse of the information collected and the fact that often it is the most disadvantaged travellers that are targeted (Bell 2013; Topak, Bracken-Roche, Saulnier and Lyon 2015). Soshana Magnet (2007) concurs, pointing out that these technologies were developed in large part due to anxieties around racialized suspect bodies such that biometrics, far from circumventing racism, are intimately connected to problematic assumptions about race, class and gender.

The growing number of racialized communities that are currently constructed as problem sites demonstrates how the tentacles of state control have shaped the lives of racialized peoples. Their criminalization, marginalization and exclusion highlight the structural entrenchment of contemporary racism and the continuing need to challenge racial inequalities. Racialized groups may be easy targets for demonstrations of state power in times of fear, insecurity and uncertainty about the future, but the legacy of disadvantage that they experience points to perilous times ahead. Only by understanding and challenging this phenomenon can we hope to undo the damage caused by denying the problems of contemporary racism.

Toward an Anti-Racist Criminal Justice System

In the last several decades, numerous reports have been produced highlighting the need to address racial bias in all parts of the justice system (Correctional Investigator of Canada 2012, 2013; Colour of Poverty — Colour of Change Network 2014; Logical Outcomes 2014). Human rights commissions, community groups, public watchdogs and quasi-judicial organizations such as the Correctional Investigator of Canada have demonstrated the presence of racial bias and provided recommendations for minimizing discriminatory treatment. Furthermore, formal public inquiries, such as the Commission of Inquiry into the Actions of Canadian Officials in Relation to Maher Arar (2006) and the Missing Women Commission of Inquiry (2012) have also concluded that law enforcement policies and practices are discriminatory. The cases that sparked these public inquiries, such as the one of Arar, highlight the dire consequences that can emerge from biased treatment. Arar is a Syrian Canadian citizen who was accused by American law enforcement of being a member of al Qaeda while en route home to Ottawa from JFK airport (Abu-Laban and Nath 2007). He was deported to Syria and, while there, subsequently detained and tortured for twelve months before being released. The inquiry cleared him of any wrongdoing and this was followed by compensation and an apology by the federal government. As the Missing Women Inquiry Commissioner, Wally Oppal, notes, "the historic and continuing racism and sexism within Canadian society is likely to be reproduced in discriminatory policies and practices within law enforcement, unless and until steps are taken to actively work toward bias-free policing" (Missing Women Commission of Inquiry 2012: 17–18).

Indeed, the argument that racism remains an enduring problem in the criminal justice system is difficult to refute despite claims that race no longer matters because racial equality has been achieved. One only has to turn to the news media to see a continuous stream of stories about tensions between racialized communities and law enforcement agencies. Increasingly, the issue is less about whether racial discrimination is present or not and more about what will be done about the differential treatment. For example, public frustrations regarding the indifference expressed by police forces toward concerns about the discriminatory use of street checks is palpable (Rusonik 2015; *Ottawa Citizen* 2015). Various op-eds have publicly called on police forces in Ottawa and Toronto to implement changes, to no avail thus far (Smith 2015; Rusonik 2015). Furthermore, the disadvantage experienced by racialized individuals as a result of institutional racism is often turned on its head, with claims that the problem of over-criminalization resides with racialized individuals who make bad decisions rather than the result of discrimination within the system. Racialized peoples are characterized as backward, less civilized and possessing flawed cultural values and beliefs, and that is why they have higher rates of criminalization (Toor 2013). Thus, while racialized communities see the criminalization of their members as commonplace and expanding, the conventional wisdom of many Whites is that racism is an aberrant and exceptional problem, not a commonplace one (Murakawa and Beckett 2010).

Clearly, the contemporary character of racism is complex, where celebrations of diversity and multiculturalism take place alongside allegations of abuses of power and differential treatment. Stephen Ostertag and William Armaline (2011: 268) add that contemporary racism endures because it is covert and sophisticated — it is able to draw on hegemonic mechanisms for the uneven distribution of power and resources despite resistance to these practices. Racial discrimination is, and will continue to be, a formidable obstacle for many people of colour in Canada who hope their claims of differential treatment in the justice system will be acknowledged or who are victims wanting recognition of their criminal victimization. The continued presence of racial bias in the criminal justice system has led some scholars to suggest that, rather than finding justice, people of colour are more likely to experience "in-justice" from the criminal justice system (Lyubansky and Hunter 2014; Tanovich 2008).

Given the long history of criminalizing racialized people in Canada, taking corrective action toward redressing disadvantaged groups will be long and painstaking, as seen in negotiations between the government and Indigenous communities. That said, many positive recommendations have been suggested for improving relations between criminal justice agencies and racialized communities. Increased representation of minority groups in positions of authority within the criminal justice system, better communication to improve community–criminal justice relations and more education around anti-racism and cultural differences will help to dampen the mistrust and suspicion of those unfairly targeted by the criminal justice system. Moreover, in this era of easy access to information, there is still insufficient awareness of the role that race plays in criminal justice proceedings and policies. As noted at the beginning of this chapter, education and awareness of how race and racial differences matter is an important first step toward racial equality.

Support for anti-racist mobilization remains high in Canada and elsewhere. This is an indication that, while racism may continue to challenge how these societies evolve, anti-racist movements will help to bring greater accountability to social institutions like the criminal justice system. There currently exists a broad range of local, national and international anti-racist initiatives that have bolstered the anti-racist movement and linked anti-racist struggles to new political and social developments, such as the demonization of asylum seekers and refugees. One important recognition has been the acknowledgement that binary constructions of difference (e.g., Black/White, male/female) fail to fully grasp how individuals are socially positioned in ways that intersect across multiple axes of difference and how this shapes their lived experiences. This makes it possible to see how immigrant women's experiences of crime and victimization can be different from those of Indigenous women or women living in poverty. Challenging the power of criminal justice authorities to name and define the problem that leads to the marginalization and exclusion of racialized groups will help to build a more inclusive and just society.

DISCUSSION QUESTIONS

1. How can we improve relationships between racialized groups in Canada and various criminal justice organizations, such as the police?
2. Would you support a move away from criminalizing minor offences for racialized groups in Canada?
3. Consider how race, gender and class characteristics shape criminal justice outcomes. Can you think of two contemporary examples where the offences were similar, but the outcomes were different?

ACTION STEPS

1. Campaign for the need to collect statistics on race and crime in Canada.
2. Find a local organization, initiative, or campaign that advocates for equitable treatment of Indigenous and racialized individuals within the criminal justice system. Get involved and help raise awareness!

Supplemental Readings

Barnett, Laura, et al. 2012. *Legislative Summary — Bill C–10: An Act to enact the Justice for Victims of Terrorism Act and to amend the State Immunity Act, the Criminal Code, the Controlled Drugs and Substances Act, the Correctional and Conditional Release Act, the Youth Criminal Justice Act, the Immigration and Refugee Protection Act and other Acts.* Ottawa: Library of Parliament, Publication No. 41-1-C10-E.

Oparah, Julia. 2005. *Global Lockdown: Race, Gender and the Prison Industrial Complex.* New York: Routledge.

Patel, Tina, and David Tyrer. 2011. *Race, Crime and Resistance.* London: Sage Publications.

Additional Resources

Canadian Civil Liberties Association <ccla.org/>.

Canadian Race Relations Foundation <crrf-fcrr.ca/en/>

Montréal Urban Aboriginal Community Strategy Network <reseaumtlnetwork. com/wp-content/uploads/2015/01/Report-on-the-Aboriginal-Justice-Research-Project.pdf>.

Truth in Sentencing Act. S.C. 2009, c. 29. Assented to 2009-10-22. <laws-lois.justice. gc.ca/eng/annualstatutes/2009_29/page-1.html>.

References

Abu-Laban, Yasmeen, and Nisha Nath. 2007. "From Deportation to Apology: The Case of Maher Arar and the Canadian State." *Canadian Ethnic Studies,* 39, 71.

Adelman, Madelaine, Edna Erez and Nadera Shalhoub-Kevorkian. 2003. "Policing Violence Against Minority Women in Multicultural Societies: 'Community' and the Politics of Exclusion." *Police and Society,* 7.

Avery, Donald. 1979. *Dangerous Foreigners.* Toronto: McClelland and Stewart.

Backhouse, Constance. 1999. *Colour–Coded: A Legal History of Racism in Canada, 1900–1950.* Toronto, ON: University of Toronto Press.

Balfour, Gillian. 2012. "Do Law Reforms Matter? Exploring the Victimization–Criminalization Continuum in the Sentencing of Aboriginal Women in Canada." *International Review of Victimology,* 1.

Banton, Michael. 1998. *Racial Theories.* New York: Cambridge University Press.

Barot, Rohit, and John Bird. 2001. "Racialization: The Genealogy and Critique of a Concept." *Ethnic and Racial Studies,* 24, 4.

Beauchamp, Diane. 2004. "Sexual Orientation and Victimization." Ottawa: Canadian Centre for Justice Statistics.

Bell, Colleen. 2013. "Grey's Anatomy Goes South: Global Racism and Suspect Identities in the Colonial Present." *Canadian Journal of Sociology,* 38, 4.

Bezusko, Adriane. 2013. "Criminalizing Black Motherhood." *Souls,* 15, 1–2.

Braidwood, Thomas. 2010. "Why? The Robert Dziekanski Tragedy." Braidwood Commission on the Death of Robert Dziekanski (B.C.).

Brannigan, Augustin, and Zhiqiu Lin. 1999. "'Where East Meets West': Police, Immigration and Public Order Crime in the Settlement of Canada from 1896 to 1940." *Canadian Journal of Sociology,* 24, 1.

Cacho, Lisa. 2012. *Social Death: Racialized Rightlessness and the Criminalization of the Unprotected.* New York: New York University Press.

Cannon, Martin. 2014. "Race Matters: Sexism, Indigenous Sovereignty and McIvor." *Canadian Journal of Women and the Law,* 26, 1.

Cao, Liqun. 2014. "Aboriginal People and Confidence in the Police." *Canadian Journal of Criminology and Criminal Justice,* 53, 1.

CBC News. 2016. "Saskatoon Law Professor Marilyn Poitras to Serve on MMIW Inquiry." August 3. <cbc.ca/news/politics/mmiw-inquiry-launch-details-1.3705346>.

___. 2015a. "Harper Says 'Overwhelming Majority' Agrees with Tories on Niqabs." March 11. <cbc.ca/news/politics/harper-says-overwhelming-majority-agrees-with-tories-on-niqabs-1.2990439>.

___. 2015b. "'Niqab Ban' Returns as Conservative Bill Planned for Parliament's Final Days." June 10. <cbc.ca/news/politics/niqab-ban-returns-as-conservative-bill-planned-for-parliament-s-final-days-1.3107975>.

___. 2015c. "Fatal Police Shooting of Andrew Loku Inspires 'Black Lives Matter' Chant." July 9. <cbc.ca/news/canada/toronto/fatal-police-shooting-of-andrew-loku-inspires-black-lives-matter-chant-1.3145049>.

___. 2015d. "UN Human Rights Committee Slams Canada for Record on Women." July 23. <cbc.ca/news/canada/un-human-rights-committee-slams-canada-s-record-on-women-1.3164650>.

___. 2012. "Conrad Black Returning to Canada on Temporary Permit." May 1. <cbc.ca/news/politics/conrad-black-returning-to-canada-on-temporary-permit-1.1141793.

___. 2011. "What's in the Tory Crime Bill — and What's Not." September 11. <cbc.ca/news/politics/what-s-in-the-tory-crime-bill-and-what-s- not-1.991873/>.

___. 2009a. "Justice System Failed Frank Paul, Left to Die of Hypothermia." March 12. <cbc.ca/news/canada/british-columbia/justice-system-failed-frank-paul-left-to-die-of-hypothermia-report-1.800186>.

___. 2009b. "Stun Guns: Facts about Stun Guns and Their Use in Canada." March 20. <cbc.ca/news/canada/facts-about-stun-guns-and-their-use-in-canada-1.810288>.

Chan, Wendy. 2005. "Crime, Deportation and Regulation of Immigrants." *Crime, Law and Social Change,* 44, 2 (September).

Chan, Wendy, and Dorothy Chunn. 2014. *Racialization, Crime and Criminal Justice in Canada.* Toronto, ON: University of Toronto Press.

Citizens for Public Justice. 2014. "The Burden of Poverty: A Snapshot of Poverty across Canada." Ottawa, ON.

Colour of Poverty — Colour of Change Network. 2014. "Racial Justice Report Card for Ontario." Toronto (June).

Comack, Elizabeth. 2015. "The Impact of the Harper Government's 'Tough on Crime' Strategy: Hearing from Frontline Workers." Winnipeg: Canadian Centre for Policy Alternatives.

___. 2012. *Racialized Policing: Aboriginal People's Encounters with the Police.* Black Point, NS: Fernwood Publishing.

Commission of Inquiry into the Actions of Canadian Officials in Relation to Maher Arar. 2006. *Report of the Events Relating to Maher Arar — Factual Background, Volume 1*. Ottawa: Public Works and Government Services.

Correctional Investigator of Canada. 2013. *A Case Study of Diversity in Corrections: The Black Inmate Experience in Federal Penitentiaries — Final Report*. Office of the Correctional Investigator.

___. 2012. *Spirit Matters: Aboriginal People and the Corrections and Conditional Release Act*. Office of the Correctional Investigator.

Cox, Kevin. 1999. "Westray Proceedings Formally Terminated." *Globe and Mail*, June 30.

Crenshaw, Kimberlé. 1991. "Mapping the Margins: Intersectionality, Identity Politics, and Violence Against Women of Colour." *Stanford Law Review*, 43.

Crichlow, Wesley. 2014. "Weaponization and Prisonization of Toronto's Black Male Youth." *International Journal for Crime, Justice and Social Democracy*, 3, 3.

D'Arcy, Stephen. 2007. "The 'Jamaican Criminal' in Toronto, 1994: A Critical Ontology." *Canadian Journal of Communication*, 32.

Davis, Jeff, Mark Kennedy and Jason Fekete. 2012. "Mulcair Blasts 'Double Standard' that Cleared Way for Conrad Black's Return to Canada." *National Post*, May 2. <news.nationalpost.com/news/canada/conrad-black-return-to-canada>.

Decoste, Rachel. 2015. "Fairness Falls Short: Carding Continues Across Canada." *Huffington Post*, June 11. <huffingtonpost.ca/rachel-decoste/carding-canada_b_7546522.html>.

Denney, David, Tom Ellis and Ravinder Barn. 2006. "Race, Diversity and Criminal Justice in Canada: A View from the UK." *Internet Journal of Criminology*. <internetjournalofcriminology.com/ijcarticles.html>.

Fergusson, Ross, and John Muncie. 2008. "Criminalising Conduct." In Allan Cochrane and Deborah Talbot (eds.), *Security: Welfare, Crime and Society*. Milton Keynes, UK: Open University Press.

Gabor, Thomas. 1994. "The Suppression of Crime Statistics on Race and Ethnicity: The Price of Political Correctness." *Canadian Journal of Criminology*, 36.

Garland, David. 2001. *The Culture of Control: Crime and Social Order in Contemporary Society*. Chicago: University of Chicago Press.

Gaynes, Elizabeth. 1993. "The Urban Criminal Justice System: Where Young + Black + Male = Probable Cause." *Fordham Urban Law Journal*, 20, 3.

Gill, Aisha. 2004. "Voicing the Silent Fear: South Asian Women's Experiences of Domestic Violence." *The Howard Journal*, 43, 5.

Gill, Sheila Dawn. 2000. "The Unspeakability of Racism: Mapping Law's Complicity in Manitoba's Racialized Spaces." *Canadian Journal of Law and Society*, 15, 2.

Gillis, Wendy. 2015. "Police Must Address Race Factor in Fatal Shootings, Says Community Groups." *Toronto Star*, July 9.

Globe and Mail. 2015. "Why Omar Khadr Deserves Bail." March 25. <theglobeandmail.com/opinion/editorials/why-omar-khadr-deserves-bail/article23620688/>.

Goodey, Jo. 2005. *Victims and Victimology: Research, Policy and Practice*. Essex, UK: Pearson.

Gotell, Lise. 2008. "Rethinking Affirmative Consent in Canadian Sexual Assault Law: Neoliberal Sexual Subjects and Risky Women." *Akron Law Review*, 41.

Green, Joyce. 2006. "From Stonechild to Social Cohesion: Anti-Racist Challenges for Saskatchewan." *Canadian Journal of Political Science*, 39, 3.

Ha-Redeye, Omar. 2015. "Getting Smart on Crime Instead of Tough." *Slaw*, June 21.

<slaw.ca/2015/06/21/getting-smart-on-crime-instead-of-tough/>.

Hall, Stuart, Charles Critcher, Tony Jefferson, John Clarke and Brian Roberts. 1978. *Policing the Crisis*. London: Macmillan.

Hesson, Ted. 2012. "Jose Antonio Vargas Challenges NYT and AP to Drop 'Illegal Immigrant." *ABC News*, September 21. <abcnews.go.com/ABC_Univision/News/jose-antonio-vargas-drop-illegal-immigrant-challenges-nyt/story?id=17291550>.

Hodgson, James. 2001. "Police Violence in Canada and the USA: Analysis and Management." *Policing: International Journal of Police Strategies and Management*, 24, 4.

Hudson, Barbara. 2006. "Beyond White Man's Justice: Race, Gender and Justice in Late Modernity." *Theoretical Criminology*, 10, 1.

Huey, Laura, and Marianne Quirouette. 2010. "Any Girl Can Call the Cops, No Problem: The Influence of Gender on Support for the Decision to Report Criminal Victimization within Homeless Communities." *British Journal of Criminology*, 50.

Hylton, John. 2002. "The Justice System and Canada's Aboriginal Peoples: The Persistence of Racial Discrimination." In Wendy Chan and Kiran Mirchandani (eds.), *Crimes of Colour*. Peterborough, ON: Broadview Press.

Janhevich, Derek, Melanie Bania and Ross Hastings. 2008. "Rethinking Newcomer and Minority Offending and Victimization: Beyond Hate Crimes." Report prepared for the Metropolis Seminar, Policing, Justice and Security in a Diverse Canada: Building an Empirical Evidence Base. Ottawa, ON.

Johnston, Philip. 1994. "Academic Approaches to Race–Crime Statistics Do Not Justify Their Collection." *Canadian Journal of Criminology*, 36.

Jones, Rachel, and Ye Luo. 1999. "The Culture of Poverty and African-American Culture: An Empirical Assessment." *Sociological Perspectives*, 42, 429.

Kennedy, Randall. 1997. *Race, Crime and the Law*. New York: Pantheon.

Khenti, Akwatu. 2014. "The Canadian War on Drugs: Structural Violence and Unequal Treatment of Black Canadians." *International Journal of Drug Policy*, 25, 2.

Kitossa, Tamari. 2012. "Criminology and Colonialism: Counter Colonial Criminology and the Canadian Context." *Journal of Pan African Studies*, 4, 10.

Kroes, Genevieve. 2008. "Aboriginal Youth in Canada: Emerging Issues, Research Priorities and Policy Implications. Workshop Report." Indian and Northern Affairs Canada, March 17.

Lawson, Erica. 2014. "Disenfranchised Grief and Social Inequality: Bereaved African Canadians and Oppositional Narratives About the Violent Deaths of Family and Family Members." *Ethnic and Racial Studies*, 37, 11.

Lentin, Alana. 2014. "Post-Race, Post Politics: The Paradoxical Rise of Culture After Multiculturalism." *Ethnic and Racial Studies*, 37, 8.

Li, Peter. 2007. "Contradictions of Racial Discourse." In Vijay Agnew (ed.), *Interrogating Race and Racism*. Toronto, ON: University of Toronto Press.

Logical Outcomes. 2014. *This Issue Has Been with Us for Ages: A Community–Based Assessment of Police Contact Carding in 31 Division — Final Report*. November. Toronto.

Lyon, David. 2008. "Biometrics, Identification and Surveillance." *Bioethics*, 22, 9.

Lyubansky, Mikhail, and Carla Hunter. 2014. "Toward Racial Justice." In Elena Mustakova-Possardt, Mikhail Lyubansky, Michael Basseches and Julie Oxenberg (eds.), *Toward a Socially Responsible Psychology for a Global Era*. New York: Springer-Verlag.

Mackay, Allison. 2016. "Troublesome Indigestion: The 'Return' of Omar Khadr and

Post-Racial Politics of Citizenship in Canada." *Topia: Canadian Journal of Cultural Studies,* 35, 107.

Magnet, Soshana. 2007. "Are Biometrics Race-Neutral?" June 5. <anonequity. org/ weblog/archives/2007/06/are_biometrics_raceneutral.php>. Maki, Krystle. 2011. "Neoliberal Deviants and Surveillance: Welfare Recipients Under the Watchful Eye of Ontario Works." *Surveillance and Society,* 9, 1/2.

Marable, Manning. 2007. *Racializing Justice, Disenfranchising Lives: The Racism, Criminal Justice, and Law Reader.* New York: Palgrave Macmillan.

McKenney, Katherine, Debra Pepler, Wendy Craig and Jennifer Connolly. 2006. "Peer Victimization and Psychosocial Adjustment: The Experiences of Canadian Immigrant Youth." *Journal of Research in Educational Psychology,* 4, 2.

Meloy, Michelle, and Susan Miller. 2011. *The Victimization of Women: Law, Policies, and Politics.* New York: Oxford University Press.

Meng, Yunlian, Sulaimon Giwa and Uzo Anucha. 2015. "Is There Racial Discrimination in Police Stop-and-Searches of Black Youth? A Toronto Case Study." *Canadian Journal of Family and Youth,* 7, 1.

Miles, Robert. 2000. "Apropos the Idea of 'Race' … Again." In Les Black and John Solomos (eds.), *Theories of Race and Racism: A Reader,* second edition. New York: Routledge.

____. 1989. *Racism.* London, UK: Routledge.

Mirchandani, Kiran, and Wendy Chan. 2007. *Criminalizing Poverty, Criminalizing Race.* Halifax, NS: Fernwood Publishing.

Missing Women Commission of Inquiry. 2012. *Forsaken: The Report of the Missing Women Commission of Inquiry — Executive Summary.* November 19. British Columbia.

Monaghan, Jeffrey. 2013. "Settler Governmentality and Racializing Surveillance in Canada's North-West." *Canadian Journal of Sociology,* 38, 4.

Mosher, Clayton. 1998. *Discrimination and Denial.* Toronto, ON: University of Toronto Press.

____. 1996. "Minorities and Misdemeanours: The Treatment of Black Public Order Offenders in Ontario's Criminal Justice System — 1892–1930." *Canadian Journal of Criminology,* 38.

Murakawa, Naomi, and Katherine Beckett. 2010. "The Penology of Racial Innocence: The Erasure of Racism in the Study and Practice of Punishment." *Law and Society Review,* 44, 3–4.

Murjui, Karim, and John Solomos. 2005. *Racialization: Studies in Theory and Practice.* Oxford: Oxford University Press.

Murphy, Christopher. 2012. "Canadian Police and Policing Policy, Post 9/11." In Karim Ismaili, Jane Sprott and Kim Varma (eds.), *Canadian Criminal Justice Policy: Contemporary Perspectives.* Don Mills, ON: Oxford University Press.

O'Grady, Bill, Stephen Gaetz and Kristy Buccieri. 2013. "Tickets … and More Tickets: A Case Study of the Enforcement of the Ontario Safe Streets Act." *Canadian Public Policy,* 39, 4 (December).

Ontario Human Rights Commission. 2003. *Paying the Price: The Cost of Racial Profiling.* Toronto, ON.

____. 1995. *Final Report on Systemic Racism in Ontario's Criminal Justice System.* Toronto, ON: Queen's Printer for Ontario.

Ormond, Aiyanas. 2013. "Jaywalking to Jail: Capitalism, Mass Incarceration and Social Control on the Streets of Vancouver." *Radical Criminology,* 3.

Ostertag, Stephen, and William Armaline. 2011. "Image Isn't Everything: Contemporary System Racism and Anti-Racism in the Age of Obama." *Humanity and Society,* 35, 3.

Ottawa Citizen. 2015. "Op-Ed: Ottawa's Strange Indifference to 'Street Checks.'" August 5. <ottawacitizen.com/news/national/op-ed-ottawas-strange-indifference-to-street-checks>.

Owusu-Bempah, Akwasi, and Paul Millar. 2010. "Revising the Collection of Justice Statistics by Race in Canada." *Canadian Journal of Law and Society,* 25, 1.

Parkes, Debra, and Abby Deshman. 2014. "The High Cost of Jailing the Innocent." *Winnipeg Free Press,* October 30. <winnipegfreepress.com/opinion/analysis/the-high-cost-of-jailing-the-innocent-280887002.html>.

Patel, Tina, and David Tyrer. 2011. *Race, Crime and Resistance.* London: Sage Publications.

Perreault, Samuel. 2009. "The Incarceration of Aboriginal People in Adult Correctional Services." *Juristat,* 29, 3.

Phillips, Coretta, and Benjamin Bowling. 2003. "Racism, Ethnicity and Criminology." *British Journal of Criminology,* 43, 2.

Randall, Melanie. 2010. "Sexual Assault Law, Credibility, and 'Ideal Victims': Consent, Resistance, and Victim Blaming." *Canadian Journal of Women and the Law,* 22, 397.

Razack, Sherene. 2012. "Memorializing Colonial Power: The Death of Frank Paul." *Law and Social Inquiry,* 37, 4.

___. 2000. "'Simple Logic': Race, the Identity Documents Rule and the Story of a Nation Besieged and Betrayed." *Journal of Law and Social Policy,* 15.

Rudin, Jonathan. 1996. *Aboriginal Peoples and the Justice System.* Ottawa: Report of the Royal Commission on Aboriginal Peoples.

Rusonik, Reid. 2015. "Police Need to Face Up to Racism Problem." *Toronto Star,* July 27. <thestar.com/opinion/commentary/2015/07/27/police-need-to-face-up-to-racism-problem.html>.

Rustin, Michael. 1991. *The Good Society and the Inner World.* London: Verso.

Sayad, Abdelmalek. 2004. *The Suffering of the Immigrant.* Cambridge: Polity Press.

Schissel, Bernard. 2006. *Still Blaming Children: Youth Conduct and the Politics of Child Hating.* Halifax, NS: Fernwood Publishing.

Simon, Jonathan. 2007. *Governing Through Crime.* New York: Oxford University Press.

Smith, David. 2008. "Criminology, Contemporary Society and Race Issues." In Hindpal Singh Bhui (ed.), *Race and Criminal Justice.* London, ON: Sage Publications.

Smith, Madeline. 2015. "A Call to Action: Black Lives Matter Toronto Continues the Fight Against Racism." *Globe and Mail,* August 1.

Snider, Laureen. 2000. "The Sociology of Corporate Crime: An Obituary (Or: Whose Knowledge Claims Have Legs?)." *Theoretical Criminology,* 4, 2.

Sprott, Jane, and Anthony Doob. 2014. "Confidence in the Police: Variation Across Groups Classified as Visible Minorities." *Canadian Journal of Criminology and Criminal Justice,* 56, 3 (April).

Symons, Gladys. 2002. "Police Constructions of Race and Gender in Street Gangs." In Wendy Chan and Kiran Mirchandani (eds.), *Crimes of Colour.* Peterborough: Broadview Press.

Tanovich, David. 2008. "The Charter of Whiteness: Twenty-Five Years of Maintaining Racial Injustice in the Canadian Criminal Justice System." *Supreme Court Law Review,* 40.

___. 2006. *The Colour of Justice: Policing Race in Canada.* Toronto, ON: Irwin Law.

___. 2003–04. "E-Racing Racial Profiling." *Alberta Law Review,* 41, 905.

Thornhill, Esmeralda. 2008. "So Seldom For Us, So Often Against Us: Blacks and the Law in Canada." *Journal of Black Studies*, 38, 3.

Toor, Sunita. 2013. "New 'Racisms' and Prejudices? The Criminalization of 'Asian.'" In Malcolm Cowburn, Marian Duggan, Anne Robinson and Paul Senior (eds.), *Values in Criminology and Criminal Justice*. Cambridge, UK: Polity Press.

Topak, Ozgun, Ciara Bracken-Roche, Alana Saulnier and David Lyon. 2015. "From Smart Borders to Perimeter Security: The Expansion of Digital Surveillance at the Canadian Border." *Geopolitics*, 20, 4.

Toronto Star. 2016. "Inquiry into Murdered and Missing Indigenous Women Must Show Results." August 3. <thestar.com/opinion/editorials/2016/08/03/inquiry-into-murdered-and-missing-indigenous-women-must-show-results-editorial.html>.

Wane, Njoki. 2013. "African Canadian Women and the Criminal Justice System." In Njoki Wane, Jennifer Jagire and Zahra Murad (eds.), *Ruptures: Anti-Colonial and Anti-Racist Feminist Theorizing*. Rotterdam: Sense Publishers.

Warde, Bryan. 2012. "Black Male Disproportionality in the Criminal Justice Systems of the USA, Canada, and England: A Comparative Analysis of Incarceration." *Journal of African American Studies*, 17.

Weaver, Vesla. 2007. "Frontlash: Race and the Development of Punitive Crime Policy." *Studies in American Political Development*, 21.

Webster, Colin. 2007. *Understanding Race and Crime*. Open University Press.

Western, Bruce. 2006. *Punishment and Inequality in American Democracy*. New York: Russell Sage Foundation.

Williams, Patrick. 2015. "Criminalising the Other: Challenging the Race–Gang Nexus." *Race and Class*, 56, 3.

Wortley, Scot. 2006. *Police Use of Force in Ontario: An Examination of Data from the Special Investigations Unit. Final Report*. Toronto, ON.

Wortley, Scot, and Akwasi Owusu-Bempah. 2011. "The Usual Suspects: Police Stop and Search Practices in Canada." *Policing and Society*, 21, 4.

___. 2009. "Unequal Before the Law: Immigrant and Racial Minority Perceptions of the Canadian Criminal Justice System." *Journal of International Migration and Integration*, 10, 4.

Zerbisias, Antonia. 1994. "Let's Not Bury our City with Vivi." *Toronto Star*, April 8.

10

SOCIAL DETERMINANTS OF NEWCOMER IMMIGRANT AND REFUGEE YOUTH'S MENTAL HEALTH

Nazilla Khanlou and Luz Maria Vazquez

In this chapter, we examine newcomer youth's experiences of racism, and its ramifications for their mental health and well-being, through the perspectives of social determinants of health and intersectionality. Youth experiences of racism in Canada are neither a new phenomenon, nor are they limited to newcomer youth. Indigenous youth were subjected to residential schools until recent decades (Kirmayer, Brass and Tait 2000; Regan 2010). The intergenerational trauma of these forced separations from their families and cultures continues to impact Indigenous Peoples today (Elias et al. 2012; Bombay, Matheson and Anisman 2014). Black Nova Scotian youth continue to be impacted by daily interpersonal and institutional racism, despite having lived in Canada since the eighteenth century (Beagan, Etowa and Thomas Bernard 2012). The internment of Japanese Canadians is an example of explicit anti-Asian government policies in the twentieth century (Day 2010).

Newcomer youth in Canada are increasingly from non-European backgrounds, representing diversities in ethnicity, racialized identities, religious beliefs and geo-sociopolitical countries of origin (Statistics Canada 2017). As a result, new waves and forms of youth experiences of racism are emerging, which are impacted by both national discourses on identity and belonging and local approaches to inclusion. In this chapter, we focus on youth (also referred to as adolescence in health and psychological literature or as the teenage period in common nomenclature) because it is an important period in identity development. Identity is impacted by racism and, at the same time, it is an important aspect of mental well-being (Williams, Aiyer, Durkee and Tolan 2014; Theron et al. 2011; Chapman and Perreira 2005; Edge and Newbold 2013).

From a developmental perspective, adolescence is a critical period in human development; it is a phase all youth share whether immigrant, refugee or Canadian-born (Khanlou and Crawford 2006). During this period, newcomer youth experience a twofold type of transition, one related to their own self and identity formation and the second to their adaptation and integration to a new society. That is, along with their migration-related transitions, newcomer youth also need to adjust to the biophysical and psychological changes characteristic of their developmental stage.

This chapter is divided into seven sections. First, we define key concepts, explain the social determinants of youth mental health, describe intersectionality and introduce discrimination, prejudice and racism. Second, we briefly present immigrant and refugee population data. Third, we discuss youth mental health and resilience. In section four the social determinants of youth mental health are considered, followed by section five where we consider youth's experiences and the impacts of discrimination and racism on their mental health. In section six, we discuss what society can do to promote newcomer immigrant and refugees' mental health, and in section seven we discuss what students can do to help newcomer immigrant and refugee youth reduce resettlement stress and barriers in adapting to their new country.

The objectives of this chapter are to:

- describe the social determinants of immigrant and refugee youth's mental health;
- pay particular attention to youth resilience; and
- examine the impacts of racism on immigrant and refugee youth's mental health.

Key Concepts

"Newcomer" is a general term that refers to people who are new to Canada. Newcomers can be individuals who have entered Canada as immigrants or who are in Canada as refugees. It is important to distinguish between the two groups, because each group has particular pre- and post- migration experiences that shape their mental health outcomes as well as their coping strategies (Khanlou 2008; Guruge and Butt 2015). Table 10.1 provides official definitions of newcomer-related terminology in Canada.

Scholars in different disciplines use other terms related to so-called "visible minorities." These include terms like race, ethnoracial, racialized, minorities (see chapter 1).

Table 10.1: Definitions of Newcomer Related Terms

- *Newcomers* or *recent immigrants* are considered to be those migrants who have been in Canada for less than five years (Statistics Canada 2013).

- *Visible minorities* are "Persons, other than Aboriginal peoples, who are non-Caucasian in race or non-white in colour" (Statistics Canada 2006).

- *Immigrant* refers to "a person who is or has ever been a landed immigrant/ permanent resident. This person has been granted the right to live in Canada permanently by immigration authorities. Some immigrants have resided in Canada for a number of years, while others have arrived recently. Some immigrants are Canadian citizens, while others are not. Most immigrants are born outside Canada, but a small number are born in Canada" (Statistics Canada 2013).

- A *refugee* "is a person who, by reason of a well-founded fear of persecution for reasons of race, religion, nationality, membership in a particular social group or political opinion,

  o   is outside each of their countries of nationality and is unable or, by reason of that fear, unwilling to avail themself of the protection of each of those countries; or
  o   not having a country of nationality, is outside the country of their former habitual residence and is unable or, by reason of that fear, unwilling to return to that country" (Immigration and Refugee Protection Act 2016).

Social determinants of health (SDOH) are those social factors and processes that have an impact on the health and well-being of individuals and groups. They are "social" because they are not biologically based — a characteristic intrinsic to the individual — but they are socially created — external to the individual — and arise out of inequities existing in society. Income is a social determinant of health because it has multiple impacts on the health of individuals, families and communities. For example, in Canada, people living in poverty have higher rates of experiencing chronic health conditions than affluent people (Balogh et al. 2015; Braveman 2014; Frohlich, Ross and Richmond 2006); they are also deprived from resources for health promotion and illness prevention and have unequal access to health services. Furthermore, we must consider racism as another SDOH that crosscuts and is intertwined in other health determinants. For example, racism within educational or work places has been shown to deepen the disadvantages faced by minority populations (Charles, Mahoney, Fox and Halse 2016; Hasford 2016; Sensoy and DiAngelo 2017; Shin 2015).

The SDOH perspective is helpful in recognizing the multiple influences on health. To analyze and individualize youth's experiences, we apply an intersectional approach. *Intersectionality* is a way of examining how different

Table 10.2: Social Determinants of Health

- income and income distribution
- education
- unemployment and job security
- employment and working conditions
- early childhood development
- food insecurity
- housing
- social exclusion
- social safety network
- health services
- Indigenous status
- gender
- race
- disability

Source: Mikkonen and Raphael 2010

influences come together to produce specific experiences at particular junctures in time and place (Crenshaw 1989). As a framework, intersectionality has three key principles: identities, power and context. *Identities* refers to the different identities we each have (e.g., gender, ethnicity, migration status, racialized status, socioeconomic status, life stage, sexual orientation). *Power* refers to the notion that we can have power to influence outcomes in any situation or we can have limited power to do so. Both our identities and level of power are dependent on the particular situation within which an experience occurs; that is, they are dependent on *context* (see Hankivsky, Cormier and de Merich 2009).

For example, in the classroom context youth's student identity is a key aspect of who they are. Particular youth may experience higher levels of power because they are, for instance, considered by their peers to be leaders or popular. In the same classroom, some youth may experience little power because they are considered to be different (for example, due to their newcomer status or accent when they speak). Outside the classroom the same youth's experiences may be quite different, again depending on context. The popular student may live with a single mother in a poor neighbourhood and experience discrimination directed at children of single mothers living in poverty. The newcomer youth may be recognized as a youth group leader by her neighbourhood peers because of her involvement on the local ethnic community radio show. Therefore, who we are (our identities) is influenced by the power we have or lack within each context. This does not diminish the prevailing impacts of such SDOH influences as social class, racism and gender, which are also important constructs from an intersectional perspective.

In summary, the SDOH perspective offers us a better understanding of the dimensions at play when trying to untangle social influences affecting youth's health (including their mental health). As an approach, intersectionality helps us understand how various factors come together for specific individuals and groups at particular places and points in time.

Discrimination, prejudice and racism constitute pervasive components of the daily experiences of minority individuals (Greene, Way and Pahl 2006; Khanlou, Koh and Mill 2008). Discrimination alludes to differential and unequal treatment of people based on their race, age, gender, socioeconomic status, ability, religion, ethnicity and migration status, among other parts of their identity (Law 2007). These processes have material repercussions because they result in the denial of access to societal opportunities for employment, education, housing, health and justice (Law 2007), resulting in social inequity and differential opportunities and rights (Khanlou, Koh and Mill 2008). Prejudice, racism and discrimination are social determinants of poor health outcomes (Edge and Newbold 2013; Priest et al. 2014).

Immigration: A Key Aspect of Canada's Diversity

Immigrants make up a significant proportion of Canada's population (table 10.3). Statistics Canada (2017) reported that, of the total population living in Canada in 2016, about 21.9 percent were immigrants, refugees and other non-permanent residents born outside Canada (7,540,830). In 2014, a total of 211,833 were permanent residents to Canada aged 15 years or older. From that total, 15 percent were youth between 15 and 24 years old. Of these youth, 18 percent were refugees and 91 percent were immigrants (CIC 2015).

Philippines, India and the People's Republic of China were the top three immigrant source countries. Statistics show that immigrants arriving to Canada are well educated and qualified to work. For example, in 2012 about 24 percent of the population entering the country held a bachelor's degree and 10 percent held master's degrees, while 65 percent were economic immigrants selected to enter Canada because of their education, English or French language abilities and work experience (e.g., skilled workers and business immigrants, among others) (CIC 2012). The above statistics underscore the increasing diversity of Canada's population, including those who are youth.

Table 10.3 Immigrant and Refugee Population in Canada

Total population living in Canada	35,151,728
Total population of immigrant, refugees and other non-permanent residents born outside Canada	21.9%
Top three immigrant source countries	Philippines India People's Republic of China
Most important provinces of destination in Canada	Ontario Québec British Columbia

Source: Statistics Canada (2017).

Mental Health: Why Resilience Matters

The notion of *mental health* applies to everyone. It is a broad concept that tends to be interpreted inconsistently by the public. For most persons, mental health appears to refer to serious mental illness (such as depression, bipolar disorder or schizophrenia). At times, it is also understood to refer to the daily ups and downs of life and our feelings associated with them (such as feeling sad, anxious or stressed). However, increasing attention is also being given to the positive aspect of mental health (i.e., mental well-being). Accordingly, the World Health Organization (WHO) recognizes mental health as a state of well-being in which individuals can cope with stress and, at the same time, have a fruitful life that they enjoy (WHO 2016).

Mental health is the capacity "to feel, think, and act in ways that enhance our ability to enjoy life" (CIHI 2009: 9), and it supports our ability to flourish (Khanlou and Wray 2014). Viewed from this perspective, mental health is a positive state. Our sense of *mental well-being* is also influenced by our social contexts. It is the result of interconnected social, environmental, economic, cultural and individual factors (CIHI 2009). To be able to have *positive mental health*, individuals need assets and resources to help them to face and navigate life's challenges.

Resilience and mental health are linked to each other (Barankin and Khanlou 2007). Resilient youth have positive mental health; vice versa, positive mental health supports resilience. It is important to reiterate that to have good mental health (or develop resilience) is not solely dependent on the personal intentions and willingness of each individual but also on the social context in which individuals develop and live. For youth, education, health and social services and the home environment are among the social systems influencing their healthy development (Khanlou et al. 2002). In other words, SDOH are a powerful influence on youth's (mental) well-being.

Studies on immigrant youth highlight that they are "remarkably resilient" (Ko and Perreira 2010). Resilience is regarded as a key element in promoting and maintaining youth mental health; it works as a buffer to threats (Khanlou and Wray 2014). Facing challenges actively and positively, and becoming stronger over time as a result of them, is a key aspect of being resilient.

Resilience entails two elements: the exposure to any type of *adversity* (physical, emotional, psychological) and the *adaptation* of an individual or a system (individual, society, ecosystem, etc.) to the challenge (Barankin and Khanlou 2007; Khanlou and Wray 2014). When that adaptation is positive, we refer to the resilience of a person or system. The process of adaptation is the result of many factors that, working together, provide the resources for youth to become resilient. Therefore, resilience cannot be conceived of solely as a personal trait or attribute; rather, it is also influenced by the supports available at family, community and societal levels. Resilient families, communities and societies together support resilient youth.

The adaptation of an individual or system depends on the type of adversity/threat/change the individual/system is experiencing. In this chapter, when we refer to newcomer youth's resilience we mean youth's overcoming of migration-related difficulties (or risk factors). Resilience also refers to the process of becoming a fulfilled individual — a young person with agency and access to resources, so she/he can thrive despite adversity. Therefore, to become resilient not only depends on the youth's individual, internal factors. It is also a systemic outcome in the sense that the processes occurring at community and societal levels (such inclusion/exclusion, equality/inequities, belonging/discrimination) also matter in supporting youth resilience and well-being.

Social Determinants of Newcomer Youth's Mental Health

Newcomer immigrants and refugees can experience threats to their social determinants of health (Mikkonen and Raphael 2010; Vissandjée and Hyman 2011; Guruge and Butt 2015). Socioeconomic status (SES) — such as living in poverty — impacts health, as do other SES factors such as employment status, or precarious and low-paid jobs. Many of the SDOH affecting youth result from impacts on their families. Among newcomer families, underemployment is a key issue (Teelucksingh and Galabuzi 2005; Walters, Phythian and Anisef 2006; Goldring and Landolt 2012;

Affiliation of Multicultural Societies and Services Agencies of BC 2013; Frank 2013). *Underemployment* refers to working in positions that do not reflect one's prior educational credentials or prior work experience. It leads to downward socioeconomic status among newcomer immigrant families in Canada. Length of stay in the host country is another determinant, because it may impact the initial knowledge immigrants have in accessing social, education and health systems, as well as the availability of social support. Racism is also another factor that creates inequities in labour market access. Research among Ghanaian and Somali youth, for example, reports barriers to employment access based on race, ethnicity and recency of immigration (Gariba 2009).

Social Determinants Shaping Mental Health Outcomes of Immigrant and Refugee Youth

The migration experiences of immigrant and refugee youth and their families can be usefully divided into three stages: pre-migration (before migration to Canada), migration (how migration takes place) and post-migration (settlement in Canada). Each stage conveys a diversity of processes that shape and impact mental health outcomes.

Pre-Migration Experiences
Pre-migration experiences refer to the cultural, social, political, economic and environmental conditions from which immigrant families come (Chapman and Perreira 2005; Ginieniewicz and McKenzie 2014; Guerrero 2014). The particular conditions of immigrants' countries of origin or refugees' countries of dislocation make immigrant and refugee populations heterogeneous (Guruge and Butt 2015). Therefore, immigrants or refugees as groups of people may come from the same "country of origin," but we cannot think of them as homogeneous social groups. Pre-migration conditions shape newcomers' perceptions and available resources and influence their migration trajectories once they make the decision to leave their countries. In this stage refugees can face challenges, such as war, internal displacement, political conflict, instability, persecution and potential prosecution, that result in them fleeing from their country (Este, Simich, Hamilton and Sato 2017; Ko and Perreira 2010; Ginieniewicz and McKenzie 2014; Guruge and Butt 2015).

The impacts of pre-migration experiences on youth's mental health are diverse. Refugees, for example, may experience trauma related to war, forced migration, violence (physical or sexual), loss of family and friends, and famine, as well as multiple displacements across refugee shelters (Este et al. 2017; Khanlou et al. 2002; Khanlou 2008). Each of these experiences elevates the risk of mental health problems such as suicide, post-traumatic stress disorder and lasting depression (Khanlou 2008). Experiences may also include family separation, which has significant impacts on child–parent interrelationships. Separation may be a source of some youth's emotional and psychological stress (Khanlou et al. 2002; Ko and Perreira 2010) and has emotional impacts on the mental health of children and youth, such as experiences of depression (Ginieniewicz and McKenzie 2014).

Forced migration, as opposed to voluntary immigration, is also important to consider. For different reasons, youth may not be consulted or take part in the decision made by their parents to migrate to another country, and this is important to consider because "those who have had immigration imposed on them may be less likely to adapt positively than those for whom immigration was a choice" (Chapman and Perreira 2005: 105).

Migration Experiences

Migration experiences are part of the journey immigrants and refugees partake in when leaving their country. Immigrant and refugee families have different resources and levels of social support they can draw from when they migrate (Khanlou 2008). Some have more social networks that help them make informed decisions about how to apply to migrate to another country or where to settle within the host country. Refugees may migrate temporarily to different countries in their journey to their final destination. In other words, refugees might have experienced multiple displacements and face lengthy transitional living circumstances before arriving at their final destination (Guruge and Butt 2015).

Post-Migration Experiences

Post-migration experiences refer to the settlement and integration experiences of immigrant and refugee populations after they arrive in their new country of residence. Newcomer families, including newcomer youth, face a number of diverse challenges, barriers and opportunities.

Cultural tensions, such as facing new social norms and values, are important processes to consider. Immigrant youth and their families encounter intergenerational concerns when negotiating their families' cultural values vis-à-vis the ones they learn from their new host society (Khanlou et al. 2002; Khanlou and Crawford 2006). Youth may have conflicting gender roles and expectations from both their families and their social context (Guerrero 2014). For example, the role and meaning of being a woman may be challenged by the factors shaping female youth's lives in their new settings. Katherine Zeiders, Adriana Umaña-Taylor and Chelsea Derlan (2013) argue that stress generated by societal gender expectations may be one of the causes of higher levels of depressive symptoms among immigrant female youth. Immigrants and refugees may experience a "generational culture clash," producing stress, anxiety, depression and identity loss that have impacts on their mental health (Islam, Khanlou and Tamim 2014). However, it is important to underscore the heterogeneity among immigrant youth and to avoid generalization. For example, other community-based studies also report positive self-esteem and mental well-being among newcomer female youth (Khanlou et al. 2002).

Language proficiency is major concern for newcomer youth for whom English is a second language (ESL), particularly for integration into school-based peer groups and mainstream classroom activity (Khanlou et al. 2002). In English speaking provinces, fluency in English influences how youth feel about themselves. Lack of fluency may promote their isolation and may also trigger what Nazilla Khanlou and Charmaine Crawford (2006: 52) define as the silenced self, "the process through which an individual disassociates from interaction with others for fear of negative consequences" (e.g., withdrawing from conversations or not sharing experiences). Their decision "not to be present" may have negative consequences on their self-esteem (ibid.). In such contexts, newcomer youth may draw their strength and peer support from other newcomer youth from different cultural backgrounds.

Lack of recognition of professional credentials of youth's parents is a well-known barrier that families face when they settle in Canada. In addition to its economic impacts, underemployment also affects parents' professional identity because they experience de-skilling, meaning they are not able to practise or keep updated in their professional field. Older youth can also face a lack of recognition of their prior learning experiences in their country of origin (Khanlou et al. 2002).

Regardless of their professional qualifications, newcomer populations increasingly face a number of economic barriers, such as occupying lower-paid and precarious jobs, which contributes to their poverty and low social mobility (Bauder 2003; Teelucksingh and Galabuzi 2005; Walters, Phythian and Anisef 2006; Reitz 2007; Li 2008). The integration of immigrant youth into the labour market depends on a variety of contingent factors, such as the age of arrival to their host country and the financial and social resources of their families. It is well documented that poverty is one of the strongest SDOH.

Social marginalization and isolation results from the lack of access to social and health services, or lack of networks such as family or friends, and is a risk factor for newcomer populations' health and well-being. For some newcomers, precarious immigration status (i.e., not having an officially recognized immigrant or refugee status) is an important concern. Social support from peers, family, communities, institutions and governments can be instrumental in reducing immigrants' marginalization and isolation. Social support has a positive impact on the health and well-being of the population (Ardiles, GermAnn and Mawani 2014); it is a key social determinant of health (Oxman-Martinez et al. 2005; Simich, Wu and Nerad 2007). Family, extended family, community members and religious organizations, for example, provide protective factors for the mental health and well-being of newcomers. Social support related to tangible support from governments and institutions, such as the provision of financial assistance, material goods or services, may constitute key social resources with positive health and well-being outcomes (Ardiles, GermAnn and Mawani 2014).

Discrimination, Racism and Mental Health

Prejudice, racism and *discrimination* can negatively affect youth's process of settlement and integration, as well as on their feelings of belonging to their new society (Khanlou, Koh and Mill 2008). They also produce socioeconomic inequities and injustices among the population (Blanchet, Browne and Varcoe 2017). Discriminatory barriers to accessing employment, for example, impact family income, mental health and well-being, and therefore positive settlement. Economic deprivation resulting from discrimination also explains the difficult challenges some Latino youth living in Toronto experience when trying to adapt to public schools (Schugurensky, Mantilla and Serrano 2009; Matute 2010). Economic hardships experienced by immigrant families may force students to find a job, which may compromise their commitment to stay in school (Matute 2010).

In the United States, studies report that nearly 50 percent of ethnic minority adolescents report daily experiences of discrimination (Zeiders, Umaña-Taylor, and Derlan 2013). In a study of 1,348 Southeast Asian adult refugees in Canada, one in five of the interviewed refugees reported experiences with discrimination (Beiser 2010). A new study also provides evidence of peer and school-based racism, which has become more salient in small urban areas in Canada, explaining that minority youth are treated differently due to their race in that context (Baker, Price and Walsh 2016).

Racism and discrimination occur at the personal or at the institutional–systemic level. Personal practices refer to individual attitudes and behaviours. Systemic discrimination is the set of practices generated by the social institutions (government agencies, schools) of any society. The school setting is a common place where discrimination is practised, not only by peer students (individual discrimination) but also by school teachers and staff (low expectations of visible minorities) (Carranza 2007; Matute 2010). Prejudice against minorities in school settings may promote feelings of social isolation and lack of belonging (Khanlou, Koh and Mill 2008). The issue of Black male students stereotyped within school settings as "at risk," as underachievers, or as needing special educational support further contributes to youth racialization and marginalization (James 2012). Furthermore, these stereotypes negatively impact youth's learning, social life and future opportunities (ibid.). The media (T.V., radio, movies, newspapers) is a key powerful source of systemic prejudice. The impacts of media are insightfully explained by a racialized female youth:

> We are from that country, we are from that religion and when we see it being discriminated so negatively on T.V. it affects us. So it rubs off on society, I mean, … now these youth … they watch T.V. and it has an effect on them and then … they may stereotype you because they have seen whatever on T.V. (18-year-old Afghan female quoted in Khanlou et al. 2002)

This quote reinforces the power that the media possesses and how it may negatively impact youth and their confidence while residing in Canada.

Racialized immigrant youth face racism and discrimination in a context where multiple personal and family transitions are also taking place, such as loss of ties with friends and family that they left behind, the building of new social networks, and their integration into the new cultural and economic systems of the host society. The youth need the support of inclusive communities and societies at large to face discriminatory practices and to resist exclusion; they cannot be expected to do this alone. In what follows, we address some actions that can be taken.

What Can Society Do to Promote Immigrant and Refugee Youth's Mental Health?

The migration experiences of newcomer youth are both sources of challenges and sources of strength. However, while it is important to recognize youth's social contexts, we need to also consider the individuals' strengths and resilience (Khanlou 2008). Resilience results from the combination of social supports, such as healthy families, youth-focused schools and caring communities (Theron et al. 2011). There are also political and socioeconomic structural changes that can be made to promote a more equitable world for immigrant and refugee youth. For example, addressing issues related to unemployment and income promote newcomer youth resilience (Khanlou and Wray 2014). Therefore, there is a need to implement structural policies aimed at addressing the risk factors that are impacting the mental health of immigrant and refugee youth in the first place. As Amélie Blanchet, Annette Browne and Colleen Varcoe (2017) explain, recognizing the existence of racism is not enough; we need to counteract racism and discrimination with specific interventions.

The School Sector

The school setting is one of the most important venues to promote youth mental health. It is one of the environments that immigrant and refugee youth first encounter, where they interact with their peers and have new experiences. The school may be the right place to promote cross-cultural events and initiatives, so youth learn about their peers' cultures (Khanlou et al. 2002). There are a number of ways to improve the services schools provide to help youth better adapt to their new society (Khanlou et al. 2002; Khanlou and Crawford 2006).

Enhancing Language Programs

English language learners (ELL) programs are offered through the Canadian school sector across the country. Language is a key barrier limiting newcomer youth's options. Not being fluent in English (or having an accent) is a source of stress as well as a contributor to youth's sense of isolation. After the completion of ELL courses, youth may still not be well-equipped to "meet the academic, social and emotional skills needed" to integrate and participate in their new society (Khanlou et al. 2002: 50). As some experiences show, the integration of "humanizing spaces" in the ELL classroom through the implementation of values such as respect, mutual trust, verbal teachings and role modelling as the foundations of teaching or learning English may have the potential to change the lives of immigrant students (Salazar and Franquiz 2008).

Inclusive Educational Curricula

Khanlou et al. (2002) highlight the need to implement multicultural, anti-sexist and anti-racist values within the school system curricula. For example, curriculum shifts may include the introduction of multicultural and diverse literature and texts, as well as the development of knowledge and skills among teachers to adopt critical literacy as a source to analyze racism with their students (McCardle 2017). Furthermore, the lack of visible minority teachers in the school system may have a negative impact on youth integration (Khanlou et al. 2002). Teachers are not neutral, and their role is key in anti-racist education (Gibson et al. 2014). Policies toward the inclusion of visible minorities in school boards and executive positions are also important to promote social change from within and, ultimately, to improve newcomer youth experiences in school settings (Gibson et al. 2014; Carr and Klassen 1997). They may also help to promote the reinforcement of anti-harassment and anti-victimization programs that result from racism and discrimination (Thomson et al. 2015).

Increase School-Based Social Activities

This is a suggestion expressed in interviews by immigrant female youth (Khanlou and Crawford 2006). The youth wanted to have activities such as field trips, so they could learn more about Canada. They wanted to better understand the Canadian way of life as part of a process of understanding their new society as well as feeling better about themselves (improving their English skills and knowledge about the country). Other recommendations include counselling and support services, welcoming and reception centres, mentoring and peer tutoring programs, among others (Khanlou et al. 2002).

Health Services

Immigrants and refugees encounter barriers to their seeking or obtaining help (Este et al. 2017; Mental Health Commission of Canada 2012), and they also under-utilize mental health services due to discrimination and other important barriers related to language, transportation and linguistically and culturally inappropriate services (Thomson et al. 2015). There is a need to integrate into the health and social service providers' (e.g., medicine, nursing, social work) education/training a comprehensive focus on culture, racialization and the social determinants of health. However, as Lorraine Culley (2006) argues, proper training should go beyond culture and ethnicity to address racism. There is a need to contest the idea that service providers offer a colourblind service (ibid.) and problematize the idea that race matters in terms of unequal access to health services, in interactions with the patient and as a determinant of the health of the population. The idea is to make racism visible and to integrate a critical understanding of ethnicity by recognizing the existence of differentiated power relations, privilege, hierarchy and dominance among social groups (Culley 2006).

Empowerment is an important element of anti-oppressive practice and service providers or educators can play a key role in promoting it among immigrant and refugee youth. *Anti-oppressive frameworks* may also "help social workers to challenge themselves to be cognizant of power differentials" among the population they are serving (Sakamoto and Pitner 2005: 436). These frameworks go beyond the individual to highlight the intersection of broader systemic processes and structures such as racism, class, gender and age, shaping inequality within and among ethnic groups (Culley 2006).

At the organizational level, there are a wide array of national and local initiatives to promote anti-racism practices. For example, the Coalition of Municipalities Against Racism and Discrimination provides a toolkit for municipalities, organizations and citizens (Canadian Commission for UNESCO 2012). The toolkit includes practical information on how to develop and monitor a Plan of Action, promote youth participation and collaborate with Indigenous communities; it also contains examples of good practices, tools to produce press releases or media advisories, and other additional resources (ibid.). At the local level there are community-based youth-led organizations that are also actively engage in promoting anti-racism such as the Antiracism Resource Centre,[1] which provides resources and information for educators, employers, students and youth on race, anti-racism and anti-discrimination.

What Can Students Do to Help Newcomer Immigrant and Refugee Youth Reduce Resettlement Stress and Barriers in Adapting to Their New Country?

Organize talks to increase awareness among students about discrimination and racism issues at school and their impacts on newcomer youth's mental health and well-being.

The school setting is a key environment to promote changes in students' social perceptions, social practices and behaviours toward newcomer youth. The first step is to initiate a dialogue. Students engaging in negative practices, beliefs or behaviours may not be aware of the detrimental impacts these may have on the mental and physical health of newcomer youth. Such students may be doing this subconsciously, or they may be replicating ideas they hear at home or through the media.

Media shapes cultural narratives, including those of respect and inclusion, or discrimination and racism, toward groups. In Canada limited empirical work has focused on the impact of cultural narratives on Black Canadian youth (Hasford 2016). Media literacy education, such as workshops run by and for youth, can help youth take a critical perspective toward the media (Scharrer and Ramasubramanian 2015).

Promote dialogue among students' families and friends to increase awareness about the difficulties and problems immigrant and refugee families face when settling into a new country.

By promoting informed dialogue with the students' social networks (family, friends) about the settlement issues newcomer youth and their families face, students may increase society's awareness. In doing so they may indirectly contribute to reducing discrimination and racism against newcomers because these are practices based on misinformed ideas about newcomers.

The steps proposed here are based on an assumption that students are individuals with agency. The youth need to be integrally involved in many such initiatives to recognize their key role in addressing the discrimination faced by their newcomer immigrant and refugee peers.

DISCUSSION QUESTIONS

1. What are the social determinants of immigrant and refugee youth's mental health?
2. What are the impacts of racism, discrimination and prejudice on im-

migrant and refugee youth's mental health?

3. What can institutions (such as the school or community-based or-
    ganizations) do to promote immigrant and refugee youth resilience?

ACTION STEPS

1. Organize talks to increase awareness among students about discrim-
    ination and racism issues at school and their impacts on newcomer
    youth's mental health and well-being.
2. Promote dialogue among students' families and friends to increase
    awareness about the difficulties and problems immigrant and refu-
    gee families face when settling into a new country.
3. Work with key stakeholders (e.g., governments, service providers,
    and policy makers/influencers) to implement structural policies
    aimed at addressing the risk factors impacting the mental health of
    immigrant and refugee youth.

Supplemental Readings

Baker, James. 2013. "Just Kids? Peer Racism in a Predominantly White City." *Refuge:
    Canada's Journal on Refugees,* 29, 1.
Guruge, Sepali, and Hissan Butt. 2015. "A Scoping Review of Mental Health Issues
    and Concerns among Immigrant and Refugee Youth in Canada: Looking Back,
    Moving Forward." *Canadian Journal of Public Health,* 106, 2.
Taylor, Alison and Harvey Krahn. 2013. "Living through Our Children: Exploring
    the Education and Career 'Choices' of Racialized Immigrant Youth in Canada.
    Journal of Youth Studies, 16, 8.

Additional Resources

Canadian Mental Health Association.
Multicultural Mental Health Resource Centre.

Acknowledgements

We wish to acknowledge startup funding provided to Nazilla Khanlou as part of
her Chair in Women's Health Research in Mental Health at York University, which
supported the writing of this chapter.

Note

1. <anti-racism.ca/node/18>.

References

Affiliation of Multicultural Societies and Services Agencies of BC. 2013. "The
    Intersection of Poverty and Immigration in BC and Canada." Info Sheet. Issue
    6. Vancouver, BC.

Ardiles, Paola, Kathy GermAnn and Fatah Mawani. 2014. "Illuminating Gender-Transformative Mental Health Promotion in the Workplace." In Lorraine Greaves, Ann Pederson and Nancy Poole (eds.), *Making It Better: Gender Transformative Health Promotion*. Toronto, ON: Canadian Scholars' Press.

Baker, James, Jonathan Price and Kenneth Walsh. 2016. "Unwelcoming Communities: Youth Observations of Racism in St. John's, Newfoundland and Labrador, Canada." *Journal of Youth Studies*, 19, 1.

Balogh, Robert, Johanna Lake, Elizabeth Lin, Andrew Wilton and Yona Lunsky. 2015. "Disparities in Diabetes Prevalence and Preventable Hospitalizations in Persons with Intellectual and Developmental Disability: A Population Study." *Diabetic Medicine*, 32, 2.

Barankin, Tatyana, and Nazilla Khanlou. 2007. "Growing Up Resilient: Ways to Build Resilience in Children and Youth." CAMH Publications. Toronto, ON: Centre for Addiction and Mental Health.

Bauder, Harald. 2003. "'Brain Abuse,' or the Devaluation of Immigrant Labour in Canada." *Antipoda*, 35, 4.

Beagan, Brenda Lorraine, Josephine Etowa and Wanda Thomas Bernard. 2012. "'With God in Our Lives He Gives Us the Strength to Carry On': African Nova Scotian Women, Spirituality, and Racism-Related Stress." *Mental Health, Religion and Culture*, 15, 2.

Beiser, Morton. 2010. "The Mental Health of Immigrant and Refugee Children in Canada: A Description and Selected Findings from the New Canadian Children and Youth Study (NCCYS)." Canadian Issues. Immigrant Mental Health in Canada/ La Santé Mentale Des Immigrants au Canada. Metropolis, Public Health Agency of Canada.

Blanchet, Amélie, Annette J. Browne and Colleen Varcoe. 2017. "Drawing on Antiracist Approaches Toward a Critical Antidiscriminatory Pedagogy for Nursing." *Nursing Inquiry*, 25, 1.

Bombay, Amy, Kimberly Matheson and Hymie Anisman. 2014. "The Intergenerational Effects of Indian Residential Schools: Implications for the Concept of Historical Trauma." *Transcultural Psychiatry*, 51, 3.

Braveman, Paula. 2014. "What Is Health Equity: And How Does a Life-Course Approach Take Us Further Toward It?" *Maternal Child Health Journal*, 18, 2.

Canadian Commission for UNESCO. 2012. "Canadian Coalition of Municipalities Against Racism and Discrimination. Toolkit for Municipalities, Organizations and Citizens." Ottawa, ON.

Carr, Paul R., and Thomas R. Klassen. 1997. "Different Perceptions of Race in Education: Racial Minority and White Teachers." *Canadian Journal of Education/ Revue canadienne de l'éducation*, 22, 1.

Carranza, Mirna E. 2007. "Building Resilience and Resistance Against Racism and Discrimination among Salvadorian Female Youth in Canada." *Child and Family Social Work*, 12, 4.

Chapman, Mimi V., and Krista M. Perreira. 2005. "The Well-Being of Immigrant Latino Youth: A Framework to Inform Practice." *Families in Society*, 86, 1.

Charles, Claire, Caroline Mahoney, Brandi Fox and Christine Halse. 2016. "School Principals and Racism: Responding to Aveling." *Discourse: Studies in the Cultural Politics of Education*, 37, 2.

CIC (Citizenship and Immigration Canada). "Canada Facts and Figures: Immigrant Overview Permanent Residents 2014." Ottawa, ON: Minister of Public Works and Government Services. <cic.gc.ca/english/pdf/2014-Facts-Permanent.pdf>.

___. 2012. "Canada Facts and Figures: Immigration Overview Permanent and Temporary Residents 2011." Ottawa: CIC.

CIHI (Canadian Institute for Health Information). 2009. "Improving the Health of Canadians: Exploring Positive Mental Health." Ottawa, ON.

Crenshaw, Kimberlé. 1989. "Demarginalizing Intersections of Race and Sex: A Black Feminist Critique of Anti-Discrimination Doctrine, Feminist Theory and Anti-Racist Politics." *Chicago Legal Forum,* 140.

Culley, Lorraine. 2006. "Transcending Transculturalism? Race, Ethnicity and Health-Care." *Nursing Inquiry,* 13, 2.

Day, Iyko. 2010. "Alien Intimacies: The Coloniality of Japanese Internment in Australia, Canada, and the US." *Amerasia Journal,* 36, 2.

Edge, Sara, and Bruce Newbold. 2013. "Discrimination and the Health of Immigrants and Refugees: Exploring Canada's Evidence Base and Directions for Future Research in Newcomer Receiving Countries." *Journal of Immigrant and Minority Health,* 15, 1.

Elias, Brenda, Javier Mignone, Madelyn Hall, Say P. Hong, Lyna Hart and Jitender Sareen. 2012. "Trauma and Suicide Behaviour Histories Among a Canadian Indigenous Population: An Empirical Exploration of the Potential Role of Canada's Residential School System." *Social Science and Medicine,* 74, 10.

Este, David, Laura Simich, Hayley Hamilton and Christa Sato. 2017. "Perceptions and Understandings of Mental Health from Three Sudanese Communities in Canada." *International Journal of Culture and Mental Health,* 10, 3.

Frank, Kristyn. 2013. "Immigrant Employment Success in Canada: Examining the Rate of Obtaining a Job Match." *International Migration Review,* 47, 1.

Frohlich, Katherine L., Nancy Ross and Chantelle Richmond. 2006. "Health Disparities in Canada Today: Some Evidence and a Theoretical Framework." *Health Policy,* 79, 2.

Gariba, Shaibu Ahmed. 2009. "Race, Ethnicity, Immigration and Jobs: Labour Market Access among Ghanaian and Somali Youth in the Greater Toronto Area." PhD dissertation, University of Toronto.

Gibson, Priscilla A., Robert Wilson, Wendy Haight, Misa Kayama and Jane M Marshall. 2014. "The Role of Race in the Out-of-School Suspensions of Black Students: The Perspectives of Students with Suspensions, Their Parents and Educators." *Children and Youth Services Review,* 47.

Ginieniewicz, Jorge, and Kwame McKenzie. 2014. "Mental Health of Latin Americans in Canada: A Literature Review." *International Journal of Social Psychiatry,* 60, 3.

Goldring, Luin, and Patricia Landolt. 2012. "The Impact of Precarious Legal Status on Immigrants' Economic Outcomes." IRPP Study #35. Toronto: Institute for Research on Public Policy.

Greene, Melissa L., Niobe Way and Kerstin Pahl. 2006. "Trajectories of Perceived Adult and Peer Discrimination among Black, Latino, and Asian American Adolescents: Patterns and Psychological Correlates." *Developmental Psychology,* 42, 2.

Guerrero, Cristina Alexandra. 2014. "Rethinking Latin@ Student Engagement: Identification, Community Engagement, and Transformative Learning through Youth Participatory Action Research." PhD dissertation, University of Toronto.

Guruge, Sepali, and Hissan Butt. 2015. "A Scoping Review of Mental Health Issues and Concerns among Immigrant and Refugee Youth in Canada: Looking Back, Moving Forward." *Canadian Journal of Public Health,* 106, 2.

Hankivsky, Olena, Renée Cormier and Diego de Merich. 2009. "Intersectionality: Moving Women's Health Research and Policy Forward." Vancouver, BC: Women's Health Research Network.

Hasford, Julian. 2016. "Dominant Cultural Narratives, Racism, and Resistance in the Workplace: A Study of the Experiences of Young Black Canadians." *American Journal of Community Psychology*, 57, 1–2.

Immigration and Refugee Protection Act. 2016. Ottawa, ON: Minister of Justice.

Islam, Farah, Nazilla Khanlou and Hala Tamim. 2014. "South Asian Populations in Canada: Migration and Mental Health." *BMC Psychiatry*, 14, 1.

James, Carl E. 2012. "Students 'at Risk': Stereotypes and the Schooling of Black Boys." *Urban Education*, 47, 2.

Khanlou, Nazilla. 2008. "Young and New to Canada: Promoting the Mental Wellbeing of Immigrant and Refugee Female Youth." *International Journal of Mental Health and Addiction*, 6, 4.

Khanlou, Nazilla, Morton Beiser, Ester Cole, Marilinda Freire, Ilene Hyman and Kensie Murphy Killbride. 2002. "Mental Health Promotion Among Newcomer Female Youth: Post-Migration Experiences and Self-Esteem." Ottawa, ON: Status of Women Canada.

Khanlou, Nazilla, and Charmaine Crawford. 2006. "Post-Migratory Experiences of Newcomer Female Youth: Self-Esteem and Identity Development." *Journal of Immigrant and Minority Health*, 8, 1.

Khanlou, Nazilla, Jane Koh and Catriona Mill. 2008. "Cultural Identity and Experiences of Prejudice and Discrimination of Afghan and Iranian Immigrant Youth." *International Journal of Mental Health and Addiction*, 6, 4.

Khanlou, Nazilla, and Ron Wray. 2014. "A Whole Community Approach toward Child and Youth Resilience Promotion: A Review of Resilience Literature." *International Journal of Mental Health Addiction*, 12, 1.

Kirmayer, Laurence J., Gregory M Brass and Caroline L. Tait. 2000. "The Mental Health of Aboriginal Peoples: Transformations of Identity and Community." *The Canadian Journal of Psychiatry*, 45, 7.

Ko, Linda K., and Krista M. Perreira. 2010. "'It Turned My World Upside Down': Latino Youths' Perspectives on Immigration." *Journal of Adolescent Research*, 25, 3.

Law, Ian. 2007. "Discrimination." In. G. Ritzer (ed.), *Blackwell Encyclopedia of Sociology*. Blackwell Publishing.

Li, Peter 2008. "The Role of Foreign Credentials and Ethnic Ties in Immigrants' Economic Performance." *Canadian Journal of Sociology/Cahiers Canadiens de Sociologie*, 33, 2.

Matute, Alexandra Arráiz. 2010. "Migration Stories: Experiences of Recently Arrived Latino Youth in the Canadian Public School System." Master of Arts Graduate Department of Curriculum, Teaching and Learning dissertation, Ontario Institute for Studies in Education, University of Toronto.

McCardle, Todd. 2017. "'The Horror' of Structural Racism: Helping Students Take a Critical Stance Using Classic Literature." *Multicultural Perspectives*, 19, 2.

Mental Health Commission of Canada. 2012. *Changing Directions, Changing Lives: The Mental Health Strategy for Canada*. Calgary, AB: Mental Health Commission of Canada.

Mikkonen, Juha, and Dennis Raphael. 2010. *Social Determinants of Health: The Canadian Facts*. Toronto, ON: York University School of Health Policy and Management.

Oxman-Martinez, Jacqueline, Jill Hanley, Lucyna Lach, Nazilla Khanlou, Swarna Weerasinghe and Vijay Agnew. 2005. "Intersections of Canadian Policy Parameters Affecting Women with Precarious Immigration Status: A Baseline for Understanding Barriers to Health." *Journal of Immigrant Health*, 7, 4.

Priest, Naomi, Ryan Perry, Angeline Ferdinand, Yin Paradies and Margaret Kelaher. 2014. "Experiences of Racism, Racial/Ethnic Attitudes, Motivated Fairness and Mental Health Outcomes among Primary and Secondary School Students." *Journal of Youth and Adolescence*, 43.

Regan, Paulette. 2010. *Unsettling the Settler Within: Indian Residential Schools, Truth Telling, and Reconciliation in Canada*. Vancouver, BC: UBC Press.

Reitz, Jeffrey G. 2007. "Immigrant Employment Success in Canada, Part I: Individual and Contextual Causes." *Journal of International Migration and Integration/Revue de l'integration et de la migration internationale*, 8, 1.

Sakamoto, Izumi, and Ronald O. Pitner. 2005. "Use of Critical Consciousness in Anti-Oppressive Social Work Practice: Disentangling Power Dynamics at Personal and Structural Levels." *British Journal of Social Work*, 35, 4.

Salazar, María del Carmen, and María E. Franquiz. 2008. "The Transformation of Ms. Corazón: Creating Humanizing Spaces for Mexican Immigrant Students in Secondary ESL Classrooms." *Multicultural Perspectives*, 10, 4.

Scharrer, Erica, and Srividya Ramasubramanian, 2015. "Intervening in the Media's Influence on Stereotypes of Race and Ethnicity: The Role of Media Literacy Education." *Journal of Social Issues*, 71, 1.

Schugurensky, Daniel, Daniela Mantilla and José Francisco Serrano. 2009. "Four in Ten: Spanish-Speaking Youth and Early School Leaving in Toronto." Toronto, ON: Latin American Research Education and Development Network, OISE, University of Toronto.

Sensoy, Özlem, and Robin DiAngelo. 2017. "'We Are All for Diversity, But...': How Faculty Hiring Committees Reproduce Whiteness and Practical Suggestions for How They Can Change." *Harvard Educational Review*, 87, 4.

Shin, Hyunjung. 2015. "Everyday Racism In Canadian Schools: Ideologies of Language and Culture Among Korean Transnational Students in Toronto." *Journal of Multilingual and Multicultural Development*, 36, 1.

Simich, L., Fei Wu and Sonja Nerad. 2007. "Status and Health Security: An exploratory Study of Irregular Immigrants in Toronto." *Canadian Journal of Public Health*, 98, 5.

Statistics Canada. 2017. *Immigration and Ethnocultural Diversity: Key Results from the 2016 Census*. Ottawa, ON. <statcan.gc.ca/daily-quotidien/171025/dq171025b-eng.pdf>.

___. 2013. "National Household Survey (NHS) Profile: 2011 National Household Survey." Ottawa, ON: Statistics Canada.

___. 2006. "Canada's Ethnocultural Mosaic, 2006 Census: Definitions." Ottawa: ON. Statistics Canada. <www12.statcan.gc.ca/census-recensement/2006/as-sa/97-562/note-eng.cfm>.

Teelucksingh, Cheryl, and Grace-Edward Galabuzi. 2005. "Working Precariously: The Impact of Race and Immigrants Status on Employment Opportunities and Outcomes in Canada." Employment Equity, Canadian Race Relations Foundation.

Theron, Linda, Catherine Ann Cameron, Nora Didkowsky, Cindy Lau, Linda Liebenberg and Michael Ungar. 2011. "A 'Day in the Lives' of Four Resilient Youths: Cultural Roots of Resilience." *Youth and Society*, 43, 3.

Thomson, Mary Susan, Ferzana Chaze, Usha George and Sepali Guruge. 2015. "Improving Immigrant Populations' Access to Mental Health Services in Canada: A Review of Barriers and Recommendations." *Journal of Immigrant and Minority Health*, 17, 6.

Vissandjée, Bilkis, and Ilene Hyman. 2011. "Preventing and Managing Diabetes: At the Intersection of Gender, Ethnicity, and Migration." In O. Hankivsky (ed.), *Health Inequalities in Canada: Intersectional Frameworks and Practices*. Vancouver, BC: UBC Press.

Walters, David, Kelli Phythian and Paul Anisef. 2006. "Understanding the Economic Integration of Immigrants: A Wage Decomposition of the Earnings Disparities Between Native-Born Canadians and Immigrants of Recent Cohorts." In M.J. Doucet (ed.), CERIS Working Paper 42. Toronto, ON.

Williams, Joanna L., Sophie M. Aiyer, Myles I. Durkee and Patrick H. Tolan. 2014. "The Protective Role of Ethnic Identity for Urban Adolescent Males Facing Multiple Stressors." *Journal of Youth and Adolescence*, 43, 10.

WHO (World Health Organization). 2016. "Mental Health: Strengthening Our Response." Fact Sheet N° 220. <who.int/mediacentre/factsheets/fs220/en/>.

Zeiders, Katherine H., Adriana J. Umaña-Taylor, and Chelsea L. Derlan. 2013. "Trajectories of Depressive Symptoms and Self-Esteem in Latino Youths: Examining the Role of Gender and Perceived Discrimination." *Developmental Psychology*, 49, 5.

11

COMBATTING RACISM THROUGH THE INTERSECTIONAL LIFE COURSE
The Filipino Community in Canada

Ilyan Ferrer

According to recent statistics in Canada, over six million people or 16.9 percent of the entire population is over the age of 65 (Statistics Canada 2017). This statistic is reflective of ongoing realities within Global North societies, where lower fertility rates, increased life expectancy and an aging baby-boomer population present new challenges for policymakers and service providers. Given these changing demographics, research and policy have paid particular attention to the health outcomes of older adults as they occur throughout their life course. In 2002, the United Nations held the Second World Assembly on Ageing to outline global priorities in addressing the aging population. Among the priorities were the promotion of health and well-being throughout life and the prevention of late-life illness and decline (United Nations 2002; Grenier 2012). Although the Canadian state has integrated some of these initiatives into some of its policies with the aim of universal applicability to its multicultural population, it is important to note these policy initiatives have paid little attention to the experiences of *racism* in its older and racialized immigrant population (Durst and MacLean 2010).

The *life course* is a commonly used perspective in social gerontology (the study of aging). Developed by Glen Elder in 1974, the life course perspective offers an ontological and holistic view of life. This approach examines how events earlier in the life course impact events in later life (see Elder 1974; Grenier 2012). Even within the field of social gerontology, little attention has focused on the issues of racism among older adults (Rozario and Chadiha 2013). Yet, older racialized adults experience forms of racism that can be explicit and direct as well as subtle and difficult to document (Shaw 2000). For instance, within institutional and service settings, racialized older adults experience forms of racism that are pervasive yet rarely acknowledged. In a study on health care access among ethnic older women, Shari Brotman (2003) notes how discourses of "race" and racism within elder care services are disguised as miscommunication between clients and service providers. Moreover, racism is presented as individual prejudice and is therefore construed as a lack of individual competency skills. Brotman (2003) notes that understandings of institutional structures, power relations and anti-racist agendas are rarely articulated within gerontological settings.

Older racialized people who settle into Canadian society face systemic barriers over their entire life course, which include racism and discrimination. Thus, the following question is raised: What can be done to contest the dominant framings that render the perception of racialized older adults invisible? This chapter discusses *systemic exclusion* of and *structural racism* against older racialized adults and immigrants in Canada. It is important to note that systemic exclusion and structural racism affect not only the aging experiences of older people but also adult children who provide care to them, as well as grandchildren who are cared for by their grandparents.

Drawing from my years as a scholar and a community organizer in the Filipino diaspora, I reflect on how notions of the *"exalted Canadian subject"* (Thobani 2007) embed themselves within state institutions and their mechanisms, such as immigration and labour policies, and continue to render invisible the contributions of older racialized people in Canada. The primary purpose of this chapter is to illuminate this *invisibility*, emphasize that it is underserved and explore how we, as activists and scholars, can engage in *anti-racist and inclusive practices*. The first part of this chapter explores how older racialized adults experience social exclusions through the life course and across different generations. I discuss the intersections between immigration and labour regimes throughout the life course, and how these intersections create hidden realities that are often unacknowledged and contribute to experiences of racism. The second half of the chapter discusses strategies and actions required to acknowledge these invisible realities and the ways in which to acknowledge and integrate the voices of older adults themselves.

Throughout the chapter, I draw from my experiences as an organizer and researcher within the Filipino diaspora in Canada. I participated in campaigns calling for the end of both the Live-in Caregiver Program and systemic barriers in the education system as Filipino youth integrated in

Canada. I use the Filipino-Canadian diaspora as a way to highlight the intersections of aging, race, immigration and labour, as well as to provide a point of comparison that can also be applied to other older racialized immigrant communities in Canada.

The objectives of this chapter are to:

- introduce the "invisibility" of older racialized people to the wider discourse on anti-racism;
- understand the lived experiences of racialized im/migrants living in Canada through an intersectional and life course perspective; and
- examine the possibilities of advocacy to contest dominant framings of older racialized im/migrants as unproductive and undervalued members of Canadian society.

Current Understandings of Ageism and Racism

In a classic study on age and race, Ken Blakemore and Margaret Boneham (1994) argue that older Black and Asian adults in the United Kingdom experience the "*double jeopardy*" of age and race discrimination, which constitute risk factors for a poor quality of life (Ajrouch and Abdulrahim 2013). That is, the dual disadvantages of age and race adversely effect the socioeconomic status and health of older racialized adults (Sin 2005). The concept of double jeopardy can be extended to triple or *multiple jeopardy* to highlight the multiple social locations and burdens related to living in industrial societies, the devaluation of old age and the economic and social constraints that older racialized people encounter in their later lives (Dowd and Bengston 1978; Markides, Liang and Jackson 1990). While the concepts of double and multiple jeopardy allow us to make sense of the sociodemographic trends and experiences that older racialized adults encounter in their later lives, they tend to reduce and essentialize experiences and relationships and ignore challenges related to poverty, poor health, discrimination and barriers to service utilization (Rosenthal-Gelman, Tompkins and Ihara 2013).

Part of the problem can be attributed to the ways in which we think about race and age. For instance, understandings of "*race*," ethnicity and age are dominated by solution-based approaches that privilege models of health promotion and continuity (Biggs and Daatland 2004; Torres 2012). Moreover, models and frameworks used to understand *aging* and "race" tend to be culturally specific and based on assumptions that communities are stable and homogenous groups (Marshall 1999). Often understated are the cumulative disadvantages that racialized older adults have experienced throughout their lives and the ways in which racism intersects with other forms of discrimination (for instance, ageism, sexism, discrimination based on sexual orientation).

Diversity in Later Life: Distinctions between Canadian-Born Racialized Older Adults and Racialized Older Immigrants

It is important to note the distinctions between *older racialized immigrants* and *older racialized adults* who were born in Canada. Identity markers for older racialized adults vary from one source to another, but for the most part, do not distinguish between racialized adults who have aged in place and those who have immigrated to Canada. For instance, Statistics Canada (2016: n.p.) defines an immigrant as:

> A person who is, or who has ever been, a landed immigrant or permanent resident. Such a person has been granted the right to live in Canada permanently by immigration authorities. Immigrants who have obtained Canadian citizenship by naturalization are included in this group.

However, data from Statistics Canada do not take into account racialized people who were born in and are subsequently aging in Canada. In this chapter, I use the term *"racialized older adult and immigrant"* to take into account the broad category of ethnocultural minority older adults in Canada. *Racialization* refers to broad social processes (including colonialism and cultural privileging) in ascribing social meaning to the term "race." This definition acknowledges how the meanings and effects of "race" shift across time and space and construct racial difference, categorization and exclusion between groups (Henry and Tator 2009).

Older immigrants are a population of growing interest to Canadian policymakers because of the recent increase in persons over the age of 65. Older immigrants include individuals who have recently arrived (in the past ten years) and those who arrived earlier in their life course and have aged in place, spending most of their lives in the adopted society. While research and activism has done much to advance our knowledge on the rights and welfare of racialized immigrants and migrants, there is a tendency to focus on young and productive immigrants and migrants who come through the economic class (an immigration class for skilled workers who become permanent residents on the basis of their economic contributions) and through the family sponsorship class (where relatives can reunify with a Canadian sponsor who is a Canadian citizen or permanent resident). Older racialized adults who have immigrated to Canada often occupy contradictory spaces where their lived experiences are largely invisible but, like their younger counterparts, they are perceived to be a threat to existing health and social services. At worst, they experience everyday forms of individual and structural discrimination that impact their everyday lives.

Taking into Account the Intersectional Life Course When Thinking about Age and Race

When taking into account the lives of older racialized people and immigrants in Canada, an increasing number of gerontological scholars have begun to incorporate intersectionality into their research on aging and diversity (see Hulko 2009; Torres 2012; Koehn et al. 2013; Coloma and Pino 2016). An intersectional perspective is imperative in understanding the experiences of racism in later life because it takes into account the wider structural barriers and the unique realities and histories that have shaped racialized communities and older people's lives (Ferrer, Grenier, Brotman and Koehn 2017). Recently, my colleagues (Amanda Grenier, Shari Brotman and Sharon Koehn) and I wrote about an "instersectional life course perspective" as a way to integrate the interplay between identity categories, individual chronological life events and the impact of institutions, policies and broader histories and systems that come to shape identities over a lifetime (see Ferrer, Grenier, Brotman and Koehn 2017). Such a frame allows us to take into account how systems of oppression such as colonialism, patriarchy and capitalism are interlinked, shaping key events over the life course and jointly constituting later life experiences (Hulko 2009). The use of an *intersectional life course perspective*

- identifies key life course events, the timing of these events and structural forces;
- takes into account local and globally linked lives;
- considers identities and categories of difference as defined through structural and institutional relations; and
- identifies instances of domination, agency and resistance.

An intersectional life course perspective thus examines interconnections between life events, transitions and systems of domination that occur over the life course and into later life. Most importantly, we can begin to understand how life course experiences are structured by experiences of racialization, patriarchy and commodified labour but are also contested, resisted and utilized by older people.

Let us take a look at the Filipino community in Canada, and how we might examine racism and exclusion of older racialized adults through the intersectional life course. The Filipino community has also been recognized as an emerging part of the diverse Canadian landscape, representing one of Canada's fastest growing racialized groups. While research and campaigns on migrant labour have rightly focused on the inequalities faced by Filipinos (Alcuitas et al. 1997), less attention has been given to its older population (Coloma and Pino 2016; Ferrer 2017). In fact, Canada's older Filipino population is oftentimes perceived as a homogenous and monolithic group. There is, however, considerable diversity along age (for instance, the experience of being 65 is different from 75 or 85), ability, sexual orientation and class lines.

The Filipino Community in Canada: Identifying Key Moments within Migration Trajectories

In adopting an intersectional life course perspective, it is important to examine key life course events, the timing of these events and the structural forces that have contributed to these moments. In the case of migration, we must carefully consider the role of *immigration policies*, as well as the impacts of relocation, including, for example, exposure to discrimination. The understanding of timing and structure provides the space to take into account age norms within a social structure and an analysis of historical and contemporary logics, systems of domination and processes of differentiation. According to Hetty Alcuitas et al. (1997), the history of Filipino settlement in Canadian society began in the 1960s when predominantly health care professionals immigrated from the United States after the expiration of their work permits. Economic, social and political instability in the Philippines, established by centuries of colonialism and propelled by the Ferdinand Marcos dictatorship, set the stage for the mass exodus of Filipinos from the Philippines (Rodriguez 2010). While the Philippines has had a history of sending its labour force outward, the state's Labor Export Program in 1972 is widely seen as the starting point for the Philippine government's structural adjustment project, which facilitated the flow of migrants to alleviate the growing income inequality in the Philippines. The impact of these structural changes was the commodification of its migrant labour force. To date, the Philippines benefits from this outward mobility, as remittances from abroad represent roughly 10 percent of the Philippines' gross national product (Rodriguez 2010). The worsening social and economic condition of the Philippines, as well as the bureaucratized streamlining of migration labour policy, have facilitated what community organizations have alluded to as "the brain drain of the Philippines" (Alcuitas et al. 1997).

The bifurcation of the labour market is commonly understood as the *primary and secondary labour market,* where the former is characterized with high-paying, secure jobs that require formal education and training. The latter is reflective of low-paying, high-turnover jobs. Racialized people in Canada experience the racializaton of poverty (Block and Galabuzi 2011), where they are consigned to the secondary and peripheral labour market because of structural barriers that make it difficult to engage in upward mobility.

The first wave of Filipino newcomers in Canada comprised predominately middle-class professionals who were medical technologists, doctors, teachers, managers and engineers, and they had some success in finding jobs that matched their degrees (Alcuitas et al. 1997). Others were unable to have their educational and professional credentials recognized and were thus relegated to the secondary labour market (Coloma et al. 2012). As first-generation immigrants settled, they petitioned their families to rejoin them through family sponsorship. However, the nature of Filipino immigration began to shift with the emergence of the Foreign Domestic Movement in 1982, which added more regulation to the previous domestic worker policies in Canada but streamlined particularly Filipina women to take on this caring labour work.

Beginning in the 1980s, the pattern of Filipino migration to Canada underwent noticeable changes. Though Canada continues to accept applications under its independent and reunification classes, the number of newcomers engaging in secondary or peripheral labour market work continues to grow; it is outpacing numbers seen by traditional immigrants who are considered to be professionals that contribute to the Canadian economy through permanent settlement in Canada. This is due, in large part, to the emergence of predominantly Filipino domestic workers and temporary foreign workers under the Temporary Foreign Worker Program and the Provincial Nominee Program, which highlight the ways in which labour broadly, and caring labour specifically, is gendered and racialized.

The historical overview of immigration and migration of the Filipino community in Canada offers an important context in understanding how logics of differentiation have occurred over time. The commonly held trope of racialized immigrants being a drain to precious state resources is so predominant (both historically and in present day) that it masks the economic contributions that immigrants make. In fact, racialized and immigrant communities who have entered Canadian borders since the late nineteenth century, and who have recently composed the largest group of incoming immigrants and migrants since the latter half of the twentieth century, are key contributors to the economy. Yet, they often face barriers in adaptation and integration within Canadian society in getting labour market opportunities commensurate to education, entering the education system or accessing social and health care services (Li 2003; Walker 2008; Knowles 2010). Questions have been raised about the extent to which racialized newcomers "belong" to Canadian society (Lee and Ferrer 2014). Sunera Thobani (2007: 8) describes this belonging as the "exalted subject" where the "figure of the national subject is a much venerated one, exalted above all others as the embodiment of the quintessential characteristics of the nation and the personification of its values, ethics, and civilizational mores." The exalted subject exists in opposition to the "Other" — to individuals who do not embody the imagined character of the nation and who are therefore deemed illegitimate members of Canadian society. In consideration of immigration policy, the Canadian immigration regime creates rigid expectations of its newcomers. Peter Li (2003), for instance, argues that Canadian immigration is often framed along specific benchmarks of adaptation, adjustment, acculturation, ethnic identification, survival and the process of change.

Moving Beyond the Individual: Taking into Account Globally Linked Lives

Another step in adopting an intersectional life course perspective is taking into account local and globally linked lives and the ways in which aging is seldom experienced in isolation but implicates multiple family members, multiple generations, intergenerational relationships and transnational contexts. The intersectional life course perspective takes into account how people organize their lives, assess their aging and formulate their identities based on relationships that occur with family and ancestors, between generations and across *transnational contexts*. Conceptualizing linked lives in this manner allows for a consideration of how multiple intersecting trajectories of immigration, migration, care and labour influence social relationships and aging. It also provides a frame to consider experience within contemporary lives that includes globalization, im/migration and transnational migration.

Realities of *intergenerational care* by and of adult children, grandchildren, and other family members are central in the lives of older racialized people and immigrants. According to Brotman (2003), care among older racialized adults is often generally perceived by service providers as constrained to the normative immediate nuclear family, where it is assumed that family members (particularly children and parents) will provide the basic necessities of care for each other (e.g., meals, coordinating care and transportation and undertaking physical tasks such as cleaning and hygiene). Seldom considered are the structural barriers that alter the composition of the family and the availability of family members to provide care (Sun 2014).

Given the challenges and changes that occur when settling into Canadian society, older Filipinos engage and renegotiate caring exchanges with their local families as well as transnational ones. One common strategy is the pooling of resources among intergenerational family members. This is especially the case for retired and retiring domestic workers who, after periods of separation from their children when entering Canada, are called upon to become primary caregivers to their grandchildren. In addition to intergenerational arrangements, different types of caring exchanges exist that transcend international borders and include members of the *transnational family*. For instance, older racialized adults and immigrants might provide financial remittances to family members in different parts of the world. In some cases, transnational family members depend on the financial contributions made by older members in Canada. Considerations of caring as a fluid exchange between older people and their families, fictive kin networks and communities allow service providers and policymakers to take on an advocacy role that moves past individual-based interventions.

Systemic Racism and the Invisibility of Older Racialized Immigrants: Considerations of Categories of Difference through Structures and Institutions

Another consideration of the intersectional life course takes into account how identities and categories of difference are defined through structural and institutional relations. This includes identities for the purposes of making claims, such as for access to services. This category thus extends the life course beyond historical events, timing and relationships to be more inclusive of the structural and institutional relations that shape lived experiences and identities. By considering categories of difference and the consequent processes of differentiation, we expand our understandings to the social processes that work to limit access among marginalized and racialized groups in Canadian society, which force these groups to rely on mechanisms such as families and extended kin networks.

How do we take into account categories of differences through structural and institutional relations? One tool is through immigration and migration programs themselves, which exclude certain populations from crossing Canadian borders from the outset. Recently the Canadian government revamped its immigration and migration programs for older applicants with the aim of instilling efficiency and accessibility into their programs (Ferrer 2015). Long wait times have been used as justification to introduce restrictions on older applicants such as the "Parent and Grandparent Supervisa," a streamlined visa program that allows older parents to temporarily reunify with their families in Canada (Ferrer 2015), and the "*Parent and Grandparent Program*," a specific reunification class for older applicants, who must meet stringent qualifying criteria. The introduction and maintenance of both programs assuage concerns about the social and financial costs of allowing incoming older people to reunify with their families whether it be on a permanent or interim basis.

Restrictions within the Parent and Grandparent Program and Parent and Grandparent Supervisa

The recent age-specific changes to its immigration programs reveal the nominal benchmark that older people are expected to meet — namely, not being a burden to the existing health and social services. An important provision of past and current sponsorship programs of older adults is the structured dependency period known as the "*twenty-year dependency period*" (previously ten-year dependency period). Under this clause, sponsors are required to assume responsibilities for the social and economic needs of their older relatives, such as food, clothing, shelter, dental and eye care, for a period of twenty years. The justification of this dependency period was to assuage concerns that sponsors, not taxpayers, remain responsible for any welfare or supplementary health care costs (Ferrer 2017; Ferrer, Brotman and Grenier 2017). Moreover, sponsors are required to meet a minimum level of income (known as the *"minimum necessary income"* depending on the number of members in the family) as proof of capacity in undertaking the sponsorship. These types of structural barriers call into question the exchanges that exist within the intergenerational family unit, the perpetuation of the cycle of poverty and the imbalanced power dynamics given the structured dependency of older parents on their adult children.

Because many racialized older people cannot meet the stringent criteria of the Parent and Grandparent Program, they are effectively forced to apply for the Parent and Grandparent Supervisa. These policies have effectively shifted conceptualizations of citizenship and family and, in turn, have structured how older im/migrants are received and managed. Moroever, we see how older applicants are coded as visitors — what Citizenship and Immigration Canada have dubbed "genuine visitor(s) to Canada who will leave by choice at the end of the visit" (cic 2012). The notion of a genuine visitor necessarily excludes older immigrants from the imagined Canadian community, and they are, therefore, rationalized to be ineligible for state-provided services and entitlements (Ferrer 2015). Perhaps the most exclusionary and stringent stipulation of the Parent and Grandparent Supervisa and Parent and Grandparent Program is that they deny access to state entitlements such as health care services and basic income-security programs such as retirement pensions and programs. The inaccessibility of Old Age Security and the Guaranteed Income Supplement exacerbates precarious financial situations, in that 25 to 40 percent of immigrant seniors under family sponsorship report no source of income (Koehn, Spencer and Hwang 2010). If we are to critically assess the Parent and Grandparent Supervisa and the Parent and Grandparent Program, it is clear that the stricter and more restrictive eligibility criteria on the older adults and their sponsors creates a tiered immigration program with expectations to meet means-tested criteria based on financial capacities.

Aging, Immigration and Retirement

Another way in which older (racialized) people in Canada are socially excluded and encounter systemic racism is through their access and entitlement to retirement provisions. Divided along three pillars, Canada's pension scheme offers basic entitlements through government transfers and contributory schemes meant to ensure and maintain a standard of living for older Canadians (Government of Canada 2014). First is the *Old Age Security* (OAS), which is a universal transfer program whose purpose is to reduce poverty in later life. This entitlement can be supplemented with a means-tested *Guaranteed Income Supplement* (GIS). The OAS and GIS are not tied to the amount of time that one has worked in Canada. Second is the *Canadian Pension Plan/Québec Pension Plan* (CPP/QPP), which all Canadian workers formally contribute to throughout their working lives in Canada. Third are private pension schemes such as the Registered Pension Plan (RPP) and the Registered Retirement Savings Plan (RRSP), which individuals contribute to voluntarily.

It is well established that women are generally more likely to be poor than men, and that older immigrant women are more likely to live in poverty than their Canadian-born counterparts (Marier and Skinner 2008; Chui 2011). This starts early in the life course and extends well into later life. When we take into consideration participation in the labour market, we see how cumulative disadvantages over the life course impact experiences in later life. Interrupted careers and low wages within the secondary labour market are two examples of how women, particularly immigrant women, are systematically excluded in later life. Retirement programs reflect the gendered and stratified labour market in Canada, where older women disproportionately access the Guaranteed Income Supplement, a maximum benefit of $17,270.40 as of April 2018 (Government of Canada 2018). With 7.6 percent of older women living below the low income cut-off (LICO) line, it is important to note that even maximum entitlements to the GIS would still situate older women well below the LICO in urban areas with populations of 500,000 and over ($24,949) and slightly above the LICO for rural ($17,175) areas (Statistics Canada 2018). Approximately 80 percent of older women (who are unattached) are living in poverty in Canada (Chui 2011; Young 2011).

The persistence of inequalities among older immigrant women is closely tied to the eligibility rules governing Canada's OAS and GIS programs, which are particularly restrictive to newcomers and have a disproportionate impact on immigrant women who cannot access and benefit from pension programs in the same way as their Canadian-born counterparts (Ferrer

2017; also see Marier and Skinner 2008). Since many immigrants from the Global South arrive halfway through their life courses, they necessarily have reduced capacity to contribute to the CPP/QPP and are more likely to identify the OAS and GIS as their main source of pension.

Another reason is the residency criteria, where older people must demonstrate that they have lived in Canada for at least forty years to receive maximum Old Age Security entitlements. For Filipino domestic workers who arrived in their twenties and thirties and who worked in the secondary labour market (where their contributions to the pension scheme are low because their wages are oftentimes minimal), receiving maximum benefits by the time they reach 65 is rare.

Acknowledging Invisible Realities, Agency and Resistance

A key feature of the intersectional life course perspective is how it takes into account *domination, agency* and *resistance*. Agency and resistance can be constructed and experienced in relation to difference, but also in response to wider systems of domination. While systems of domination shape and structure experience, they can, at the same time, be overturned by strategies that respond to the structural forces that perpetuate oppression and marginalization. The *social exclusion* of racialized older immigrants reinforces dominant perceptions of racialized older immigrants, whose realites are largely rendered invisible from the wider discourse on aging. Acknowledging these experiences is a necessary first step in combatting social exclusion and systemic racism (Hulko, Brotman and Ferrer 2017). In my activist and scholarly work with retired and retiring domestic workers, I note how domestic workers I have worked with criticized their pension entitlements as not being enough to sustain their late-life activities. In fact, many disclosed how they were barely surviving and relied heavily on the support of their intergenerational families and community networks.

Part of the difficulty can be attributed to the implicit barriers mentioned earlier; for instance, at the time of arrival into Canada, domestic workers entered under the Foreign Domestic Movement during their mid-lives and therefore could not meet the residence criteria to reach the maximum OAS/GIS benefit. The implications of not having adequate retirement provisions are particularly devastating for those living at or under the poverty line. Some domestic workers I worked with must, out of necessity, continue to work in the secondary labour market or underground economy to survive, even past the age of 65. Opportunities come in the form of untaxed labour in the *underground economy*, where older domestic workers are able to leverage pre-existing relationships with employers into modified work schedules and tasks (Ferrer 2017; Ferrer, Grenier, Brotman and Koehn 2017). While continuing to engage in domestic work presents its own unique set of risks, many older Filipino domestic workers speak about how they are able to benefit from better work conditions such as having a reduced work schedule and being compensated without having to pay taxes.

Experiences of domestic workers highlight intersections between immigration and *income insecurity*. The constant caring labour provided by retired domestic workers in the informal economy, as well as unpaid caring labour within their own families, is emblematic of the gendered nature of caring labour throughout the life course — especially for women from the Global South. Such engagements are notable when considering how the trajectory of caring provision begins early in the life course when domestic workers migrate from the Philippines to take on paid domestic work/care while sending money to their families in the homeland (Pratt and pwc-bc 2012).

Upon arrival in Canada, domestic workers endure years of separation from their families, causing generational traumas. Once reunified, domestic workers find themselves struggling to support their families as their children encounter difficulties integrating into Canadian educational institutions (Pratt 2004). Racialized poverty (see chapter 5 and Galabuzi 2006) is key in unravelling how and why retired domestic workers continue working in the underground economy to ensure the survival of the intergenerational/transnational family. It becomes clear that, in working for affluent (and sometimes middle-class) Canadian families, these domestic workers play an important yet unrecognized role in providing care for families across racial and class lines. Immigration and retirement policies serve to organize and structure the lives of older domestic workers so that "retirement" is not the end of work but simply the point when the work moves underground and is extended.

Imagining an Anti-Racist Future with Older Racialized People

Moving forward, we must think about the ways in which our perceptions of older adults contribute to and sustain the dominant imagery of older people being a burden to Canadian society, and how social policies impact experiences over the life course (Hulko, Brotman and Ferrer 2017). Such considerations allow us to render visible the invisible realities of aging and take into account advocacy links, both locally and transnationally. Some examples might include accounting for caring networks such as the intergenerational family, the transnational family and local fictive kin. By doing so, we expand our support to racialized older immigrants in a way that both acknowledges their everyday realities and challenges as well as combats the structural barriers that perpetuate cycles of marginalization and racism.

It is clear that the confluence of immigration, retirement and labour policies punitively impact older adults striving for survival. Given the restrictive immigration clauses which tie older people to their sponsors for a period of time (for example, the twenty-year dependency period that commits the sponsor to provide all amenities), policies must acknowledge how these dependencies impact older people. In host societies where the primacy of the immediate nuclear family prioritizes the spouse or adult child for care services, and where family and community networks are not as extensive as they are in the homeland, a caregiving context that is both unfamiliar and challenging is created. Even when family members are reunited in a host society, the dynamics are such that adult children are working in the labour market for longer hours and often in lower-paying jobs than their Canadian-born contemporaries. As such, when we engage in advocacy work and campaigns on the rights and welfare of older racialized immigrants, we must think of how this work transcends their generation and encompasses many generations.

Expanding our work to include multiple generations also means looking at *local and transnational spaces*. In my research with older Filipinos, I noted how care exchanges also include local and extended kin. These networks emerge in the absence of formal provisions from the state or when care from normative caregiving sources such as spouses or adult children are limited or unavailable. *Networks* provided within local community organizations represent part of an organic growth within the Filipino community in response to gaps in services, where community stakeholders are creating opportunities to address the loneliness and isolation that some Filipinos encounter in their later lives. Even informal networks created by older people themselves serve to ensure that their caring needs are addressed, for example, when older people are dropped off at the mall and then picked up at the end of the day. In a sense, these local spaces serve as makeshift care providers.

Considerations of how older adults move across transnational spaces, and how these care exchanges and relationships develop meaning, offer an important opportunity for understanding the structural and spatial inequalities that exist within and across aging racialized immigrant communities in Canada. Given these realities, social services and advocacy work must be inclusive in terms of how they address assessments and interventions with older people. Social services are generally predicated on individual life course events where older adults are seen as individuals without necessarily considering the contributions of the family. As such, interventions that involve family members and fictive kin offer an important starting point that takes into account everyday realities. Providing information about immigration and retirement eligibility and entitlements would help in terms of collective planning and coordination of care. Thus, anti-racist practice should be developed to account for the types of geographic mobility that older people are likely to engage in, without risk to eligibility or service delivery. Next, creating programs that involve the community is important. While the tendency is to off-load services to voluntary sectors, more connections need to be made by state institutions that have the resources to support informal community organizations that are doing on-the-ground work.

DISCUSSION QUESTIONS
1. What were your perceptions of racialized older immigrants in Canada before you read this chapter?
2. What are the past and present policies that directly impact racialized older immigrants in Canada?
3. How do we integrate the voices of multi-generations in our campaigns and advocacy work?

ACTION STEPS
1. Consider the intersectional life course perspective when working with older racialized immigrants. For instance, think about the policies and programs that impact older racialized immigrants over the life course and how they impact people in their later lives (as well as their local and transnational families and support networks).
2. Advocate for anti-poverty initiatives such as better provisions and access to Old Age Security and the Guaranteed Income Supplement.
3. Engage and work with informal community organizations that support older racialized adults and older racialized immigrants.

Supplemental Readings

Hulko, Wendy, Shari Brotman and Ilyan Ferrer. 2017. "Counterstory Telling: Anti-Oppression Social Work with Older Adults." In Donna Baines (ed.), *Doing Anti-Oppressive Practice: Social Justice Work,* third edition. Black Point, NS: Fernwood Publishing.

Alcuitas, Hetty, Luningning Alcuitas-Imperial, Cecilia Diocson and Jane Ordinario. 1997. *Trapped: "Holding on to the Knife's Edge": Economic Violence against Filipino Migrant/Immigrant Women.* Vancouver, BC: The Feminist Research, Education, Development and Action Centre.

Young, Claire. 2011. "Pensions, Privatization, and Poverty: The Gendered Impact." *Canadian Journal of Women and the Law,* 23, 2.

Additional Resources

Lived Experiences of Aging Immigrants: A Narrative-Photovoice Project 2014–17 <mcgill.ca/soc-gerontology/research/lived-experiences-aging-immigrants>.

Institute for Research on Public Policy (2015 Report) that seeks a National Seniors Strategy <irpp.org/research-studies/report-2015-10-07/>

Ng, Edward, Daniel W.L. Lai, Aliza T. Rudner and Heather Orpana. 2012. "What Do We Know About Immigrant Seniors Aging in Canada? A Demographic, Socio-economic and Health Profile." CERIS Working Paper Series, Toronto, ON. <elderabuseontario.com/wp-content/uploads/2014/03/What-do-we-know-about-immigrant-seniors-aging-in-Canada.pdf>.

Note

This chapter has been drawn from my previous work and doctoral dissertation (see Ferrer 2015, 2017; Ferrer, Grenier, Brotman and Koehn 2017; Ferrer, Brotman and Grenier 2017).

References

Ajrouch, Kristine, and Sawsan Abdulrahim. 2013. "Intersections Among Gender, Race, and Ethnicity: Implications for Health." In Keith Whitfield and Tamara Baker (eds.), *Handbook of Minority Aging.* New York: Springer.

Alcuitas, Hetty, Luningning Alcuitas-Imperial, Cecilia Diocson and Jane Ordinario. 1997. *Trapped: "Holding on to the Knife's Edge": Economic Violence against Filipino Migrant/Immigrant Women.* Vancouver, BC: The Feminist Research, Education, Development and Action Centre.

Biggs, Simon, and Sven Daatland. 2004. "Ageing and Diversity: A Critical Introduction." In Sven Daatland and Simon Biggs (eds.), *Ageing and Diversity: Multiple Pathways and Cultural Migrations.* Bristol, UK: Policy Press.

Blakemore, Ken, and Margaret Boneham. 1994. *Age, Race and Ethnicity: A Comparative Approach.* Philadelphia, PA: Open University Press.

Block, Sheila, and Grace-Edward Galabuzi. 2011. *Canada's Colour-Coded Labour Market: The Gap for Racialized Workers.* Canadian Centre for Policy Alternatives and the Wellesley Institute. <policyalternatives.ca/sites/default/files/uploads/publications/National%20Office/2011/03/Colour%20Coded%20Labour%20Market.pdf>.

Brotman, Shari. 2003. "The Limits of Multiculturalism in Elder Care Services." *Journal of Aging Studies,* 17, 2.

Chui, Tina. 2011. *Women in Canada: A Gender-Based Statistical Report: Immigrant Women.* Ottawa, ON: Statistics Canada, Social and Aboriginal Statistics Division. Catalogue no. 89-503-X.

CIC (Citizenship and Immigration Canada). 2012. "Parent and Grandparent Super Visa a Great Success." <news.gc.ca/web/article-en.do?nid=675029>.

Coloma, Roland Sintos, and Bonnie McElhinny, Ethel Tungohan, John Paul C. Catungal and Lisa M. Davidson (eds.). 2012. *Filipinos in Canada: Disturbing Invisibility.* Toronto, ON: University of Toronto Press.

Coloma, Ronald Sintos, and Fritz Luther Pino. 2016. "'There's Hardly Anything Left': Poverty and the Economic Insecurity of Elderly Filipinos in Toronto." *Canadian Ethnic Studies,* 48, 2.

Dowd, James, and Vern L. Bengston. 1978. "Aging in Minority Populations: An Examination of the Double Jeopardy Hypothesis." *Journal Gerontology,* 33, 3.

Durst, Douglas, and Michael MacLean (eds.). 2010. *Diversity and Aging among Immigrant Seniors in Canada: Changing Faces and Greying Temples.* Calgary, AB: Detselig Enterprises.

Elder, Glen H. 1974. *Children of the Great Depression: Social Change in Life Experience.* Chicago, IL: University of Chicago Press.

Ferrer, Ilyan. 2017. "Aging Filipino Domestic Workers and the (In)adequacy of Retirement in Canada." *Canadian Journal on Aging,* 36, 1.

___. 2015. "Examining the Disjunctures between Policy and Care in Canada's Parent and Grandparent Supervisa," *International Journal of Migration, Health and Social Care* 11, 4.

Ferrer, Ilyan, Shari Brotman and Amanda Grenier. 2017. "The Experiences of Reciprocity among Filipino Older Adults in Canada: Intergenerational, Transnational and Community Considerations." *Journal of Gerontological Social Work,* 60, 4.

Ferrer, Ilyan, Amanda Grenier, Shari Brotman and Sharon Koehn. 2017. "Understanding the Experiences of Racialized Older People through an Intersectional Life Course Perspective." *Journal of Aging Studies,* 41, 10.

Galabuzi, Grace-Edward. 2006. *Canada's Economic Apartheid: The Social Exclusion of Racialized Groups in the New Century.* Toronto, ON: Canadian Scholars' Press.

Government of Canada. 2018. "Table of Benefit Amounts." Employment and Social Development Canada: Ottawa, ON. <canada.ca/content/dam/canada/employment-social-development/migration/documents/assets/portfolio/docs/en/cpp/oas/sv-oas-apr-jun-2018.pdf>.

___. 2014. "Action for Seniors Report." <canada.ca/en/employment-social-development/programs/seniors-action-report.html>.

Grenier, Amanda. 2012. *Transitions and the Lifecourse: Challenging the Constructions of "Growing Old."* Bristol, UK: Policy Press.

Henry, Frances and Carol Tator. 2009. *Racism in the Canadian University: Demanding Social Justice, Inclusion and Equity.* Toronto, ON: University of Toronto Press.

Hulko, Wendy. 2009. "The Time and Context Contingent Nature of Intersectionality and Interlocking Oppressions." *Affilia,* 24, 1.

Hulko, Wendy, Shari Brotman and Ilyan Ferrer. 2017. "Counterstory Telling: Anti-Oppression Social Work with Older Adults." In Donna Baines (ed.), *Doing Anti-Oppressive Practice: Social Justice Work,* third edition. Black Point, NS: Fernwood Publishing.

Knowles, Caroline. 2010. "Theorising Race and Ethnicity: Contemporary Paradigms and Perspectives." In Patricia Hill Collins and John Solomos (eds.), *The Sage Handbook of Race and Ethnic Studies*. London, ON: Sage.

Koehn, Sharon, Sheila Neysmith, Karen Kobayashi and Hamish Khamisa. 2013. "Revealing the Shape of Knowledge Using an Intersectionality Lens: Report on a Scoping Review on the Health and Health Care Access and Utilization of Ethnocultural Minority Older Adults." *Ageing and Society*, 33, 3.

Koehn, Sharon, Charmaine Spencer and Eunju Hwang. 2010. "Promises, Promises: Cultural and Legal Dimensions of Sponsorship for Immigrant Seniors." In Douglas Durst and Michael MacLean (eds.), *Diversity and Aging among Immigrant Seniors in Canada: Changing Faces and Greying Temples*. Calgary, AB: Detselig Enterprises.

Lee, Edward Ou Jin, and Ilyan Ferrer. 2014. "Examining Social Work as a Canadian Settler Colonial Project: Colonial Continuities of Circles of Reform, Civilization, and In/visibility." *Journal of Critical Anti-Oppressive Social Inquiry*, 1, 1.

Li, Peter. 2003. *Destination Canada: Immigration Debates and Issues*. Don Mills, ON: Oxford University Press.

Marier, Patrik, and Suzanne Skinner. 2008. "The Impact of Gender and Immigration on Pension Outcomes in Canada." *Canadian Public Policy*, 34, Special Supplement on Private Pensions and Income Security in Old Age: An Uncertain Future.

Markides, Kyriakos, J. Liang and James S. Jackson. 1990. "Race, Ethnicity, and Aging: Conceptual and Methodological Issues." In Robert Binstock and Linda George (eds.), *Handbook of Aging and the Social Sciences*, third edition. New York: Academic Press.

Marshall, Victor. 1999. "Analyzing Social Theories of Aging." In Vern L. Bengtson and K. Warner Schaie (eds.), *Handbook of Theories of Aging*. New York: Springer.

Pratt, Geraldine. 2004. *Working Feminism*. Philadelphia, PA: Temple University Press.

Pratt, Geraldine, and PWC-BC (Philippine Women Centre of B.C.). 2012. *Families Apart: Migrant Mothers and the Conflicts of Labor and Love*. Minneapolis, MN: University of Minnesota Press.

Rodriguez, Robyn Magalit. 2010. *Migrants for Export: How the Philippine State Brokers Labor to the World*. Minneapolis, MN: University of Minnesota Press.

Rosenthal-Gelman, Caroline, Catherine Tompkins and Emily Ihara. 2013. "The Complexities of Caregiving for Minority Older Adults: Rewards and Challenges." In Keith Whitfield and Tamara Baker (eds.), *Handbook of Minority Aging*. New York: Springer.

Rozario, Philip, and Letha A. Chadiha. 2013. "Introduction: Social work and Minority Aging." In Keith Whitfield and Tamara Baker (eds.), *Handbook of Minority Aging*. New York: Springer.

Shaw. Alison. 2000. *Kinship and Continuity: Pakistani Families in Britain*. Amsteldijk, Amsterdam: Harwood Academic Publishers.

Sin, Chih Hoong. 2005. "Experiencing Racism: Reflections on the Practice of Research with Minority Ethinic Older People in Britain." *International Journal of Social Research Methodology*, 8, 2.

Statistics Canada. 2018. "Low Income Cut-offs (LICOs) before and after Tax by Community and Family Size in Current Dollars." <www150.statcan.gc.ca/t1/tbl1/en/tv.action?pid=1110024101&pickMembers%5B0%5D=2.2>.

___. 2017. "Census Topic: Age and Sex." <www12.statcan.gc.ca/census-recensement/2016/rt-td/as-eng.cfm>.

___. 2016. "Dictionary, Census of Population, 2016." <www12.statcan.gc.ca/

census-recensement/2016/ref/dict/pop221-eng.cfm?>.

Sun, Ken Chih-Yan. 2014. "Reconfigured Reciprocity: How Aging Taiwanese Immigrants Transform Cultural Logics of Elder Care." *Journal of Marriage and Family*, 76, 4.

Thobani, Sunera. 2007. *Exalted Subjects: Studies in the Making of Race and Nation in Canada*. Toronto, ON, and Buffalo: University of Toronto Press.

Torres, Sandra. 2012. International Migration: Patterns and Implications for Social Exclusion in Old Age." In Thomas Scharf Norah Keating (eds.), *From Exclusion to Inclusion in Old Age: A Global Challenge*. Bristol, UK: Policy Press.

United Nations. 2002. *Political Declaration and Madrid International Plan of Action on Ageing*. New York: United Nations.

Walker, Barrington (ed.). 2008. *The History of Immigration and Racism in Canada: Essential Readings*. Toronto, ON: Canadian Scholars' Press.

Young, Claire. 2011. "Pensions, Privatization, and Poverty: The Gendered Impact." *Canadian Journal of Women and the Law*, 23, 2.

12

RADICAL RESILIENCE
Islamophobia and the
New Canadian Muslim Reality

Mahdi Qasqas

Like other forms of hate, racism and bigotry, *Islamophobia* — the irrational fear of Islam and/or Muslims — is a serious threat not only to Muslims but to all who wish to live in a healthy, safe and prosperous society. Islamophobia has been more prominent since 9/11 and has seen a dangerous and dramatic increase in Canada and around the world over the last decade. For example, relatively recent reports suggest that a significant percentage of Canadians have negative views of Islam and Muslims (Canadian Race Relations Foundation 2012; Angus Reid Global 2013), a dynamic that requires critical examination to understand the source of these negative views in hopes of positively transforming them. Furthermore, a pronounced *culture of fear* has promoted closed and stereotypical views of Islam and Muslims, leading to increased acts of hate, discrimination and violence against Muslims of many races and ethnicities. Unfortunately, the discrimination is systemic and requires a deep analysis of Islamophobia, which is introduced in this chapter.

However, the challenge of understanding and ultimately ending *systemic discrimination* is that, unlike *individual discrimination* or overt acts of racism, systemic discrimination is much subtler and thus receives less widespread attention and outrage from the public. When six Muslims are murdered while they are praying in a mosque, or a Canadian-born Muslim woman of African descent is harassed and denied employment because of her gender, race or religion, it is much easier to condemn and carry out actions against the aggressors. Contrarily, since systemic discrimination is implicit in the operations of well-established and powerful structures in society (Carmichael and Hamilton 1967), such as government institutions and media outlets, it cannot be eliminated without massive collective action by people with power. John Graham, Cathryn Bradshaw and Jennifer

Trew (2009a) contend that, in the context of professional service provision, although some anti-oppressive and cultural competency models can serve as tools to prevent discrimination, the major limitation of these approaches is that the onus of change lies in the hands of each individual. That same limitation applies in combatting Islamophobia; thus, individuals with power must accept that the onus of change lies in their hands.

About fifty years after Stokely Carmichael[1] and Charles Hamilton (1967) coined the term *"institutional racism,"* parliamentary officials in Canada are still pondering over how to eliminate such systemic discrimination and have added the term "Islamophobia" in the recent drafting of Motion 103. Motion 103, which was a private member's motion calling on the members of the House of Commons to acknowledge and condemn Islamophobia, was born out of a petition signed by about seventy thousand Canadians and stated three main points (Parliament of Canada 2017a). These points, verbatim, are as follows:

- Islam is a religion of over 1.5 billion people worldwide. Since its founding more than 1,400 years ago, Muslims have contributed, and continue to contribute, to the positive development of human civilization. This encompasses all areas of human endeavours including the arts, culture, science, medicine, literature, and much more;
- Recently an infinitesimally small number of extremist individuals have conducted terrorist activities while claiming to speak for the religion of Islam. Their actions have been used as a pretext for a notable rise of anti-Muslim sentiments in Canada; and
- These violent individuals do not reflect in any way the values or the teachings of the religion of Islam. In fact, they misrepresent the religion. We categorically reject all their activities. They in no way represent the religion, the beliefs and the desire of Muslims to co-exist in peace with all peoples of the world.

Essentially, the motion asks the government to stand in solidarity with Canadian Muslims to recognize that Islamophobia is a real phenomenon that has had, and continues to have, negative consequences on Canadians and to take action against it. A Liberal Member of Parliament, Iqra Khalid, took this petition forward and launched Motion 103. This motion references the petition and requests that the government engage in research to combat all forms of systemic racism and religious discrimination, including Islamophobia (Parliament of Canada 2017b). Although this is not the first time policymakers addressed such an issue, it is the first time Islamophobia was recognized at the parliamentary level, and its impact is yet to be seen. The motion, although not even a binding bill, passed with a 201 to 91 vote.

Nevertheless, this form of massive action could not be possible without individuals who pushed for systemic change. Thus, the position taken in this chapter is that systematic racism requires individuals in positions of power to increase their knowledge and contact with the groups that are impacted by systemic discrimination. To do so, strategies commonly used to promote factual understanding and meaningful contact are promoted in this chapter as pragmatic first steps, starting with increasing one's authentic knowledge of Islam and Muslims and avoiding biases and overgeneralizations.

Learning more about a population can serve to reduce negative views and enhance greater understanding; education is perhaps one of the most important elements for the primary prevention of discrimination. In some cases, hopefully in most, knowing the roots and impact of Islamophobia may lead to preventing discrimination against Muslims. When knowledge is turned to action, we become more inclined and able to engage in meaningful contact with diverse populations as we hope to coexist in a world without bias, prejudice and discrimination. The first step in that journey is being more knowledgeable about an often-misunderstood population. In this chapter it is posited that, not only are the demographics and sociopolitical challenges important to know but so are the resiliency-based dynamics of the Muslim population in the face of systemic discrimination.

Positionality

For the most part, I write this as an academic endeavour. However, as a practice of transparency and respect, I make my position clear for a variety of reasons. First, this is a topic that I have been intimately involved with since before September 11, 2001. I still recall what life was like before that world-changing date and what a difference the aftermath has made on the Muslim community, so I will often refer to it and other personal experiences. Second, it is important to know that my views here are my own and in no way represent those of the entire Muslim community despite my leadership and advisory role spanning the province of Alberta and over twenty major organizations representing the majority of Muslims in Alberta. Third, I have been privy to many responses from various Muslim communities after they were attacked or threatened, and I am still awe-struck by the *radical resiliency* that they have portrayed. This response is often overlooked and unwritten and thus I cannot point to a reference for when I begin to discuss their radical resiliency. Fourth, as one of the very few Arabic-speaking, Muslim psychologists in the province of Alberta, I have a more nuanced view on the centrality of culture in relation to mental health challenges and treatments and the lack of readiness of many professionals to engage with this population. It is primarily for that reason that I chose to focus on Islamophobia and its impact on the Muslim community, noting that Muslim women are the bravest of them all.

The objectives of this chapter are to:

- describe the demographics and diversity of Canadian Muslims;
- explore major issues confronting Muslims in Canadian society along with the unintended positive outcomes of these socio/geopolitical challenges; and
- provide practical strategies that are both reflective and action-based to reduce closed-minded views about non-dominant populations in general, and Muslims in particular, to promote inclusive and anti-discriminatory attitudes.

Reducing Tension through Enhancing Knowledge

Let us begin with the solution first. When irrational negative attitudes toward Muslims are left unchecked and unchallenged, Islamophobia is allowed to survive in the minds of the uninformed. An irrational fear of Islam and Muslims seems to grow in public forums resulting in many authors forming opinions and reviving knowledge on a construct called Islamophobia. This fear can be explained by examining the link between uncertainty and anxiety. Based on a simple description of the core principles of anxiety and uncertainty management theory (Gudykunst 2005), uncertainty is directly and positively related to anxiety; thus, as uncertainty levels rise, so too do anxiety levels. A high degree of uncertainty leads to fear, and fear leads to avoidance. In light of 9/11 and current geopolitical issues (e.g., ISIS, homegrown terrorism), the high levels of uncertainty among the population about Muslims may contribute to the existing culture of fear in the so-called war on terror. This fear is likely to prevent people from trying to further understand Muslims, so they remain uninformed about the vast differences and dynamics within this population. As a corrective, being informed reduces uncertainty, which is likely to reduce the degree of anxiety in a person and ultimately prevent a fear-based approach to looking at Muslims while avoiding meaningful contact. The same application can be used for any population, but that is beyond the scope of this chapter.

Hence, I echo the call of social justice scholars such as David Este (2007: 96) that we "need to be informed about different cultural and racial groups." Although Muslims are the population this chapter focuses on, the same sentiment applies to personal or professional interactions with ethnoracial individuals, groups and populations.

Graham, Bradshaw and Trew (2009a), for example, state that there is a crucial need to engage in research on Muslims to inform ethical and effective engagement with Canadian Muslim individuals or groups. The vast diversity of this population makes it clear that there are no quick and simple rules to apply. In the process of becoming informed, Graham, Bradshaw and Trew offer the following starting point to anyone working or interacting with Muslims (e.g., co-workers, employees, research participants, communities and so on):

- seek knowledge on the diversity within the Muslim population;
- understand the sociopolitical issues facing Muslims;
- avoid all stereotypes and biases; and
- understand and use the strengths Muslims derive from their faith and communities.

These starting points set the foundation for individuals to develop the knowledge and capacity to effectively identify and subsequently combat the systemic racism and Islamophobia that currently prevails in Canadian society.

Global Muslim Demographics

The Pew Research Center (2011) has conducted research on the global Muslim population that showcases the diversity within this massive population. The global Muslim population is around 1.6 billion, accounting for almost one-fifth of the world's population. Islam is not bound by nationality and its adherents can be found living in all nations of the world (with the exception of the Vatican). About 1.3 billion Muslims live in over fifty countries that are considered Muslim majorities, while 300 million live as minorities in other nations across the world (Pew Research Center 2009).

Although there is a historical connection between Islam and Arabs (Dwairy 2006), it is important to note that Muslims are very ethnically and racially diverse. In fact, there are more Muslims living in China than Muslims living in the Arab countries of Jordan, Kuwait, Lebanon, Palestine and Qatar combined. Over half of the Muslims in the world reside in five non-Arab countries: Indonesia, Pakistan, India, Bangladesh and Nigeria (Pew Research Center 2011). Hence, sweeping generalizations tend to ignore the vast diversity within the population.

Muslims in Canada

Logically, changing demographics and dynamics are essential to understanding the reality of a population. That is, Muslims in Canada are not the same as they were in 2001 and will not be the same in 2030. Muslims in Canada make up a large and growing demographic and are ethnically and racially diverse, as they are globally. Muslims from many countries migrated westward to North America and Europe; many have made Canada their new home. The multicultural heritage of Muslims is mirrored in the multicultural heritage of Canadians. The Muslim population in Canada is currently over one million (3.2 percent of the Canadian population) (Statistics Canada 2013).

In Canada, Islam is the second-largest religion, compared to 67.3 percent of people reporting Christianity and 23.9 percent reporting no religious affiliation (Statistics Canada 2013). In addition, it is considered the fastest-growing religion. According to Statistics Canada (2013), most Canadian Muslims live in Ontario and Québec, with 424,925 in the Greater Toronto Area, 65,880 in Ottawa and 221,040 in Montréal. Alberta has 113,445 Muslims, mostly divided between Calgary (58,310) and Edmonton (46,125), whereas Vancouver has 73,215 Muslims. In 1971, there were approximately 33,000 Muslims in Canada (Qasqas and Chowdhury 2017). Muslim communities have more than doubled in size in nearly all provinces since 2001 and are expected to grow to about 3.3 million by 2031 (Statistics Canada 2010).

Growth Due to Fertility Rates and Immigration

The growth is only partially due to fertility rates and largely due to immigration (Kazemipur 2014). Fertility rates account for some of the increase, as the average number of children per female is 2.4 for Muslims compared to 1.6 for the nation (Statistics Canada 2013). Moreover, Muslims are young: the median age of Muslims is 28.9 years compared to 40.6 years across the nation, and 48.7 percent of Muslims are female (Statistics Canada 2013).

In 2011, 6,775,800 people in Canada (20.6 percent of the Canadian population) were considered foreign-born, excluding refugee claimants and those on a work or study visa (Statistics Canada 2013). Of those who migrated to Canada, about 10.6 percent (or 720,125) are Muslims, 54.2

percent are Christian, and 20.1 percent report no affiliation. Thus, the majority of Muslims in Canada (68.3 percent) are foreign-born. Prior to 1971, 0.7 percent of immigrants were Muslim, 78.4 percent were Christian, and 16 percent reported no affiliation. However, between 2006 and 2011, 17.4 percent of immigrants were Muslims, 47.5 percent were Christian, and 19.5 percent reported no affiliation (Statistics Canada 2013). The majority of foreign-born Muslims in Canada are of Pakistani origin. Between 2006 and 2011, Muslims from Pakistan made up the largest immigrant group among Muslims (Statistics Canada 2013). Approximately 36,000 more migrants from Pakistan arrived between 2011 and 2016, although their religious orientation is not recorded in the new census data (Statistics Canada 2017). It is worth noting, however, that about 96.4 percent of Pakistan is Muslim (Pew Research Center 2011).

When scanning the national statistics on religion and ethnic origin, I found that Muslims were very ethnically diverse, with immigrants hailing from nearly all countries. Significant numbers originate from other parts of Southeast Asia (e.g., India, Bangladesh), the Middle East (e.g., Iran, Lebanon, Palestine and Egypt), Africa (e.g., Somalia, Morocco, Libya, Algeria and Tunisia) and Europe (e.g., Bosnia, Turkey), as well as about 21.7 percent having been born in Canada who are either first- or second-generation Canadians (Statistics Canada 2013). Muslim community websites demonstrate how diverse these communities really are. For example, the website of the Al-Rashid, an organization that has operated in Edmonton since the 1930s, reports that its members are made up of about sixty-two different ethnicities (Al-Rashid Mosque 2017).

Furthermore, these statistics on Muslim demographics do not take into account the sects and denominations within the Muslim community as well as several other within-group differences. They also do not account for an often-overlooked group within the Muslim population who are converts to the faith from other ethnic origins (Canadian-born and immigrants), and data is not readily available.

Furthermore, Muslim community leaders and the websites of Islamic organizations offer higher numbers than are found from Statistics Canada. For example, according to the Muslim Council of Calgary, there are over eighty thousand Muslims in Calgary (MCC 2017) and the Al-Rashid mosque places Edmontonian Muslims at more than sixty thousand (Al-Rashid Mosque 2017). In addition, the recent influx of refugees from Syria are not included in these latest statistics. Finally, there is little research completed on Islamic organizations in Canada despite their contributions to society, diversity and heritage spanning over seventy years (Nimer 2002; Yousif 2008; Qasqas and Chowdhury 2017). Despite the aforementioned gaps, one solid fact is that Muslims are both growing and are ethnoculturally diverse; therefore, it is difficult to make any sweeping generalizations.

Muslim Differences

Acknowledging *within-group differences* is another important ingredient in understanding Muslims and other racialized groups. John Stanfield (1994) recognizes that no singular voice or narrative represents an entire population, and Veronica Williams (2005) has suggested that one major misconception regarding Muslims is the assumed homogeneity within the community. Assuming the Muslim community to be monolithic and static, rather than diverse and dynamic, is one such misconception that has been characterized as a *closed-minded view of Islam* and Muslims (Runnymede Trust 1997). It has already been shown that all Muslims are not Arabs and not all Arabs are Muslims. This is one misconception that can easily be refuted through census data and other demographic evidence. This diversity also extends to sectarian differences, ethnic origins, nationalities and acculturation differences among Muslims; that is, not all Muslims are immigrants either. Assuming all Muslims are immigrants is yet another critical oversight that Wanda Thomas Bernard and Jemell Moriah (2007) have generally cautioned against. They state that cultural competency is not just a matter of dealing with immigrants but also with citizens who have lived in the country for many years. Although Muslims continue to migrate to (or seek asylum in) Canada, many are also born and raised in Canada, making it necessary to consider the experiences of first- and second-generation Canadians and converts to the faith as part of the new Canadian Muslim reality that is diverse and dynamic.

Furthermore, assuming that all Canadian Muslims perceive Islam or interpret Islamic scripture in the same way is an irrational and illogical misconception that has been elaborated on in the extant literature (see Ramadan 2004; Graham, Bradshaw and Trew 2009a, 2010). The assumption that all Muslims think alike is erroneous, yet it may be a major factor in why, according to one survey, 51 percent of Canadians view Islam as being more likely to promote violence than any other religion (Angus Reid Institute 2015). This is another strong reason why understanding the diversity within a community is an essential step in reducing stereotypes consistent with discrimination and Islamophobia.

Unpacking Islamophobia

Islamophobia is a major issue facing Muslims in Canada and requires some unpacking. But first, let us do the same for the general issue of discrimination.

Stigma

One way of unpacking factors that lead to discrimination and preventing it early on is by examining the variables that contribute to the construction of stigma. Erving Goffman (1963: 9) defines *stigma* as "the situation of the individual who is disqualified from full social acceptance." Stigma consists of four main sequential variables: attitudes, stereotypes, prejudice and then discrimination (Corrigan, Roe and Tsang 2011).

In short, an attitude can be positive or negative and formed in many ways. A *stereotype* is an attitude formed against a group based on overgeneralizations and possibly born out of a negative experience. *Prejudice* is a negative attitude toward a group based on the acceptance of stereotypes. One important point when it comes to vulnerable populations that Anne Bishop (2002: 86) states is, "all groups are stereotyped to some degree, but those with power cannot be hurt by them as much as those with less power." Finally, *discrimination* is the only observable manifestation of the conceptual factors of stigma that can have legal ramifications and is a result of acting on prejudicial attitudes. By looking at discrimination as the outcome of a series of attitudinal changes, it becomes possible to implement strategies that deal with its determinants (stereotypes and prejudices), which will prevent the outcome (discrimination).

Prejudice

Prejudice as a construct has been researched extensively and several perspectives, theories and models have emerged (Dion 2003). Each of these theories allows us to identify theoretical and practical factors related to the (attitudinal) determinants of discrimination. According to Gordon Allport (1979), ethnic prejudice is primarily derived from irrational and rigid thoughts about a population; more specifically, it can be conceptualized as negative attitudes and biases against a specific group and its members (Dion 2003).

Defining Islamophobia

To Wayne Martino and Goli Rezai-Rishti (2008: 414), Islamophobia occurs when Islam is perceived to be "monolithic, separate, and without any common values with other cultures and as being essentially barbaric and sexist." At the United Nations, factors contributing to Islamophobia were debated and myths were debunked. According to statements made at a United Nations seminar, four contributing factors also considered myths were as follows (United Nations 2004: 30):

- Islam is a monolithic whole;
- Islam wants to rule the Western world;
- Islam is anti-Western; and
- Islam is against modernity and democracy.

It is important to note that these myths about Islam have, in fact, existed for centuries (see Said 1978).

Contrarily, a discourse emerged on whether the term "Islamophobia" was the best to use. Peter Gottschalk and Gabriel Greenberg (2008: 5) questioned whether Islamophobia could be appropriately compared to other anxiety disorders such as "acrophobia, arachnophobia, or xenophobia." Others have distinguished Islamophobia from the common notion of Western racism based on race and ethnicity (Marranci 2004). Some argued that, although Islam is not a race, the same behaviours and attitudes involved in ethnic prejudice are apparent in Islamophobia — for example, feelings of superiority, inferiority, "Othering" and overgeneralizations by people who are usually suspicious and distrusting of outsiders (Dunn, Klocker and Salabay 2007). In other forums, new phenomena and directions were proposed to define the same construct of Islamophobia. Still others proposed that it should be called "anti-Islamism because, similar to anti-Semitism, it focused on the agony of the victims while Islamophobia reflected the state of mind of those who felt threatened" (United Nations 2004: 31). These discourses and dialogues are useful in that they have contributed to our knowledge on the sociopolitical climate Muslims live in today, and they provide a rationale on how discrimination against Muslims can be multi-faceted. However, the heart of the solution lies in enhancing knowledge about Muslims that is accurate and objective and reduces the need to rely on superficial knowledge based on simplistic stereotypes, biased information or overgeneralizations. Preventing bias and prejudice may be the single most important and practical intervention to prevent the dangerous outcomes of discrimination and, in our case here, the dangers of Islamophobia. With respect to systemic discrimination against Muslims, if people in power are unwilling or unable to challenge their closed-minded views of Islam, then Islamophobia will live on. It is optimistically hoped that the opposite is also true; if *open-minded views of Islam* are prevalent in society and especially among people in power, then Islamophobia will weaken and eventually be eliminated.

Major Challenges Facing Muslims in Canada

Perhaps the most devastating and horrendous act ever committed against Muslims in Canada was the Québec City mosque massacre. On January 29, 2017, a Québecer by the name of Alexandre Bissonnette murdered six Muslims and injured many others while they were praying in the Islamic Cultural Centre of Québec. He was found guilty on six counts of first-degree murder, which the Canadian Prime Minister called a terrorist attack (Prime Minister of Canada 2017; *CTV News* 2018). Québecers have been known to have negative views of Muslims and this massacre should be a wake-up call to all Canadians. In 2009, about 15 percent of Québec residents stated in a survey that they held a favourable view of Islam, whereas in 2013 this number had increased to 32 percent (Angus Reid Institute 2017). We cannot assume that the 68 percent of Québecers who hold unfavourable views, or anyone who holds an unfavourable view of Islam, are Islamophobic; that would be too simple, and many arguments can be made regarding their right for contempt. Also, we cannot know precisely whether or not those with unfavourable views have authentic knowledge of Islam or Muslims or any meaningful contact with their fellow Canadian Muslims that could lead to more open-minded views. What is of interest is how much of their attitude is logically prejudiced or represents the closed-minded views by the many years of media exposure and government policies addressing the irrational threat of Islam and Muslims, especially those riddled with misconceptions.

One misconception that is more in line with explaining, perhaps, why many Canadians have a negative view of Muslims is the assumption that very few or no similarities exist in terms of concepts, morals and beliefs between the Muslim and non-Muslim world (of course, no such monolithic non-Muslim world exists and so usually the term refers to the West or OECD countries). In addition to the assumed separation, "Islam is seen as hermetically sealed off from the rest of the world, with no common roots and no borrowing or mixing in either direction" (Runnymede Trust 1997: 6). Rather, the reality is that a myriad of shared values and experiences, as well as "incidentally shared problems and weaknesses" (6), exist between Muslims and Western society.

In a liberal democratic society that values multiculturalism, like Canada, the strengths of each culture are supposed to be harnessed and supported. The process of "*Othering*" is usually accompanied with claims of us (the non-Muslims) and them (the Muslims). The "Other" is considered "primitive, violent, irrational, scheming, disorganized, oppressive" while the "us" is seen to be "civilized, reasonable, generous, efficient, sophisticated, enlightened, non-sexist" (Runnymede Trust 1997: 6). However, an open-minded view of Islam would not reduce the cultural differences to a simplistic categorization of "us" versus "them" but rather perceive all as different but equal.

Bernard Lewis notes in his essay, "The Roots of Muslim Rage" (1990: 48) that Islam is not a monolith and that it "inspired a great civilization in which others besides Muslims lived creative and useful lives and which, by its achievement, enriched the whole world." To this end, the aforementioned open-minded views of Islam are in line with Lewis's statements. However, following this quote he says, "*But* [emphasis added], Islam, like other religions, has also known periods when it inspired in some of its followers a mood of hatred and violence" (Lewis 1990: 48). In doing so, he engages in what Teun Van Dijk (1992: 98) explains as the discourse of denial in which "the denial often serves as the face-keeping move introducing a generally negative assertion following the invariable *but*." He later introduces two terms that are indicative of closed views of Islam; "Islamic fundamentalism" and the "*Clash of Civilizations*." On these lines, those with closed-minded views of Islam see it as clashing with societal norms because it is "violent and aggressive, firmly committed to barbaric terrorism, and implacably hostile to the non-Muslim world" (Runnymede Trust 1997: 7). During a time when the Government of Canada should have been safeguarding Canadian Muslims by standing in solidarity against Islamophobia, Public Safety Canada under the Harper government stated that violent Islamist extremism is the leading threat to Canada's national security, and there were many other instances reinforcing that the so-called war on terror might have been simply code for a war on Islam (Government of Canada 2013).

One is left wondering how this sentiment toward Islam was interpreted in the minds of the general public and what factors would inoculate the average citizen from overgeneralizing Muslims and accepting a "clash of civilizations" narrative or any other closed-minded view of Islam and Muslims? Based on a recent survey conducted by Angus Reid (2017), a little less than half of Canadians (46 percent) view Islamic clothing less favourably than other religious attire dawned by adherents of religions such as Judaism, Christianity, Buddhism and Sikhism. In addition, the survey also showed that Islam has been gaining the favour of Canadians from about 25 percent in 2013 to about 33 percent in 2017. It appears as though many Canadians don't have a problem with Muslims, but they do have a problem with how they dress, particularly how women dress (this intersectionality is discussed later in the chapter).

Some have argued that the increase in favourable views of Islam (in Québec at least) may have come from sympathy rather than genuine understanding and meaningful contact — that is, because the survey was conducted two weeks after Bissonnette, a White man, murdered six Muslims while they were praying in a mosque and wounded many others. The Canadian prime minister declared it a terrorist attack and both the premier of Québec and other political leaders immediately showed solidarity with Canadian Muslims. This type of solidarity is what is constantly needed and, although it may not eliminate systemic discrimination, it is likely to influence the minds of the general public — and perhaps it did.

In the Muslim community, I often hear criticisms of how the RCMP has not laid *terrorism* charges on Bissonnette, which supports a sentiment in the community reflecting systemic discrimination. That is, had he been Muslim and had it been anywhere else, he would have been immediately assumed to be a terrorist. Notwithstanding these claims and the legal definition of terrorism, the challenges faced by Muslims due to Islamophobia have their roots in years of anti-Islamic discourse stemming back to 9/11. According to the Runnymede Trust (1997), *anti-Muslim discourse* in society becomes normalized rather than challenged, contributing to Islamophobia. For this reason, it is important to go back to September 11, 2001, to begin telling the story.

The terrorist attacks of September 11 had an extreme impact on both the United States and the world. At the time, the US government immediately declared the culprits to be of Arab and Muslim backgrounds, which in and of itself was not problematic. The problem was how this was interpreted by the masses. Perhaps due to a lack of understanding of Muslim culture, it led to widespread negative attitudes against Islam and Muslims by the general public that resulted in a severe backlash against Muslims in many parts of the world (Inayat 2007; Ali, Milstein and Marzuk 2005; Hassouneh and Kulwicki 2007). In 2002, the Council on American–Islamic Relations documented 1,500 reported incidents of attack and discrimination against

US Muslims including twelve murders, a hate rape and other forms of illegal attacks (Kwan 2008). In the US, Muslims have been repeatedly singled out as a problematic segment of society and constantly questioned about violence and terror while being victims of it (Salaita 2006; Welch 2006; Gottschalk and Greenberg 2008). The current Trump administration and its stance against Muslims is beyond the scope of this chapter. Nonetheless, the backlash from the 9/11 atrocities have found their way into Canadian society via the mass media.

In Canada, several legal ramifications of 9/11 emerged, such as the creation of the *Anti-Terrorism Act* in October 2001, which included a pre-emptive detention clause, made suspicion a basis for an investigation and expanded the surveillance power of authorities (Wark 2006). The Act received Royal Assent on December 18, 2001. I recall this being a major issue in the Muslim community, as peaceful protest was no longer a civic right but rather something that Muslims became afraid of joining due to the fear of having a Canadian Security Intelligence Services (CSIS) officer visit their home or request a meeting. On the face of it, and to those uninitiated to the Muslim reality, it does not appear to be a big deal; after all, we have rights and illegal search, seizure and detention are not acts committed in a democratic and just Canada. The Muslim community did not believe this to be true and it became a regular part of our reality to think that CSIS was always watching. I still recall frantic university students being approached by security agents at their home during exam time. Needless to say, they were not guilty of anything other than being Muslim and democratically active. Sadly, this happened more than once and few of them have returned to social activism again. It is also important to note that the pressures on young Muslims to stay out of the public eye was perhaps more a factor of the fear their parents had of the authorities than a real fear of being detained under a draconian security certificate. Nevertheless, despite these new powers being criticized as being incompatible with the *Charter of Rights and Freedoms*, the damage was done.

Not surprisingly, Canadian Muslim communities have experienced a negative backlash post-9/11 (Barkdull et al. 2011) that lives on until this day. In Ahmad Yousif's (2008) work, it was stated that, after 9/11, Islam's association with terrorism became portrayed more often in the public spheres, with media's negative reporting only serving to exacerbate the situation. Furthermore, an increase in discrimination and hate crimes was reported. This had a tremendous impact on the local Muslims as there was a higher sense of fear and anxiety, especially among visibly identifiable Muslims such as women wearing hijabs and men with a dark complexion and a beard. No studies can possibly report how many Muslim women removed their veils, how many men shaved off their beards, or the number of other forms of shedding of any identifiable religious and cultural symbols that were considered to be stigmas. However, this became part of the post-9/11 Muslim reality in Canada despite no acts of terror being demonstrated and no clear threats made against Canada by Muslims at the time.

Research demonstrates that negative media attention against an identifiable group can create bias and prejudicial attitudes against that group (Persson and Musher-Eizenman 2005). Perhaps the responsible thing for the government and news agencies to do would have been to encourage the public to not overgeneralize and panic but to remain safe and vigilant in productive ways, thus possibly preventing the onslaught against innocent Muslims, but this was not the case. The negative impact of Islamophobia was clear, and the community would often complain of the biased views and images of Muslims in the media.

The accessibility principle can explain what happened. The accessibility principle holds that repeated and recurring exposure to a certain thought or mental picture causes that thought or mental picture to be more available in the future (Shrum 2002). Since most mainstream media outlets in northern European nations and North America continued to reinforce anti-Muslim stereotypes and biased information (Poynting and Mason 2006), widespread biases against Muslims were formed. It is likely that these images were internalized by many because the there was no pre-existing knowledge of Muslims that could be used as counter-examples — this further supports the need for authentic knowledge of Islam and Muslims and meaningful contact to serve as counter-examples to biased media reporting. Despite the challenges, many Muslims maintained their identity and forged the beginning of a new Muslim reality in Canada: one of radical resilience.

Radical Resilience

For some, in the crisis of 9/11 there was opportunity for growth and development. Yousif (2008: 117) states that, despite the backlash of 9/11, "it should be noted that there has been no mass feeling on the part of Muslims in Ottawa that Canada is no longer a good place for Muslims to live." This is a sentiment I can testify to here in Alberta. Rather, after 9/11, there was also a greater interest in Islam from the public, an increase in inter-faith dialogue, more attempts toward unbiased media and an increase in collaboration with government officials and law enforcement. Although many Muslims I spoke to were quite wary of trusting csis, they did not have a problem working with the local police and government officials to address the issues at hand.

Carenlee Barkdull and colleagues (2011) found that many of their participants found a sense of resilience in their faith. Many participants have also added that the role of Muslim organizations in the building of the nation should be promoted, and Muslims should do more to build bridges with others, hold more events, conduct more programs and provide more services. These sentiments of doing more in the face of adversity should not be ignored as a characteristic of the new Muslim reality. Muslim organizations and leaders continually put a wealth of resources into correcting misinformed views of Islam to the public, even at the expense of core social programs within the community. Two acts of radical resiliency are important.

Mrs. Valerio Stands in Solidarity with Muslim Women Wearing the Hijab

On November 8, 2016, a man was lingering around an Edmonton LRT station with a noose in his hand, approaching only Muslim females wearing the *hijab* and telling them that the noose was intended for them. Nakita Valerio of the Alberta Muslim Public Affairs Council created a radically resilient response (*Edmonton Journal* 2016). She had mobilized a group to hand out flowers to every Muslim woman wearing the hijab at the same LRT station on December 7, 2016. This show of solidarity, in my opinion, is worthy of mention because after an incident like this, far too often the undocumented statements heard in the community usually surround retreating and not showing observable signs of being Muslim to stay safe.

This notion of isolating or avoiding the public out of fear ultimately leads to various psychological difficulties for Muslim women. In one study, Muslim women wearing the hijab became more afraid of being out alone (Kwan 2008). Wahiba Abu-Ras and Zulema Suarez (2009: 58) also conducted a study on Muslim women post-9/11 and concluded that Muslim women who wore the hijab "were more likely to express a reluctance to leave home." Furthermore, because these women felt they were easily identifiable as Muslims, they were also "easier targets for harassment" (Abu-Ras and Suarez 2009: 58). Such prejudice, harassment and discrimination can be serious stressors contributing to mental health problems (Asvat and Malcarne 2008).

This is why Mrs. Valerio's response and other acts of standing in solidarity with Muslim women wearing the hijab are so crucial; they have the power to reduce stressors for these women. This incident is one that I believe contributes to the new Muslim reality, one in which Muslims and those of other faiths stand in solidarity against racism, bigotry and Islamophobia and counter the post-9/11, anti-Muslim discourse both within the Muslim community and in society at large.

Mr. Iqbal Promotes Compassion, Dialogue and Understanding

Shortly after the Québec City mosque massacre, another incident occurred on the steps of a Red Deer mosque. Although the incident did not place anyone in direct harm and was targeted at the institution, it was the response from the community that attests to radical resilience. In Red Deer, Alberta, the main mosque in the city had been victimized by a possible hate-crime. Instead of calling for authorities to punish the criminal, an adult male whose ethnicity, race or religious orientation were not highlighted, they offered to invite him for tea (CBC News 2017). Mr. Iqbal, the mosque's spokesperson, stated, "We would like to invite him for tea and just understand why he left that message and why he has so much anger and resentment toward Muslims." He went on to summarize several current events that perhaps contributed to the recent rise in Islamophobia as well a rational counter-argument:

> I think what's happening around the world, south of the border, as well as what's happening in Canada with this Motion 103 being discussed in Parliament. People have this perception their rights or freedoms to express themselves will be taken away and there is this wrong idea Muslims are behind this and Muslims want to shut down any criticism of their religion, that's not true.

Mr. Iqbal and many other community leaders have attested that anger does not help and neither does feeling afraid and victimized; rather, the best way forward for Canadian Muslims is "through compassion and dialogue and understanding." These are three core Islamic principles Mr. Iqbal believes in and, ultimately, they are additional elements of preventing discrimination and promoting meaningful coexistence.

Being uninformed about a population has negative ramifications, especially if they are a population that is already marginalized and negatively impacted by systemic discrimination. Thus, the demographics and characteristics of a community are not the only important things to know and neither is simply that the population is experiencing severe challenges. In my opinion, the dynamic nature of the community and the resilience found within it is also essential. Simply put, "recognizing the strengths that exist in all cultures" (CASW 2005: 4) is essential to a better understanding of a population. Muslim women in particular are perhaps the best to examine in relation to the strengths they derive from their cultures.

Islamophobia and Muslim Women

With the rapid increase of Islamophobia after 9/11, *Muslim women* were the most likely recipients of many hate-motivated incidents (Jiwani 2004; Martino and Rezai-Rashti 2008) probably because those who wear the hijab are more easily identifiable as Muslim and also because they are women. After 9/11, the media played a major role in producing the stereotypes of Muslim women. Two consistent biases included the perception of Muslim women being victimized in Muslim society and in need of being saved from oppression and the appearance of being associated with anti-Canadian values and terrorism.

For example, in Edmonton, an ad campaign on the exterior of public transit buses singled out Muslims and Islam as being directly related to honour killings that were reported by CBC *News* on October 29, 2013. The ad reads "Is Your Family Threatening You? Is There a Fatwa on Your Head?" and above these questions is written "Muslim Girls Honor Killed by Their Families." The ads were sponsored by the American Freedom Defense Initiative (AFDI) as part of their Stop Islamization of America campaign. Although to some it may be obvious that there is nothing Islamic nor honourable about this barbaric and senseless form of violence against women, to others it may not be. It is unclear what uninformed Edmontonians thought of seeing these ads on their public transportation; more so, it is unclear how Muslim women felt when they saw these ads. What is clear is that the ads were offensive and legally deemed to not meet the requirements of freedom of speech. The ads were soon removed, the sponsors got their money back and the city of Edmonton was taken to court for curtailing freedom of speech but three years later, in 2016, the courts rejected the AFDI's claim that their charter right to free speech was infringed upon (Malik, Watson and Wong 2016). It is of note that the AFDI justified their erroneous claims under the pretence that they were trying to save Muslim women.

Discrimination against Muslim women is perhaps most evident in the workplace. Research by Judy Vashti Persad and Saolme Lukas (2002) discovered that Muslim women donning the hijab experience barriers and discrimination when applying for jobs across various sectors. More recently, the National Council of Canadian Muslims, a non-partisan Muslim advocacy group, states that, in the context of hate-crime statistics, those who have been targeted the most have been Muslim women. A significant portion of those women are also of African descent, thus adding race as a third dimension to the systemic discrimination.

If you take one thing from this chapter, it is this: Muslims are diverse, and part of that diversity includes different intersections that we need to understand if we are to truly understand populations and individuals. Muslim women, however, are by far the most likely to be attacked. We should not automatically stereotype them as helpless and in need of saving, but rather as the bravest Muslims in the community who should be honoured and owed our solidarity. Moreover, much of that bravery stems from their commitment to their identity and faith.

Radical Resilience: Faith-Based Virtues

Although only the hijab is used as an example here, others have identified Islamic practices such as prayer, faith-based coping mechanisms, family cohesion and many other factors derived from Islamic belief and practices as having a positive impact on its adherents and as being important to fully understanding the Muslim reality (Al-Krenawi and Graham 2000). Many Muslim women refer to their hijabs as an important faith-based virtue. For example, in Persad and Lukas (2002: 18), in response to being pressured to compromise aspects of their Islamic identity, one of the hijab-wearing respondents stated, "It is unthinkable, I will never even think of taking off my hijab to find work." The function of Islam on the lives of its adherents has been shown in several publications (see Hodge 2005; Graham, Bradshaw and Trew 2009a, 2009b, 2010; Carter 2010). For example, Nadia Caidi and Susan Macdonald (2008) surveyed 120 Muslim post-secondary students across several of Toronto's institutions and identified that many young Muslims consider Islam to be a major part of their identity.

Understanding the positive impact of faith on the lives of Muslims in general and Muslim women in particular is essential to those working with Muslims (Graham, Bradshaw and Trew 2009a; Qasqas and Jerry 2014). The hijab has many positive factors that contribute to positive well-being for Muslim women. These factors include "a sense of security, a reminder of commitment, a sense of space and the right of scrutiny" (Franks 2000:

918). Myfanwy Franks concludes that despite those who label Muslims who wear the hijab as "passive victims," in actuality "they have to be bold and intrepid" (2000: 920). Many Muslim respondents in Franks' study felt that the hijab empowered women in framing discussions with men "by narrowing the area of the body open to exchange in the public arena to the 'face and brain,' the body can no longer be viewed as a series of 'more or less sexual sites or sights'" (2000: 921).

Not only do these women have to face sexist and often misogynistic interactions with men, but they also have to combat inherent Islamophobia as well. Franks' study also reported that a Canadian-born Muslim woman advised the University of Essex Islamic Society website that,

> in the Western world, the hijab has come to symbolize either forced silence or radical, unconscionable militancy. Actually, it's neither. It is simply a woman's assertion that judgment of her physical person is to play no role whatsoever in social interaction. (Franks 2000: 924)

Franks' study also found that Muslim women wearing the hijab chose to wear the hijab as a personal choice and not because they were forced by family, local culture or the state.

Another study showed that Québec groups had advocated for banning Muslim girls' wearing of the hijab in schools as a way of freeing "young women from oppression imposed on them by their families" (Martino and Rezai-Rashti 2008: 420). The groups calling for the ban apparently identified as feminists, but rather than supporting the girls' right to self-determination, they were inadvertently stifling it. Nonetheless, the study concluded that the Muslim women "chose to wear the veil because they identified it as part of their religion" (Martino and Rezai-Rashti 2008: 420). This study also showed that Muslim women who wore the hijab did not feel that they had to compromise their Islamic faith or identities when engaging within the public sector of society. Also, they did not feel forced to embrace patriarchal values and roles that are common to some cultural traditions found in some Muslim communities; rather, they were expressing their own agency and power even if mainstream society could not see it.

At the private-school level, Jasmin Zine (2006) focuses on Muslim girls who wear the hijab and attend an Islamic school in Ontario. Zine notes that none of the girls were forced to wear the hijab and many viewed it as a form of Islamic expression and modesty. Furthermore, these girls indicated that they felt that the hijab allowed them "to feel freer to shape their own identity without the peer pressure to conform to more popular and less modest norms of clothing" (Zine 2006: 248).

With the rise of Islamophobia and the negative portrayal of the hijab in the media, "debates on the hijab often construe the wearing of the veil as a sign of limited agency and the incompatibility between Islamic and western values" (Korteweg 2008: 438). Anna Korteweg also notes that it is important to accept that women's agency can be embedded in religion, and it is problematic to not recognize this.

Diversity and Anti-Islamophobia

Clearly, there is great diversity of Muslims — in Canada and globally. Such knowledge is essential in combatting stereotypes and biases linked to Islamophobia. In particular, the troubling sociopolitical backlash emanating from 9/11 and the current heightened Islamophobia across Canada are ingredients in understanding the new reality of Canadian Muslims.

At face value, Muslim communities doing more to promote positive stories, reclaim their own narrative and show the general public that they are not against Canadian values, along with the radical resilience demonstrated in the community, appears to be a good solution to a societal problem. Certainly, it has led to more massive action in the form of petitions and civic engagement to end all forms of systemic discrimination. It is also a major factor in understanding the new Canadian Muslim reality, as these communities continue to contribute because they "want to" and not because they "have to." The journey of characterizing the new Muslim reality is far from over and part of that new reality is further understanding radical resiliency as well as celebrating the champions who promote it.

Nevertheless, is it really fair and just to make it the job of the victim to prove her or his innocence or to beg the public to not engage in unjust guilt by association? Rather, I believe the problem of Islamophobia is a shared Canadian problem, not just a Muslim problem and not just a social justice advocate's problem either. Instead, preventing Islamophobia requires one to be knowledgeable about the Muslim population and not allow ignorance to lead to prejudice and discrimination. More importantly, one must not allow uncertainty to turn into fear and avoidance of meaningful contact with Muslims. This should hold not only for politicians and journalists, but for anyone who has any power over another human being. In sum, given the subtle and often difficult nature of changing systemic discrimination, the onus of change remains in the hands of each individual with power to confront and challenge closed-minded views of Muslims and any other racialized or marginalized group, as our collective journey toward a just and prosperous Canada continues.

DISCUSSION QUESTIONS

1. Should Muslim leaders condemn acts committed by Muslims even if they are not affiliated with the person or the act? Try to provide an argument for and against this statement. How would you know if they were or were not already doing so?
2. What sources do you consider valid and reliable to consult when wanting to learn about Muslims (or others)? What makes these sources valid and reliable to you?
3. How would you respond to another student who says, "your people [Muslims]" should be doing more to stop this, or "your people [Muslims] should be speaking out against it"?
   a.   What if you were told this by a supervisor at your job, instructor on campus, or any other person in a position of power over you? Would your response change?
   b.   What if it were grounds for being investigated by authorities if you made public statements that this is unfair treatment of your people? Would you still say it publicly?

ACTION STEPS

1. Read an online article from a major news source on any topic regarding Muslims and review the comments section. Identify oppressive discourses (e.g., Islamophobia, racism, sexism), then discuss with a close friend, classmate or instructor ways that these issues could be reframed from an anti-oppressive lens.
2. Visit a local mosque and express your interest in learning more about the Muslim community and Islam. Engage in a respectful conversation and ask questions to increase your authentic knowledge to challenge biases and stereotypes you may have.

Supplemental Readings

Fisher-Borne, Marcie, Jessie Montana Cain and Suzanne L. Martin. 2015. "From Mastery to Accountability: Cultural Humility as an Alternative to Cultural Competence." *Social Work Education*, 34, 2.

Kazemipur, Abdolmohammad. 2014. *The Muslim Question in Canada: A Story of Segmented Integration*. Vancouver, BC: University of British Columbia Press.

MacDonald, Erin Geneva. 2015. "Muslims in Canada: Collective Identities, Attitudes of Otherment and Canadian Muslims Perspectives on Radicalism." *Islamophobia Studies Journal,* 3, 1.

Perry, Barbara. 2015. "'All of a Sudden, There Are Muslims': Visibilities and Islamophobic Violence in Canada." *International Journal for Crime, Justice and Social Democracy,* 4, 3.

Additional Resources

National Council of Canadian Muslims. 2016. *National Council of Canadian Muslims 2016 ODIHR Hate Crime Report.* Ottawa, ON: NCCM. <nccm.ca/wp-content/uploads/2017/07/2016-Hate-Crime-Report-National-Council-of-Canadian-Muslims.pdf>.

Qasqas, Mahdi J., and Tanvir Chowdhury. 2017. *A Diverse Portrait of Islamic Religious Charities Across Canada: A Profile Analysis of Organizational Dynamics.* The Tessellate Institute. <tessellateinstitute.com/wp-content/uploads/2017/09/Portrait-of-Islamic-Charities.pdf>.

Notes

I would like to acknowledge Dr. David Este for his encouragement and mentorship in developing this chapter and Christa Sato for her insights and editing. I would also like to acknowledge my supervisory committee, Drs. Graham, Chowdhury and Kazemipur, for their ongoing support and permission to take a break from writing my dissertation. In addition, I'd like to acknowledge Mrs. Amal Qutb, a future leader and scholar, for her review, comments and contributions to this chapter. Most importantly, I'd like to acknowledge my wife Deema Qasqas for her kindness, patience and support, who recently gave birth to our fourth child while still pursuing her own career and academic trajectory, Alhamdulillah.

1. Stokely Carmichael later changed his name to Kwame Ture.

References

Abu-Ras, Wahiba M., and Zulema E. Suarez. 2009. "Muslim Men and Women's Perception of Discrimination, Hate Crimes and PTSD Symptoms Post 9/11." *Traumatology,* 15, 3.

Al-Krenawi, Alean, and John R. Graham. 2000. "Islamic Theology and Prayer: Relevance for Social Work Practice." *International Social Work,* 43, 3.

Al-Rashid Mosque. 2017. "About Us: History." Edmonton, AB. <alrashidmosque.ca/history/>.

Ali, Osman M., Glen Milstein and Peter M. Marzuk. 2005. "The Imam's Role in Meeting the Counseling Needs of Muslim Communities in the United States." *Psychiatric Services,* 56, 2.

Allport, Gordon W. 1979. *The Nature of Prejudice (25th Anniversary Edition).* Cambridge, MA: Perseus Books.

Angus Reid Institute. 2017. "Religious Trends: Led by Quebec, Number of Canadians Holding Favourable Views of Various Religions Increases." <angusreid.org/religious-trends-2017/>.

___. 2015. "Religion and Faith in Canada Today: Strong Belief, Ambivalence and Rejection Define Our Views." <angusreid.org/faith-in-canada/>.

___.2013. "Canadians View Non-Christian Religions with Uncertainty,

Dislike." <http://angusreid.org/canadians-view-non-christian-religions-with-uncertainty-dislike/>.

Asvat, Yasmin, and Vanessa L. Malcarne. 2008. "Acculturation and Depressive Symptoms in Muslim University Students: Personal–Family Acculturation Match." *International Journal of Psychology*, 43, 2.

Barkdull, Carenlee, Khadija Khaja, Irene Queiro-Tajalli, Amy Swart, Dianne Cunningham and Sheila Dennis. 2011. "Experiences of Muslims in Four Western Countries Post-9/11." AFFILIA: *Journal of Women and Social Work*, 26, 2.

Bishop, Anne. 2002. *Becoming an Ally: Breaking the Cycle of Oppression in People*, second edition. Halifax, NS: Fernwood Publishing.

Caidi, Nadia, and Susan MacDonald. 2008. "Information Practices of Canadian Muslims Post 9/11." *Government Information Quarterly*, 25, 3.

CASW (Canadian Association of Social Workers). 2005. *Guidelines for Ethical Practice*. Ottawa, ON: CASWE.

Canadian Race Relations Foundation. 2012. "Canadians Regard the Internet as the Place Where Racism Is Most Prevalent." <crr.ca/images/stories/pdf/Racism_and_Prejudice_Sources_Trust_and_Blame.pdf>.

Carmichael, Stokely, and Charles V. Hamilton. 1967. *Black Power: Politics of Liberation*. New York: Vintage.

Carter, Brianne Goodman. 2010. "The Strengths of Muslim American Couples in the Face of Religious Discrimination Following September 11 and the Iraq War." *Smith College Studies in Social Work*, 80, 2–3.

CBC News. 2013. "ETS Pulls Controversial 'Honour Killings' Advertisements." October 29. <cbc.ca/news/canada/edmonton/ets-pulls-controversial-honour-killings-advertisements-1.2287819>.

___. 2017. "From Hatred to Handshakes: Red Deer Muslims Want to Meet Mosque Vandal." February 23. <cbc.ca/news/canada/calgary/red-deer-islamic-center-vandal-tea-1.3996029>.

Corrigan, Patrick W., David Roe and Hector W.H. Tsang. 2011. *Challenging the Stigma of Mental Illness: Lessons for Therapists and Advocates*. Chichester, West Sussex, UK: Wiley-Blackwell.

CTV News. 2018. "Transcript of Letter Alexandre Bissonnette Read Out in Quebec Courtroom." *The Canadian Press*, March 28. <ctvnews.ca/canada/transcript-of-letter-alexandre-bissonnette-read-out-in-quebec-courtroom-1.3863306>.

Dion, Kenneth L. 2003. "Prejudice, Racism, and Discrimination." In Theodore Millon and Melvin J. Lerner (eds.), *Handbook of Psychology: Personality and Social Psychology*. New York: Wiley.

Dunn, Kevin M., Natascha Klocker and Tanya Salabay. 2007. "Contemporary Racism and Islamophobia in Australia: Racializing Religion." *Ethnicities*, 7, 4.

Dwairy, Marwan. 2006. *Counseling and Psychotherapy with Arabs and Muslims: A Culturally Sensitive Approach*. New York: Teachers College Press.

Edmonton Journal. 2016. "Muslim Group Denounces Edmonton LRT Incident as 'Hate Crime,' Calling It 'Absolutely Horrifying.'" December 7. <edmontonjournal.com/news/crime/muslim-group-denounces-edmonton-lrt-incident-as-hate-crime-calling-it-absolutely-horrifying>.

Este, David. 2007. "Cultural Competence and Social Work Practice in Canada." *Canadian Social Work Review*, 24, 1.

Franks, Myfanwy. 2000. "Crossing the Borders of Whiteness? White Muslim Women Who Wear the Hijab in Britain Today." *Ethnic and Racial Studies*, 23, 5.

Goffman, Erving. 1963. *Stigma: Notes on the Management of Spoiled Identity.* New York: Simon and Schuster.

Gottschalk, Peter, and Gabriel Greenberg. 2008. *Islamophobia: Making Muslims the Enemy.* New York: Rowman and Littlefield.

Government of Canada. 2013. "Building Resilience Against Terrorism: Canada's Counter-Terrorism Strategy." Ottawa, ON: Author.

Graham, John R., Cathryn Bradshaw and Jennifer L. Trew. 2010. "Cultural Considerations for Social Service Agencies Working with Muslim Clients." *Social Work,* 55, 4.

___. 2009a. "Addressing Cultural Barriers with Muslim Clients: An Agency Perspective." *Administration in Social Work,* 33, 4.

___. 2009b. "Adapting Social Work in Working with Muslim Clients." *Social Work Education,* 28, 5.

Gudykunst, William B. 2005. *Theorizing about Intercultural Communication.* Thousand Oaks, CA: Sage.

Hassouneh, Dena, and Anahid Kulwicki. 2007. "Mental Health, Discrimination, and Trauma in Arab Muslim Women Living in the US: A Pilot Study." *Mental Health, Religion, and Culture,* 10, 3.

Hodge, David R. 2005. "Social Work and the House of Islam: Orienting Practitioners to the Beliefs and Values of Muslims in the United States." *Social Work,* 50, 2.

Inayat, Qulsoom. 2007. "Islamophobia and the Therapeutic Dialogue: Some Reflections." *Counselling Psychology Quarterly,* 20, 3.

Jiwani, Yasmin. 2004. "Gendering Terror: Representations of the Orientalized Body in Quebec's Post-September 11 English-Language Press." *Critique: Critical Middle Eastern Studies,* 13, 3.

Kazemipur, Abdolmohammad. 2014. *The Muslim Question in Canada: A Story of Segmented Integration.* Vancouver, BC: University of British Columbia Press.

Korteweg, Anna C. 2008. "The Sharia Debate in Ontario Gender, Islam, and Representations of Muslim Women's Agency." *Gender and Society,* 22, 4.

Kwan, Mei-Po. 2008. "From Oral Histories to Visual Narratives: Re-Presenting the Post-September 11 Experiences of the Muslim Women in the USA." *Social and Cultural Geography,* 9, 6.

Lewis, Bernard. 1990. "The Roots of Muslim Rage: Why So Many Muslims Deeply Resent the West, and Why Their Bitterness Will Not Easily Be Mollified." *The Atlantic.* <theatlantic.com/magazine/archive/1990/09/the-roots-of-muslim-rage/304643/>.

Malik, Ola, Jeff Watson and Holly Wong. 2016. "No Offence, But I Hate You: American Freedom Defence Initiative v Edmonton (City)." <ablawg.ca/wp-content/uploads/2016/12/Blog_OM_etal_AFDI.pdf>.

Marranci, Gabriele. 2004. "Multiculturalism, Islam and the Clash of Civilizations Theory: Rethinking Islamophobia." *Culture and Religion,* 5, 1.

Martino, Wayne, and Goli M. Rezai-Rashti. 2008. "The Politics of Veiling, Gender and the Muslim Subject: On the Limits and Possibilities of Anti-Racist Education in the Aftermath of September 11." *Discourse: Studies in the Cultural Politics of Education,* 29, 3.

MCC (Muslim Council of Calgary). 2017. "About MCC." <yycmuslims.ca/news-details.php?news=155>.

National Council of Canadian Muslims. 2016. *National Council of Canadian Muslims 2016 ODIHR Hate Crime Report.* Ottawa, ON: NCCM. <nccm.ca/wp-content/

uploads/2017/07/2016-Hate-Crime-Report-National-Council-of-Canadian-Muslims.pdf>.

Nimer, Mohamed. 2002. *The North American Muslim Resource Guide: Muslim Community Life in the United States and Canada*. New York: Routledge.

Persad, Judy Vashti, and Salome Lukas. 2002. "No Hijab Is Permitted Here: A Study on the Experiences of Muslim Women Wearing Hijab Applying for Work in the Manufacturing, Sales and Service Sectors." Toronto, ON. <http://atwork. settlement.org/downloads/no_hijab_is_permitted_here.pdf>.

Persson, Anna V., and Dara R. Musher-Eizenman. 2005. "College Students' Attitudes Toward Blacks and Arabs Following a Terrorist Attack as a Function of Varying Levels of Media Exposure." *Journal of Applied Social Psychology*, 35, 9.

Pew Research Center. 2011. "The Future of the Global Muslim Population Projections for 2010-2030." <pewforum.org/2011/01/27/the-future-of-the-global-muslim-population/>.

___. 2009. "Mapping the Global Muslim Population: A Report on the Size and Distribution of the World's Muslim Population." <pewforum.org/2009/10/07/mapping-the-global-muslim-population/>.

Poynting, Noel, and Victoria Mason. 2006. "'Tolerance, Freedom, Justice and Peace'? Britain, Australia and Anti-Muslim Racism Since 11 September 2001." *Journal of Intercultural Studies*, 27, 4.

Prime Minister of Canada. 2017. "Statement by the Prime Minister of Canada on the Fatal Shooting in the City of Québec." January 29. <pm.gc.ca/eng/news/2017/01/29/statement-prime-minister-canada-fatal-shooting-city-quebec>.

Qasqas, Mahdi J., and Tanvir Chowdhury. 2017. *A Diverse Portrait of Islamic Religious Charities across Canada: A Profile Analysis of Organizational Dynamics*. The Tessellate Institute. <tessellateinstitute.com/wp-content/uploads/2017/09/Portrait-of-Islamic-Charities.pdf>.

Qasqas, Mahdi J., and Paul Jerry. 2014. "Counselling Canadian Muslims: A Culture-Infused Anti-Discriminatory Approach." *Canadian Journal of Counselling, and Psychotherapy*, 48, 1.

Parliament of Canada. 2017a. "E-petitions: E-411 (Islam)." Ottawa, ON: House of Commons. <petitions.ourcommons.ca/En/Petition/Details?Petition=e-411>.

___. 2017b. "Members of Parliament: Iqra khalid — Private Members' Motions — Current Session (Filtered Results)." Ottawa, ON: House of Commons. <ourcommons.ca/Parliamentarians/en/members/Iqra-Khalid(88849)/Motions?documentId=8661986%2520>.

Ramadan, Tariq. 2004. *Western Muslims and the Future of Islam*. New York: Oxford University Press.

Runnymede Trust. 1997. *Islamophobia: A Challenge for Us All*. London, UK.

Salaita, Steven. 2006. *Anti-Arab Racism in the USA: Where It Comes from and What It Means for Politics Today*. London: Pluto Press.

Said, Edward. 1978. *Orientalism*. New York: Pantheon Books.

Shrum, L.J. 2002. "Media Consumption and Perceptions of Social Reality: Effects and Underlying Processes." In Jennings Bryant and Dolf Zillmann (eds.), *Media Effects: Advances in Theory and Research*. Hillsdale, NJ: Lawrence Erlbaum.

Stanfield, John H. II. 1994. "Ethnic Modeling in Qualitative Research." In Norman K. Denzin and Yvonna S. Lincoln (eds.), *Handbook of Qualitative Research*. Thousand Oaks, CA: Sage.

Statistics Canada. 2017. "Immigration and Ethnocultural Diversity Highlight Tables,

2016 Census." <www12.statcan.gc.ca/census-recensement/2016/dp-pd/hlt-fst/imm/index-eng.cfm>.

___. 2013. "2011 National Household Survey." <www5.statcan.gc.ca/bsolc/olc-cel/olc-ccl?catno=99-004-X&lang=eng>.

___. 2010. "Projections of the Diversity of the Canadian Population, 2006 to 2031." <statcan.gc.ca/pub/91-551-x/91-551-x2010001-eng.pdf>.

Thomas Bernard, Wanda, and Jemell Moriah. 2007. "Cultural Competency: An Individual or Institutional Responsibility?" *Canadian Social Work Review*, 24, 1.

United Nations. 2004. "Confronting Islamophobia." *UN Chronicle*, 4.

Van Dijk, Teun. 1992. "Discourse of the Denial of Racism." *Discourse and Society*, 3, 1.

Wark, Wesley. 2006. "National Security and Human Rights Concerns in Canada: A Survey of Eight Critical Issues in the Post-9/11 Environment." Toronto, ON: Canadian Human Rights Commission. <chrc-ccdp.gc.ca/eng/content/national-security-and-human-rights-concerns-canada-survey-eight-critical-issues-post-911>.

Welch, Michael. 2006. *Scapegoats of September 11th: Hate Crimes and State Crimes in the War on Terror*. New Brunswick, NJ: Rutgers University Press.

Williams, Veronica. 2005. "Working with Muslims in Counselling: Identifying Sensitive Issues and Conflicting Philosophy." *International Journal for the Advancement of Counselling*, 27, 1.

Yousif, Ahmad. 2008. *Muslims in Canada: A Question of Identity*, second edition. Ottawa, ON: Legas Publishing.

Zine, Jasmin. 2006. "Unveiled Sentiments: Gendered Islamophobia and Experiences of Veiling among Muslim Girls in a Canadian Islamic School." *Equity and Excellence in Education*, 39, 3.

13

FROM MULTICULTURALISM
TO CRITICAL
MULTICULTURALISM

Christa Sato and David Este

> Multiculturalism without a transformative political agenda can
> just be another form of accommodation to the larger social order.
> (McLaren 1995: 126)

The 2016 census data on immigration and diversity found that over 7.6
million Canadians identified themselves as belonging to a visible minority group as defined by the *Employment Equity Act*. Visible minorities
represented more than one-fifth (22.3 percent) of the Canadian population. Of this number, 30 percent were born in Canada (Statistics Canada
2017). Combined, the three largest visible minority groups — South Asians,
Chinese and Blacks — accounted for 61.2 percent of the visible minority population in 2016. The National Household Survey (NHS) of 2011
reported that the vast majority of visible minorities (70 percent) lived in
the three largest cities: Toronto, Montréal and Vancouver. From a language
perspective, of the immigrants who had a single mother tongue, close to
one-quarter (23.8 percent) reported English as their mother tongue and 3.9
percent reported French. Among those whose mother tongues were neither
English nor French, Chinese languages were the most common, followed
by Tagalog, Spanish and Punjabi. The 2011 NHS also collected information
on religious affiliation: the largest religion was Christianity, with just over
two-thirds (67.3 percent) reporting that they were affiliated with a Christian
religion. Given the changing patterns of immigration, there were growing
proportions of the population affiliated with Muslim, Hindu, Sikh and
Buddhist religions. In 2011, 7.2 percent of Canada's population reported an
affiliation with one of these religions, which represented an increase from
4.9 percent reported in the 2001 census data. Finally, 23.9 percent reported
no religious affiliation (Statistics Canada 2013).

According to the 2017 Annual Report to Parliament on Immigration,

Canada admitted 246,346 new permanent residents in 2016, which constituted an increase from 2015 (Government of Canada 2017). Persons admitted under the economic class represented 53 percent; 26 percent were in the family reunification category; and 20 percent were protected persons, with 1 percent in the humanitarian category (Government of Canada 2017). It is anticipated that, from 2018–20, the number of individuals that will be allowed to migrate to Canada will be 980,000 (Government of Canada 2017).

Clearly, we live in a diverse, multicultural reality. Canada is a nation where multiculturalism is enshrined as an official policy, which has contributed to a mosaic representing a plethora of different cultures, languages, religions and so forth. Broadly, most Canadians accept the ideology of multiculturalism, where citizens take pride in upholding associated values of respect for diversity, inclusion and equality. Yet, in recent decades, multiculturalism has been subjected to considerable criticism (Fleras and Elliott 2002; James 2010; Fleras 2011a, 2014; Leung 2011; Guo and Wong 2015). While multiculturalism was once embraced as a legitimate approach in dealing with issues of diversity, recently the relevance of multiculturalism within nation-states is questioned as the world becomes more interconnected through globalization and transnationalism. Further, some scholars maintain that one of the limitations of Canadian multiculturalism is that it does not address the issue of racism, which racialized and Indigenous people experience on a constant basis. Augie Fleras and Jean Leonard Elliot (2002) contend that multiculturalism ghettoizes minorities and their aspirations and commodifies culture by using cultural solutions to address structural problems. In the face of an ever-changing social, political and cultural landscape, we contend that critical multiculturalism is an alternative approach that can be adopted in Canada (McLaren 1995; Awad 2011).

The objectives of this chapter are to:

- describe Canada's multicultural policy and how multiculturalism discourse is constructed and situated within the Canadian context;
- set out critiques of traditional conceptualizations of multiculturalism and discuss critical multiculturalism as an alternative approach; and
- suggest strategies for adopting a critical multiculturalism approach for addressing issues of racism in Canada.

Multicultural Paradigms

Multiculturalism is both a complex reality and a contested idea. Peter McLaren (1995) and David Nylund (2006), for example, distinguish between conservative, liberal and critical multiculturalism. *Conservative multiculturalism* "is an assimilationist model of cultural diversity" (Nylund 2006: 29). This form of multiculturalism is congruent with the approach adopted by the United States. Those who adopt a conservative multicultural approach maintain that multiculturalism promotes a discourse of tolerance rather than acceptance, which is centred around differences rather than commonalities that bind Canadians together (Bissoondath 2002). Further, Neil Bissoondath (2002) raises concerns that multiculturalism leads to ghettoization and lack of social cohesion at the expense of national unity. However, critics argue that those who adopt a conservative multicultural approach fail to recognize how the dominant Eurocentric hegemony is the point of reference from which all other ethnic and cultural groups are judged (Nylund 2006), which imbues "the self-serving, self-congratulatory, and profoundly imperialist attitude of Europe and North America" (McLaren 1995). In other words, the "White cultural elite" constructs a "common culture" that serves as the "invisible norm" to which other cultural minorities are expected to adhere (McLaren 1995: 121–22). As such, "conservative multiculturalism tends to marginalize and dismiss the different experiences of [peoples] of color and avoid a power analysis of institutional forms of racism" (Nylund 2006: 29).

Proponents of *liberal multiculturalism* maintain the belief that there is "a natural equality" that exists among various racial and ethnic groups (McLaren 1995: 124). Underlying this view is the assumption that, in spite of racial differences, each group has the same opportunities available to compete for economic, political and social resources in a capitalist society because they are perceived as being "equal" (McLaren 1995). With that said, liberal multiculturalism does acknowledge and celebrate cultural differences; yet, it tends to categorize ethnic and racial minorities into fixed identities, which in effect actually reproduces stereotypes by essentializing difference (Nylund 2006). This is affirmed by Stephen May and Christine Sleeter (2010: 4), who maintain that the focus of liberal multiculturalism "is on getting along better, primarily via a greater recognition of, and respect for, ethnic, cultural, and/or linguistic differences, while the approach adopted is a problem-solving one." Consequently, this type of multiculturalism tends to "ignore the historical and cultural situatedness of difference … removed from social and historical constraints" (McLaren 1995: 125). Examples of the social and historical differences that are ignored by liberal multiculturalism are how in the seventeenth and eighteenth centuries, Indigenous Peoples and people of African descent were subjected to slavery. At the turn of the twentieth century, Chinese migrants continued to pay the head tax to venture to Canada. In the 1930s, members of the Jewish faith in cities such as Montréal and Toronto were excluded from some social clubs or resorts, and opportunities to attend universities such as McGill were limited. The historical and cultural experiences of racialized groups and their relationship with the nation-state must be examined in order to understand how forms of racial inequality were produced and continue to be reproduced in Canada. However, liberal multiculturalism tends to ignore or minimize the role of racism within current state laws, policies and practices and instead focuses on essentialized differences between cultures. In its current form, liberal multiculturalism aligns closely with the approach in Canada, and this is the form that we are referring to when we discuss multiculturalism in this chapter (unless otherwise stated).

Critical multiculturalism is a response to criticisms of conservative and liberal multiculturalism. McLaren (1995) advanced the concept of critical multiculturalism which he also termed "*resistance multiculturalism.*" Critical multiculturalists contend that multiculturalism ought to "historicize racism and critically engage with a more nuanced and complex analysis of culture, one that links diversity of education with social justice and includes power analysis" (Nylund 2006: 29). Accordingly, critical multiculturalism "doesn't see diversity itself as a goal but rather argues that diversity must be affirmed within a politics of cultural criticism and a commitment to social justice" (McLaren 1995: 126). A salient example is how current liberal discourse on multiculturalism espouses a rhetoric of diversity as strengthening Canada's economy; yet current immigration policies paradoxically prevent this diverse pool of talent from utilizing their knowledge and skills upon entry, and instead immigrants are often relegated to jobs far below their education and skill levels. While liberal multiculturalists might view Canada's diversity as something positive in and of itself (Kymlicka 1995), critical multiculturalists recognize the injustice embedded within institutions and structures that perpetuate racial inequality and actively work to dismantle these systems in pursuit of social justice for those most affected (McLaren 1995; Nylund 2006; May and Sleeter 2010). Critical multiculturalism, therefore, is highly politicized. On the other hand, conservative and liberal multiculturalism are often construed as being *depoliticized*, which "occurs when an issue of social concern is removed from the realm of public debate through claims that the issue has dissolved or is not the responsibility of the state, naturalizing the absence of legitimate contention" (Grant 2016: 2). In other words, dialogue about anti-racism and anti-oppression are minimized or non-existent in conservative and liberal multiculturalism discourse. This is highly problematic within the current liberal multicultural context, because cultural groups (i.e., racialized groups) are thought to be in competition between different but equal groups rather than competing within differential power, hierarchies and oppressions that are not easily identifiable in liberal multicultural discourses. In contrast, critical multiculturalism's central aim is to dismantle structures of oppression embedded within systems and institutions that reproduce racial inequality and promote a structure grounded in principles of social justice and equity (McLaren 1995; May and Sleeter 2010; Awad 2011).

What Is Multiculturalism?

There are numerous definitions and conceptualizations that exist in relation to multiculturalism, particularly in the Canadian context (Bauder 2000; Mookerjea 2011; Fleras 2011b; Chiasson 2012; Guo and Wong 2015). John Berry (2011) maintains that there is a national social framework of institutions (called the larger society) that accommodates the interests and needs of numerous cultural groups, which are fully incorporated into the national framework. Ilene Hyman, Agnes Meinhard and John Shields (2011: 2) define multiculturalism as

> a system of beliefs and behaviours that recognizes the presence of all diverse groups in an organization or society, acknowledges and values their sociocultural differences and encourages and enables their continued contribution within an inclusive society; an ideological aspiration celebrating diversity, a set of policies aimed at managing diversity; or a process by which ethnic and racial groups leverage support to achieve their aspirations.

According to Miriam Chiasson (2012: 2), an essential aspect of multiculturalism "is the idea that Canadians regardless of race, ethnicity, language, or religion are all equal." More simplistically, given the diversity that exists in Canada, multiculturalism is considered a descriptive fact (Fleras 2011b; Mookerjea 2011). The profile at the beginning of the chapter demonstrates this diversity.

Fleras (2011b: 312) advanced the following detailed conceptualization, in which multiculturalism

> is a belief that a society of many cultures is possible as a basis for living together with differences under four ideal typical scenarios: (1) differences are rejected, (2) differences are tolerated, (3) differences are taken into account, and (4) differences are taken seriously.

Fleras and Elliot (2002, 2007) stressed that multiculturalism in Canada can be viewed as an ideology. A critical assumption underlying this conception of multiculturalism is the "belief that people are social beings whose well-being depends on shared cultural identity" (Fleras and Elliot 2002: 307).

Table 13.1: Principles of Multiculturalism

• Differences among groups are important and of benefit to both the individuals and society at large if properly managed.
• Cultural differences are endured as integral components of a national mosaic, a reflection of the Canadian ideal and a source of unity.
• Multiculturalism, as an ideal, builds on the principles of cultural relativism. This doctrine holds that all cultural practices are relative to a particular time and place, take their meaning from this context and must be understood accordingly.
• A commitment to multiculturalism is predicated on the premise that those confident in their cultural background will concede a similar tolerance to others.

Source: Adapted from Fleras and Elliot 2002: 307.

Multiculturalism, both as a concept and a policy, is complex. Similarly, Ho Hon Leung (2011: 20) asserts, "multiculturalism is neither a static concept nor a simplistic idea. It is not only a moving target, but it is also a multidimensional entity." The dynamic and changing nature of multiculturalism is reflected in the next section, which outlines its evolution as an official policy.

The Evolution of Canada's Multicultural Policy

Although Canada prides itself as a multicultural society, historically Canada has deliberately excluded racialized, non-European Canadians. Chinese immigration was discouraged with the introduction of a "head tax" that was levied starting in 1885 (Edwards and Calhoun 2011). In 1923 the migration of Chinese was completely eliminated with the passing of the

Chinese Immigration Act (Edwards and Calhoun 2011). The influx of African Americans to the Prairie provinces, particularly Alberta and Saskatchewan beginning in 1907, resulted in a vigorous campaign to deny "Blacks" the right to migrate to Canada. The Liberal government, under the leadership of Wilfrid Laurier in 1911, passed an order-in-council barring Blacks from entering Canada. The order was never acted upon and was repealed the fall of that same year (Shepard 1983). These are just a few examples of how racism was manifested in Canada's past.

Since the early 1970s, Canada has become an increasingly diverse society, with the country's immigration policy being a major contributor to racial, ethnocultural, linguistic and religious diversity. A critical question from a state perspective that espouses a liberal multiculturalism approach is: How does a nation such as Canada manage such diversity so that harmony is encouraged and conflict discouraged?

Since 1971, the major mechanism employed by the federal government is the *Multiculturalism Policy*. This policy had its origins in the mid-1960s under Prime Minister Lester B. Pearson, whose government proposed a policy of bilingualism designed to address concerns put forth by the people of Québec for real and greater recognition of French Canadians. As a result, the policy of bilingualism implemented in 1969 was intended to ensure that French Canadians would be able to conduct business with any federal government department and their regional offices in French. Moreover, it gave French Canadians a way of preserving their language and culture. Essentially, the policy officially recognized that there were two founding nations of Canada — English and French (Fleras and Elliot 2002, 2003; Dewing 2013).

Not surprisingly, this simple representation dichotomizing Canada as a French and English nation garnered considerable criticism, as it did not represent the diversity within the Canadian population (Bauder 2000; Fleras and Elliot 2003). For example, the policy ignored the existence of Indigenous Peoples and the incredible diversity of those communities. Also, the fact that several racial and ethnocultural communities had existed in Canada for many decades (such as the Chinese and Black Canadians) was neglected. Finally, the bilingualism policy failed to acknowledge the reality that, for an increasing number of Canadians, their first language was neither French nor English. The excluded groups felt the policy ignored how these communities contributed to the development of Canada as a nation-state, and they wanted to be recognized in the same manner as their French and English counterparts (Fleras and Elliot 2007; Dewing 2013).

As a response, in 1971 the federal government under the leadership of Prime Minister Pierre Trudeau decided to implement "an official policy of multiculturalism with a bilingual framework" (Minister of State, Multiculturalism 1978: 10). In announcing the new policy, Trudeau stated,

> There cannot be one cultural policy for Canadians of British and French origin, another for the original peoples, and yet a third for all others. For although there are two official languages, there is no official culture, nor does any ethnic group take precedence over any other. No citizens or group of citizens is other than Canadian and should be treated fairly. (Minister of State, Multiculturalism 1978: 10)

The policy included four state objectives:

- assisting cultural groups to support and promote cultural retention;
- overcoming barriers to full participation in Canadian society for members of cultural groups;
- enhancing national unity through the promotion of cultural exchange and interaction among Canadian cultural groups; and
- assisting members of cultural groups, particularly immigrants, in learning at least one official language.

The policy was founded on the assumption that encouraging individuals to maintain and promote their cultures through art, writing and music would facilitate better integration into Canadian society. Another assumption within the policy was that promoting various cultures enabled all Canadians to become aware of the diverse communities in the nation, thereby enhancing respect and understanding (Minster of State, Multiculturalism 1978).

Multiculturalism has developed in three distinctive phases (Dewing 2009;

Figure 13.1: Three Distinctive Phases of Multiculturalism

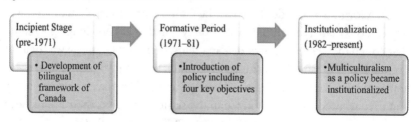

Source: Adapted from Dewing 2013.

also see Fleras and Elliot 2002; Dewing 2013). The first — *Incipient Stage* (pre-1971) — was highlighted in the discussion focused on the bilingual framework of Canada as a nation. The second — the *Formative Period* (1971–81) — primarily dealt with the introduction of the policy including the four key objectives. A series of steps was implemented to help the policy achieve its objectives (Dewing 2013). For example, two major developments included, in 1971 investing approximately $200 million for special initiatives in language and cultural maintenance, which represented core elements of the policy. The second development occurred in 1973 with the creation of the Ministry of Multiculturalism, which was tasked with the responsibility of monitoring how well government departments were implementing multicultural initiatives.

Institutionalization (1982 to the present) — the third phase — has concentrated on multiculturalism as a policy being institutionalized through a number of key events. The adoption of the *Canadian Charter of Rights and Freedoms* in 1982 strengthened multiculturalism as a critical attribute of Canadians. Michael Dewing (2013: 4) stressed that the multicultural heritage of Canadians was recognized in the constitution as stated in section 27 of the Charter: "this Charter shall be interpreted in a manner consistent with the preservation and enhancement of the multicultural heritage of Canadians."

The passing of the Canadian *Multiculturalism Act* in 1988 represented a major milestone in the development of Canada as a multicultural society. According to Dewing (2013: 4), "the Act sought to assist in the preservation of culture and language, to reduce discrimination, to enhance cultural awareness and understanding and to promote culturally sensitive institutional change at the federal level." The Act served as a catalyst for changing the focus of multiculturalism in the 1990s. Instead of being centred on cultural preservation and intellectual sharing through ethnic media and activities such as festivals, the new focus stressed cross-cultural understanding and the attainment of social and economic integration through institutional change and the removal of discriminating barriers such as racism in Canadian institutions (Dewing 2013).

However, prompted by increasing criticism that the policy was not dealing with systemic and structural discrimination encountered by racialized Canadians, in 1997 the Secretary of State for Multiculturalism introduced a new program that focused on social justice (building a fair and equitable society), civic participation (ensuring that Canadians of all origins participate in the shaping of our communities) and identity (fostering a society that recognizes, respects and reflects a diversity of cultures so that people of all backgrounds feel a sense of belonging to Canada). Examples of programs that received fiscal support included those that assisted in the development of strategies designed to facilitate the full and active participation of ethnic, racial, religious and cultural communities. Programs that increased public awareness and understanding with respect to multiculturalism, racism and cultural diversity received priority attention (Dewing 2013: 6).

Key developments in Canadian multiculturalism from 2000–12 included the following (Dewing 2013):

- the establishment of the Canadian Race Relations Foundation in 1997;
- the announcement of a five-year investment of $56 million for Canada's Action Plan Against Racism in 2005; and
- three new objectives in 2010, with two directly focused on Canadian society
  - to build an integrated, socially cohesive society;
  - to improve the responsiveness of institutions to meet the needs of a diverse population; and
  - to actively engage in discussions on multiculturalism and diversity at an international level.

Given the array of changes to multiculturalism since becoming a policy, we maintain that the policy will continue to be fluid in nature.

Criticisms of Multiculturalism

Critiques of Canadian liberal multiculturalism have surfaced. In Canada, multiculturalism is embedded within the nation's policy; it is an ideology that a large majority of citizens value as a core characteristic of our national identity. However, over the last two decades, multiculturalism has been increasingly critiqued (Fleras and Elliott 2002; James 2010; Fleras 2011a; Leung 2011; Fleras 2014; Guo and Wong 2015). The major criticisms of liberal multiculturalism are as follows:

- it does not deal with the issue of racism embedded within Canadian multicultural policies and practices;
- it is outdated; and
- it is idealized — yet, paradoxically, these ideals are not congruent with how multiculturalism is actually practised in Canada.

Most Canadians take pride in the fact that our country is known for being multicultural. The idea of individuals and families from various different cultures coming together and living in harmony is indeed alluring. However, more often than not multiculturalism is trivialized. Too often it reduces culture to simply the inclusion of music, dance, food and art (Henry and Tator 2010; Kubota 2015; Stewart 2014). Eve Haque puts it this way:

> Canadian state-sanctioned multiculturalism can be viewed as a liberal national imaginary as it mainly functions to construct national characteristics of tolerance and accepting dispositions. Yet, the official policy of multiculturalism within a bilingual framework is far from apolitical in that it endows and privileges the two white founding groups with collective linguistic rights, while marginalising other racialised and visible minority groups without the same rights (Haque 2012).

Moreover, we must go beyond the superficial celebration of liberal multiculturalism and engage in critical open discussion on racial and other forms of inequality that exist in our social system (Kubota 2015: 9). Unfortunately, liberal multiculturalism has failed to produce the harmony that it promises because the country's leaders, and subsequently its citizens, are reluctant to address *racism* and *racial inequality* embedded within society. This manifests in a variety of ways. The dominant White society has benefited from Canada's racist past and employs strategies that depoliticize issues of race when it comes to multiculturalism. For example, Bonita Lawrence and Enakshi Dua's (2005) note that dominant groups use racialized groups to be complicit in the ongoing project of colonization of Indigenous Peoples to keep marginalized groups alienated and oppressed. In proposing strategies to decolonize anti-racism, Rita Dhamoon (2015: 33) cautions against being trapped in the "Oppression Olympics in which groups compete for the mantle of most oppressed (e.g., genocide against Indigenous peoples versus migratory processes between the Global South and Global North) because this ultimately consolidates tactics, discourses, and institutions of domination." However, these are issues that fail to be examined within discourses of liberal multiculturalism; instead, it has been reduced to the idea of being tolerant of cultural diversity. Yet, beyond this superficial celebration of differences, inequity for racialized populations persists.

If racism is raised as a concern, it tends to be associated with personal prejudice on the part of individuals, thereby stifling and stigmatizing dialogue about race and racism in Canadian society (Kubota 2015). The problem with multiculturalism being practised in this way is that it makes it very difficult to talk about issues of power and oppression where a clear social hierarchy exists (along the intersections of race, gender and socio-economic status). Scholars have noted that, because multiculturalism as an idea is largely accepted in Canada, few individuals will openly discuss their racist views because they know it is contrary to accepted norms (Henry and Tator 2010). However, racist attitudes surface in the behaviours and actions that are hard to explicitly label as racist, such as employment practices in companies. For example, during an economic downturn, an oil and gas company may lay off its part-time or seasonal employees who are mostly racialized men that are skilled immigrants. The rationale provided by the employer is that they were laid off due to the struggling economy, even though their White male counterparts who started only a couple days earlier were able to keep their jobs and the racialized men took on a larger work-load. Rather than attributing the layoffs to racism within the labour market, the employers deny that it has anything to do with race and instead defend their actions as being economicaly motivated due to the downturn. In this example, the employer's decision to fire racialized employees illustrates how *neoliberal ideology* can serve as an excuse to justify the employer's actions.

According to Frances Henry and Carol Tator (2010: 16), "in the last thirty years, classic liberalism has given birth to the doctrines of neoliberalism, a political and economic ideology linked to the main tenets of capitalism, the rule of the marketplace, globalization, corporate deregulation, and freedom of trade." Collectively, these forms of neoliberalism perpetuate what Carl Grant (2016) argues is the depoliticization of the language of social justice, multiculturalism and multicultural education. Essentially, discourses of neoliberalism reinforce racism or the concept of neoliberal racism, where "individual freedom focuses on the disconnection between notions of the public good, fairness, civic responsibility and social justice" (Henry and Tator 2010: 16), as illustrated in the example provided above.

Another major criticism of liberal multiculturalism is that, at the first sign of conflict or disruption, the values underpinning multiculturalism are quickly abandoned and regarded as a threat to the nation's cohesive-ness (Ang 2011; Stewart 2014). This was endemic during the 2015 federal election, where the issue of wearing niqabs during citizenship ceremonies sparked considerable controversy among political parties and Canadians in general. At the time, "[Prime Minister Stephen Harper] suggested during a response regarding niqabs, coverings that veil most of a woman's face, that Islam is anti-woman" (Payton 2015). Essentially, this issue was politicized as a way of propagating fear that Islam was fundamentally in opposition to Canadian values, with the nation's leader going so far as to say, "I believe, I think most Canadians believe, it is offensive that someone would hide their identity at the very moment they are committing to join the Canadian family" (CBC News 2015). A policy was introduced in Parliament to ban face coverings during the public, ceremonial citizenship oaths, which was subsequently struck down as the Federal Court declared the rule "unlawful" (Gollom 2015; Hopper 2015). A public opinion poll conducted by Léger Marketing (commissioned by the Harper government) during that time period revealed that 82 percent of Canadians favoured the policy requiring that women remove face coverings during citizenship ceremonies, while only 15 percent were opposed (Beeby 2015; Levitz 2015). Though there was backlash from the opposing parties, it was a chilling reminder of how "Othering" cultural and religious practices of ethnic minority groups could so easily be used as a political platform by national leaders, despite the nation's official commitment to multiculturalism.

Media portrayals tended to frame this issue in a way that propagated liberal ideologies by emphasizing the success of one Muslim woman (Zunera Ishaq), winning a case enabling her to obtain Canadian citizenship and emphasizing her decision to wear a niqab as her personal choice rather than a political issue (CBC News 2015; Hopper 2015; Black 2015). It demonstrates how these issues, when brought to the public realm, actually serve the hegemonic society, while rendering racial and ethnic groups silent and/or voiceless (Grant 2016).

If multiculturalism is an ideal that we want to engender, then it requires a commitment to hold on to these values even during difficult times. As Canadians, we need to reclaim the multicultural values that we hold so dearly as central to the fabric of our nation, but we need to do so in ways that demonstrate to the rest of the world and ourselves that we stand by these principles. With multiculturalism embedded in our country's history and politics, we cannot simply "talk the talk" but it is incumbent upon us to also "walk the talk" and be international leaders who respond in socially just and ethical ways.

Canada's multicultural policy has also been criticized for being outdated. Fleras (2011a: 19) posits, "Canada's urban landscape appears to have outgrown both the traditional model of multiculturalism and the mosaic metaphors once used to describe Canadian society." Since its inception in 1971, the multicultural landscape has significantly changed in terms of Canada's diverse ethnic, linguistic and religious composition.

Finally, in highlighting the paradox of multiculturalism as a policy and how it is actually practised in Canada, Anthony Stewart (2014: 16) maintains,

> Even as Canada's general population makeup changes, its composition at the decision-making levels stays remarkably the same, and its commitment to engage publicly with the issues that necessarily arise with population changes remains rudimentary at best. What's more, many Canadians continue to believe that Canada does not have any problems with respect to issues of race, that these are the problems of other countries.

In examining the cabinet of the federal government at the time of writing, there is gender parity; however, there appears to be limited representation from Canada's various ethnoracial communities. A brief scan of the cabinet's ethnoracial composition includes one Indigenous female, four South Asians (three male and one female), one female of Afghani ancestry and one African male from Somalia (Parliament of Canada n.d.). While there are no official statistics on the ethnoracial composition, only 20 percent or six out of the thirty cabinet members appear to be ethnoracial minorities. This closely mirrors the national statistics of visible minorities (22.3%) reported in the 2016 census (Statistics Canada, 2017); however, it does not account for the White colonial structures like the federal government within which racialized minorities operate. Recognizing the paradox of Canada's multicultural rhetoric and the lack of representation of racialized representatives in decision-making positions at the federal level illustrates how *structural racism* is entrenched within our institutions.

Canada is a self-professed world leader of multiculturalism, yet there are inherent contradictions in the ways that multiculturalism is discussed by Canadians and how it is actually practised within nation-states. As proponents of multiculturalism, Canadians tend to blindly accept multiculturalism as the best approach in dealing with diversity, while attributing cultural conflict to problems of other countries (Leung 2011; Stewart 2014; Kubota 2015). Critics highlight some of the major challenges that come with adopting multiculturalism, which are important to consider and may have relevance within the Canadian context. Therefore, we maintain that criticism could be a valuable learning tool that critically informs us about strategies for carving out our vision of multiculturalism — one that embodies the values of this ideology in a way that is distinctly Canadian. The reluctance to embrace multiculturalism in other countries provides part of the basis for articulating our vision for an anti-racist Canada embedded in critical multiculturalism.

In discussing (conservative) multiculturalism within the United States, May and Sleeter (2010) point out that, over the last couple of decades, there has been major retrenchment of principles of multiculturalism. In a country that traditionally prefers assimilation as an approach to dealing with diversity in contrast to integration or pluralism, it is not coincidental that, for many American citizens, "ethnic, linguistic, and cultural diversity are no longer something to be celebrated, but rather feared" (May and Sleeter 2010: 1). Intrinsically, there is fear that the increasing diversity poses a threat to the nation's core democratic values and identity, as eloquently depicted by Ien Ang (2011: 28):

> In the aftermath of 9/11, however, this model of multicultural-ism has fallen out of favour. Some opponents even blame it for the violence that was unleashed on that fateful September day: from this point of view, multiculturalism validated the pursuit of incompatible "parallel lives" that then were turned against the dominant, western culture.

Not surprisingly, contemporary manifestations of multiculturalism do not provide the mechanisms to unpack these root issues underlying the fear and perceived threat associated with difference.

As a result, *anti-multiculturalism sentiments* have been manifesting in various Western nations. During the past fifteen years, there has been a growing backlash against multiculturalism in the United Kingdom. For example, Leo McKinstry (2013: n.p.) remarked,

> We are paying a terrible price for the creed of left-wing politi-cians. They pose as champions of progress yet their fixation with multiculturalism is dragging us into a new dark age. In many of our cities, social solidarity is being replaced by divisive tribalism, democracy by identity politics. Real integration is impossible when ethnic groups are encouraged to cling to customs, practices, even languages from their homeland.

Several factors have contributed to growing criticism of multiculturalism in the United Kingdom. The bombings by four Islamic terrorists that occurred on July 7, 2005, in the London subway system and killed fifty-two people and injured over seven hundred — known as the "7/7 attacks" — sparked considerable negativity. Second, as the United Kingdom has become more racially, linguistically and culturally diverse, there is a growing sentiment that the distinct British culture and traditions are being diminished and hence there is a need to reverse this trend.

In 2011, British Prime Minister David Cameron declared that multiculturalism in the United Kingdom was a failure. In his address, Cameron stressed that the United Kingdom needed a stronger national identity to deal with various types of extremism:

> Under the doctrine of state multiculturalism, we have encouraged different cultures to live separate lives, apart from each other and apart from the mainstream. We've failed to provide a vision of society to which they feel they want to belong. We've even tolerated these segregated communities behaving in ways that run completely counter to our values. (Gov. UK 2011)

This discourse on multiculturalism shows the limits and hidden values of conservative and liberal multiculturalism. Further, it exemplifies the real problem in the failure of liberal multiculturalism, and neoliberal capitalism in general, to produce results, because it never addressed the racism or structural inequality that these systems perpetuate.

Although multiculturalism is a term that has been used in so many ways, it essentially has lost its meaning (Ang 2011); it is used in reference to policy, ideology, values, fact and practice (Bauder 2001; Fleras and Elliott 2002, 2007; Dewing 2013; Fleras 2011b; Mookerjea 2011; Chiasson 2012). The ambiguity and overuse of the term has garnered skepticism from both the political right and left (Awad 2011). The right-wing parties argue that multiculturalism assumes the idea of cultural relativism — a doctrine positing that all cultural practices are relative to a particular time and place, take their meaning from this context and must be understood accordingly (Fleras and Elliot 2002) — which threatens the values and stability of the nation. Similarly, the left-wing parties view multiculturalism as a threat because it opposes the idea of universality by serving the interests of cultural minorities. Benhabib (1999: 404) highlights some of the contradictions within political liberalism:

> On the one hand, the liberal imagination dictates that we are all "equal" in the eyes of the law vis-à-vis certain rights and claims; on the other hand, this promise of universal equality is daily

contradicted by the existence of relations of oppression, domination, marginalization, exploitation, and denigration.

This quote highlights the ambiguity inherent in multiculturalism that garners criticism from both right-wing and left-wing parties.

Fleras (2011a: 26) posits that, in a *postnational era* — where conventional forms of governance by the nation-state based on a shared national identity have become less important — societies are challenged with "a new game with a different set of rules for belonging, identity, and unity in a radically sceptical world where everything is relative and contested because nothing is absolute and definitive." Despite the overutilization and manipulation of the concept, some scholars urge that, rather than discarding multiculturalism altogether, critical multiculturalism should be advanced (Nylund 2006; May and Sleeter 2010; Awad 2011). For example, in distinguishing liberal forms of multiculturalism from critical multiculturalism, Isabel Awad (2011: 44) stresses the importance of moving beyond the superficial toward a focus on structural forces embedded within society:

> The politics of minority groups should not be equated to the promotion of a minority language, food, religion, and music; their interests cannot be reduced to an aggregation of individual preferences, nor to the mere demand for cultural preservation. What is in the interest ... is the advancement of structural changes that would allow them to speak the language they speak ... eat the food they want to eat and listen to the music they want to hear ... and, *at the same time*, be fully enfranchised with respect to the law, as well as to educational, occupational, material, and political resources. (Emphasis in the original)

At its core, the emphasis of critical multiculturalism is on how various racialized groups should participate in broader institutions, notwithstanding the right to practise cultural traditions as a means of cultural preservation. This is exemplified by Richard Gwyn (1995) and Bissoondath (2002), who argue that multiculturalism produces ethnic enclaves or ghettos that confine ethnoracial groups from participating in the larger Canadian society. To meaningfully engage diverse groups, institutions need to ensure that the voices of diverse cultural groups are meaningfully represented and included without being tokenistic. Furthermore, facilitating this type of structural and institutional change requires a critical analysis of dynamics of power and oppression (McLaren 1995; Awad 2011; Kubota 2015) that will hopefully lead to a more equitable society.

Accordingly, we argue that shifting from liberal multiculturalism toward critical multiculturalism equips everyday citizens, groups and communities with the knowledge and skills to take action toward a shared vision of Canada without racism. In essence, "ideal nation-building should be a collective process" (Leung 2011: 28).

Critical Multiculturalism

In simple terms, critical multiculturalism compels citizens to think beyond the notion of liberal multiculturalism as being tolerant and accepting of different cultures. Instead, proponents of critical multiculturalism challenge us to identify the underlying systems and structures that engender intersecting "isms," including racism, and take action to change societal inequities (racial, gendered, economic and so forth) in pursuit of more socially just policies and institutions.

Ryuko Kubota (2015: 3) ascertains, "close examinations of social structures and everyday experiences will reveal that racism indeed exists in various corners of everyday life, reflecting and reinforcing relations of power." The heart of critical multiculturalism is connecting everyday experiences of racism with its dynamic relationship to social injustice, power and oppression. More importantly, there is a need to act on this knowledge by addressing social inequities that exclude those who are marginalized and disadvantaged. The concept of critical multiculturalism is used primarily in the context of multicultural education within schools (see Nylund 2006; May and Sleeter 2010; Hikido and Murray 2016; Park 2016). It is also applied more broadly at a national or societal level (McLaren 1995; Awad 2011), which is the approach that we advance.

Critical multiculturalism has its roots in *critical theories*, with influences by intellectuals such as Paulo Friere, Henry Giroux, bell hooks and Peter McLaren (cited in Nylund 2006). In a book chapter entitled, "White Terror and Oppositional Agency: Towards a Critical Multiculturalism," McLaren (1995:125) contends, "critical multiculturalism understands representations of race, class, and gender as the result of larger social struggles over signs and meanings ... [it] stresses the central task of transforming the social, cultural, and institutional relations in which meanings are generated." By making clear distinctions from traditional forms of multiculturalism, conflict is emphasized as a vital component of this alternative conceptualization:

Resistance [critical] multiculturalism also refuses to see culture as non-conflictual, harmonious and consensual. Democracy is understood from this perspective as busy — not a seamless, smooth or always harmonious political and cultural state of affairs. Resistance multiculturalism doesn't see diversity itself as a goal but rather argues that diversity must be affirmed within a politics of cultural criticism and a commitment to social justice. (McLaren 1995: 126)

Fundamentally, critical multiculturalism challenges citizens to examine diversity with particular attention to power and privilege. Proponents of this approach insist that the failure of other multicultural approaches to address systemic issues pertaining to power and privilege is a major weakness. This is affirmed by May and Sleeter (2010: 10), who remark,

Each theoretical analysis of oppression usefully unpacks the workings and institutionalization of unequal power relations, although focusing on one axis of oppression only offers a partial analysis. We need to learn to build solidarity across diverse communities, both academically and professionally, which can only happen when all of us learn to embrace the struggles against oppression that others face. This also centrally includes locating ourselves, and our own individual and collective histories, critically and reflectively in these wider discourses, and their associate power relations.

Therefore, critical multiculturalism aligns with an intersectionality lens (Crenshaw 1989), where various social identities intersect and position members of society according to the power that is associated with their particular social status. *Intersectionality* was a term first coined by Kimberlé Crenshaw (1989), who called into question feminist and racial discrimination discourses at the time, which insisted that the demands and needs of Black women were filtered through single categorical analyses. Such single-axis analysis denies the multi-dimensionality of experiences and serves as a mechanism to further marginalize those who experience intersecting oppressions (for more on intersectionality see chapter 1). Thus, connecting critical multiculturalism to an intersectionality framework can be useful in understanding the ways in which systems of oppression such as racism, colonialism, neoliberalism and so forth operate to produce a "matrix of domination" (Collins 2000, cited in Dhamoon 2015). As illustrated in the section on the evolution of Canada's multicultural policy, ethnoracial groups and Indigenous populations have not equitably benefited from the institutionalization of multiculturalism as a policy and practice in Canada. To move toward transformational changes characterized by critical multiculturalism, identifying and dismantling these systems of oppression embedded within liberal multicultural discourses is paramount.

It is easy to place blame on minority populations or focus on the ways in which an ever-increasingly diverse nation is negatively impacting the everyday lives of citizens. In her work, Maggie Ibrahim (2005) argues that discourses of *migrants as threats* to nations' security have been normalized and legitimized in liberal societies and consequently justify unequal relations of power that, in effect, are inherently racist. Examples of migrant-as-threat discourses date back to the "*yellow peril*" discourses, which originated in the late 1800s in reference to Chinese and Japanese people who arrived as labourers in the US and Canada, and perceiving Asians as "'unfit' for Canadian society and a 'danger' to national security," which justified further restriction on Asian immigration (Sismondo 2017). Yellow peril discourses were also apparent during World War II, when fear of Japanese Canadians as a threat rekindled xenophobia and, consequently, they were placed in internment camps (CBC *Radio* 2017). Ibrahim (2005) uses the example of the backlash that resulted from the entry of Chinese boat people in the province of British Columbia in 1999, which was fuelled by media that constructed these "illegal" migrants as a threat to Canada's security. The primary perceived threats were of "health risk, increased criminality, and the potential collapse of the welfare state" (Ibrahim 2005: 174).

More recently, similar concerns about *domestic or "homegrown" radicalization* emerged in the mid to late 2000s, especially in the aftermath of 9/11 (McCoy and Knight 2015). The fear of domestic radicalization has been a concern in many Western nation-states (e.g., after the 2004 Madrid transit bombings, the 7/7 attacks in London and the Charlie Hebdo attack in Paris). Until recently, Canada was considered relatively safe from these threats; however, two separate events in late October 2014 occurred within two days and had significant implications: Martin Couture-Rouleau deliberately struck two Canadian Armed Forces (CAFs) personnel with his vehicle resulting in the death of Warrant Officer Patrice Vincent (a twenty-eight-year veteran of the CAF) (CBC *News* 2014); and Michael Zehaf-Bibeau, a 32-year-old Canadian citizen, shot and killed a CAF reservist, Corporal Nathan Cirillo, at the Canadian National War Memorial in Ottawa. Zehaf-Bibeau subsequently entered the Canadian Parliament, where he was shot and killed by Paul Vickers, the Sergeant-at-Arms of the House of Commons Canada (Horowitz 2014).

These events were a reminder that Canada is not exempt from the political, economic, social or cultural concerns directed at the Western world. These issues are disembedded from their particular contexts and are reframed to demonize Islam and serve the particular interests of the hegemony (Monaghan 2014). In examining three cases of homegrown radicalization in Canada to help shed light on how individuals from the West are physically drawn to social movements, John McCoy and Andy Knight (2015) argue that it is important to understand how the al Qaeda movement at a global level has influenced patterns of terrorism and violence in Canada in the post-9/11 environment. Instead of focusing on the "root causes" of radicalization, discourses have been influenced by an emotional response to the shock of 9/11 and subsequent securitization of Islam, producing a mix of definitions and frameworks for understanding political and contemporary violence (Monaghan 2014; McCoy and Knight, 2015). As a result, security agencies along with government departments and agencies have legitimized this discourse through laws, policies and practices that have disproportionately impacted some groups, particularly Muslims. Accordingly, many individuals from the Muslim and Islamic communities feel alienated, "Othered" and targeted in Canada — a country that prides itself on being tolerant and accepting of differences. However, as noted earlier, Canada is a country that has historically used regulation and control to shape hegemonic and ultimately racist discourses about migrants as threats, and this has continued in current sociopolitical contexts. Therefore, "by setting mechanisms in place to reject 'threatening' migrants in order to secure Canadian liberties, these liberties come at the expense of justice" (Ibrahim 2005: 183). From a critical multiculturalism perspective, the challenge is to connect everyday experiences of racial and religious injustice to broader societal and structural issues — moving the discourse beyond the issues that only directly affect our ethnic groups/communities or us as individuals. Therefore, articulating different pathways forward must incorporate intersectional and social justice lenses.

Another salient illustration of incorporating intersectionality and *social justice* lenses in critical multiculturalism is exemplified by Kubota, who highlights the importance of considering multiple social perspectives to gain a more holistic picture of the intersections and complexities of living in a multicultural society. In describing a racist encounter with two White working-class males in Vancouver, Kubota (2015: 4) explained how she was mistakenly assumed at first to be a Chinese tourist while taking a photo of the sunset on the harbour on her way home from a conference. As they engaged further, their conversation revealed that one of the males was a janitor at a school who constructed her as a "wealthy Asian Canadian looking down upon a working-class white man." Kubota (2015: 7) expressed, "clearly, my narrative shows individual expressions of racist prejudice as well as racial and linguistic superiority, but the underlying resentment is also caused by capitalist and neoliberal effects on economic gaps between rich and poor, which threatens working-class whites." In her ability to critically analyze this experience not simply as an individual case of prejudice directed against her, Kubota (2015) identifies how neoliberalism as an unjust political system has contributed to an increasingly unequal society in which low income, working-class White citizens are also negatively impacted.

Although the two working-class White men are privileged in terms of their gender and race, this does not negate the fact that they are suffering the consequences of unequal distributions of wealth perpetuated by neoliberal capitalism. Just because an individual is White does not automatically imply that he or she is privileged in all ways; rather, the example must be understood structurally — the perpetrated racism occurs in the context of economic inequality. Consequently, the powerlessness of invisible structures of racism manifest in such a way that racialized groups are blamed rather than capitalism for the economic oppression of the White working class. Similarly, despite being a racialized female, Kubota occupies positions of privilege as an educated, middle-class citizen. Race and racism are complex and intersectional and the strategies for dealing with these issues within a multicultural society will be similarly complex:

> In encountering white racism in whatever form, we tend to position the victim and victimiser or people of colour and whites in a binary fashion. This positioning essentialises and dichotomises these two groups, while colonial relations of power that have existed between the victims of white racism are neglected. People of colour or "visible minorities," who typically occupy the centre stage of the anti-racist movement, are in fact settlers of Canada. (Kubota 2015: 5)

This quote underscores the importance of acknowledging the complex intersections and paradoxes whereby racialized minorities who advocated for anti-racism are also settlers on colonized land who have benefited from this at the expense of Indigenous Peoples.

Increasingly, there has been recognition that Indigenous perspectives have been largely excluded or neglected from *anti-racist theory and discourses.* Lawrence and Dua (2005: 123) contend that "antiracism is premised on an ongoing colonial project" by ignoring the ongoing colonization of Indigenous Peoples in the Americas and failing to integrate an understanding of Canada as a colonialist state into anti-racist frameworks. Accordingly, Lawrence and Dua (2005: 134) discuss the complex dynamics between people of colour, Indigeneity and colonialism that situates people of colour as settlers on colonized land, "where Aboriginal peoples are denied nationhood and access to their own lands." Accordingly, Lawrence and Dua (2005: 133–34) contend that, despite being marginalized by "a white settler nationalist project," as citizens, racialized people are "implicated in colonial actions," particularly with respect to immigration and multiculturalism.

Building on Lawrence and Dua's notion of *decolonizing anti-racism,* Dhamoon (2015) highlights inherent anxieties associated with decolonizing racism in anti-racist, feminist spaces and offers ways of rethinking transnationalism, intersectionality and settler colonialism. The three anxieties identified by Dhamoon (2015: 20) are as follows:

- the tension among feminists between the nation as a site of liberation or conversely a site of oppression;
- how to navigate differentials of power within various interconnected forms of heteropatriarchical and neoliberal racism and colonialisms; and
- the simultaneity of being a member of an oppressed group and being structurally implicated in "Othering."

The following paragraph summarizes the ways in which these anxieties can be confronted:

Specifically, *transnationalism* prompts urgent issues about how to navigate gendered, capitalist, colonial global forces of neoliberalism and racism, settler formations of the nation-state, and non-state formations of nationalism simultaneously. *Intersectionality* provokes issues of whether the gender-race-class mantra will be displaced to account for colonialism "in the margins" … *Settler colonialism* raises questions about the epistemic and material violences that implicate non-Indigenous peoples in Indigenous dispossession, and how far feminists of colour (Third Word feminists in western and non-western places, transnational feminists, postcolonial feminists, and anti-racist feminists) might navigate subjectivity and collective action in the colonial formations of heteropatriarchial, racial capitalism, and concurrent systemic implications in settler colonialism. (Dhamoon 2015: 33–34, emphasis in the original)

A commitment on the part of anti-racist scholars to confront the historical and contemporary colonization of Indigenous populations in current multicultural discourses offers a promising way forward that ensures we are not complicit in reinforcing structural inequalities.

Additionally, an analysis of how power is distributed within and among cultural groups (including "White" culture) in ways that are oppressive to some while benefiting others can reveal valuable insights about how to move forward in realizing the critical multicultural society envisioned for Canada. Working toward a more just and equitable nation is not just an issue affecting racialized populations. Unjust systems and institutions can also affect White citizens. They, too, are a part of the Canadian fabric and their voices — keeping in mind that they are not monolithic but rather diverse and heterogeneous — need to be heard in conjunction with racialized minorities and Indigenous populations, because power and oppression within a multicultural society are intricately linked, laying the foundation to critical dialogue. Fundamentally, this begins with education and assisting all citizens with capacity in terms of knowledge, skills and tools to mobilize and demand change.

Implications for an Anti-Racist Canada

At the beginning of this chapter, a major critical question was posed with respect to liberal multiculturalism from a state perspective: How does a nation such as Canada manage such diversity so that harmony is encouraged and conflict discouraged? Conflict does happen, is happening, and will continue to happen. What we can control is how we deal with the conflict that arises, and this has to be grounded in principles of social justice. In attempting to address this from a critical multicultural perspective, Awad (2011: 45–45) argues,

> Group interests do not necessarily conflict with the interests of the broader community. On the contrary, to the extent that a group's claims are targeted against structural inequalities, they are claims of justice and, as such, they may become interests shared by the community at large ... The point here is not to say that all group-based politics fit into a structural justice-oriented model, but that — in its critical form — multiculturalism is concerned with cultural

claims that are actually tied to structure and are fundamentally justice oriented.

This conceptualization of critical multiculturalism strongly resonates with us because we are both social workers and social justice is a core principle embedded in our professional practice (CASW 2005). Structural inequities must be addressed in multiculturalism rather than simply defaulting to cultural relativism or superficial cultural celebrations. Similarly, the practice of multiculturalism cannot be reduced to advancing the needs of specific cultural minority groups over others. Of particular value is connecting critical multiculturalism to issues of social justice so that those occupying marginalized positions as a result of inequality have a fairer share of resources. For this to happen, real conversations need to begin where issues of power are discussed and citizens are given opportunities to openly criticize various aspects of cultures (such as class, gender, race) within a multicultural society. This does not mean criticizing other cultures into dichotomies of good/bad, better/worse or superior/inferior in comparison to one's own culture. Rather, we need to be able to look constructively at particular practices embedded within cultures and question them.

As a means of providing a concrete example of how critical multiculturalism can be used as a tool for emancipation, we have crafted a case example based on our professional experiences working with diverse, multicultural teams. With Canada's ever-expanding, diverse landscape, working in racially diverse contexts is becoming more of a reality in Canada. Our intention is to describe and analyze dynamics of power and oppression from a critical multicultural lens and propose ways that transformative social action can lead to liberation grounded in principles of social justice.

Navigating Power and Oppression on a Diverse Team

Agency X received funding to implement an anti-racist initiative within its organization, which provides services to ethnocultural families. More specifically, the two-year project was designed to ensure that the agency developed and implemented anti-racist policies and practices, which in turn aimed to strengthen the agency's ability to work effectively with the families it serves. As the team was formed, it included individuals from diverse (according to age, gender, migration status, socioeconomic status, language and religious affiliation) and multicultural backgrounds. It was led by a racialized female (Keisha), who had worked with Agency X for four years and had considerable experience in issues related to diversity in organizations. The balance of the team included a White female (Samantha) with two years' work experience and three racialized males, who were respectively Latin American (Jorge) with six years' experience, South Asian (Mr. Singh) with fifteen years of experience and Chinese (Victor) with three years of experience.

In the first six months of the project, Keisha had concerns about the way that she and Samantha were being treated by some of her male colleagues. She noticed that, during meetings, the men tended to be quite dominant and assertive, often assuming leadership roles while she and Samantha played more passive and complacent roles, such as being expected to set up the room, organize refreshments and take meeting minutes. Some of the males maintained patriarchal beliefs and behaviours that reinforced hegemonic patriarchy, which made it difficult for the women to share their views and perspectives. There was an instance when Keisha shared an idea that she had with Mr. Singh; at the following team meeting, Mr. Singh claimed the idea as his own without giving any credit to Keisha. When confronted, Mr. Singh explained in private to Keisha that, in his culture, good women build up the character of the males to promote their success. Hence, he had no concern passing ideas that she had shared as his own, viewing it as his right.

Throughout the duration of the project, micro-aggressions continued on an ongoing basis, where Keisha's leadership abilities were consistently questioned and challenged. Despite reinforcing workplace expectations or attempting to hold people accountable, Keisha would be dismissed and rendered invisible. For example, she would send emails to her male colleagues asking them to provide a list of their activities and how they achieved them but would receive no response. When Keisha raised these concerns to her White, male executive director, he sent an email reminding the team to complete the task, and he immediately received the response and the work that Keisha had requested in her earlier email. Further, during meetings, Keisha would suggest anti-racist ideas and strategies to adopt in their work with ethnocultural families, but most of her team members ignored her or the room would go silent, then one of the males would quickly change the conversation topic. Conversely, if any male member on the team said the exact same thing Keisha said earlier but in a different way, their contributions would instantaneously be validated. Mr. Singh, Jorge and Victor formed a sub-group and often tried to intimidate the females in a variety of ways, such as raising their voices to talk over the women, staring at them intensely with their arms crossed leaning back into their chairs and being on their phones and laptops whenever they were talking.

Paradoxically, two of the males were quick to identify the oppression they encountered due to having been born outside of Canada. For instance, Jorge had to essentially re-do his whole university education in Canada to be certified as a social worker, even though he felt that he was overqualified for this current position. Victor had experienced a similar issue as an international student who had to pay higher tuition than his Canadian-born counterparts before becoming a permanent resident. Mr. Singh had to take a series of exams, including English language competency, pay to get his professional credentials assessed and take a licensing exam to prove his qualifications. However, they failed to see how they used patriarchy as a way to assert dominance over female team members. At the most basic level, they were unable to see beyond their own everyday experiences of oppression, unwilling to tackle issues that extended beyond their own.

Keisha became disillusioned as a result of the attitudes and behaviour manifested by male team members. She became increasingly critical of her colleagues, identifying mistakes and shortcomings and overemphasizing the poor quality of the work. While she knew that her reactions were excessive and harsh at times, she instinctively reacted this way as a means of feeling a sense of control and mitigating the complete powerlessness she felt when she came to work. Keisha tried to reach out to Samantha, who explained that she did not want to get involved because she feared the situation would worsen or that she might be accused of being racist (aware that she was the only White person on the team). On numerous occasions, Keisha tried to raise these issues with the entire team. She even spoke to Agency X's executive director (a White male), who listened and empathized but did not take any action to address the problems. The executive director's responses were diplomatic, stating that the agency is culturally competent and respects the diversity of people from different cultural backgrounds. Further, he was concerned that if the agency was perceived to be experiencing racial issues within the team, it could jeopardize the funder's perception that Agency X was anti-racist and they might decide to cease funding, or it could impact future funding. The executive director explained to Keisha that the anti-racist policies and practices that were being adopted by the agency should be focused on the work with ethnocultural families rather than issues that occurred among the staff. The inability to talk about the underlying issues led Keisha to completely withdraw because the lines of communication had failed. Workplace dynamics had reached a point where the majority of team members felt the tension was so high and felt guarded in being able to safely express the root issues.

In looking at this example from a social justice perspective, we can see multiple manifestations of domination and subordination. For example, despite working with Agency X for four years and Keisha's competency in the area of anti-racism and diversity in organizations, she was delegitimized because she is a racialized female. She was silenced by the other racialized team members because she is a female. Each person wanted to advance their own personal interests and often failed to see how doing so might have negative implications for others on the team. Furthermore, while fighting for more power and social and material resources, few colleagues were willing to examine the unearned privilege each employee possessed (e.g., the executive director's status as a White male; Jorge, Mr. Singh and Victor being males; Samantha being White; Keisha being Canadian-born) and were reluctant to take action to mitigate these inequitable distributions of power.

From a critical multicultural perspective, an ideological shift must happen where these depoliticized concepts of *colourblindness* (refusing to acknowledge the colour of one's skin on the premise that one only sees individuals rather than their races) and avoiding conflict under the pretence that "everybody should just get along" are no longer practised. These are mechanisms used to justify inaction and maintain the status quo, which reinforces negative elements of liberal multiculturalism as a way of dismissing racism by assuming it does not (should not) exist. Injustice and manifestations of power and oppression need to be confronted within racial/ethnocultural groups, across racial/ethnocultural groups and with the broader mainstream society. Most importantly, power has to be confronted within each of us, internally. Only discussing these issues in private further exacerbates the politics of difference and, as a result, individuals, groups, communities and the broader Canadian society will continue to hold prejudices and racist beliefs toward those who are ethnoculturally, religiously and linguistically different. Ang (2011: 29) keenly observes, "after many generations of immigration history, migrants and their descendants are no longer containable within a fixed and internally homogeneous category of 'ethnic community', as tended to be assumed in the formative years of state-sponsored multiculturalism." As such, our conceptualizations of culture need to shift with the acknowledgement that there are no monolithic cultures because essentialized notions about particular ethnoracial groups perpetuate stereotypes and reinforce racist ideologies. Having fixed concepts of identity and culture effectively serves as a barrier toward realizing critical multiculturalism.

Similarly, taking a colourblind position also hinders individual and collective efforts toward realizing a nation without racism. These strategies employed under liberal multiculturalism are mechanisms that essentially attempt to depoliticize multiculturalism (Grant 2016) by taking issues of race and racism out of multiculturalism. However, as demonstrated throughout this chapter, multiculturalism as practised in Canada is, indeed, highly political in nature. We must be able to engage in real (albeit sometimes painful and uncomfortable) conversations to build understanding rather than risk silencing those who express their opinions, ideas and beliefs (social perspectives). Rather than attacking individuals based on the ideas that they have, we need to foster an environment that allows one to express their ideas openly; however, the expression of ideas must be in tandem with reflective dialogue that breaks down misconceptions, biases and racial discrimination as a means of creating opportunities to engage in meaningful, constructive conversations. It is also important to keep in mind that individuals and groups with differing social positioning and related experiences (e.g., a right-wing, poor, working-class, White man in relation to a left-wing, upper-middle-class, university educated woman) may not be equipped with the "politically correct" language to enter conversations about racism in a context that is skewed toward liberal discourses. Because of this, we emphasize that the *ideas* are being challenged, not the individual who expresses these ideas. Challenging the individual shuts down opportunities for conversation and may further entrench racist ideologies. Also, these conversations cannot be confined to those who think similarly on issues. Dialogue involves both articulating and, more importantly, listening (which, in our opinion, is often overlooked), especially when it comes to conversing with those who have polarizing perspectives. To move toward social and political transformation, we contend there has to be willingness to not only engage in meaningful dialogue but to act upon it.

Critical multiculturalism demonstrates the complex interactions and various manifestations of power and oppression that inevitably surface when analyzing and resolving such conflict; it is not always clear-cut with concrete solutions. Fundamentally, strategies and actions aimed at changing unjust racial practices are rooted in an analysis of power and oppression within a social justice framework. The principles of social justice need to be determined through transformative dialogue involving diverse citizens who are representative of the changing cultural, linguistic and religious Canadian demographics. Critical multicultural policy must extend beyond the scope of the nation-state and consider its relationship within a broader, global, transnational, international context (Ang 2011; Fleras 2011a; Leung

2011). While we recognize this is ambitious and idealistic, we contend that we need a collective vision to aspire toward. In the meantime, we provide some concrete strategies and preliminary steps that can be taken in the short-term to work toward this broader goal.

Within and across different cultural groups, we need to create the conditions necessary to foster conversations on how our social and political histories are linked. One way to do this is to include as many different *social perspectives* in our overall understanding of the formation of Canada — not just those understandings that shed light on the positive aspects, but also those that reconcile the past injustices that were done and continue to be done to marginalized members of our society. Given our sociocultural, political and historical contexts, as a nation we need to accept the past and learn from it to transform society, but we cannot to blame individuals or cultures for past atrocities. This entails taking ownership, but also acknowledging that most of us, who are settlers on colonized land, are complicit in perpetuating both oppression and unearned power relations. We can simultaneously be both oppressors and oppressed.

Individuals are taught what it means to be a citizen in Canada within public institutions such as schools. Here, young people are socialized about behaviours and norms that prepare them to be citizens in the larger society. Traditional multicultural education has been criticized for reinforcing the status quo with its focus on cultural retention and intercultural harmony, offering short-term programs and curriculum focused on individual strategies to address racism (see chapter 7). Instead, critical multiculturalism with a focus on anti-racism and anti-oppression can be taught and practised within schools. Accordingly, schools, staff and administration need to be equipped with knowledge and skills that strengthen their capacity to adopt a critical multicultural framework within the current education system. It is well documented that teachers do not feel adequately prepared to engage in critical dialogues about issues of race and racialization in the classrooms (Daniel 2008; Watkins and Noble 2016). To move beyond simplified understandings of culture toward a closer examination of the deep-seated and underlying structural issues affecting Canadians on a daily basis, ongoing training of educators is required. Furthermore, the responsibility cannot rest solely on the teachers; holistically, the support of the education system itself and the existence of anti-racist champions at the administrative and frontline levels are paramount. This requires a fundamental shift and commitment on the part of administration, decision makers and policy influencers (e.g., Ministries of Education) toward restructuring schools within an anti-racist, anti-oppressive, critical multicultural framework. At the frontlines, teachers and educators have a vital role in preparing students and citizens to respond to oppressive conditions and act on the students' knowledge gained from lived experience (Daniel 2008). While this is no easy feat, there are a few examples where critical multicultural discourse has been used in the classroom context and has produced some effective outcomes in terms of facilitating a deeper anti-racist, anti-oppressive analysis of institutional racial inequality that disrupts traditional multicultural education in classrooms (see Nylund 2006; May and Sleeter 2010; Bickmore and Parker 2014; Park 2016).

Extending to public institutions beyond the school, governments at the municipal, provincial and federal levels have a central role in working toward an anti-racist society. The federal government should implement a *critical* multiculturalism policy, which phases out the policy in its current liberal form. For example, in 2017 a report was released entitled, "A Better Way Forward: Ontario's 3-Year Anti-Racism Strategic Plan." One of the key pillars of the plan is implementing a target public education and awareness campaign with the goal of "deepening the public's understanding of many new forms of racism, including a focus on anti-Black racism, anti-Indigenous racism, anti-Semitism, Islamophobia and other forms of racism against racialized groups such as Sikhs" (Government of Ontario 2017: 32). Governments at all levels in Canada should invest in resources to develop similar campaigns.

In addition, coordination among the various governmental bodies is vital, as communication and synchronization facilitate seamlessness across intergovernmental bodies. Recognizing the unique positions of provincial and especially municipal governments, these institutions are often better positioned than federal bodies to know how policies are directly impacting the everyday lives of their citizens. As such, they can utilize citizens' local knowledge to inform the federal government, thus ensuring an ongoing feedback process ensues — one that inclusively and meaningfully incorporates the knowledge and skills reflective of its diverse citizens.

To move toward this, Canadians need to first acknowledge the existence of racism in their country, bring these conversations into the public sphere and live up to our claims of multiculturalism by taking action to include those who occupy marginalized positions (e.g., along the spectrum of various "isms") in decision-making processes. Recently, Alberta Premier Rachel Notley asked Minister of Education David Eggen to "gather input on the ways that government can fight racism, foster acceptance, and promote an inclusive society" (Government of Alberta 2017). As part of this initiative, Minister Eggen led a series of conversations with community organizations and leaders about racism in the province and to determine practical steps the government can take to help Albertans who experience racism. During consultations, topics and questions were posed to various ethnoracial communities/organizations (Personal communications, Teresa Woo-Paw, August 2017):

- how do members of your organizations experience racism;
- which community and government initiatives are working (and which are less successful);
- which existing community initiatives should government be supporting;
- how can government engage ethnoracial communities/organizations more effectively;
- what is working in other jurisdictions that could be adopted and adapted to suit Alberta;
- how can our government promote diversity and inclusion, including through recruiting to, and advancing within, the public service and government's agencies, boards and commissions; and
- how does government remain attuned to the dynamic multicultural nature of Alberta to ensure laws are passed and inclusive?

This illustrates how conversations about racism can be brought to the public realm in a way that attempts to include those who are most affected and yet often excluded from such conversations.

Conclusion

It is time to rethink multiculturalism. Cultures are not fixed, static entities. They are fluid, dynamic, ever changing and evolving. As well, culture is not limited to ethnicity and there is considerable heterogeneity within a culture. As we illustrate in this chapter, hierarchies based on the intersecting "isms" exist within all cultures and identities.

In discussing multiculturalism in the Canadian context, we cannot divorce ourselves from the colonial past and injustices that were done to Indigenous populations and other racialized minority groups such as Blacks, Chinese, Japanese and Muslims. This is a part of our history, but to create a socially just and anti-racist future for Canada, we as a nation must include these realities in narratives about our multicultural reality instead of simply denying, glossing over or omitting them. This culture of denial, if left unexamined, continues to permeate across generations and manifests itself in contemporary issues pertaining to race and racism in Canada. Racism exists. It is everywhere and manifests itself in our everyday lives, within our communities and in the broader societal context. The sooner we can admit that and accept that, the sooner we can begin to identify the underlying issues and subsequently take action to create real change and move toward an anti-racist society.

In this chapter, we were intentionally provocative as a way of encouraging people to think radically differently about the society in which we live. Given that we all come from different social locations or perspectives, it is important that we can collectively engage in dialogue — beyond conversations with those who are similar to us — and identify inequality within our own racial communities and among different racial populations. As such, we all need to work together in the struggle against all forms of inequality, as they support and perpetuate one another. If critical and meaningful dialogue is not fostered, then individuals, groups, communities and the broader society will continue to make misinformed decisions based on superficial and discriminatory prejudices.

A deeper level of understanding about different cultures and cultural practices is vital to creating an anti-racist Canada that holds true to the values of multiculturalism. At the core of this critical approach is a willingness and commitment on the part of citizens and in Canadian institutions to critically examine aspects of cultures and subsequently take transformative action that challenges social injustice. As a society, our perspectives and views on liberal multiculturalism can shift toward those of critical multiculturalism and we can reconnect with our values of social justice, inclusion and equity.

DISCUSSION QUESTIONS

1. Please describe and compare the concepts of liberal multiculturalism and critical multiculturalism.
2. Reflecting on the case example presented in this chapter, how would you deal with the issues presented in the case study?
3. Identify a practice in your culture you think is socially unjust. What are the reasons you think it is unjust? What do you think could be changed to make this practice more equitable?

ACTION STEPS

1. Attend an annual multicultural event in your community. Using anti-racist and anti-oppressive lenses, generate a list of recommendations that the organizers could do to better promote critical multiculturalism. Contact the organizers and share your recommendations.
2. Organize a panel discussion where invited speakers with differing views debate on the issue of multiculturalism in Canada. Following the debate, facilitate a critical dialogue with attendees.

Supplemental Readings

Awad, Isabel. 2011. "Critical Multiculturalism and Deliberative Democracy: Opening Spaces for More Inclusive Communication." *Javnost-the Public: Journal of the European Institute for Communication and Culture*, 18, 3.

Leung, Ho Hon. 2011. "Canadian Multiculturalism in the 21st Century: Emerging Challenges and Debates." *Canadian Ethnic Studies*, 3, 11.

Nylund, David. 2006. "Critical Multiculturalism, Whiteness, and Social Work." *Journal of Progressive Human Services* 17, 2. <http://www.drdavidnylund.com/uploads/CriticalMulticulturalism.pdf>.

Additional Resources

Permanent Culture Now. "Exploring Models of Education: Critical Multiculturalism." <permanentculturenow.com/exploring-models-of-education-critical-multiculturalism/>.

Canadian Multicultural Education Foundation <cmef.ca/>.

Multicultural History Society of Ontario <mhso.ca/wp/multi-faceted-websites/>.

References

Ang, Ien. 2011. "Ethnicities and Our Precarious Future." *Ethnicities*, 11, 1.

Awad, Isabel. 2011. "Critical Multiculturalism and Deliberative Democracy: Opening Spaces for More Inclusive Communication." *Javnost-the Public: Journal of the European Institute for Communication and Culture*, 18, 3.

Bauder, Harold. 2001. "Employment, Ethnicity and Metropolitan Context: The Case of Young Canadian Immigrants." *Journal of International Migration and Integration*, 2, 3.

Bauder, Julien. 2000. "Multiculturalism, Cultural Community: Is It about Culture or Ethnicity? The Canadian Approach." *International Journal of Cultural Policy*, 7, 11.

Beeby, Dean. 2015. "Poll Ordered by Harper Found Strong Support for Niqab Ban at Citizenship Ceremonies. *CBC News,* September 24. <cbc.ca/news/politics/canada-election-2015-niqab-poll-pco-1.3241895>.

Benhabib, Seyla. 1999. "The Liberal Imagination and the Four Dogmas of Multiculturalism." *The Yale Journal of Criticism*, 12, 2.

Berry, John W. 2011. "Integration and Multiculturalism: Ways towards Social Solidarity." *Papers on Social Representations*, 20.

Black, Debra. 2015. "Woman at Heart of Niqab Debate Becomes Canadian Citizen."

Toronto Star, October 9. <thestar.com/news/canada/2015/10/09/woman-at-heart-of-niqab-debate-becomes-canadian-citizen.html>.

Bickmore, Kathy, and Christina Parker. 2014. "Constructive Conflict Talk in Classrooms: Divergent Approaches to Addressing Divergent Perspectives." *Theory and Research in Social Education,* 42, 3.

Bissoondath, Neil. 2002. *Selling Illusions: The Cult of Multiculturalism in Canada* (Revised and Updated Version). Toronto, ON: Penguin.

CASW (Canadian Association of Social Workers). 2005. "Code of Ethics." Ottawa: CASW.

CBC News. 2015. "Niqab Ban at Citizenship Ceremonies Unlawful, as Ottawa Loses Appeal: Appeal Court Rules so Woman Has Chance to Take Oath and Vote on Oct. 19." September 15. <cbc.ca/news/politics/niqab-ruling-federal-court-government-challenge-citizenship-ceremonies-1.3229206>.

____. 2014. "Martin Rouleau, Quebec Driver Shot by Police, 'Radicalized': RCMP: Hit and Run that Injured 2 Soldiers Raised in House of Commons as 'Possible Terror Attack.'" October 21. <cbc.ca/news/canada/montreal/martin-rouleau-quebec-driver-shot-by-police-radicalized-rcmp-1.2806104>.

CBC Radio. 2017. "Canada's 'Yellow Peril': It Happened Before, It Could Happen Again." *The 180 with Jim Brown,* April 2. <cbc.ca/radio/the180/the-cult-of-innovation-let-s-legalize-heroin-and-who-s-housing-the-middle-class-1.4048195/canada-s-yellow-peril-it-happened-before-it-could-happen-again-1.4048791>.

Chiasson, Miriam. 2012. *A Clarification of Terms: Canadian Multiculturalism and Quebec Interculturalism.* First of Five Reports prepared by Miriam Chiasson for David Howes and the Centaur Jurisprudence Project, Centre for Human Rights and Legal Pluralism, McGill University, August 2012. <canadianicon.org/wp-content/uploads/2014/03/TMODPart1-Clarification.pdf>.

Crenshaw, K. 1989. "Demarginalizing the Intersection of Race and Sex: A Black Feminist Critique of Antidiscrimination Doctrine, Feminist Theory, and Anti-Racist Politics." *University of Chicago Legal Forum,* 14.

Daniel, CarolAnn Louise. 2008. "From Liberal Pluralism to Critical Multiculturalism: The Need for a Paradigm Shift in Multicultural Education for the Social Work Practice in the United States." *Journal of Progressive Human Services,* 19, 1.

Dewing, Michael. 2013. *Canadian Multiculturalism* (revised version). Ottawa, ON: Library of Parliament.

____. 2009. *Canadian Multiculturalism.* Ottawa, ON: Library of Parliament.

Dhamoon, Rita. 2015. "A Feminist Approach to Decolonizing Anti-Racism: Rethinking Transnationalism, Intersectionality, and Settler Colonialism." *Ferral Feminisms: Complicities, Connections, and Strruggles: Critical Transnational Feminist Analysis of Settler Colonialism,* 4.

Edwards, Jason, and Lindsay Calhoun. 2011. "Redress for Old Wounds: Canadian Prime Minister Stephen Harper's Apology for the Chinese Head Tax." *Chinese Journal of Communication,* 4, 73–89.

Fleras, Augie. 2014. *Racism in a Multicultural Canada.* Waterloo, ON: Wilfrid Laurier Press.

____. 2011a. "'From Mosaic to Multiversality': Repriming Multicultural Governance in a Postnational Canada." *Canadian Ethnic Studies,* 43, 1–2.

____. 2011b. *Unequal Relations: An Introduction to Race, Ethnic and Aboriginal Dynamics in Canada,* seventh edition. Toronto, ON: Pearson Canada Inc.

Fleras, Augie, and Jean Leonard Elliot. 2007. *Unequal Relations: An Introduction* to *Race Ethnic and Aboriginal Dynamics in Canada*, fifth edition. Toronto, ON: Pearson.

———. 2003. *Unequal Relations: An Introduction to Race and Ethnic Dynamics in Canada*, fourth edition. Toronto, ON: Prentice-Hall.

———. 2002. *Engaging Diversity: Multiculturalism in Canada*. Toronto, ON: Nelson Thompson Learning.

Gollom, Mark. 2015. "Niqab Controversy: Judge Struck Down Ban without Referring to the Charter." CBC *News*, March 16. <cbc.ca/news/politics/niqab-controversy-judge-struck-down-ban-without-referring-to-charter-1.2994954>.

Gov. UK. 2011. "PM's Speech at Munich Security Conference." February 5. <gov.uk/government/speeches/pms-speech-at-munich-security-conference>.

Government of Alberta. 2017. "Promoting Diversity and Inclusion in Alberta." July 5. <alberta.ca/release.cfm?xID=47223C31F67DD-0630-278D-3746529451BC28D5>.

Government of Canada. 2017. "2017 Annual Report to Parliament on Immigration." Ottawa, ON: Immigration, Refugees and Citizenship Canada. <canada.ca/en/immigration-refugees-citizenship/corporate/publications-manuals/annual-report-parliament-immigration-2017.html>.

Government of Ontario. 2017. "A Better Way Forward: Ontario's 3-Year Anti-Racism Strategic Plan." Toronto, ON: Government of Canada. <files.ontario.ca/ar-2001_ard_report_tagged_final-s.pdf>.

Grant, Carl A. 2016. "Depoliticization of the Language of Social Justice, Multiculturalism, and Multicultural Education." *Multicultural Education Review*, 8, 1.

Guo, Shibao, and Lloyd Wong. 2015. *Revisiting Multiculturalism in Canada: Theories, Policies and Debates*. Rotterdam, Netherlands: Sense Publishers.

Gwyn, Richard. 1995. *Nationalism Without Walls: The Unbearable Lightness of Being Canadian*. Toronto, ON: McClelland and Stuart.

Haque, Eve. 2012. *Multiculturalism within a Bilingual Framework: Language, Race, and Belonging in Canada*. Toronto, ON: University of Toronto Press.

Henry, Frances, and Carol Tator. 2010. *The Colour of Democracy: Racism in Canadian Society*, fourth edition. Toronto, ON: Nelson Education.

Hikido, Annie, and Susan B. Murray. 2016. "Whitened Rainbows: How White College Students Protect Whiteness through Diversity Discourses." *Race Ethnicity and Education*, 19, 2.

Hopper, Tristin. 2015. "Zunera Ishaq — The Woman Who Fought to Overturn Niqab Ban — Took Citizenship Oath Wearing One." *National Post*, October 9. <news.nationalpost.com/news/canada/zunera-ishaq-the-woman-who-made-the-right-to-wear-a-niqab-during-citizenship-ceremonies-a-primary-campaign-issue-is-now-a-canadian-citizen>.

Horowitz, Alana. 2014. "Ottawa Gunman Identified as Michael Zehaf-Bibeau." *Huffington Post*, October 22. <huffingtonpost.com/2014/10/22/michael-zehaf-bibea-ottawa_n_6031064.html>.

Hyman, Ilene, Agnes Meinhard and John Shields. 2011. "The Role of Multiculturalism in Addressing Social Inclusion Processes in Canada." Toronto, ON: Centre for Voluntary Sector Studies, Ted Rogers School of Management, Ryerson University.

Ibrahim, Maggie. 2005. "The Securitization of Migration: A Racial Discourse." *International Migration*, 43, 5.

James, Carl E. 2010. *Seeing Ourselves: Exploring Race, Ethnicity and Culture*, fourth edition. Toronto, ON: Thompson Educational Publishing, Inc.

Kubota, Ryuko. 2015. "Race and Language Learning in Multicultural Canada: Towards Critical Antiracism." *Journal of Multilingual and Multicultural Development*, 36, 1.

Kymlicka, Will. 1995. *Multicultural Citizenship: A Liberal Theory of Minority Rights.* Claredon Press.

Lawrence, Bonita, and Enakshi Dua. 2005. "Decolonizing Antiracism." *Social Justice*, 32, 4.

Leung, Ho Hon. 2011. "Canadian Multiculturalism in the 21st Century: Emerging Challenges and Debates." *Canadian Ethnic Studies*, 3, 11.

Levitz, Stephanie. 2015. "Majority of Canadians Agree with Conservatives over Niqab Ban, Poll Finds." *National Post*, September 24. <news.nationalpost.com/news/canada/canadian-politics/majority-of-canadians-support-conservatives-niqab-ban-poll-finds>.

May, Stephen, and Christine Sleeter. 2010. "Introduction Critical Multiculturalism: Theory and Praxis." In S. May and C. Sleeter (eds.), *Critical Multiculturalism Theory and Praxis.* New York: Routledge.

McCoy, John, and Andy Knight. 2015. "Homegrown Terrorism in Canada: Local Pattern, Global Trends, Studies in Conflict and Terrorism." *Studies in Conflict and Terrorism*, 38, 4.

McKinstry, Leo. 2013. "A Multicultural Hell Hole, That We Never Voted For." *Express*, November 18. <express.co.uk/comment/columnists/leo-mckinstry/443677/A-multicultural-hell-hole-that-we-never-voted-for>.

McLaren, Peter. 1995. "White Terror and Oppositional Agency: Towards a Critical Multiculturalism." In P. McLaren (ed.), *Critical Pedagogy and Predatory Culture: Oppositional Politics in a Postmodern Era.* New York: Routledge.

Minister of State, Multiculturalism. 1978. "Statement by the Prime Minster, House of Commons, October 8, 1971." In *Multiculturalism and the Government of Canada.* Ottawa, ON: Minister of Supply and Services.

Monaghan, Jeffrey. 2014. "Security Traps and Discourses of Radicalization: Examining Surveillance Practices Targeting Muslims in Canada." *Surveillance and Society*, 12, 4.

Mookerjea, Sourayan. 2011. "Multiculturalism and Egalitarianism." *Canadian Ethnic Studies*, 3–1.

Nylund, David. 2006. "Critical Multiculturalism, Whiteness, and Social Work." *Journal of Progressive Human Services*, 17, 2. <http://www.drdavidnylund.com/uploads/CriticalMulticulturalism.pdf>.

Park, Jie Y. 2016. "Going Global and Getting Graphic: Critical Multicultural Citizenship Education in an Afterschool Program for Immigrant and Refugee Girls." *International Journal of Multicultural Education*, 18, 1.

Parliament of Canada. n.d. "The Ministry (Cabinet)." Ottawa, ON: House of Commons. <ourcommons.ca/Parliamentarians/en/ministries>.

Payton, Laura. 2015. "Harper Says 'Overwhelming Majority' Agrees with Tories on Niqabs: NDP Leader Charges PM, Liberal Leaders of Using Inflammatory Language to Divide People." *CBC News*, March 11. <cbc.ca/news/politics/harper-says-overwhelming-majority-agrees-with-tories-on-niqabs-1.2990439>.

Shepard, Bruce. 1983. "Diplomatic Racism Canadian Government and Black Migration from Oklahoma, 1905–1912." *Great Plains Quarterly*, 1738, 5–16.

Sismondo, Christine. 2017. "What Canada's 'Yellow Peril' Teaches Us about This Migrant Moment." *MacLeans*, March 19. <macleans.ca/news/canada/

what-canadas-yellow-peril-teaches-us-about-this-migrant-moment/>.

Statistics Canada. 2017. *Immigration and Ethnocultural Diversity: Key Results from the 2016 Census*. Ottawa, ON: Minister of Industry. Catalogue no. 11-001-X.

___. 2013. *Immigration and Ethnocultural Diversity in Canada: National Household Survey 2011*. Ottawa, ON: Minister of Industry. Catalogue no. 99-010-X2011001.

Stewart, Anthony. 2014. *Visitor: My life in Canada*. Black Point, NS, and Winnipeg, MB: Fernwood Publishing.

Watkins, Megan, and Greg Noble. 2016. "Thinking Beyond Recognition: Multiculturalism, Cultural Intelligence, and the Professional Capacities of Teachers." *Review of Education, Pedagogy, and Cultural Studies*, 38, 1.

14

RACIALIZED AND INDIGENOUS YOUTH
A Call for Change

Clark Carreon-Alarcon, Aviaq Johnston,
Bryan (last name not provided),
Brittany Walker and Emma Maryam Bronson

What does a racialized Canada look like from the standpoints of racialized and Indigenous youth, and how does our national context/s impact their hopes, aspirations and everyday lives? What meanings are created and reinforced through structural inequality that imposes itself as a masquerade of inevitability?

A racist Canada, analyzed and understood through the intersectional narratives presented in this book, is one that racialized and Indigenous children and youth must navigate. It is a national climate that can best be defined as systemic violence, where fortitude and resilience are required for daily survival of the onslaught of micro- and macro-aggressions; where meritocracy is mythologized and the edict of hard work, extolled as a method to individual success, cannot compensate for the "stacked deck" privileging some and marginalizing others. This has existed, and has evolved in its sophistication, for more than five hundred years.

These five separate vignettes, individually constructed by each author, were brought together as a final narrative of this book. Each of the young contributors were recruited by four contributors to the book. The authors were asked to respond to two general questions: "What are your thoughts and experiences about racism in Canada today?" and "What changes are needed or possible in order to create a Canada without racism?" Their responses are unique, thought provoking and alarming. The courage and complexity of analysis of the five writers engender hope. As youth are frequently the teachers of those who precede them, the final words in this text belong to them.

The objectives of this chapter are to:
- share perspectives and experiences of racialized and Indigenous youth in Canada;
- promote an intersectional understanding of racism in Canada through the writing of youth who are diversely located in geography, gender and sexual identity, age and lived experience; and
- highlight the recommendations of youth with regards to the question of building a future for Canada that is without racism.

Clark Carreon-Alarcon — Montréal, Québec

Oppressed

A Spoken Word Piece by Clark Carreon-Alarcon
For a while now, I've noticed
Any skin tone is hopeless unless it's European-descended
So, the struggles of a minority begs the question
What's hue? What's man?
What's human?
These words spoken by a true man
With an Illmatic legacy
But the history books will never remember him
Cause he ain't rape and pillage
Or glorify colonizing a village
See, they tell us we wouldn't have nothing if they ain't bring us here
But materialism and ego my biggest fear
And, ain't like I'm living good
The American dream my parents visualized was never to live in the hood
For my father to be breaking his back
Or my homies to be addicted to crack
Or my mother to be worried if I'm out late
Scared if a copper decide to take her son's fate
And that's true, tell the truth
I really fear the colour blue
And the judges scales tipped more toward the wealthy
So, me and my friends are hanging out, moving stealthy
And just last week, I got stopped again
By another racist pig, this situation they locked us in

Is truly hurtful to the soul
And the stares feel so cold
Man, you ever seen an old lady cross the street
Just 'cause you was walkin behind her, whistling a beat
With no ill intent or thought of malice
What these people don't realize is the damage
It causes to young minds, 'cause I been tempted to mug her just to prove
her right
Think about it, I mourn the life I could've had had my pigment matched
snow
Or the rice I eat
And this slang I speak ain't meant for disrespect
It's all love so why they breathin on my neck
Waiting for me to slip up, do something stupid
So they can file me as another number
The system had taken us under beneath the rubbles of struggle I already
shoulder
My back's hurtin and my life's within a cursor
So, aim steady, breathe slow and squeeze the trigger
My whole life been led to think I ain't meant to do bigger
Than more than five figures, I figured
My petals are dead and withered
But woes fall on deaf ears and pointin fingers
It's hard to think, I often drink and splurge on unnecessary vices
To handle stress and pain of relatable crisis
My strife is miles long, took off where pops left off
And nothin changed, we still oppressed
Forever a blemish, irrelevant to a foreign country's texts
But, this where I'm from, I was born here
So why does my heritage elicit your fear
You should look in the mirror.

My Experiences of Racism
When I wrote this piece, I was thinking about the hardships that I go
through as a minority person living in Montréal. These events are a part
of life, but I constantly question whether they should be happening in the
first place. The piece about the older woman clutching her purse happened
when I was fourteen or fifteen years old. I was walking home at night, and
I noticed this older lady looking back at me. She walked a bit faster, but I

eventually matched her pace. Right away, she crossed the street … right away. I understand her reasons for doing what she did, but I felt *I was the victim*. In fact, I wasn't doing anything. I didn't have any ill intent in mind. I was just doing me. And when she crossed the street so quickly, I didn't know how to react. It was one of those times that I realized that people looked at me as someone who *could do* something malicious. I notice that people tend to judge you based on how you look, but when you speak to them in a well-mannered way, or when you're eloquent when you speak, they suddenly forget that they are being racist. When you put a label on a box, it's hard not to look at that box as something other than the label. There is power in the label, and it's hard to ask people to think outside the box.

Growing up, my parents were involved in activism. I remember going to rallies, and seeing my mom hold this huge megaphone up and demanding for rights. It impacted me to my core. I guess you never really realize how people mistreat you until someone says it to you out loud. My parents were really loud people. I was ten when my parents told me we were going to this rally to support a Filipino kid who got in trouble for eating pizza with utensils. His teacher told him it wasn't the proper way to eat pizza and he told her it was how he was raised to eat in the Philippines. I guess his teacher thought he was getting smart with her and kicked him out of class. I remember my mom was so mad, she asked me, "Is it fair for the boy's mom to work every day to be able to pay rent and come home to that?" She later told me, "Never forget where you came from." I never really thought about what she said until I had my first experience with racism.

As I got older, I got more involved with people who weren't really bad people but they did bad things. You can't help it, really. My dad is the smartest man I know. He's a born leader, but he and his friends formed a gang as a way to survive and to protect themselves. Who else can you make friends with when everyone in your hood is doing the same things? Maybe the gangs were different people, but the motive was the same: survive. Seems to me, it was all for acceptance. No one wants to be a target and no one wants to be alone. This brings me to the issue of the police. Police come to our hood a lot … Whether we are walking, or driving, they stop us … They ask us questions … Search us … Anything they could do to find something to throw us in their car … It's constant … We have to be gazelles keeping an eye out for predators. I once got questioned for being out late at night, and the cops just wouldn't leave me alone. They couldn't believe I was just walking home. When I got home and told my mom about it, she told me she wanted me to start coming home earlier. "You never know with the police," she said. She told me maybe if she had stayed in school, she would be able to provide us with a better life. But being a person of colour in the White man's stolen land is always gonna have problems. If I could speak to the cops who harass us, there is a better part of me that wants to educate them, to explain how being small-minded affects a young person of colour. How their surveillance belittles and makes someone feel inferior and bitter. But at the same time, do I have the patience? Is it my responsibility to educate, when all I want to do is survive? I would feel a lot better if I could tell them, straight up, "Man, fuck you!"

On a Future Without Racism in Canada

Canada without racism? Whether we like it or not, a lot of people are going to be backwards with their mentality. There is going to be people who have inner hatred. But if we really need to eliminate racism in the world, it's something that everyone has to agree to. What is needed is a mutual understanding of the human soul. Because struggle is something that everybody can relate to. But there are varying degrees and levels of struggle. If you lived your life with a silver spoon, you can't really relate to eating instant noodles every day for lunch. If we can make my situation your situation, and your situation mine, then I think we would get more understanding.

And this is something I think about for my own kids if I have them. I would like to think that my kids won't suffer to the same degree that me or my parents did, but they definitely will get profiled in some way. It's a cold and sad reality, but I'd tell them the truth. If I didn't it would be like me saying that you're never going to struggle in your life. That's not true. It's a burden that generations before haven't been able to cash out of yet.

Maybe the next generation will have it better. For me right now, I focus on my survival. And I survive through writing. Writing is my outlet for anything that I go through. If I write or speak out, then it's off my chest. I survive that way.

Aviaq Johnston — Igloolik, Nunavut

"Annagunnarninga" (Resilience)

When people learn that I am an Inuk, it usually builds interest and begins a long conversation in which I am often answering questions about where I grew up, my culture and traditional practices, my language and the problems my community faces. All these questions I don't mind talking about. To educate others on my territory and culture is something I enjoy, but there are some things I always try to make clear: I am not the voice of all Inuit, I have lost parts of my language and culture and, most of all, Inuit identity is not rooted in our social problems.

Of course, I do end up talking extensively about the problems. They are what is talked about in the media and in meetings between Inuit organizations and the government, and they are what is taught most often in schools. It is inevitable that it will come up sooner or later. Almost every paper I've ever written seems to have a line that lists the social problems in Inuit Nunangat. This is the list: housing, food insecurity, suicide, accessible health care, education, language and cultural loss, climate change, intergenerational trauma, physical abuse, emotional abuse, sexual abuse, substance and alcohol abuse, mental health, anti-sealing campaigns, employment, high cost of living, isolation … and it goes on.

Though I do say that our identities are not rooted in our social problems, they are intertwined. These problems have been imposed on families in the Arctic for millennia, as different groups of people came in big ships. These groups — explorers, whalers, traders, missionaries — brought change, new ways of life to the people. They brought tools, commerce, employment and divine salvation. And Inuit, naturally, adapted to the changes.

Inuit have always been an adaptable people. One cannot survive in the frigid Arctic, next to ferocious polar bears and vicious winds, without the ability to assess a situation and evolve with it. So, they accepted the metal tools from the White men from across the sea, they traded their fox pelts in exchange for guns and flour, they fed the whalers who almost decimated the bowhead whale population, and they began to practise Christianity.

Before that, my ancestors lived nomadically, following the animals across the tundra and vast ocean, making their seasonal homes on the ice and hillsides. They believed that the environment was made up of spirits and deities. Shamans were the spiritual leaders in villages, making sure that the spirits remained satisfied, that taboos were not broken. Families thrived on partnership, men could not live without women and vice versa. Men provided for their families and their village, they taught little boys how to build an igloo and how to hunt, they made tools from the bones and skin of the animals they caught, from the rocks surrounding them, from the bounty of the earth. Women took care of the young and the old, they sewed beautiful and purposeful clothing for each season, even creating a waterproof stitch, they taught young girls how to take care of a family. Neither the men or women were whole without the other, but sometimes that meant there were men with two wives or women with two husbands.

Because the Inuit lived unrestricted by the strict principles and modesty of Christianity, missionaries came and introduced a world of sin to the Inuit. To practise shamanism, to be polyamorous, to throat-sing and drum dance were sins. They provided health care and education, though their intentions were more for their own gain as they tried to win the most souls for heaven. Priests developed a syllabic writing system and translated the bible into Inuktitut. Before that, Inuit passed down information through storytelling. These stories, ancient legends of giants, of dwarves, of shapeshifters, creatures of the spirit world, and the magnificent feats of shamans, are ingrained in Inuit society still to this day. The only difference is that they are told as myths, their once-truth forgotten as our society accepted the ways of Western civilization.

From then on, other systems were introduced to Inuit lives: settlements, law enforcement, social programming, residential school. Traumatic events in lives that were once completely autonomous. When the dog teams of Inuit men were taken away from them and slaughtered, it took away the man's ability to feed his family, a role that was vital in Inuit lives and brought status to men. When children were taken from their parents for residential school, parents lost their purpose in life and their future. Children lost their culture. In one generation, Inuit livelihood changed dramatically: from nomadic life to settlements, to grocery stores and sin.

So, why am I taking all this time to address racism? It is obvious that these changes were imposed because of Western society's lack of understanding, lack of respect and superiority complexes toward other civilizations, other skin colours, other cultures. This has been an issue since Ancient Greece. Why the history lesson of the colonization of Inuit?

Because, in the grand scheme of things, in the grand scheme of time, colonization of Inuit is incredibly recent. My grandparents were not the ones put into residential schools, my aunts and uncles were. Sure, there may have been a long history of interaction between Inuit and Europeans and changes being brought into Inuit homeland, but the sticky and slimy fingers of colonialism began to bring harm during the time of the Second World War. As the Government of Canada began to claim sovereignty over the Arctic, they began to damage the lives of the families who lived there. This damage is still felt today. I am reinforcing my earlier point that Inuit identity is not rooted in our social problems. Again, I say this because it's not, but it is intertwined. Closely.

What I mean is that hardship has been a part of Inuit lives since time immemorial. In the old days, before the very first explorers brought their complicated values and desire for fame and fortune to the Arctic, Inuit already struggled to make a living. They hunted every day, in months without the sun rising above the horizon, in freezing winters. They travelled treacherous terrain, withstood nasty weather and were constantly looking for ways to survive. This hardship is only a part of our lives. The most important thing to consider in Inuit identity is not our hardships but our resilience.

Inuit resilience is in the children who are growing up eating our traditional food, speaking our language and learning the traditional practices that the church said were sinful. It is in the hunters who continue harvesting the animals that provide more nutrients than anything that can be bought in our expensive grocery stores. It is in the women who are reclaiming the tattoos that represented strength and beauty. It is in our sense of humour, in our blood, in our love for those little towns on the coastlines of Nunavut.

In that generation of change, Inuit had to stop their nomadic lives and learn to live in communities. They learned to live within the system, to create their own style of government that ensured the opportunity to create an economy within our cultural practices and conserve our environment and wildlife.

And now, when I think of all the pain, all the horrible things my ancestors, my great-grandparents, grandparents and parents went through, I am angry. But if you spoke to the Elders who were there, who those things happened to, many times they will shrug and say, "that's just the way life was."

So, I've begun to reflect more on the anger that I feel toward systems that have been put in place. These systems that place Western values and White culture higher than those of any other.

To succeed in the world, one must be a good student throughout life, one must be able to relate to others, one must have the ability to think critically and share their ideas. Traditionally, this is how Inuit survived, and these skills are interchangeable with surviving in the modern world. To live a good life, one must be able to carry their culture within both systems. I've begun to ask myself, how can I fit into Western culture while still holding onto my Inuit culture? How can I firmly hold onto my traditions, while standing firmly in the modern world where the prime value in life seems to be placing yourself in a position of wealth? My own interpretation of wealth is in the relationships I hold in my community, not in the numbers of my bank account.

Practising reflection has changed a lot in my life. It's changed the way I talk to people about my culture, about the issues my community faces. I used to talk about these problems as if they were the only things you would see in Nunavut communities, neglecting to mention that we are also known to have the highest rate of artists per capita in Canada. I would always mention that we have high dropout rates, high unemployment, high suicide rates, all these horrible things, but that was all. I'd give you the numbers, not the people, not the truth behind those numbers. So, now when I talk about these problems, I always try to talk about them in the most human way possible, because numbers are overwhelming, so much so that when we hear the high percentages, they wash over us in a way that is incomprehensible.

Now, when I talk about these problems, I emphasize that it is not only Inuit or Indigenous populations in general who are suffering from these issues. It is not only Indigenous Peoples who have substance and alcohol abuse problems, who struggle in Western educational styles, who have high rates of domestic violence. It is universal; these problems are seen in Indigenous and non-Indigenous communities. The difference is poverty, systemic oppression, the slanted lens in which people who live in poverty are seen. Those who live in poverty are seen as failures, as those who couldn't mould themselves into the baking pans that the government deems to be correct.

You know, if you look back at those black-and-white photos of Inuit, their whole lives depended on the environment around them. No one was wealthy nor impoverished. If one person had more than they needed, they shared with those who were struggling. If one person was impoverished, it was likely that the whole village was also impoverished. Life was hard, but people were happy, at peace with the world. When non-Inuit came to our homeland, they saw Inuit as a rare species, barbaric and ancient. And a lot of the time, that is how we are still seen, a people who have gone extinct.

As times changed, as schools and hospitals and governance came into the Arctic, Inuit values were expected to change, too. To assimilate with the rest of White Canada, learn from reading words not in our mother tongue or navigate the maze-like infrastructures and bureaucracy that governments thrive on. As Inuit were put in schools and jobs and struggled to learn and follow all those little meaningless rules, the system told those Inuit that they were dumb, even though Inuit have been non-verbal, visual learners since the beginning of time. Children learned how to hunt, sew, cook, craft, child rear and everything else by watching what their parents and Elders did, without asking questions.

And suddenly, people who survived and thrived in one of the harshest environments in the world for thousands of years were deemed to be stupid because papers and pens somehow meant intelligence. I see the irony as I am writing this down, but I know Inuit who are illiterate and intelligent in ways much more productive to the betterment of my community than this would seem. Our communities need the hands-on approach, because the political and bureaucratic approach oftentimes reaches a standstill and fails us.

The government is slowly starting to right the horrible wrongs they committed in the fifties, sixties, seventies and eighties, but there is still a lot of work to be done. As truth and reconciliation becomes more and more important, as it gains more public attention, the government is taking the steps to go in that direction. To acknowledge the truth of those situations and to reconcile. However, as the government apologizes for the hurt, as they offer compensation, as they promise that they will *talk* to us about our problems, all I see is band-aids. No investment.

I've been to plenty of conferences that focus on mental health and suicide prevention, and I have seen the work that dozens of scholars and researchers have put into studying Inuit customs and lives. I've heard their stories of developing mental health and wellness programs for youth, adults and Elders, how much those programs could benefit Inuit communities, but the end is always the same. Once those researchers and scholars leave, the funding leaves too, then we are back at square one. More mental health programs need to be developed, and local community members need to be trained to run those programs and to provide them in Inuktitut, to empower Inuit. Many Inuit have the potential to pursue this opportunity, but they cannot due to issues that stem from systemic oppression and other factors that come from the isolation and poverty that our communities face.

Many organizations are beginning the process of truth and reconciliation. Indigenous studies is being brought into classrooms in middle schools and high schools and becoming a mandatory course in colleges and universities. My best hope is that these courses are being taught in an engaging way for both the Indigenous students and the non-Indigenous students. (As well, I hope the heavy parts are told in a serious way, but with hints of resilient Indigenous humour sprinkled in to alleviate that weight).

Truth and reconciliation is important, but there is a fine line between reconciliation and tokenization. When you thank the Indigenous Peoples of the land you're on at the beginning of a speech or conference, is it just a line you are memorizing, a trend you are following, or is it something that you are feeling? Do you understand the historic significance of those words and what they mean to the offspring of the ancestors the land was stolen from?

As great as it is that so many people have adopted truth and reconciliation into their ways of doing business, I think that, most of the time, it is only partially practised. So quick we are to reconcile, to move past our differences and to start thinking of solutions and ways to move forward. However, little time is put into acknowledging the truth of Indigenous history. At a workshop I attended recently, an Indigenous Elder spoke about how it is hopeful that we are working on reconciliation, but how truth cannot be overlooked anymore. She said something powerful enough to make me tear up, and I still get goosebumps when I think of her words. I don't remember what she said exactly, but she spoke of how we are forgetting the truth. To paraphrase her words, when asked to do opening prayers for events or to be a consultant for different meetings for reconciliation, it is not the Indigenous person who struggles to look into the eyes of the non-Indigenous people at the meetings, it is them who cannot look at us.

And that is where truth begins. Not in taking the blame for the historical and contemporary treatment of Indigenous Peoples, but to take the time to acknowledge that those things happened and are still happening, to be comfortable enough to accept that as part of you — even if it is a small, tiny, almost insignificant piece of you — has been raised to look at Indigenous folks as a lesser people, as people who are not deserving of equality in their own homeland. This is not targeting non-Indigenous people, because many Indigenous communities have internalized their oppression and have practised lateral oppression. Many young Inuit are told that they are not Inuit if they are too pale or if they don't understand their language and culture. This needs to be acknowledged among the Inuit community as a whole; it needs to be discussed, and it needs to be addressed.

If we begin there, we can move forward and work on creating programs that acknowledge the dark history of Canada. Once we acknowledge this, we can think of new and innovative strategies to undo those wrongs. To create hands-on training programs so that Indigenous people can thrive in the workplace, to start developing oral testing rather than always using pen and paper, to develop creative programs in which Indigenous youth can show their excellence without being burdened by trying to grasp the difficult language and jargon that Western culture seems to love so dearly.

Another way to move forward is to stop putting the onus on Indigenous people to be the ones working on the change. It's not an Indigenous problem, it is a Canadian problem. It is not fair that Indigenous students in classrooms must be the subject of hard questioning, having to explain why residential school is still a problem in our lives today, being an ambassador for Indigenous Peoples everywhere, walking the thin line of stigma and stereotyping and being on their best behaviour at all times. Our teachers, our peers, our coworkers need to actively take on a role of welcoming, of acknowledging that they are not an expert, but that they can take some of that weight off the student.

As a student who has been pursuing post-secondary education for the last six years, I have enjoyed talking about Indigenous life and issues, but I am no expert. It grows exhausting to talk about these issues without my professors backing me up, it grows tiring when someone asks, "what's the big deal with missing and murdered Indigenous women" or, "was residential school really that bad?" If it's created this many problems for decades, I think the answer is pretty clear, don't you?

My last piece of advice is for you to take responsibility, whether you are Indigenous or not, for changing the conversation. Remember to acknowledge the truth, remember that sometimes we just have to talk about these things before we can start solving our problems. Accept when an Indigenous person tells you that something you've said hurt them, and apologize. We can't forget the trauma of our country, but we can learn to live with it. Taimalu. That's it.

Bryan (last name not provided) — Montréal, Québec

My name is Bryan, I'm twenty-one years old and I'm a queer and trans person of colour (QTPOC). I'm an anti-racist and a trans activist. I fought for the rights of trans citizens in Québec via Bill 35 so that, as trans citizens, we would have the right to change our gender marker and legal name on our birth certificate and other ID. Lots of people think I'm not born here and that I'm an immigrant. But the truth is that I was born here. My mom is Venezuelan and has Canadian citizenship and my father was born in Québec. I never met my dad. Unfortunately, he died a few years ago. But, I found some cousins from my father's side of the family and have a great relationship with them! I consider myself to be a Latino-Québecer or Latino-Canadian. I am 100 percent Canadian and 100 percent Venezuelan.

As a Brown Latino trans guy, I have to deal with institutional racism, transphobia and cissexism. This affects me everywhere I go, especially in the gay village. When I go in some bars, people often think I'm Arab because of my skin colour. Sometimes I have to deal with insults when I walk in the street or into a gay bar because I'm Brown. For me, racism in the gay village is when I walk on the street and only see gay, White, cisgender guys on the publicity for gay bars. It's when Fierté Montréal invites the police to walk in the gay parade, while we all know that LGBT people of colour are at risk of being racially profiled by the police for trying to survive in a world that constantly excludes us. It's also when LGBT people allow a racist LGBT person to take up the space in the media, acting like our community is inclusive while only White people really have full representation within our legal institutions.

For me, racism in activist LGBT groups is when we don't give up space to LGBT people of colour to talk about racism. It's also when we ignore that trans migrants have been fighting for their rights. Some LGBT people do help out when it comes to LGBT immigration issues. But some don't care. For example, trans migrants living in Québec often have to wait many years before becoming legally recognized as citizens and being able to change their gender marker on their IDs. Some trans migrants have to work undocumented so they can have food in their stomach and pay for the papers that the government requires them to pay for. Sometimes, they end up in detention centres where they are put in the wrong-gendered cell, which makes it dangerous for them to be in there and also outs them to the inmates. I don't live that situation, but I have many QTPOC friends who have to live or have already lived in that situation.

For me, not talking about racism when I talk about transphobia is a bit like ignoring that these two kinds of oppressions are interconnected. It's ignoring the fact that I can experience racism and transphobia in the same situation. For example, when I go on Grindr to find a date, I'm often hyper-sexualized because I'm Latino and also because I'm trans. I can be asked to talk in Spanish because my language is so hot or be touched in places I mentioned clearly to not be touched. It's like a double kind of exoticization.

But, on the other hand, it can also be hard within Latinx communities to be accepted as who I am. I grew up as a trans boy but was perceived as a cis girl, so people forced me to socialize as if I was a cis girl. This means that I was taught to dance, eat and act in specific ways that still have an impact on my social life. So, I have lived experience of how misogyny and racism can impact women and trans men or gender non-conforming people who are not still out as trans.

When I was younger, I went into a youth centre because I had problems with my mom about how I dressed, and she used to beat me because of that. I was always perceived to be affiliated with gang members or as having bad friends (they didn't have any proof), even if I was at the youth centre because of being connected to child welfare and not because I committed a criminal act. White people with friends and family members in the Hells Angels that were there were never told that they were affiliated with gangs or had bad friends (even with proof). It was clearly a form of racial profiling. I was not able to wear yellow clothes because they said it was a symbol for being a gang member. This wasn't true at all. Wearing that colour could result in being placed in an isolation chamber for twelve to twenty-four hours consecutively with no bed and no blanket, just a cold room with a cold floor. The workers were also allowed to do a full body search while I menstruated to see if "I wasn't hiding a dangerous object" in my vagina. I was treated like a criminal when I wasn't one. I was supposed to be there to be protected from an abusive mother who couldn't accept the fact I liked wearing men's clothing.

Now, as a man, I experience racism in a whole different way. I can be perceived as a potential rapist or drug dealer by the police. I see that, when I walk on the streets, women will walk to the sidewalk on the other side of the street, because they feel scared by my presence, without knowing that I am also targeted for sexual violence when I'm outed as a trans guy. The gendered violence I live as a trans man is being touched in parts that I don't consent to be touched. When I disclose that I'm trans, they try to see if I have a penis. When I share these experiences with my White trans friends, they often tell me to hit the person, but the problem is that if I hit a transphobic person, I could be charged for assault and not be believed by the police because of the fact that I'm Brown.

I've also had to deal with housing problems. These have been some of the worst moments of racism and transphobia in my life. I've had roommates (and their friends) that were racist. I've also had to deal with roommates that misgendered me or didn't respect the fact that I am a man, which makes me really anxious and triggered. There were times that I was so scared that I locked myself in my bedroom. In the past two years, I have had to move out at least six times because I didn't feel safe enough in my home. These are some examples about how racism or racial profiling can hurt us even when we are citizens and/or born in Canada.

I dream that, one day, some of these issues will be addressed and spoken about publicly in the media so we can change things and make the country I was born in as inclusive as we pretend it is. I also wish that trans migrant people of colour can be treated with dignity, have their voices respected within LGBT spaces and be recognized for their contribution to LGBT activism!

Brittany Walker — Calgary, Alberta

I am a seventeen-year-old Black female living in Calgary. Throughout the years, I have become more familiar and more aware of the profiling that happens in my streets and my surrounding neighbourhoods. My neighbourhood is known as the "hood" of Calgary. People believe that the school I go to is unsafe and that I am risking my life every day just by living where I live. This is an unfair stigma attached to my neighbourhood and school. Many of the students in my school have gone on to attend amazing schools and pursue so many of their wildest dreams, despite living in the "hood." I, too, have dreams that are so much bigger than myself, and I will break free of the stigma that is attached to a young Black female.

Most people wouldn't know that, when you come from the "hood," whatever you succeed in seems to matter so much more — not only to your family but to yourself as well. Despite this being a US statistic, we are no different here in Canada: Black children living with high levels of poverty have a 76 percent chance of graduating high school, while White children living in these same neighbourhoods have an 87 percent chance (*Huffington Post* 2011).

In my own household, I am the youngest, and only, child that will graduate from high school. When my parents divorced, nobody guessed that I would grow up and be as mature and grateful as I am. Nobody expected me to stick to my studies and stay on track to graduate. I proved everyone wrong by doing what I knew was best for me and ignoring those who doubted me. In fact, I am now in grade twelve and I am perfectly on track to graduate and move on to post-secondary.

Despite the major leaps made by Black people and in our society, there are still more cons than pros. I can only speak about myself, but does seeing police, in any neighbourhood, make your heart race and your blood run cold? I instantly get nervous and begin to be on my best behaviour. When driving, I keep two hands visibly on the wheel and do my best to stay below the speed limit. Once I pass them, I constantly look in my mirrors to see if they've started to follow me once they saw who was driving.

My last encounter with police ended with me driving away with my first ticket, within just two weeks of having my licence. I had failed to stop completely before turning right on a red light. Of course, I went to Youth Court and did what I could to have the ticket dismissed, but when I walked into the courtroom, something didn't seem right. There were only White officers, and not one White child. It seemed that only people of colour were there. I kept my thoughts to myself.

Throughout my life, I've been around police. I was there when my father was arrested, and I am around an officer five days a week while at school. I believe that if someone respects you, they deserve respect back, especially police. It is no secret that I dislike police; however, I will always obey them because I am aware of what they can do. The events that have been happening in the US involving innocent Black civilians have done nothing but make me feel disgusted with who we are choosing to protect us.

We are forced to respect and obey police and, because of this, they feel that they can be the judges, jury and prosecutors of innocent people. Section 11(d) of Canada's *Charter of Rights and Freedoms* states, "Any person charged with an offence has the right to be presumed innocent until proven guilty according to law in a fair and public hearing by an independent and impartial tribunal" (Government of Canada 2017). The idea of being innocent until proven guilty is somehow forgotten. This is also shown in the US constitution, "The Fifth Amendment provides that citizens not be subject to criminal prosecution and punishment without due process" (White House n.d.). Somehow, police forget this, or they just ignore it.

Profiling has never gone away. Blacks are perceived to steal, lie and end up in jail. Schools that have a large number of Black students are always thought to have more trouble. In my school, the Black students are not usually the issue. Quite honestly, they are rarely the issue.

For me, school is a great place to be. I feel safe because I know that I am not alone, and I can relate to a lot of the other students and what they feel. However, teachers in my school always seem to have a problem with my honesty. In every social studies class I bring up the fact that I still haven't learned anything about Black culture. The response that I get always seems to have something to do with the curriculum and the fact that class time is limited.

I go to a school where White people are the minority. Our school is made up of mostly Arabs, followed by those of African descent. I find it outrageous that, somehow, we cannot learn about where we're from unless we are White. We are forced to learn about the Germans and Hitler but not about where most of us come from. Unfortunately, as I have been told time and time again, teachers do not get to choose what they can and cannot teach, as they are given instruction by Alberta's curriculum.

As I am slowly closing this chapter of my high-school life, and moving on to post-secondary, there will never be a day where I say that I am not proud to be Black. My melanin will always be my signature no matter what anyone does to me or the people I love. I will always be who I am. I am very aware that it is not only me who struggles with this opinion. I read an article in the *Toronto Star* that resonated with me. It expressed exactly how I feel: "As we enter early adulthood we are collectively realizing that, despite what many think, blacks in Canada cannot speak about their lived experience and the ongoing injustices they face without being met with silencing indifference, dismissal and sometimes hostility" (Morgan 2015). Even with these unfortunate truths about moving into adulthood, I still proudly demonstrate my Black pride.

If we want to see change, the first step will have to be stopping police brutality. We need to stop letting these officers abuse us just because they have a badge and sirens. Respect needs to be given both ways. Police should be trained in the same way across the country, and they should face the same penalties that we do. I understand that their jobs are to serve and protect, but no one that I know has ever felt served or protected by the police. I am aware that not all police are like this; however, the numbers of those who are like this shows more evidently. A statistic from the Crime Prevention Research Center states, "police are killing young blacks at 2.3 times the rate that they kill young whites" (Crime Prevention Research Center 2014). I try by writing this, but I cannot fight this on my own, nobody can. But if we all come together to realize that our justice system needs to change, then we will be creating a better society and future for everyone.

Your skin colour cannot tell your story. However, police Canada-wide seem to particularly target those of colour. It should be unfair to simply target someone because they are not White. In cases where White people have done something wrong, there tends to be some sort of disregard for their actions, and the case gets thrown out or they receive a lesser charge. However, if a Black person were to do the same thing, they would be charged and thrown in jail for a number of years: "A [US] Department of Justice study of the federal system between 1995 and 2000 found that of 159 cases that federal attorneys approved for death-penalty prosecution, 72 percent involved minority defendants" (Constitutional Rights Foundation 2017: n.p.). Most Black people call the police "pigs" and are the first to be defiant. This is because of the way they treat us. Police are part of a system that specifically targets Black people, and that needs to change.

The Canadian government needs to recognize the injustice that is prevalent in this society and do something to change it. A government is made up of many levels of hierarchy, and it is understandable that they need to go through many levels to understand the federal sectors. At a municipal level, police need to be reprimanded for targeting non-White people for no reason. One of the things that we study in social class is the differences and principles of individualism and collectivism. A principle that stood out to me is the "rule of law." This means, "all people and institutions are subject to and accountable to law that is fairly applied and enforced" (Dictionary.com 2017). The rule of law was created to ensure that someone who has power cannot get away from punishment after committing a crime. However, when a White police officer murders an innocent Black person, they do not get punished for their actions. It is crucial for this to be applied to every individual, regardless of his or her social class or colour. The federal government needs to be aware of municipal affairs. I cannot speak about the RCMP, as I live within city limits, but I believe that Trudeau, as a newly elected prime minister, should get to know those who vow to risk their lives to serve and protect us. If they are not shown that what they're doing is wrong, they will never have a reason to change. When police take off their uniforms, they are the same people that we are.

People assume that Canada is a country free of racism and prejudice. Despite this universal thought, Canada was created on a great many lives lost and blood spilled. Historically, discrimination is often at the root of many problems; it is always one nation or culture wanting to dominate another. We can start by educating people on what discrimination really is. Discrimination of any type is merely a demonstration of an individual's ignorance. Racism is not born, it is taught. It is important for everyone to know that racism is not solely comments or opinions; it is about acting on your comments and opinions to belittle someone else. A Canada free from racism is possible, but unfortunately it is not something that will happen in my lifetime; it is something that hopefully my great-grandchildren will see. To achieve our goal, we must work together and use every resource that we have. It is interesting to see that blood has still been shed because of our government and police, and it is often blood of colour. In my adulthood, I will absolutely face challenges and stereotypes, but I will surmount them by keeping my goals and aspirations at the front of my mind. As I move on in life, I will break free of this negative stigma and work toward changing one person at a time.

Emma Maryam Bronson — Montréal, Québec

My experience with race and sexuality has been an extremely diverse and complicated one, something I have had to actively think about every day for the past seventeen years. Last semester I had a teacher who asked us to describe our ethnic identity in one sentence and it was the hardest assignment I had all semester. I am mixed: Mauritian, Indian and Anglo-Canadian but have lived my entire life in Montréal, Québec. I'm a Brown girl but have grown up around mostly White lesbians, having two mothers, which made it both easy and difficult for me to explore my own queerness and sexuality. I've always tried to avoid strict labels because I feel like I embody and live between so many intersections that I choose broad terms to identify with, since I don't really fit in any specific boxes. So, this is my experience as a queer Brown girl from Montréal.

I've always distanced myself from identifying as a Canadian or as a Québecer because of the intolerance of racialized and queer people, which I don't find as much in Montréal as in the rest of Canada. Though, I am rethinking the idea that Montréal has much more diverse and accepting ways of thinking; with the increase in hate crimes around the city, this may be fiction and with the rise of fascism in the United States, things may not get better. It's ignorant and a privilege to believe that Canada is a land of promise and tolerance compared to the States, as if what happens across the border doesn't affect us. However, most of my experiences with racism have come from Francophones. The French language itself is limited in its vocabulary about race, gender, sexuality and oppression. It is almost like the language is erasing these topics and experiences, just like it erases Québec's history of oppression, colonialism and genocide of Indigenous Peoples.

I went to a French-Catholic high school. However, most of my friends were rich White Anglophones. I don't know if that was because it's what I was used to with my mother's family, or if it was because I was distancing myself from the questions I knew I would get from the rich White Francophones, who, maybe, were more secluded from the real world. The school itself was just a mess, filled with racist and sexist teachers and faculty, not to mention the impact that it had on the students. In my last year, my religion teacher said, "Not all Muslims are terrorists, but all terrorists are Muslim." If students are fed this kind of information for five years from the people they are supposed to be learning from, why would they question it? Both my parents are militants and human rights activists; open conversation about race and sexuality were had every night at dinner when I was growing up, and they taught me to always think critically.

In elementary and in the first few years of high school, I assimilated myself, mostly by trying to lighten my skin with lemons or by putting bows all over my hair. I don't know why, but it made me think that I was fitting in. I hated that I looked different than everyone. I grew up around mostly White kids (and White adults), and the media was no better. I felt ashamed of my Brown skin and hated things about my body that I didn't see on other (White) kids, like the darkness of my elbows, knees and armpits or the darkness and thickness of my body hair. These are things that are directly linked with being a Brown woman and that I have found pride in today.

It was in ninth grade that I was introduced to the QTBIPOC (queer, trans, black, indigenous, people of colour) Montréal community by my older sister. The conversations that I was having in these spaces made me develop the vocabulary to call out injustices at my high school. I wrote a letter to the principal about the unaddressed racism that the few students of colour were facing. I remember him pulling me out of class and completely invalidating and denying everything I had expressed in my letter. He said "What do you mean there's no diversity? We have a lot of German and French people" and, "Well you're always going to be a person of colour, so you're gonna have to get used to this." This was all in French, and this conversation was very difficult for me to have in French, again because of the lack of vocabulary. Graduating from such a toxic space and going to CEGEP[1] was great. And though there was still a fair share of bigotry, it wasn't what the school was founded on, so it wasn't predominant and nothing near what I was used to.

That's why I don't think it's possible to have a Canada without racism and oppression. The entire country is built on racism and the oppression of Indigenous Peoples. Until real reparations are made to the people whose land we stole, we are nowhere near that goal. Like my high school, Canada was founded on White supremacy, so it is dominant. A way to reduce it is to give a voice and a platform to the oppressed so the privileged stop speaking for them. This means in our media but also in everyday life, to question ourselves: "Who are we silencing? Who are we giving a voice to?" Stop erasing marginalized experience as if it doesn't exist. The more representation we have, the more people will be able to listen and learn. I don't think it is going to eliminate racism from Canadian society because racism is embedded in it. However, it might reduce it and allow the oppressed to have a voice and place here.

Passing the Anti-Racist Torch

This chapter centres the experiences and voices of racialized and Indigenous youth in Canada today, sharing perspectives that are socially and geographically diverse. We see this as symbolically passing the torch from the book's authors to the youth who represent Canada's future. We also see our book as a call to action and a call for significant, structural and durable change. This requires a deep faith and trust in the next generations, those who are growing and learning in spaces where racism, sexism, heterosexism, classism and other oppressions have become expected and normalized.

The collective contributions by the youth in this chapter reveal that various forms of oppression, including racism, are pervasive in Canadian society. Their experiences and insights, as well as concrete steps designed to resist these oppressions, show that they will be at the forefront in the struggle to create a more equitable and just society.

DISCUSSION QUESTIONS

1. What are the key concerns expressed by the youth writers in this chapter?
2. What systems and policies negatively impact racialized and Indigenous youth in Canada today?
3. What changes need to be implemented so that racialized and Indigenous youth are treated with equity and fairness, and their human rights are respected?

Note

1. Editor's note: The CEGEP system was founded in Québec during the late 1960s and is a publicly funded pre-university college. The purpose of this system is to make post-secondary education more accessible in Québec, as well as to provide proper academic preparation for university (Youth Encyclopedia of Canada 2018).

References

Constitutional Rights Foundation. 2017. "The Color of Justice." <crf-usa.org/brown-v-board-50th-anniversary/the-color-of-justice.html>.
Crime Prevention Research Center. 2014. "Grossly Misleading Claims about Black Teens Being 'Vastly More Likely To Be Killed by Police Than Whites Even after Adjusting for Crime Rates.'" October 12. <crimeresearch.org/2014/10/inflammatory-and-misleading-claims-about-black-teens-being-vastly-more-likely-to-be-killed-by-police-than-whites-even-after-adjusting-for-crime-rates/>.
Dictionary.com. 2017. "Rule of Law." <dictionary.com/browse/rule-of-law>.
Government of Canada. 2017. "Constitution Act, 1982: Canadian Charter of Rights and Freedoms." *Justice Laws Website*. <laws-lois.justice.gc.ca/eng/Const/page-15.

html>.

Huffington Post. 2011. "Children Living in Low-Income Neighborhoods Less Likely to Graduate High School: Study." October 4. <huffingtonpost.com/2011/10/04/children-low-income-neighborhoods-high-school_n_994580.html>.

Morgan, Anthony. 2015. "The Suffocating Experience of Being Black in Canada." *The Star,* July 31. <thestar.com/opinion/commentary/2015/07/31/the-suffocating-experience-of-being-black-in-canada.html>.

White House. n.d. "The Bill of Rights." <whitehouse.gov/1600/constitution#bill>.

Youth Encyclopedia of Canada. 2018. "CEGEP Education: Colleges and Universities. Historical Foundation of Canada."

INDEX